D1426917

KA 0279688 0

A W. B. Yeats Chronology

Author Chronologies

General Editor: **Norman Page**, Emeritus Professor of Modern English Literature, University of Nottingham

Published titles include:

J. L. Bradley
A RUSKIN CHRONOLOGY

Gordon Campbell
A MILTON CHRONOLOGY

Martin Garett
A BROWNING CHRONOLOGY
ELIZABETH BARRETT BROWNING AND ROBERT BROWNING

A. M. Gibbs
A BERNARD SHAW CHRONOLOGY

J. R. Hammond
A ROBERT LOUIS STEVENSON CHRONOLOGY
AN EDGAR ALLAN POE CHRONOLOGY
AN H. G. WELLS CHRONOLOGY
A GEORGE ORWELL CHRONOLOGY

John McDermott
A HOPKINS CHRONOLOGY

John S. Kelly
A W. B. YEATS CHRONOLOGY

Norman Page
AN EVELYN WAUGH CHRONOLOGY

Peter Preston
A D. H. LAWRENCE CHRONOLOGY

Author Chronologies Series
Series Standing Order ISBN 0–333–71484–9
(*outside North America only*)

You can receive future titles in this series as they are published by placing a standing order. Please contact your bookseller or, in case of difficulty, write to us at the address below with your name and address, the title of the series and the ISBN quoted above.

Customer Services Department, Macmillan Distribution Ltd. Houndmills, Basingstoke, Hampshire RG21 6XS, England

A W. B. Yeats Chronology

John S. Kelly
Professor of English
Oxford University
Fellow and Tutor
St John's College, Oxford

First published 2003 by
PALGRAVE MACMILLAN
Houndmills, Basingstoke, Hampshire RG21 6XS and
175 Fifth Avenue, New York, N.Y. 10010
Companies and representatives throughout the world

PALGRAVE MACMILLAN is the new global academic imprint of the Palgrave
Macmillan division of St. Martin's Press, LLC and of Palgrave Macmillan Ltd.
Macmillan® is a registered trademark in the United States, United Kingdom
and other countries. Palgrave is a registered trademark in the European
Union and other countries.

ISBN 0–333–46006–5

This book is printed on paper suitable for recycling and made from fully
managed and sustained forest sources.

A catalogue record for this book is available from the British Library

Library of Congress Cataloging-in-Publication Data
Kelly, John S., 1942–
    A W. B. Yeats chronology/John S. Kelly
        p. cm – (Author chronologies)
    Includes bibliographical references and indexes.
    ISBN 0–333–46006–5
    1. Yeats, W. B. (William Butler), 1865–1939 – Chronology. 2. Poets, Irish –
19th century – Chronology. 3. Poets, Irish – 20th century – Chronology. I. Title.
II. Author chronologies (Palgrave Macmillan (Firm))

PR5906 .K45 2003
821'.8–dc21

                                                                2002035540

10   9   8   7   6   5   4   3   2   1
12 11 10 09 08 07 06 05 04 03

Printed and bound in Great Britain by
Anthony Rowe Ltd, Chippenham and Eastbourne

Contents

General Editor's Preface

Most biographies are ill adapted to serve as works of reference – not surprisingly so, since the biographer is likely to regard his function as the devising of a continuous and readable narrative, with excursions into interpretation and speculation, rather than a bald recital of facts. There are times, however, when anyone reading for business or pleasure needs to check a point quickly or to obtain a rapid overview of part of an author's life or career; and at such moments turning over the pages of a biography can be a time-consuming and frustrating occupation. The present series of volumes aims at providing a means whereby the chronological facts of an author's life and career, rather than needing to be prised out of the narrative in which they are (if they appear at all) securely embedded, can be seen at a glance. Moreover whereas biographies are often, and quite understandably, vague over matters of fact (since it makes for tediousness to be forever enumerating details of dates and places), a chronology can be precise whenever it is possible to be precise.

Thanks to the survival, sometimes in very large quantities, of letters, diaries, notebooks and other documents, as well as to thoroughly researched biographies and bibliographies, this material now exists in abundance for many major authors. In the case of, for example, Dickens, we can often ascertain what he was doing in each month and week, and almost on each day, of his prodigiously active working life; and the student of, *say, David Copperfield* is likely to find it fascinating as well as useful to know just when Dickens was at work on each part of that novel, what other literary enterprises he was engaged in at the same time, whom he was meeting, what places he was visiting, and what were the relevant circumstances of his personal and professional life. Such a chronology is not, of course, a substitute for a biography; but its arrangement, in combination with its index, makes it a much more convenient tool for this kind of purpose; and it may be acceptable as a form of 'alternative' biography, with its own distinctive advantages as well as its obvious limitations.

Since information relating to an author's early years is usually scanty and chronologically imprecise, the opening section of some volumes in this series groups together the years of childhood and adolescence. Thereafter each year, and usually each month, is dealt with separately. Information not readily assignable to a specific month or day is given as a general note under the relevant year or month. The first entry for each month carries an indication of the day of the week, so that when necessary this can be readily calculated for other dates. Each volume also contains a bibliography of the principal sources of information. In the chronology itself, the sources of many of the more specific items, including quotations, are identified, in order that the reader who wishes to do so may consult the original contexts.

NORMAN PAGE

Introduction and Acknowledgements

T. S. Eliot said that Yeats was 'one of those few whose history is the history of their own time, who are a part of the consciousness of an age which cannot be understood without them'. That age was one of profound and far-reaching change, and this Chronology bears witness not only to Yeats's deep engagement with poetry, drama and the arts, but also with the historical, social and cultural processes that helped to shape the evolving sensibilities of his time. Keenly aware of the significance of contemporary artistic movements, he embraced as a young man the Pre-Raphaelite rejection of High Victorianism, and in the course of his life was introduced to Aestheticism by Oscar Wilde, Craft Socialism by William Morris, and to French Symbolism by Arthur Symons. Inspired by Standish O'Grady's mythological histories and John O'Leary's library of Irish literature, as well as by the contemporary growth of interest in folklore and comparative mythology, he helped to create the movement that became known as the Celtic Twilight. This was superseded by the Irish dramatic movement, which he was chiefly instrumental in transforming from a modest amateur enterprise into the internationally renowned Abbey Theatre Company – a transformation that involved sometimes relentless and often contentious artistic, managerial and administrative demands, as well as the creation of a repertoire of poetic drama. Writing for the stage, together with his friendship with John Synge, H. J. C. Grierson and Ezra Pound, caused him to reshape his poetic style, and he lived through the cultural upheavals of Post-Impressionism, Cubism, Imagism, Futurism and the politicized arts of the thirties. He was personally acquainted with many of the leaders of these and other movements, as well as with G. B. Shaw, Lady Augusta Gregory, James Joyce, T. S. Eliot, and Sean O'Casey: indeed, as this Chronology demonstrates, he seems to have met almost everyone who was a moving force in the literary life of his time.

He was no less alert to political developments, living through the rise and fall of Charles Stewart Parnell, the Imperialist expansion of the late nineteenth century, the Boer War, the First World War, the Easter Rising in Ireland, the Anglo-Irish War and Irish Civil War, and the rise of Soviet Communism, Italian Fascism and the German Nazi Party. It is part of Yeats's genius that he was peculiarly alert to these historical forces and to their public and private manifestations and this Chronology indicates the extent to which he himself was drawn into the various public debates of the period, meeting leading politicians in Britain, Ireland and the United States. The list of his achievements are awe-inspiring: poet, of course, but also public polemicist, dramatist and theatre director, occultist, literary critic, lover, Senator, and Nobel laureate who continued to be creative and outspoken to his dying day. The ambition of the present work is not only to trace and register these multiple interests, but also to show how they were pursued simultaneously, and how apparently disparate activities impacted on each other to produce a rich, energetic and ultimately coherent canon.

The main sources for this Chronology are the over 8000 largely unpublished letters by Yeats distributed in libraries and private collections throughout the world – in particular those to the various members of his family and Lady Gregory, but also including correspondence with his publishers T. Fisher Unwin, A. H. Bullen and Macmillan, as well as his agent A. P. Watt, 'AE' (George Russell), Mabel Beardsley, Gordon Craig, Edmund Dulac, T. S. Eliot, Frank and William Fay, Maud Gonne, T. W. Horton, James Joyce, Ethel Mannin, Ottoline Morrell, Ezra Pound, John Quinn, Lennox Robinson, J. M. Synge, Shree Purohit Swami, Rabindranath Tagore and Dorothy Wellesley. It also calls heavily upon unpublished and published collections of letters to Yeats – notably those from Lady Gregory, George Yeats, J. B. Yeats, AE, John Quinn, Annie Horniman, T. Sturge Moore and Dorothy Wellesley. Other sources of essential information include, of course, Yeats's own *Autobiographies* and *Memoirs*, as well as his published and unpublished diaries and Occult Notebooks. Lady Gregory's Diaries and Journals have also been invaluable, as have the published and unpublished Diaries of Joseph Holloway, Charles Ricketts, William Rothenstein and Sidney Cockerell. I have drawn gratefully on Roy Foster's magisterial official biography of Yeats and Terence Brown's *The Life of W. B. Yeats*. George Harper's detailed work on Yeats's Vision Notebooks has also been of the greatest value, as have William M. Murphy's immaculately researched writings on J. B. Yeats and the Yeats family, Ann Saddlemyer's splendid editions of Synge's Letters and Plays, as well as her life of George Yeats and Peter Jochum's awesomely inclusive *W. B. Yeats: a Classified Bibliography of Criticism*. Besides these, I have also made use of other diaries, reminiscences, autobiographies and biographies of Yeats's contemporaries too numerous to list.

In locating this material, as well as many smaller collections, I am indebted to librarians in many countries, some of whom have gone to trouble well above and beyond the call of duty. I also owe an immense debt to Michael Yeats, the late Anne Yeats, Joann M. Andrews, Francis A. Brennan, Jim Edwards, Roy Foster, Warwick Gould, Terry Halladay, William F. Halloran, George Harper, Peter Jochum, Declan Kiely, Mark Samuels Lasner, Brenda Maddox, Catherine Morris, William M. Murphy, James Pethica, Ron Schuchard, Colin Smythe, Deirdre Toomey, George Watson and Anna MacBride White.

Given the extent and complexity of Yeats's canon, the Chronology provides not only dates and details of his first publications (in both periodical and book form), but also attempts where possible to supply the dates at which individual poems, plays and essays were actually composed. First editions of books published uniquely in America are cited; otherwise, American editions of English publications are not normally listed, nor are minor or 'acting' editions of his various plays. Since Yeats's range of friends and acquaintances was so large, the index gives brief identifying biographies of each of them as they appear in the story and should in this sense be used as an adjunct to the main text. To save unnecessary confusion, the names of Yeats's poems, plays and prose writings are cited and indexed under their final, canonical titles. The titles of Yeats's reviews are given in the text but the authors and names of the books reviewed appear in full in the index.

From late 1917 onward Yeats and wife spent much time taking down the automatic writing which was to from the basis of *A Vision*. So extensive were these sessions that is has only been possible to list the more important of them in this Chronology, and the curious are referred to the splendidly detailed 4-volume edition of *Yeats's Vision Papers* under the general editorship of George Mills Harper (Palgrave 1992–2001) and George Mills Harper's 2-volume *The Making of Yeats's 'A Vision'* (Macmillan, 1987).

Works by W. B. Yeats

Ah. Sweet Dancer: W. B. Yeats Margot Ruddock, A Correspondence, ed. Roger McHugh (1970).
Autobiographies (1955).
The Collected Letters of W. B. Yeats, vol. 1, ed. John Kelly (1986).
The Collected Letters of W. B. Yeats, vol. 2, eds Warwick Gould, John Kelly, and Deirdre Toomey (1997).
The Collected Letters of W. B. Yeats, vol. 3, eds John Kelly and Ronald Schuchard (1994).
Essays and Introductions (1961).
Explorations, sel. Mrs W. B. Yeats (1962).
The Letters of W. B. Yeats, ed. Allan Wade (1954).
Letters on Poetry from W. B. Yeats to Dorothy Wellesley, ed. Dorothy Wellesley (1940).
Letters to the New Island, eds George Bornstein and Hugh Witemeyer (New York, 1989).
Memoirs, ed. Denis Donoghue (1972).
Mythologies (1959).
The Oxford Book of Modern Verse, ed. W. B. Yeats (1936).
Prefaces and Introductions, ed. William H. O'Donnell (1988).
The Secret Rose, Stories by W. B. Yeats: a Variorum Edition, ed. Warwick Gould, Phillip L. Marcus and Michael J. Sidnell (1981, rev. 1992).
The Senate Speeches of W. B. Yeats, ed. Donald R. Pearce (1961).
Theatre Business, ed. Ann Saddlemyer (1982).
Uncollected Prose, ed. John P. Frayne, vol. 1 (1970), vol. II, eds John P. Frayne and Colton Johnson (1975).
Under the Moon, ed. George Bornstein (1995).
The Variorum Edition of the Poems of W. B. Yeats, eds Peter Allt and Russell K. Alspach (1957, rev. 1966).
The Variorum Edition of the Plays of W. B. Yeats, ed. Russell K. Alspach (1966).
A Vision (1925, new edn 1937).
W. B. Yeats and T. Sturge Moore, Their Correspondence 1901–1937, ed. Ursula Bridge (1953).
W. B. Yeats and W. T. Horton: the Record of an Occult Friendship, ed. George Mills Harper (1980).
W. B. Yeats Interviews and Recollections, ed. E. H. Mikhail, 2 vols (1977).
Yeats Annual nos 1–11 (1982–94).

Other works

William Blake, *The Works of William Blake Poetic, Symbolic, and Critical*, eds Edwin John Ellis and William Butler Yeats, 3 vols (1893).
Terence Brown, *The Life of W. B. Yeats, A Critical Biography* (1999).
A Bibliography of the Writings of W. B. Yeats, eds Allan Wade, rev. Russell K. Alspach, 3rd edn (1968).
Wilfrid Scawen Blunt, *My Diaries*, 2 vols (1919, 1920).

George Moore, *Hail and Farewell*, ed. Richard Cave (Gerrards Cross, 1976, rev. 1985).

George Russell (AE), *Letters from AE*, ed. Alan Denson (1961).

W. G. Fay, *The Fays of the Abbey Theatre* (1935), W. G. Fay and Catherine Carswell.

Michael Field *Works and Days*, eds T. and D. C. Sturge Moore (1933).

Elizabeth, Countess of Fingall, *Seventy Years Young: Memories as Told to Pamela Hinkson* (1937).

R. F. Foster, *W. B. Yeats: a Life*, vol. 1: *The Apprentice Mage* (1997).

Harper, George Mills Harper, *The Making of Yeats's 'A Vision'*, 2 vols (1987); *Yeats's Golden Dawn* (1974).

Hogan and Kilroy, *The Modern Irish Drama*, eds Robert Hogan and James Kilroy, vols I–V (Dublin, 1975–84).

Joseph Holloway, *Joseph Holloway's Abbey Theatre*, eds Robert Hogan and Michael J. O'Neill (Carbondale, IL, 1967).

J. M. Hone, *W. B. Yeats 1865–1939*, rev. edn (1962).

Ellic Howe, *Magicians of the Golden Dawn* (1972).

K. P. S. Jochum, *W. B. Yeats: a Classified Bibliography of Criticism*, rev. edn (Urbana, IL: 1990).

The Letters of John Quinn to William Butler Yeats, ed. Alan B. Himber (Ann Arbor, MI: 1983).

Letters to W. B. Yeats, eds Richard J. Finneran, George Mills Harper, William M. Murphy, with Alan B. Himber, 2 vols (1977).

William M. Murphy, *Prodigal Father: the Life of John Butler Yeats 1839–1922* (1978).

Lady Gregory, *Our Irish Theatre: a Chapter of Autobiography* (Gerrards Cross, 1972); *Lady Gregory's Diaries 1892–1902*, ed. James Pethica (Gerrards Cross, 1996); *Lady Gregory's Journals* 2 vols (Gerrards Cross, 1978, 1987) ed. Daniel J. Murphy; *Seventy Years: Being the Autobiography of Lady Gregory*, ed. Colin Smythe (Gerrards Cross, 1974); *Visions and Beliefs in the West of Ireland*, collected and arranged by Lady Gregory (Gerrards Cross, 1970).

Maud Gonne MacBride, *A Servant of the Queen*, rev. edn (Gerrards Cross, 1994); *The Gonne–Yeats Letters 1893–1938*, eds Anna MacBride White and A. Norman Jeffares (1992).

Brenda Maddox, *George's Ghosts* (1996).

John Masefield, *Some Memories of W. B. Yeats* (Dublin, 1940).

Edward O'Shea, *A Descriptive Catalog of W. B. Yeats's Library* (New York, 1985).

Charles Ricketts, *Self-Portrait*, eds T. Sturge Moore and Cecil Lewis (1939).

The Selected Letters of Somerville and Ross, ed. Gifford Lewis (1989).

Elizabeth A. Sharp, *William Sharp (Fiona Macleod), a Memoir* (1910).

G. Bernard Shaw, *Bernard Shaw Collected Letters*, ed. Dan H. Lawrence, 5 vols (1972–90).

Frank Pearce Sturm, *Frank Pearce Sturm: His Life, Letters and Collected Works*, ed. Richard Taylor (Urbana, IL: 1969).

J. M. Synge, *The Collected Letters of John Millington Synge*, ed. Ann Saddlemyer, 2 vols (Oxford, 1983, 1984); *J. M. Synge Collected Works*, 4 vols (1962–68).

J. B. Yeats, *Letters to his Son W. B. Yeats and Others*, ed. Joseph Hone (1944).

W. B. Yeats and W. T. Horton: The Record of an Occult Friendship, ed. George Mills Harper (1980).

Yeats and the Theatre, eds Robert O'Driscoll and Lorna Reynolds (1975).

List of Abbreviations for Persons, Institutions and Works Cited

Persons frequently referred to

Those listed below appear frequently and are designated by initials after the first entry.

AE   George William Russell (1867–1935), poet, journalist and essayist, who wrote under the pseudonym AE, attended the Metropolitan School of Art with WBY and became one of his closest friends. In 1897 he joined the Irish Agricultural Organisation and later edited the Society's journal, the *Irish Homestead*. In 1923 he was appointed editor of the *Irish Statesman*, and he helped WBY found the Irish Academy of Letters in 1932.

FF   Florence Farr Emery (1860–1917), actress and author, had divorced her actor husband, Edward Emery, in 1894. WBY discovered her beautiful speaking voice in amateur productions; in 1890 and in 1894 she acted in his *The Land of Heart's Desire*. She was also associated with WBY in the Golden Dawn and from 1900 to 1910 frequently accompanied his experiments in speaking verse to the psaltery, a lyre-like instrument. Between 1905 and 1908 their friendship became a physical relationship and in September 1912 she emigrated to Sri Lanka (Ceylon), where she became the principal of a girls' school, took up vegetarianism and immersed herself in Tamil culture.

AG   Lady Augusta Gregory (1852–1932), Irish folklorist and playwright, was WBY's closest friend, patron and correspondent from 1897, when he began to spend his summers at her house, Coole Park, in County Galway. She helped initiate the Irish dramatic movement, became a Director of the Abbey in 1905 and helped organize and oversee a number of transatlantic tours. WBY greatly admired her version of the Irish myths, *Cuchulain of Muirthemne* and *Gods and Fighting Men*, and he contributed to her collection of folklore, *Visions and Beliefs in the West of Ireland*. Her only son, Robert, was shot down over Italy in 1918 and she devoted the later part of her life to a campaign to have a collection of modern paintings made by her nephew, Hugh Lane, restored to Dublin.

MG   Maud Gonne (1866–1953), the daughter of a British army officer, got to know Ireland when her father was stationed in Dublin. Shortly after his death she moved to Paris, where she became the mistress of the lawyer and politician Lucien Millevoye by whom she had two children. She cast herself in the role of an Irish Joan of Arc and met WBY in January 1889. He fell in love with her immediately, but she turned down his proposals of marriage; he was devastated by her marriage to John MacBride in 1903 and gave her help during its acrimonious break-up in 1905–06. Their relationship seems to have been briefly consummated in 1908 and in 1916, after the execution of MacBride, he again asked her to marry him. She refused and he transferred his affections to Iseult, her daughter by Millevoye. WBY tried to assist her and her family during the politically troubled times from 1918–23 and thereafter, despite fundamental political differences, they remained distant friends.

ESH   Edith Shackleton Heald (1885–1976) became a journalist at the suggestion of her brother Ivan, a well-known humorous writer, and, after a brief period in Manchester, joined the *Evening Standard*, where she wrote editorials and succeeded Arnold Bennett as its main book reviewer. She was introduced to WBY by Edmund Dulac in April 1937 and they immediately became friends and later lovers.

AEFH   Annie Elizabeth Fredericka Horniman (1860–1937), occultist and patron of drama, was the daughter of a wealthy Manchester tea merchant. She was a fellow-member of the Golden Dawn and in March 1894 she anonymously put up money for productions of WBY's *The Land of Heart's Desire* and plays by Todhunter and Shaw. In 1904 she became the benefactress of the Abbey Theatre, but quarrelled with members of the Company and finally with WBY and in 1908 she transferred her interest to the Gaiety Theatre, Manchester, ceasing to subsidize the Abbey in 1910.

JO'L   John O'Leary (1830–1907), President of the Supreme Council of the Irish Republican Brotherhood, who returned to Ireland in 1885 after 20 years in prison and exile for his part in the Fenian movement. He exerted a powerful political, moral and literary influence on WBY, especially in the years 1885–93, during which he loaned him books from his extensive library of Anglo-Irish works, encouraged him to contribute to Irish periodicals, and organized the subscriptions for *The Wanderings of Oisin*.

LR   Esmé Stuart Lennox Robinson (1886–1958), writer, playwright and theatre director, grew up in Co. Cork. His first play, *The Clancy Name*, was produced at the Abbey in 1908 and in 1909 he was appointed director and manager of the Theatre. Thereafter he contributed plays regularly to the Abbey and was principal director from 1910 to 1914 and from 1919 to 1934. He was appointed a Director of the Abbey Company in 1923.

OS   Olivia Shakespear, née Tucker (1864–1938), novelist and playwright, married Henry Hope Shakespear in 1885. WBY met her in 1894, through her cousin, Lionel Johnson, and had a brief affair with her in 1895–96; thereafter they became close friends and WBY saw her frequently in London. Her daughter, Dorothy, married Ezra Pound in 1914, and her brother, Henry Tudor Tucker, married Mrs Edith Ellen Hyde-Lees, whose daughter George became WBY's wife in 1917.

KT Katharine Tynan (1859–1931) poet, novelist and journalist, was born near Dublin, the daughter a substantial farmer who encouraged her literary ambitions. WBY met her for the first time in June 1885 and thereafter they saw each other regularly to discuss and review each other's work. WBY began to wonder if it was his duty to marry her but in 1893 she married Henry Hinkson and settled down in London, where she turned her hand to pot-boiling novels, serials and reviews. Although they met less frequently, the friendship with WBY survived, and in 1906 he edited a selection of her poems. In 1914 Hinkson was appointed Removeable Magistrate in Mayo, where KT remained until his death in 1919. In the following years she travelled widely in Britain and on the Continent, occasionally meeting WBY on her visits to Ireland.

DW Dorothy Violet Wellesley, née Ashton (1889–1956), poet, married Lord Gerald Wellesley, the third son of the 4th Duke of Wellington, in 1914. Although estranged from her husband, she became the Duchess of Wellington in 1943. She met WBY in 1934 and quickly became a surrogate Lady Gregory for him; he stayed at Penns in the Rocks, her house in Sussex, on his frequent trips to England, where they discussed poetry and collaborated on various literary projects.

ECY Elizabeth Corbet ('Lolly') Yeats (1868–1940), WBY's second sister, was the third of JBY's surviving children. From 1903 she ran the Cuala Press with WBY as literary advisor, but the relationship between them was often difficult and the enterprise always financially precarious.

GY Bertha Georgie Yeats, née Hyde-Lees (1892–1968), married WBY in November 1917. She was born in Hampshire, and went to school with Dorothy Shakespear, later Mrs Ezra Pound, who remained one of her best friends. She met WBY in 1910 and helped him with a number of psychic experiments before their marriage, and on their honeymoon began the automatic writing which was to constitute *A Vision*. After her marriage she adopted the name 'George' and WBY's nickname for her was 'Dobbs'.

JBY John Butler Yeats (1839–1922) gave up a career as a barrister to become a painter after his marriage to Susan Pollexfen. He moved his family regularly between Ireland and England, but settled more permanently in London from 1887 until Susan Yeats's death in 1900. In October 1901 he returned to Dublin where he was joined by his two daughters. He accompanied SMY on a supposedly brief visit to New York in late 1907, but he remained there for the rest of his life, living mainly off benefactions from the lawyer John Quinn, which WBY helped partly to off-set by the sale of his manuscripts.

SMY.   Susan Mary ('Lily') Yeats (1866–1949) was the elder of WBY's two surviving sisters, and particularly close to the poet. She learned embroidery from William Morris and his daughter May, and subsequently designed and executed embroidery work for Cuala Industries.

Institutions frequently referred to

Abbey	The Abbey Theatre, Dublin
IAOS	Irish Agricultural Organisation Society
GD	Order of the Golden Dawn
NLS	National Literary Society, Ireland
INTS	Irish National Theatre Society
ILS	Irish Literary Society, London
ILT	Irish Literary Theatre
INA	Irish National Alliance
IRB	Irish Republican Brotherhood
TCD	Trinity College Dublin

Works frequently referred to

The standard abbreviations for the titles of Yeats's works have been used. They are also identified at their time of first publication by genre and, where appropriate, major reprintings are also cited.

Aut	*Autobiographies* (1955)
The Countess Kathleen	*The Countess Kathleen and Various Legends and Lyrics* (1892)
CP	*Collected Poems* (1933)
CW	*Collected Works*, 8 vols (1908–09)
DUR	*Dublin University Review*
E & I	*Essays and Introductions* (1961)
Expl	*Explorations*, sel. Mrs W. B. Yeats (1962)
FFT	*Fairy and Folk Tales of the Irish Peasantry* (1889)
LNI	*Letters to the New Island*, ed. George Bornstein and Hugh Witemeyer (New York, 1989)
Mem	*Memoirs*, ed. Denis Donoghue (1972)
Myth	*Mythologies* (1959)
OBMV	*The Oxford Book of Modern Verse*, ed. W. B. Yeats (1936)
Oisin	*The Wanderings of Oisin, and Other Poems* (1889)
Per Amica	*Per Amica Silentia Lunae* (1918)
UM	*Under the Moon*, ed. George Bornstein (1995)
UP I	*Uncollected Prose*, ed. John P. Frayne, vol. 1 (1970)
UP II	*Uncollected Prose*, ed. John P. Frayne and Colton Johnson, vol. 2 (1975)

Visions and Beliefs	*Visions and Beliefs in the West of Ireland*, collected and arranged by Lady Gregory (1920)
VP	*The Variorum Edition of the Poems of W. B. Yeats*, ed. Peter Allt and Russell K. Alspach (1957, rev. 1966)
VPl	*The Variorum Edition of the Plays of W. B. Yeats*, ed. Russell K. Alspach (1966)
VSR	*The Secret Rose, Stories by W. B. Yeats: A Variorum Edition*, ed. Warwick Gould, Phillip L. Marcus, and Michael J. Sidnell (1981, rev. 1992)
Wade	*The Letters of W. B. Yeats*, ed. Allan Wade (1954)
YA	*Yeats Annual*
Yeats Annual	*Yeats: An Annual of Critical and Textual Studies.*
YL	Edward O'Shea, *A Descriptive Catalog of W. B. Yeats's Library* (New York, 1985)

A William Butler Yeats Chronology (1865–1939)

1865

June
13   William Butler Yeats (WBY), eldest child of John Butler Yeats (JBY) and Susan Mary Yeats (née Pollexfen), born at Georgeville, Sandymount Avenue, Dublin.

1866

January
        JBY called to the Irish Bar.

August
25   Susan Mary (Lily) Yeats (SMY), sister, born at Enniscrone, Co. Sligo.

1867

Late February/early March
        JBY gives up the law and moves to London to enrol at Heatherley's Art School.

Late July
        Susan Yeats, WBY, SMY, and Isabella Pollexfen (aunt) join JBY at 23 Fitzroy Road, Regent's Park.

1868

March
11   Elizabeth Corbet (Lollie) Yeats (ECY), sister, born in Fitzroy Road.

Summer
        Family holiday in Sligo.

1869

Summer
        Family holiday in Sligo; children remain there until December.

1870

March
27   Robert Corbet (Bobbie) Yeats, brother, born in Fitzroy Road.

April
        WBY ill with scarlatina (scarlet fever).

Summer
        Family holiday in Sligo.

1871

August
29   John Butler (Jack) Yeats, brother, born in Fitzroy Road.

September
        Short family holiday in Sligo.

1872

July
23   Yeatses leave London for Sligo where Susan Yeats and the children remain for more than two years, living with her parents.

1873

March
3   Bobbie Yeats dies suddenly in Sligo.

October–December
        JBY painting portraits at Muckross Abbey.

1874

Winter–Spring
        JBY painting portraits at Stradbally Hall; rejoins his family in Sligo in the summer.

Late October
        Yeatses move back to London, settling at 14 Edith Villas, North End (West Kensington).

1875

August
29   Jane Grace Yeats, sister, born at Edith Villas.

1876

June
6   Jane Grace Yeats dies of bronchial pneumonia; the same month, WBY's paternal grandmother Jane dies of cancer in Dublin.

Summer

Yeatses holiday in Sligo. JBY returns alone to London and, having decided to abandon portrait-painting for landscapes, spends extended periods at Burnham Beeches.

Autumn

WBY joins his father at Burnham Beeches, lodging with the Earles in Farnham Royal.

1877

January

Susan Yeats and the other children return to Edith Villas.

26   WBY enrolled at the Godolphin School, Iffley Road, Hammersmith.

1879

Spring

Yeatses move to 8 Woodstock Road, Bedford Park.

Summer

Family holiday at Branscombe, Devon.

1880

June

13   Confirmed by the Bishop of London at Christ Church, Ealing.

1881

Easter

WBY leaves the Godolphin School.

Summer

JBY's chronic financial difficulties worsen; in the autumn he moves to Dublin and rents a studio at 44 York Street.

Late autumn

JBY brings his family (except Jack, who is living permanently in Sligo with his grandparents) to Dublin where they settle at Balscaddan Cottage in Howth. WBY enrolled at the Erasmus Smith High School, Harcourt Street, Dublin.

1882

Spring

Yeatses move from Balscaddan Cottage to Island View, Harbour Road, Howth.

Autumn

WBY meets his distant cousin, Laura Armstrong, and is attracted to her.

1883

November

22   Attends lecture by Oscar Wilde in Dublin.

December

Leaves the Erasmus Smith High School.

1884

January

8   Begins play, 'Vivien and Time', for Laura Armstrong.

Early Spring

Yeats family forced by financial pressures to leave Howth for 10 Ashfield Terrace, in the south Dublin suburb of Terenure.

March

8   WBY writes unpublished poem 'Behold the man ...' (*UM*, 35).

May

Enrols as a student at Metropolitan School of Art, Kildare Street, Dublin.

August

10   Laura Armstrong apologises for being out when he called.
12   Laura Armstrong invites WBY to call on her at 60 Stephen's Green that afternoon. WBY writing *The Island of Statues*.

September

Laura Armstrong marries Henry Byrne.

1885

January

19   The Fenian John O'Leary (JO'L) returns from exile in Paris; WBY meets him a little later in the year.

March

WBY's first publications, 'Song of the Faeries' (poem; *VP*, 643–4) and 'Voices' (poem, later 'The Cloak, the Boat and the Shoes';*VP*, 69–70), published in the *Dublin University Review* (*DUR*).

April–July

The Island of Statues (play; *VP*, 644–79) published in *DUR*.

May

'Love and Death' (poem; *VP*, 680) published in *DUR*.

June

2   Attends an evening meeting in C. H. Oldham's rooms in TCD to discuss how to bring a national spirit into *DUR* with F. J. Gregg, Douglas Hyde and George Coffey among those present. Meeting continues until after midnight.

16   First meeting of Dublin Hermetic Society, WBY presiding.

Late June

Oldham introduces WBY to Katharine Tynan (KT) at her house in Clondalkin.

August

Death of Matthew Yeats, JBY's uncle and his agent on the Thomastown estate; JBY's money problems increase.

September

The Seeker (dramatic poem; *VP*, 681–5) published in *DUR*.

October

'An Epilogue To "The Island of Statues" and "The Seeker"' (poem, later 'The Song of the Happy Shepherd'; *VP*, 64–9) published in *DUR*.

November

21   The Contemporary Club founded by C. H. Oldham.

December

13   WBY and Hyde attend a social evening at the Coffeys'.

18   Attends a meeting of the Young Ireland Society to hear a paper by Oldham, after which he spends three hours talking to Hyde in Oldham's rooms.

1886

January

'In a Drawing Room' (poem; *VP*, 685–6) published in *DUR*.

February

'Life' (poem; *VP*, 686) published in *DUR*.

March

'The Two Titans. A Political Poem' (poem; *VP*, 687–8) published in *DUR*.

April

'On Mr. Nettleship's Picture at the Royal Hibernian Academy' (poem; *VP*, 688–9) published in *DUR*. WBY leaves the Metropolitan School of Art.

10, 11 Attends William Morris's lecture in Dublin and meets him at the Contemporary Club.

June

Mosada (play; *VP*, 689–704) published in *DUR*. Writes 'The Meditation of the Old Fisherman'.

July

'Remembrance' (poem; *VP*, 704–5) published in the *Irish Monthly*.

October

Mosada WBY's first publication in book form, privately printed in Dublin. Begins first part of 'The Wanderings of Oisin'. 'Miserrimus' (poem, later 'The Sad Shepherd'; *VP*, 67–9) and 'From the Book of Kauri the Indian – Section V. On the Nature of God' (poem, later 'The Indian upon God'; *VP*, 76–7) published in *DUR*. 'Meditation of the Old Fisherman' (poem; *VP*, 90–1) published in the *Irish Monthly*.

9 The first part of 'The Poetry of Sir Samuel Ferguson' (article; *UP* I. 81–7) published in the *Irish Fireside*.

November

The second part of 'The Poetry of Sir Samuel Ferguson' (article; *UP* I. 87–104) published in *DUR*.

24 Attends social evening at JO'L's house in Leinster Street, Dublin, with George Sigerson, Rose Kavanagh, KT, George and Mrs Coffey.

27 First part of 'The Poetry of R. D. Joyce' (article; *UP* I. 104–9) published in the *Irish Fireside*.

December

'The Stolen Child' (poem; *VP*, 86–9) published in the *Irish Monthly*, and 'An Indian Song' (poem, later 'The Indian to His Love'; *VP*, 77–8) in *DUR*.

3 Spends three hours in the afternoon with Hyde discussing and reciting their poetry; afterwards attends a debate on Archbishop Walsh's manifesto on the Irish Land Question at the Contemporary Club.

4	Second part of 'The Poetry of R. D. Joyce' (article; *UP* I. 109–14) published in the *Irish Fireside*.
7	Attends Roman Lipmann's conversazione at the Russell Hotel. Hyde, J'OL, Ellen O'Leary, the two Johnstons and their sisters also present.
11	Discusses historical drama with Hyde at the Contemporary Club, claiming that dramatists have licence to violate historical truth.
15	Attends a social evening at JO'L's house with KT, Rose Kavanagh, George Sigerson, Mrs Sigerson, Hester Sigerson, ECY, SMY, J. F. Taylor, and Hyde. They read and discuss contributions to the forthcoming *Poems and Ballads of Young Ireland*.
25	Gives ECY *The Poetical Works of John Greenleaf Whittier* for Christmas.

1887

January

10	(Mon) Accompanies KT to a meeting of the Protestant Home Rule Association at which T. W. Rolleston speaks.
25	Has tea in Hyde's college rooms with KT and her sister.
23	Goes with Hyde to visit KT at Clondalkin.
30	Visits Edward Dowden, Professor of English at TCD.

February

5	(Sat) 'A Dawn-Song' (poem; *VP*, 705–6) published in the *Irish Fireside*.
15	Calls to ask KT for another sitting to his father for a portrait begun the previous summer.
26	'Ephemera' (poem; *VP*, 79–81) published in *North & South*.

March

	'The Fairy Pedant' (poem; *VP*, 706–8) published in the *Irish Fireside*.
2	(Wed) Visits the Misses Gill at Roebuck House, Dublin.
3	JBY goes to London to arrange for his family's return there.
5	'Song of Spanish Insurgents' (poem; *YA3*, 179–81) published in *North & South*.
6	WBY and his sisters visit KT in Clondalkin.
12	'Clarence Mangan' (article; *UP* I. 114–19) published in the *Irish Fireside*.

April

3	(Sun) Last visit to KT before moving to London. After this the family joins JBY in England, WBY lodging at 6 Berkeley Road, Regent's Park, London, until the family house is ready, and

experiments with dining cheaply. Spends the month writing poems and an article on Finn Mac Cumhaill for the *Gael*.

27   'Finn Mac Cumhaill' (article; *Yeats Annual* II. 85–91) published in the *Gael*.

May

Early this month WBY moves into the new family home, Eardley Crescent, South Kensington.

6   (Fri) Attends a debate at House of Commons in which Timothy Healy denounces *The Times'* attack on John Dillon. Later in the month he meets Ernest Rhys and, although out of sorts, works on reviews, articles and poems at the Art Library, South Kensington (later the Victoria and Albert) Museum. Pays his first visit to the theosophist Madam Blavatsky, lately arrived in London.

June

11   (Sat) 'The Celtic Romances in Miss Tynan's New Book' review; *Yeats Annual* II. 98–114) published in the *Gael*.

19   Hears H. H. Sparling lecture on 'Irish Rebel Songs' at William Morris's house in Hammersmith; meets May Morris. Thereafter regularly attends Morris's 'Sunday Nights'.

23   Calls on the journalist Boyd Montgomerie Ranking.

26   Has supper at the Morrises; William Morris asks him to write for his periodical *Commonweal*.

29   Obtains a reader's ticket for the British Museum Reading Room.

July

1   (Fri) Writing on Irish poets for the *Leisure Hour*.

9   'Miss Tynan's New Book' (review; *UP* I. 119–22) published in the *Irish Fireside*.

August

8   (Mon) Sees Montgomerie Ranking again. Early this month writes the poem 'Love Song' (*VP*, 717).

6   'How Ferencz Renyi Kept Silent' (poem; *VP*, 709–15) published in the *Boston Pilot*.

9   Sails for Sligo by the Liverpool boat.

11   Arrives in Sligo at 2 am to stay with his uncle, George Pollexfen, at Rosses Point; working on 'Oisin'. Susan Yeats suffers her first stroke.

12   Reading Philip Bourke Marston's *For a Song's Sake*.

13   Collecting fairy and folk lore in the neighbourhood of Sligo.

14   Writes poem, 'The Fairy Doctor'.

15   Again searching for fairy stories.

September

'King Goll' (poem, later 'The Madness of King Goll'; *VP*, 81–6) published in the *Leisure Hour* and 'She Who Dwelt among the Sycamores' (poem; *VP*, 715–16) in the *Irish Monthly*.

10   (Sat) 'The Fairy Doctor' (poem; *VP*, 716–17) published in the *Irish Fireside*.

October

Moves into Sligo town to stay with his grandparents. Trying to finish 'The Wanderings of Oisin'.

November

18   (Fri) Finishes 'Oisin'.

19   'The Protestants' Leap' (poem; *Yeats Annual* II. 121–3) published in the *Gael*.

22   To Dublin where he stays with KT at Clondalkin. Sees much of the O'Learys and other Dublin friends; JO'L begins to organize subscriptions for *The Wanderings of Oisin*.

26   Writes to the *Gael* to complain of misprints in 'The Protestants' Leap'.

December

11   (Sun) Brings AE (George Russell) to Clondalkin to reintroduce him to KT; Hyde and Hannah Lynch also there. Later this month Susan Yeats and SMY go to stay with Elizabeth Pollexfen Orr at Denby near Huddersfield; Susan Yeats suffers another stroke and falls down a back stair.

24   'How Ferencz Renyi Kept Silent' published in the *Gael*.

1888

January

Early this month WBY experiences severe nervous disturbance at a Dublin séance. JBY decides to look for a house in Bedford Park.

*c.*25   (Wed) The O'Learys hold a farewell party for WBY.

26   Returns to London.

28   'The Prose and Poetry of Wilfrid Blunt' (article; *UP* I. 122–30) published in *United Ireland*.

February

Early this month commissioned by Rhys to edit *Fairy and Folk Tales of the Irish Peasantry* (*FFT*).

8   (Wed) Calls on Madam Blavatsky, but finds she has gone away for her health.

11   Meets Alexander Middleton, a cousin who has fled Ireland because of financial impropriety, in a London hotel.

| 12 | Discusses poetry with John Todhunter. In the evening meets George Bernard Shaw at William Morris's house. Busy compiling 50 pages of folklore. |
| 23 | H. H. Sparling introduces him to the Irish song-writer and humorist Francis Fahy at the British Museum. Late this month he copies out *Oisin* and organizes subscriptions for the book. Reads Sir Samuel Ferguson's work most evenings. |

March

6	(Tue) Todhunter recommends *Oisin* to the publisher Kegan Paul.
11	Meets Mrs Cunninghame Graham at the Morrises.
12	Takes the MS of *Oisin* to Kegan Paul, who accepts it but tells WBY he requires at least 50 more subscribers.
13	Polishes *Mosada* and notices that his is 'not the poetry of insight and knowledge but of longing and complaint – the cry of the heart against neccesity' (to KT).
20–1	Working at the British Museum on material which gives him the theme for 'The Ballad of Father O'Hart' (*VP*, 91–3).
21	Pays his first visit to the Southwark Irish Literary Club, where he hears Daniel Crilly, MP, lecture on Fanny Parnell.
22	Visits Herbert Horne at the office of the *Hobby Horse*.
24	The Yeats family moves to 3 Blenheim Road, Bedford Park.

April

	During this month WBY begins attending French lessons at the Morrises and goes regularly to the British Museum to read about the eighteenth century for a romance.
8	(Sun) Meets the radical politician John Elliot Burns at Morris's house.
10	Todhunter reads him part of his poem 'The Fate of the Sons of Usna'.
11	Reading John Mitchell's *History of Ireland*.
12	His mother and SMY arrive at Bedford Park from Denby.
15	Meets Shaw for a second time at the Morrises after a lecture on 'Anarchism'; they both stay on to supper with Sparling, Emery Walker, the artist J. M. Strudwick and May Morris.
16	Consults Kegan Paul about the publication of *Oisin*.
17	Suffers a physical collapse and does not go to the British Museum.
19	Accompanies Mrs Todhunter to a Women's Political Association meeting, where he hears the Irish politician and journalist T. P. Gill make a speech and meets the novelist Mabel Robinson.
28	Attends a Home Rule party given by the Hancocks and goes afterwards to a French class at the Morrises.
30	Reads the proofs of Todhunter's *The Banshee* with admiration.

May

1   (Tue) Publication of *Poems and Ballads of Young Ireland*. Early this month WBY begins to write the story 'John Sherman'.

18   Sees Sparling.

27   'A Legend of the Phantom Ship' (poem, later 'The Phantom Ship'; *VP*, 718–19) published in the *Providence Sunday Journal*.

June

13   (Wed) Lectures to the Southwark Irish Literary Club on 'Sligo Fairies'.

c.15   The commission for *FFT* is confirmed and he spends the next two months collecting material for it and finishing 'John Sherman'.

17   Attends a performance of William Morris' play, *The Tables Turned*.

20   The Irish artist Sarah Purser calls to sketch SMY.

July

         Spends most of July desperately collecting and reading material for *FFT*, which has to be delivered by the end of the month.

22   (Sun) Calls on Lady Wilde, but she is resting.

28   Spends the morning at the British Museum reading Sir William Wilde's *Irish Popular Superstitions*. In the afternoon goes to Lady Wilde's Saturday 'At Home' and thereafter attends them regularly.

August

11   (Sat) In Oxford for a week copying out Caxton's edition of Aesop's *Fables* at the Bodleian; stays in York Powell's rooms in Christ Church. Lives mainly on currant buns but dines a couple of times with the Fellows and meets the critic and controversialist Churton Collins.

22–3   Back in London and resting from copying Aesop. Later this month he meets the poet and editor W. E. Henley.

29   The Sigersons call to see the Yeatses.

September

2   (Sun) 'The Poet of Ballyshannon' (article; *LNI* 71–8) published in the *Providence Sunday Journal*.

6   Receives £5 for copying Aesop. First proofs of *Oisin* arrive. WBY reads aloud all evening to JBY.

15   Proofs of *FFT* arrive; later he goes to Madam Blavatsky's where he sees Charles Johnston and meets the American aesthete Edmund Russell, to whom he talks until 1 am.

18   John Davidson visits 3 Blenheim Road and argues with WBY and JBY over metaphysics.

19   York Powell, historian and neighbour, visits the Yeatses.

22   In the afternoon Todhunter calls to help WBY with his proofs; in the evening WBY goes to W. E. Henley's where he meets the

Australian poet Douglas Sladen. Is reading George Meredith's poems with admiration.

c.26   *Fairy and Folk Tales of the Irish Peasantry (FFT)* published.

27   The Todhunters come to tea, but WBY has to borrow 3 shillings from them to pay for the food.

28   Hears at Madam Blavatsky's that his school friend Charles Johnston is to marry her niece Vera Zhelikhovskaya.

October

2   (Tue) York Powell calls and sees WBY.

3   To dinner with the Todhunters.

7   JBY's model, Nelly Whelan, calls.

8   Finishes the first draft of 'John Sherman'.

10   Pays the family tax bill out of his Aesop money; later Todhunter calls.

13   Goes to the Irish Exhibition and in the evening accompanies Jack Yeats to a performance of *Dr. Jekyll and Mr. Hyde*.

20   Harry Hall at the Yeatses in the evening.

27   Harry Hall and David Hardy and his wife at the Yeatses.

30   Goes with the other Yeats children to a performance of Barnes's *Prince Karl* at the Lyceum.

31   Takes part in Halloween games at Blenheim Road.

November

WBY being pursued by the 39-year-old Comtesse de Brémont, a singer, novelist and journalist, who proposes to him.

3   (Sat) Reads 'John Sherman' to Edwin Ellis who suggests important alterations.

4   Edmund Russell comes to tea at the Yeatses and in the evening WBY takes him to the Morrises.

5   Jack Yeats takes WBY's poem 'A Legend' and his own illustrations to the editor of the *Vegetarian*, who accepts them. WBY reading Stevenson's *The Black Arrow*.

6   T. W. Lyster, the Dublin librarian, at Blenheim Road with May Morris, Sparling and Todhunter. WBY reading Meredith's *Diana of the Crossways*.

14   Final set of proofs of *Oisin* arrive. WBY reading Tolstoy's *Anna Karenina*.

18   Visits the Arts and Crafts Exhibition with the other Yeats children.

19   James Legge and William Crook come to supper at the Yeatses and discuss politics and art until 11 pm.

22   Attends Todhunter's lecture on Irish Fairy Tales, which makes liberal use of *FFT*.

23   Dines with ECY at the Todhunters.

26   SMY starts work as an embroidress at May Morris's.

27   Calls to see Edwin Ellis.

| 30 | WBY and ECY attend a French class at the Morrises. Late this month WBY is attacked by 'lunar influences'. Joins Esoteric Section of the Theosophical Society. |

December

4	(Tues) WBY and SMY dine at Aunt Isabella Varley's.
12	Chairs a lecture by Sparling on 'The Literature of '98' at the Southwark Irish Literary Club.
15	Sees Todhunter and asks for a copy of *The Banshee* for Hyde. Composes 'The Lake Isle of Innisfree'.
20	Writing an unpublished article on the eighteenth-century Gaelic poet Heffernan the Blind.
22	'A Legend' (poem; *VP*, 724–5) published in the *Vegetarian*.
24	A Christmas gift of £25 to Susan Yeats from her father enables the Yeatses to pay outstanding wages to their servants, as well as buy JBY new clothes.
25	WBY spends Christmas Day with the Oscar Wildes in Tite Street.
26	The Yeatses dine at their neighbours the Gambles and WBY talks of Theosophy.

1889

January

2	(Wed) Goes with Jack to a performance of Gilbert and Sullivan's *The Yeoman of the Guard*.
c.10	*The Wanderings of Oisin* published.
13	Goes to Madam Blavatsky's.
14	WBY and ECY attend a lecture on Delsartian gesture by Edmund Russell's wife Theodora.
15	'Irish Fairies, Ghosts, Witches. Etc' (article; *UP* I. 130–7) published in *Lucifer*. In the evening WBY and JBY dine with the Pagets.
18	Accompanies ECY to a French class at the Morrises.
19	Sends a presentation copy of *Oisin* to May Morris, in the hope that she will show it to William Morris.
22	The first reviews of *Oisin* appear. In the evening Edmund Russell calls.
23	Meets William Morris, who praises *Oisin* and promises to review it. Late this month the Yeats family financial problems are particularly acute.
c.28	Sees Edwin Ellis, who reads him his play *Fate in Arcadia* and discusses WBY's style.
30	Meets Maud Gonne (MG) for the first time when she visits Blenheim Road and 'the troubling of my life began' (*Aut*).
31	Dines with MG and her sister and cousin in London.

February

2	(Sat) Writes the poem 'In the Firelight'. Early this month he begins writing *The Countess Kathleen*.
3	Goes to Madam Blavatsky's with SMY and her friend Katie Browne.
5	Upset by a carping review of *Oisin* in the *Freeman's Journal*.
7	Attends Lady Wilde's 'At Home'.
9	The Yeatses attend 'Tableaux Vivants', depicting a comic history of England interspersed with songs, in the studio of the artist Sydney Hall.
10	'Dr. Todhunter's Latest Volume of Poems' (article; *LNI*, 79–90) published in the *Providence Sunday Journal*.
20	A social evening with May Morris, Sparling, the Nashes, York Powell and W. M. Crook at the Yeatses.
26	Excitement over Richard Pigott's disappearance from the Parnell Commission.
c.28	Meets James Legge at Herbert Horne's.

March

2	(Sat) 'Scots and Irish Fairies' (article, *Myth* 106–9) published in the *Scots Observer*. Attends a reception given by the novelist 'John Strange Winter' (Mrs Stannard).
3	Spends the night at the Ellises' to discuss a proposed edition of *The Works of William Blake*.
16	Goes into London with Jack Yeats.
30	'Irish Wonders' (article; *UP* I. 138–41) published in the *Scots Observer*.

April

6	(Sat) Has his portrait painted by H. M. Paget and is also being painted by JBY. Early this month he begins to contribute literary notes to the *Manchester Courier*.
c.18	Dines with the Coffeys at their in-laws, the Lawrences.
c.20	Writes the poems 'In Church' and 'A Summer Evening' for the Religious Tract Society. Beginning to read the Irish novelist William Carleton for a selection from his work.

May

1	(Wed) In Oxford copying material, including Blake's *The Book of Thel*, in the Bodleian.
5	Returns to London.
6	Reads a scene from *The Countess Kathleen* to Florence Farr (FF).
7	Makes revisions in Edwin Ellis's copy of *Oisin*.
11	'Village Ghosts' (article; *Myth*, 15–21) published in the *Scots Observer*.

| 26 | Paints the ceiling of his bedroom with the help of Jack Yeats. |
| 29 | Lectures on Mangan to the Southwark Irish Literary Society. |

June

8	(Sat) 'In Church' (poem; *VP*, 735–6) published in the *Girl's Own Paper*.
15	'Kidnappers' (article; *Myth*, 70–6) published in the *Scots Observer*.
16	Sarah Purser at the Yeatses.
28	The American journalist, Margaret Sullivan, visits the Yeatses to meet York Powell, Sydney Hall and Sarah Purser.
29	Attends Lady Wilde's 'At Home'.

July

1	(Mon) Meets KT off the Oxford train and brings her to stay for a week at Blenheim Road.
6	'A Summer Evening' (poem; *VP*, 736–7) published in the *Girl's Own Paper*.
7	'Irish Wonders' (article; *LNI*, 91–7) published in the *Providence Sunday Journal*.
10	Writing a column for the *Boston Pilot*.
14	Visits the poet and teacher Emily Hickey.
16	Sees the painter John Nettleship.
19	Delivers the copy for his *Stories from Carleton*.
20	KT at Blenheim Road to meet Nettleship, and she stays the night.
21	WBY inscribes KT's copies of *Oisin* and *FFT*.
26	Delivers his introduction to *Stories from Carleton*, and returns to writing *The Countess Cathleen*.

August

3	(Sat) 'Irish Writers who are Winning Fame' (article; *LNI*, 9–12), published in the *Boston Pilot*.
6	In Oxford copying the Elizabethan translation *The Strife of Love in a Dream* for the publisher David Nutt. Continues writing *The Countess Cathleen* and reading the Irish novelist Charles Kickham for an anthology, *Representative Irish Tales*.
11	Walks 16 miles in the Oxfordshire countryside.
16	Returns to London.
23	WBY's edition of *Stories from Carleton* published.

September

1	(Sun) Dines in London with Sir Charles Gavan Duffy.
3	Takes JO'L to Madam Blavatsky's.
7	Writing a column for the *Boston Pilot*.
28	'Some Forthcoming Irish Books' (article; *LNI*, 13–16), published in the *Boston Pilot*.
30	Attends an evening party at the publisher's John Lane.

October

5   (Sat) 'Columkille and Rosses' (article, later entitled 'Drumcliffe and Rosses'; *Myth*, 88–94) published in the *Scots Observer*.

15   Ellen O'Leary dies in Cork.

19   'William Carleton' (article; *UP* I. 141–6) published in the *Scots Observer*.

20   Sees JO'L, who is passing through London on way back from Paris following his sister's death.

21   Calls on MG who is in London on her way to Paris.

22   Sees JO'L and agrees to proof-read his late sister's book of poems.

31   Writing his column for the *Boston Pilot*.

November

2   (Sat) 'The Ballad of the Foxhunter' (poem; *VP*, 97–9) published in *East and West*, and 'Popular Ballad Poetry of Ireland' (article; *UP* I. 146–62) in the *Leisure Hour*.

16   WBY and SMY at Lady Wilde's 'At Home'.

17   Jack Yeats persuades WBY to shave off his beard.

23   'What the Writers and Thinkers are Doing' (article, *LNI*, 17–21), published in the *Boston Pilot*.

December

5   (Thu) Writing his column for the *Boston Pilot*.

7   Attends Col. Olcott's lecture on 'Theosophy and the Law of Life' at the Bedford Park Club.

20   Meets with Annie Besant and other members of the Esoteric Section of the Theosophical Society to renew their pledges to Mme Blavatsky.

*c.*22   Ellis and WBY discover the MS of Blake's hitherto unpublished *Vala* at the Linnells' house in Redhill, Surrey.

27   Has breakfast with the Coffeys, who are visiting London.

28   'Chevalier Burke – Shule Aroon' (article; LNI, 22–6), published in the *Boston Pilot*.

1890

January

1   (Wed) Receives £3 for contributions to the *Boston Pilot*.

3   Writes to the *Nation* (Dublin) to defend the Irish novelist William Carleton against charges of being anti-National.

4   'Bardic Ireland' (article; *UP* I. 162–6) published in the *Scots Observer*. WBY ill with Russian influenza.

7   Receives 10s. for contributions to the *Manchester Courier*.

11   Founds the Rhymers' Club with Ernest Rhys.

13–15   Writes his poem 'A Cradle Song'.

| 19 | Elected secretary to the Research Committee of the Esoteric Section of the Theosophical Society. |
| 23 | Writing his column for the *Boston Pilot*. |

February

1	(Sat) Experiments in clairvoyance with Mrs Besant and the medium Monsey. These experiments continue intermittently throughout the month.
3	Receives 6s. for contributions to the *Manchester Courier*.
9	The Rhymers' Club meets at Herbert Horne's and Wilde calls in afterwards.
22	'Browning' (article; *LNI*, 27–30) published in the *Boston Pilot*.
27	Calls on Lady Wilde. In the evening WBY's cousin, Edith Wise, calls with her new husband. JBY is painting a large portrait of WBY.

March

1	(Sat) 'Tales from the Twilight' (article; *UP* I. 169–73) published in the *Scots Observer*. Revised version of 'Street Dancers' (poem; *VP*, 731–3) published in the *Leisure Hour*.
2	After a supper party at the Todhunters he takes part in a reading of Todhunter's play *A Sicilian Idyll* with FF, E. H. Heron, and H. M. Paget.
4	Receives £1. 3s. for contributions to the *Boston Pilot*.
7	Initiated into the Hermetic Order of the Golden Dawn (GD) in Moina Bergson's studio, 17 Fitzroy Street.
16	Delivers the MS of *Representative Irish Tales*.

April

3	(Thu) Receives 8s. 6d. for contributions to the *Manchester Courier*.
8	Receives £2. 2s. for contributions to the *Scots Observer*.
19	'A Cradle Song' (poem; *VP*, 118) published in the *Scots Observer*.
21	Writes his column for the *Boston Pilot*.

May

3	(Sat) Receives 2s. 6d. for contributions to the *Manchester Courier*.
5	Attends performance of Todhunter's *A Sicilian Idyll* at the Club House in Bedford Park.
11	Calls on Alice and Wilfrid Meynell.
13	Writing his column for the *Boston Pilot*.
17	'Irish Writers Ought to Take Irish Subjects' (article; *LNI*, 31–5) published in the *Boston Pilot*. 'Dr. Todhunter's New Play' (review) published in the *Nation*.
28	Receives £1. 1s. for contributions to the *Scots Observer*.
30	Works on Blake manuscripts at the Linnells' house in Chelsea. A paperback edition of *Poems and Ballads of Young Ireland* published late this month.

June

8   (Sun) '*A Sicilian Idyll* – Dr. Todhunter's New Play' (article *LNI*, 98–101) published in the *Providence Sunday Journal*.

14   'Dr. Todhunter's *Sicilian Idyll*' (article; *LNI*, 36–9) published in the *Boston Pilot*.

15   The American poet and biographer Louise Imogen Guiney calls on the Yeatses and WBY sees her several times after this. 'A Scholar Poet' (article; *LNI*, 102–7) published in the *Providence Sunday Journal*.

19   Receives £2 for contributions to the *Boston Pilot*.

July

5   (Sat) 'Father Gilligan' (poem, later 'The Ballad of Father Gilligan'; *VP*, 132–4) published in the *Scots Observer*. WBY working on an unpublished book on Irish Duellists and Adventurers.

14   Receives £4 for contributions to the *Boston Pilot*.

15   Visits the occultist MacGregor Mathers at the Horniman Museum in Forest Hill, London.

August

          Spends most of this month working on Blake.

22   (Fri) Ellis signs contract with Quaritch for publication of *The Works of William Blake*.

September

20   (Sat) Receives £3 for contribution to the *Illustrated London News*.

21   Sees the American aesthete Fred Holland Day.

26   Presents a revised copy of *Oisin* to Edward Garnett.

October

4   (Sat) 'Irish Fairies' (article; *UP* I. 175–82) published in the *Leisure Hour*. Receives £2 for contributions to the *Scots Observer*.

5   JO'L leaves after staying with the Yeatses for a few days.

11   Publication of the first number of the short-lived *Weekly Review* to which WBY and other Rhymers contribute. In the middle of this month WBY is asked to resign from the Esoteric Section of the Theosophical Society. Later in the month and through the Autumn he is in a state of semi-collapse; a slight heart ailment is diagnosed.

26   'An Exhibition at William Morris's' (article; *UP* I. 182–6) published in the *Providence Sunday Journal*.

November

1   (Sat) Receives £2 for contributions to the *Weekly Review*.

15   'The Old Pensioner' (poem; *VP*, 131–2) published in the *Scots Observer*.

18   WBY receives £1. 2*s.* for contributions to the *Providence Sunday Journal*. The verdict in the O'Shea divorce case, finding

Parnell the co-respondent, precipitates a political crisis in the Irish Party.

December
1   (Mon) The Irish Party begins to debate the leadership crisis which ends on 6 December in a split between the Parnellite and anti-Parnellite factions.

13   'The Lake Isle of Innisfree' (poem; *VP*, 117) published in the *National Observer*.

1891

January
During this month WBY puts off everything else in a desperate attempt to finish his work on Blake. Contributes 'The Priest of Coloony' (later 'The Ballad of Father O'Hart'; *VP*, 91–3) to a new edition of Sparling's *Irish Minstrelsy*.

29   (Thu) Attends a meeting of the Rhymers' Club at 20 Fitzroy Street; Wilde and Walter Crane also present.

31   Visits Louise Guiney in Hampstead.

February
7   (Sat) 'The Man who Dreamed of Faeryland' (poem; *VP*, 126–8) published in the *National Observer*.

25   Receives £2, probably for contributions to the *National Observer*.

28   'Irish Folk Tales' (article; *UP* I. 186–90) published in the *National Observer*.

March
5   'In the Firelight' (poem; *VP*, 737) published in the *Leisure Hour*. (Thu) Meets Rhys and his new wife Grace, who are visiting from Wales. *Representative Irish Tales* published early this month.

13   Attends the first British performance of Ibsen's *Ghosts*, given by the Independent Theatre at the Royalty Theatre.

17   Writes his column for the *Boston Pilot*. Later this month Unwin agrees to publish *John Sherman and Dhoya* and *The Works of William Blake* begins to go through the press in various sections.

April
1   (Wed) Visits Mathers at the Horniman Museum, Forest Hill. Receives £3 for undisclosed literary work.

11   'Rose Kavanagh' (article; *LNI*, 40–4), published in the *Boston Pilot*.

18   'Gypsy Sorcery' (article; *YA3*, 182–9) published in the *National Observer* and 'Some Recent Books by Irish Writers' (article; *LNI*, 45–9) in the *Boston Pilot*.

23   Receives £20, probably for *Representative Irish Tales*.

May

4   (Mon) Invites Richard Le Gallienne and Todhunter to an 'At Home'.

8   Mme Blavatsky dies in London.

15   Attends a performance of Todhunter's plays *The Poisoned Flower* and *A Sicilian Idyll* at the Vaudeville Theatre.

19   Receives £2 for contributions to the *Boston Pilot*. Later this month he writes an essay on 'The Necessity of Symbolism' for *The Works of William Blake*, and goes through it with Ellis.

June

26   (Fri) Attends a meeting of the Rhymers' Club at John Lane's house to discuss a proposed anthology of their work.

27   Writes an article for the *Boston Pilot*.

29   Attends a gathering at the house of the novelist Nora Vynne.

July

11   (Sat) 'Plays by an Irish Poet' (review; *UP* I. 190–4) published in *United Ireland*.

13   Writes an article for the *Providence Sunday Journal*.

c.17   Arrives in Dublin and stays with KT in Clondalkin.

22   Meets MG in Dublin and his love for her revives. Calls at the *United Ireland* office and discusses possible literary articles with the sub-editor John McGrath.

23   Arrives at Ballykilbeg House near Downpatrick, Co. Down, to stay with Charles Johnston for ten days. Spends the evening launching fire balloons. While at Ballykilbeg he writes articles on Ellen O'Leary, Frances Wynne and KT for A. H. Miles's anthology *The Poets and the Poetry of the Century*.

26   'The Poetic Drama' (article; *LNI*, 11–15), published in the *Providence Sunday Journal*.

August

1   (Sat) 'Dr. Todhunter's New Play' (article; *LNI*, 50–2) published in the *Boston Pilot*. During this month he writes several poems (including 'To a Sister of the Cross and the Rose' and 'No Daughter of the Iron Times') as part of a never-published series of poems, 'The Rosy Cross Lyrics' inspired by MG.

3   Returns to Dublin from Ballykilbeg and stays at a lodging house at 54 Lower Mount Street. Asks MG to marry him but she refuses.

4   Visits Howth with MG.

5   Writes 'The Pathway', an early version of 'He Wishes for the Cloths of Heaven'.

10   Stays with KT at Clondalkin until 16 August.

17   Conducts psychic experiments at the Sigersons'.

22   'Clarence Mangan's Love Affair' (article; *UP* I. 194–8) published in *United Ireland*.

*c.*28	Moves from 54 Lower Mount Street to the headquarters of Dublin Theosophists at 3 Upper Ely Place. MG returns to Paris where her son, Georges, is desperately ill.
31	MG's son Georges dies in Paris.

September
1	(Tue) Writes an early version of 'He tells of the Perfect Beauty'.
12	'A Faery Song' (poem; *VP*, 115–16) published in the *National Observer*, 'A Reckless Century' (article; *UP* I. 198–202) in *United Ireland*, and 'The Celt in Ireland. A Ballad Singer' (article; *LNI*, 53–6) in the *Boston Pilot*.
15	Attends the inaugural meeting of the Young Ireland League, organized by WBY and JO'L to unite various Irish literary societies.
26	'Oscar Wilde's Last Book' (article; *UP* I. 202–5) published in *United Ireland*.

October
3	(Sat) 'An Irish Visionary' (article, later 'A Visionary'; *Myth*, 11–14) published in the *National Observer* and 'The Young Ireland League' (article; *UP* I. 206–8) in *United Ireland*. During this month he writes 'The Sorrow of Love' (*VP*, 119–20), 'He who bids' and 'A Dream of a Life' (*UM*, 96–7) as part of 'The Rosy Cross Lyrics'.
7	Charles Stewart Parnell dies in Brighton.
10	WBY's elegy for Parnell, 'Mourn – And Then Onward!' (poem; *VP*, 737–8), published in *United Ireland*.
11	Parnell's funeral in Dublin. MG returns to Dublin from Paris.
20	Writes poem 'When You are Old' (*VP*, 120–1). Presents MG with a vellum notebook containing seven lyrics, which he entitles 'The Flame of the Spirit'. She subsequently goes to London.
*c.*28	WBY returns to London.
31	'Kathleen' (poem, later 'The Countess Cathleen in Paradise'; *VP*, 124–5) published in the *National Observer*.

November
2	(Mon) MG is initiated into the GD.
3	MG returns to Paris.
6	Ellis takes a further instalment of the Blake book to the printers. Early in this month *John Sherman and Dhoya* published.
9	T. W. Rolleston and his wife, Arthur Lynch, Todhunter and his wife, Charles Johnston and his wife and Sergius Stepniac and his wife at the Yeatses' 'Monday Evening'.
13	WBY attends a meeting of the Rhymers' Club.
15	Writes 'He who measures gain and loss' for 'The Rosy Cross Lyrics'.
18	Writes 'A Song of the Rosy Cross' for 'The Rosy Cross Lyrics'.

22   Writes 'An Epitaph' for 'The Rosy Cross Lyrics'.
23   Calls on Elkin Mathews with G. A. Greene and Lionel Johnson,
            to discuss the publication of *The Book of the Rhymers' Club*.
25   Delivers the copy for *The Countess Kathleen* to Unwin.
28   Receives £10 as first instalment of payment for *John Sherman
            and Dhoya*.

December
12   (Sat) 'An Epitaph' (poem, later 'A Dream of Death'; *VP*, 123)
            published in the *National Observer* and 'A Poet We Have
            Neglected' (article; *UP* I. 208–12) in *United Ireland*.
28   Meeting at Blenheim Road to plan an Irish Literary Society in
            London.

1892

January
2   (Sat) 'Rosa Mundi' (poem, later 'The Rose of the World';
            VP, 111–12) published in the *National Observer*. 'Poems
            by Miss Tynan' (article; *UP* II. 511–14) published in the
            Dublin *Evening Herald*. WBY planning a new 'Library of
            Ireland'.
13   Attends a meeting at the Clapham Reform Club which formally
            decides to establish an Irish Literary Society in London.
16   'The New "Speranza"' (article; *UP* I. 212–15) published in *United
            Ireland*. WBY is correcting proofs of *The Countess Kathleen*.
17   Lectures on 'Nationality and Literature' to the Clapham Branch
            of the Irish National League.
18   Borrows the MS of Blake's *An Island in the Moon* from Charles
            Fairfax Murray.
23   'Dr. Todhunter's Irish Poems' (article; *UP* I. 215–18) published
            in *United Ireland*.
30   'Clovis Huges on Ireland' (article; *UP* I. 218–21) published in
            United Ireland.

February
4   (Thu) Pays Kegan Paul the £2. 3s. 10d. owing on the first edition
            of *Oisin* and takes possession of the unsold stock of 25 bound
            copies and 73 unbound quires.
8   Signs a contract whereby Unwin takes over the unsold stock
            of *Oisin*.
9   Inscribes a copy of the just published *The Book of the Rhymers'
            Club* to MG.
13   Present with Barry O'Brien, Rolleston, Hyde, Crook and others,
            at a meeting of the Irish Literary Society (ILS) which elects

12 Vice-Presidents. 'The Peace of the Rose' (poem, later 'The Rose of Peace'; *VP*, 112–13) published in the *National Observer*.

17 Lunches with Hyde and Edward Garnett; in the evening Hyde visits the Yeatses and meets Todhunter.

22 Appointed Stolistes (Keeper of Robes and Purifying Water) in the Outer Order of the GD, and retains this office until 23 September.

c.28 Writes the poem 'When You are Sad' (*VP*, 738).

March

26 (Sat) Attends a dinner at the Chapham Reform Club in recognition of D. J. O'Donoghue's services to Irish literature, and proposes the toast, 'The Future of Irish Literature'.

April

Spends much of the month finishing *The Works of William Blake* and revising proofs of *The Countess Kathleen*.

23 (Sat) 'The Rhymers' Club' (article; *LNI*, 57–60) published in the *Boston Pilot*.

May

Irish Fairy Tales published early this month.

6 (Fri) Attends a copyright performance of *The Countess Kathleen* at the Athenaeum Theatre, Shepherd's Bush.

7 'The White Birds' (poem; *VP*, 121–2) published in the *National Observer*.

c.10 Arrives in Dublin to help found a central Irish Literary Society.

12 Elected to the Committee of the ILS at an inaugural General Meeting at the Caledonian Hotel, London, although he is not present.

14 Joins in a public debate on 'The Irish Intellectual Capital: Where Is It?' with a letter to *United Ireland*.

21 'Fergus and the Druid' (poem; *VP*, 102–4) published in the *National Observer*. WBY passes an examination towards the 5° = 6° grade of the GD.

24 Speaks at a meeting at the Wicklow Hotel to consider the setting up of a National Literary Society in Dublin.

25 Unwin publishes a second edition of *Oisin*, comprising the copies unsold by Kegan Paul.

31 Attends a meeting of the Provisional Committee of the National Literary Society (NLS).

June

7 (Tue) Attends a meeting of the Provisional Committee of the NLS and discusses details of the administration of the Society.

9 Attends the public Steering Committee meeting of the NLS held at the Rotunda and delivers a speech along with MG, Sigerson, Ashe King, Count Plunkett and others.

11   'The Death of Cuchulain' (poem, later 'Cuchulain's Fight with the Sea'; *VP*, 105–11) published in *United Ireland*.
14   WBY and MG appointed to the Libraries Sub-committee of the NLS.

July

2   (Sat) 'Sight and Song' (review; *UP* I. 225–7) published in the *Bookman*.
9   Writes an article for the *Boston Pilot*.
23   'Some New Irish Books' (review; *UP* I. 228–30) published in *United Ireland*.
25   Attends a General Meeting of the NLS at Costigan's Hotel to adopt rules and appoint officers.
30   As a member of the Provisional Committee of the NLS, WBY meets with Sir Charles Gavan Duffy to discuss the publication of Irish national books. 'Dublin Scholasticism and Trinity College' (article; *UP* I. 231–4) published in *United Ireland* and 'The New "Speranza"' (article; *LNI*, 61–3) published in the *Boston Pilot*.

August

8   (Mon) Speaks at a public meeting at the Mansion House, Dublin, to discuss the revival of Irish literature, the foundation of a publishing company and the circulation of books.
16   Speaks after Sigerson's address to the Inaugural Meeting of the NLS at the Antient Concert Rooms with Gavan Duffy in the chair.
18   Elected to the Council of the NLS as a vice-president.
c.20   *The Countess Kathleen and Various Legends and Lyrics* published.

September

3   (Sat) 'A New Poet' and '"Noetry" and Poetry' (reviews; *UP* I. 234–7; 237–9) published in the *Bookman*.
6   Joins in a controversy over the proposed National Publishing Company with a letter to the *Freeman's Journal*.
8   Publishes another letter on the National Publishing Company controversy in the *Freeman's Journal*.
10   Contributes a third letter on the National Publishing Company controversy to the *Freeman's Journal*.
15   Attends a Committee Meeting of the NLS which sets up a Library Sub-committee with WBY, JO'L and MG among its members.
22   Appointed secretary of the Library Sub-committee of the NLS.
24   Issues a public circular setting out a scheme for founding lending libraries in small Irish towns and appealing for donations towards this.

29   Attends a Committee Meeting of the NLS. 'When You are Old' (poem; *VP*, 120–1) published in the *Independent* (NY).

October

1   (Sat) 'A Mystical Prayer to the Masters of the Elements' (poem, later 'The Poet pleads with the Elemental Powers'; *VP*, 174–5) published in the *Bookman*.

2   WBY's grandmother, Elizabeth Pollexfen, dies in Sligo; WBY is present and is asked to represent the family at the funeral. He remains in Sligo, where his grandfather is also seriously ill.

14   Invokes fairies at Rosses Point with his uncle George Pollexfen and cousin Lucy Middleton.

15   'Invoking the Irish Fairies' (article; *UP* I. 245–7) published in the *Irish Theosophist*, and 'Hopes and Fears for Irish Literature' (article; *UP* I. 247–50) in *United Ireland*.

18   Finishes his introduction to 'The Irish Adventurers' and sends it to Unwin.

29   Rolleston and Gavan Duffy begin negotiations with Unwin for establishing a New Irish Library, a proposal first broached by WBY.

November

5   (Sat) Contributes an unsigned article on the vacant Poet Laureateship to the *Bookman*. In the course of this month writes 'The Fiddler of Dooney'.

6   Writes an article for the *Boston Pilot*.

9   Alarmed to discover that Duffy and Rolleston are stealing his plans for a series of Irish books by opening negotiations with Fisher Unwin.

10   The NLS takes rooms at 4 College Green, Dublin.

12   William Pollexfen dies in Sligo. 'The Rose in my Heart' (poem, later 'The Lover tells of the Rose in his Heart'; *VP*, 142–3) published in the *National Observer*.

15   Attends the funeral of his grandfather.

16   Writes to Unwin warning him against Duffy's and Rolleston's proposal for a New Irish Library.

19   'The New National Library' (article; *LNI*, 64–7), published in the *Boston Pilot*.

20   Returns to Dublin from Sligo and takes room at Lonsdale House, Clontarf.

24   Attends a Committee Meeting of the NLS.

25   Attends Hyde's inaugural lecture, 'The Necessity for De-Anglicizing Ireland', at the NLS.

26   'The Devil's Book' (story, later 'The Book of the Great Dhoul and Hanrahan the Red'; *VSR*, 183–97) published in the *National Observer*.

December

1	(Thu) Attends an NLS Committee Meeting.
3	'The Death of Oenone' (review; *UP* I. 251–4) and 'The Fiddler of Dooney' (poem; *VP*, 178–9) published in the *Bookman*.
8	Attends an NLS Committee Meeting.
15	Attends an NLS Committee Meeting.
16	Attends George Coffey's illustrated lecture to the NLS on 'The Antiquities of Tara'.
*c.*18	Goes to London to confer with Unwin and the Committee of the ILS about the rival schemes for the New Irish Library. While in London he prepares for the Portal examination of the GD.
24	'The Twisting of the Rope' (story; *Myth*, 225–33) published in the *National Observer*.

1893

January

7	(Sat) Attends a Committee Meeting of the ILS to discuss editorial arrangements for the New Irish Library.
20	Undergoes the Portal Ritual for entry to the Second Order of the GD at the Vault in Clipstone Street, London; he also takes the 1st Point part of the 5° = 6° grade, the lowest grade of the Second Order.
21	Takes 2nd and 3rd Points of the GD 5° = 6° grade.
22	Returns to Dublin.
23	Travels to Cork with Hyde to promote the NLS at a public meeting. Shown round the Royal College and is Denny Lane's guest at a Philharmonic Society dinner.
26	Reads his poem 'To Ireland in the Coming Times' and extracts from *The Countess Kathleen* at a social meeting of the NLS.
27	Discusses Gavan Duffy's proposals for the New Irish Library at a Committee Meeting of the NLS which is so contentious that it is adjourned until 2 February. Late this month Quaritch issues a small-paper version of the Yeats-Ellis 3-vol. *The Works of William Blake*; the large-paper version appears in mid-February.

February

2	(Thu) Attends another contentious Committee Meeting of NLS at which he and JO'L are appointed members of an Advisory Committee for the New Irish Library.
4	'The Vision of MacConglinne' (review; *UP* I. 261–3) published in the *Bookman*.
8	Lectures to the Dublin Lodge of the Theosophical Society on 'William Blake and the Symbolism of the Bible'.

16	Attends an NLS Committee Meeting.
*c.*17	Visits Sligo where he stays with George Pollexfen.
24	Returns to Dublin.

March

4	(Sat) Delivers the address at the National Club, Dublin, on the anniversary of the birth of Robert Emmet; Arthur Griffith and Henry Dixon also speak.
17	Visits KT at Clondalkin with JO'L.
21	Formal agreement for publication of the New Irish Library signed by Unwin and Gavan Duffy. Later this month WBY returns to Sligo.

April

1	(Sat) 'The Wandering Jew' (review; *UP* I. 263–6) published in the *Bookman*.
4	Writes 'The Ballad of Earl Paul'.
8	'The Ballad of Earl Paul' (poem; *VP*, 739–42) published in the *Irish Weekly Independent*.
15	'The Heart of the Spring' (story; *Myth*, 171–6) published in the *National Observer*.
20	Back in Dublin, attends an NLS Committee Meeting.
30	Goes with Hyde for the last time to KT's house for a farewell party before she leaves Ireland to be married in London.

May

4	(Thu) KT marries Henry Albert Hinkson in London. WBY attends an NLS Committee Meeting.
6	'The Last Gleeman' (story; *Myth*, 47–53) published in the *National Observer*, and 'The Danaan Quicken Tree' (poem; *VP*, 742–3) in the *Bookman*.
18	Attends an NLS Committee Meeting.
19	Lectures on 'Nationality and Literature' to the NLS at the Leinster Hall.
*c.*23	Returns to London.
27	Text of 'Nationality and Literature' (lecture; *UP* I. 266–75) published in *United Ireland*, and 'Out of the Rose' (story; *Myth*, 157–64) in the *National Observer*.
30	Attends a Council of Adepts at the Second Order of the GD, Clipstone Street, where he continues to pay regular visits that summer until his return to Dublin in mid-September.

June

16	(Fri) At the GD, Clipstone Street from 3 to 10 pm.
19	At the GD from 8.30 to 11 pm.
21	Visiting publishers and working at the British Museum.

23	Sees Constance Gore-Booth.
28	At the GD at 1 pm. and from 6 to 10 pm.
29	Censured by the Committee of the NLS for inefficiencies in his running of the Library Sub-committee.

July

9	(Sun) At the GD with Percy Bullock.
14	At the GD.
16	JO'L, Lionel Johnson, and Elkin Mathews visit the Yeatses.
17	Lectures to the Chiswick Lodge of the Theosophical Society on 'The Nature of Art and Poetry in Relation to Mysticism'.
20	At the GD from 6 pm.
21	At the GD from 7 pm.
22	Attends an Adepts Meeting of the GD, Clipstone Street, from 3 pm. W. W. Westcott issues him with 'Flying Roll XII'. 'A Bundle of Poets' (review; *UP* I. 276–9) published in the *Speaker*.
23	At the GD with Westcott, Bullock and FF.
29	'The Celtic Twilight' (poem, later 'Into the Twilight'; *VP*, 147–8) published in the *National Observer*.
31	The Gaelic League founded in Dublin.

August

1	(Tue) At the GD with FF and Bullock.
4	At the GD with FF and others.
5	'The Curse of the Fires and of the Shadows' (story; *Myth*, 177–83) published in the *National Observer*, and 'The Writings of William Blake' (review; *UP* I. 280–3) and 'The Moods' (poem; *VP*, 142) in the *Bookman*.
15	At the GD.
16	At the GD.
19	'The Message of the Folk-lorist' (review; *UP* I. 283–8) published in the *Speaker*.
23	At the GD.
26	At GD. 'Two Minor Lyrists' (review; *UP* I. 288–91) published in the *Speaker*.
29	Begins a small white notebook in which many of the poems to be published in *The Wind Among the Reeds* are drafted, and starts composing 'The Hosting of the Sidhe'. Later goes to the GD.
30	At the GD. Writing 'The Everlasting Voices'.
31	At the GD.

September

5	(Tue) Writes the poem 'On a Child's Death' (*UM*, 99).
6	At the GD from 7 to 9.30 pm.
7	At the GD from 1.30 to 5 pm and again from 6.30.
8	At the GD from 12 to 1 pm.

9	Spends most of the day at the GD.
11–14	At the GD every day.
*c.*18	Returns to Dublin with Lionel Johnson, to make plans for an Irish literary magazine; they stay with WBY's medical friend, J. P. Quinn, at 56 North Circular Road.
21	Attends an NLS Committee Meeting.
28	Calls with Johnson on the Dublin printer and publisher George Bryers to discuss the production costs of the proposed Irish literary periodical.

October

1	(Sun) Writes the poem 'The Stolen Bride'. Later this month an illustrated edition of *Irish Fairy and Folk Tales* is published.
4	Present at the Annual General Meeting of the NLS.
7	'The Faery Host' (poem, later 'The Hosting of the Sidhe'; *VP*, 140–1) published in the *National Observer*, 'The Ainu' (review; *UP* I. 295–8) in the *Speaker*, and 'Old Gaelic Love Songs' (review; *UP* I. 292–5) in the *Bookman*.
14	Speaks at a Commemoration for Thomas Davis organized by the Young Ireland League at the National Club.
21	'An Impression' (article, later 'A Knight of the Sheep'; *Myth*, 31–3) published in the *Speaker*.

November

4	(Sat) '"Reflections and Refractions" by Charles Weekes' (review; *UP* I. 302–5) published in the *Academy*, and 'The Stolen Bride' (poem, later 'The Host of the Air'; *VP*, 143–5) in the *Bookman*.
11	'Our Lady of the Hills' (article; *Myth*, 101–3) published in the *Speaker*. 'Preface to the Celtic Twilight' (article) published in *United Ireland*.
16–18	Laid up in Dublin with a feverish cold.
21	Travels by the 2 pm train to Belfast and lectures to the Belfast Naturalists' Field Club on 'Irish Fairy Lore'.
22	Climbs Cave Hill outside Belfast with Alice Milligan and others.
23	Back in Dublin, attends an NLS Committee Meeting with Hyde. Later this month he publishes *The Poems of William Blake*.

December

2	(Sat) 'Wisdom and Dreams' (poem; *VP*, 743) published in the *Bookman*.
5	Attends an NLS Committee Meeting.
8	Introduces Alice Milligan to several members of the NLS and accompanies her to Richard Ashe King's lecture on 'The Silent Sister'. WBY speaks after the lecture.
*c.*10	*The Celtic Twilight* published.

24   'Michael Clancy, the Great Dhoul, and Death' (story, *UP* I.
            310–17) published in *The Old Country*. WBY returns to London
            later this month.
29   Working at the GD in Clipstone Street.

1894

January
1   (Mon) Spends most of this month writing his play *The Land of
            Heart's Desire*.
20   Sees the Irish journalist and publisher Edmund Downey about
            publishing an Irish literary magazine.

February
3   (Sat) 'Seen in Three Days' (review; *UP* I. 317–20) published in
            the *Bookman*.
7   Repays JO'L £1 of a £7. 10s. debt. Goes to Paris, staying with the
            Matherses, and sees MG, Verlaine and a number of French men
            of letters.
9   Sees Mrs Rowley, an Irish friend of MG's living in Paris.
10   Calls on MG, who is ill and, although he does not know this,
            pregnant.
24   Acts as Hegemon (Keeper of the Portal) at a GD ceremony at
            Mathers' Ahathoor Temple in Paris.
25   Calls to see Stéphane Mallarmé but discovers he is in London.
26   Accompanies MG to a performance of Villiers de l'Isle-Adam's
            Axël at the Théâtre de la Gâité.
c.29   Returns to London where he begins rewriting *The Shadowy Waters*.

March
2   (Fri) Sees Johnson about the proposed literary quarterly, now
            to be named *Irish Home Reading Magazine*.
10   Writes the poem 'I will not in grey hours ...' (*UM*, 100) in the
            small white MS book. For rest of the month he is preoccupied
            with rehearsals of *The Land of Heart's Desire*.
17   Gives a St Patrick's Day lecture. 'Cap and Bell' (poem, later
            'The Cap and Bells'; *VP*, 159–61) published in the *National
            Observer*.
24   'A Crucifixion' (story, later 'The Crucifixion of the Outcast';
            Myth, 147–56) published in the *National Observer*.
29   *The Land of Heart's Desire* produced with Todhunter's *The
            Comedy of Sighs* at the Avenue Theatre, London, to a rowdy
            and hostile reception. Nevertheless, both plays run until 14
            April. WBY loses his glasses and is in the hands of his oculist
            for two weeks.

April

7   (Sat) 'The Song of the Old Mother' (poem; *VP*, 150–1) and 'A Symbolical Drama in Paris' (drama review; *UP* I. 320–5) published in the *Bookman*.

14   *The Land of Heart's Desire* and *The Comedy of Sighs* close at the Avenue Theatre.

15   Goes to see Ernest and Grace Rhys.

16   Meets Olivia Shakespear (OS) at a *Yellow Book* Dinner.

20   *The Land of Heart's Desire* (play; *VPl*, 180–213) published and WBY inscribes a copy for MG.

21   *The Land of Heart's Desire* revived at the Avenue Theatre with Shaw's *Arms and the Man*.

May

       'Regina, Regina, Pigmeorum, Veni' (article; *Myth*, 54–6) published in the *Irish Home Reading Magazine*.

12   (Sat) *The Land of Heart's Desire* ends its run at the Avenue Theatre.

18   Returns his contract for the already published *The Land of Heart's Desire* to Unwin.

20   Attends a reception given by Unwin for London booksellers at Clifford's Inn.

June

2   (Sat) 'The Evangel of Folk-Lore' (review; *UP* I. 326–8) published in the *Bookman*. Later this month *The Second Book of the Rhymers' Club*, with WBY's contributed poems, is published and he meets Lady Augusta Gregory (AG) briefly for the first time.

c.23   Takes Dora Sigerson to see *Arms and the Man*.

24   Sarah Purser at the Yeatses.

27   Calls on the Matherses, who are visiting from Paris.

July

       Spends most of this month working on his anthology, *A Book of Irish Verse*.

16   (Mon) Attends the unveiling of a bust of John Keats at Hampstead Church.

21   'Those Who Live in the Storm' (story, later 'The Rose of Shadow'; *UP* I. 328–32) published in the *Speaker*.

31   WBY, Mrs Paget and a mediumistic chemist's assistant conduct psychical experiments at FF's apartment.

August

4   (Sat) 'Kathleen-Ny-Hoolihan' (story, later 'Hanrahan and Cathleen, the Daughter of Houlihan'; *Myth*, 234–7) published in the *National Observer*, and 'Some Irish National Books' and 'A New Poet' (reviews; *UP* I. 332–5; 335–9) in the *Bookman*.

5	Sees FF.
6	Has tea with Fred Holland Day. MG's daughter, Iseult, born in France.
15	Writes the Preface to *A Book of Irish Verse*.
23	Attends the wedding of Jack Yeats and Mary Cottenham ('Cottie') White at Emmanuel Church, Gunnersbury.

September

8	(Sat) 'An Imagined World' (review; *UP* I. 341–3) published in the *Speaker*.
29	'The Curse of O'Sullivan the Red upon Old Age' (story, later 'Red Hanrahan's Curse'; *Myth*, 238–45) published in the *National Observer*.

October

6	(Sat) 'The Stone and the Elixir' (review; *UP* I. 344–6) published in the *Bookman*.
8	The publisher Elkin Mathews makes an offer for WBY's proposed *Poems*.
9	WBY discusses terms for the publication of *Poems* with Unwin.
10	Arrives in Dublin, staying again with J. P. Quinn at 56 North Circular Road.
11	Writes to Unwin setting out his terms for the publication of *Poems*.
19	Further negotiations with Unwin by letter about the terms for the publication of *Poems*.
23	Goes to stay with George Pollexfen in Sligo, where he spends much time over the coming months revising poems and plays for his collected edition, *Poems*, and in writing *The Shadowy Waters*.
24	Writes to Robert Louis Stevenson to thank him for a letter praising 'The Lake Isle of Innisfree'.

November

5	(Mon) Signs and returns Unwin's contract for the publication of *Poems*.
19	Writes the poem 'To his Heart...' in small white MS book.
*c.*20	Goes to stay with the Gore-Booths at Lissadell for a few days.

December

1	(Sat) Back in Sligo, he gets into the routine of writing new poems during the day and revising old ones (including 'The Wanderings of Oisin') after dinner.
*c.*9	Returns to stay at Lissadell, and then at the Parsonage there. Contemplates asking Eva Gore-Booth to marry him. Collects folklore and lectures on fairy tales. Later this month he reads Anthony Hope's *The Prisoner of Zenda* and OS's *The Journey of High Honour*.

1895

January

6   (Sun) Writing the story 'Wisdom'.

20   Puts other work aside while he revises the material (including *The Countess Kathleen*) for *Poems*.

26   Joins in a public controversy over Edward Dowden's disparagement of Irish literature with a letter to the Dublin *Daily Express* and contributes further letters to the discussion on 30 January and 7 February.

27   Writes to Unwin stipulating the design for *Poems*.

February

2   (Sat) 'Battles Long Ago' (review; *UP* I. 350–1) published in the *Bookman*.

27   Initiates a discussion in the Dublin *Daily Express* on 'The Best 30 Irish Books'. Late this month both he and George Pollexfen ill with influenza.

March

2   (Sat) 'An Excellent Talker' (review; *UP* I. 354–5) published in the *Bookman*.

c.7   *A Book of Irish Verse* published.

8   Contributes a further letter to the Dublin *Daily Express* on 'The Best 30 Irish Books'.

16   Contributes a letter to *United Ireland* on 'The Best 30 Irish Books'.

24   Finishes the Preface for *Poems*.

27   Finishes the revision of *Poems* and sends the MS to Unwin.

April

13   (Sat) Leaves Sligo to visit Hyde at Frenchpark, Co. Roscommon.

16   Visits Castle Rock in Lough Key, which he later imagines as the centre for the Celtic Mystical Order.

May

1   (Wed) Returns to Sligo from Frenchpark.

4   Leaves Sligo for Dublin *en route* to London. 'To Some I have Talked with by the Fire' (poem; *VP*, 136–7) and 'Dublin Mystics' (review; *UP* I. 356–8) published in the *Bookman*.

19   Calls on Oscar Wilde to offer sympathy and support during his trial; Wilde is not there but WBY sees his brother.

20   Wilde's trial begins.

June

1   (Sat) 'The Story of Early Gaelic Literature' (review; *UP* I. 358–9) published in the *Bookman*. WBY spends most of the month correcting the proofs of *Poems*. Passes further GD exams.

July

1	(Mon) Returns proofs of *Poems* to Unwin.
6	'Irish National Literature I: From Callanan to Carleton' (article; *UP* I. 359–64) and 'The Three Sorrows of Story Telling' (review; *UP* I. 364–6) published in the *Bookman*.
16	Visits Mrs Valentine Fox at Beckenham, Kent, with OS.
*c.*17	Sees Henley and tries to persuade him to publish stories and articles by Standish James O'Grady.
18	In the evening calls to see Louise Imogen Guiney who has recently arrived from the USA.
*c.*28	Sees the publisher Dent about possible books on Blake, JBY's illustrations and O'Grady's books.

August

2	(Fri) Impecunious and works all day at a story, 'Costello the Proud'.
3	The Mathews visit the Yeatses and WBY reads them his new story. 'Irish National Literature II: Contemporary Prose Writers' (article; *UP* I. 366–73) and 'That Subtle Shade' (review; *UP* I. 373–5) published in the *Bookman*.
4	Visits Gleeson White.
5	At FF's all morning and later borrows 2*d.* from SMY to call on the novelist Nora Vynne.
10	Visits W. E. Henley wearing a new black coat.
11	The poet Nora Hopper calls and WBY reads her his story 'Costello the Proud'. Subsequently reads an article he has written on Standish O'Grady to JO'L, and later the artists Nash and Paget call in.
13	Takes 'Costello the Proud' to be typed. Uncle John Pollexfen calls unexpectedly.
14	Brings FF home to tea; in the evening, York Powell, Paget, Nash and JO'L (who stays the night) call in.
17	JBY suffering from an illness which is to persist for much of the Autumn. WBY working hard at poems and stories.
20	Receives an advance copy of *Poems*.
22	Writes 'The Twilight of Forgiveness' (later 'The Lover asks Forgiveness') in the small white MS book. In the evening meets George Moore's brother, Augustus.
23	Writes another draft of 'The Twilight of Forgiveness'.
24	Working at the British Museum. Revises 'The Twilight of Forgiveness'.
26	Inscribes an advance copy of *Poems* to AE. In the afternoon Nora Hopper, Imogen Guiney, Lionel Johnson, and Jack and Cottie Yeats call at Blenheim Road.
29	Revises poem 'The Everlasting Voices' (*VP*, 141). Sees the artist Faulks.
31	Nora Vynne comes to tea and stays for the evening at the Yeatses.

September

1   (Sun) SMY meets WBY on the way home, deep in the throes of a new poem. In the evening WBY reads aloud from Edwin Ellis's play, *Sancan the Bard*.

3   OS calls at Blenheim Road together with Nora Hopper, Louise Imogen Guiney, Dora Sigerson and Elkin Mathews.

4   WBY having his portrait painted by Faulks.

7   'Irish National Literature III: Contemporary Irish Poets' (article; *UP* I. 375–82) published in the *Bookman* and 'Wisdom' (story, later 'The Wisdom of the King'; *Myth*, 165–70) in the *New Review*.

13   Aunt Agnes Pollexfen Gorman arrives at Blenheim Road, having escaped from a mental home. Her husband, Robert Gorman, is summoned the next day and recommits her. WBY visits KT, whose newly born son is dying.

14   Visits Jack and Cottie Yeats at Chertsey.

24   Writes 'He bids his Beloved be at Peace'.

October

5   (Sat) Delivers the address at a Parnell Commemorative Meeting at the Arbitration Rooms, Chancery Lane. 'Irish National Literature IV: a List of the Best Irish Books' (article; *UP* I. 382–7) and 'A Song of the Rosy Cross' (poem; *VP*, 744) published in the *Bookman*. Early this month WBY leaves the family home and takes rooms with Arthur Symons in Fountain Court, the Temple.

13   Paget and York Powell at the Yeatses when WBY comes in delighted with his new apartment.

15   SMY leaves London for Hyères where she is to be a governess.

November

2   (Sat) 'The Twilight of Forgiveness' (poem, later 'The Lover asks Forgiveness because of his Many Moods'; *VP*, 162–3) published in the *Saturday Review* and 'The Life of Patrick Sarsfield' and 'The Chain of Gold by Standish O'Grady' (reviews; *UP* I. 387–9; *UP* II. 515) in the *Bookman*. Later this month WBY writes 'The Lover speaks to the Hearers of his Songs in Coming Days' (*VP*, 173) and rereads Edmund Gosse's play *King Erik*.

December

1   (Sun) 'St. Patrick and the Pedants' (story, later 'The Old Men of the Twilight'; *Myth*, 191–5) published in the *Weekly Sun Literary Supplement*, for which WBY receives £6. In the course of this month he writes 'He tells of the Perfect Beauty' (*VP*, 164).

11   WBY goes to tea with his family at Bedford Park and stays on until 11 pm.

29	Calls in to the family house at Bedford Park for a book, and reveals that he has had no dinner because Arthur Symons has borrowed all his money.
31	Attends a New Year's party at the Gosses'.

1896

January
1	(Wed) Sends KT's *Miracle Plays* to SMY as a New Year's gift.
4	'The Shadowy Horses' (poem, later 'He bids his Beloved be at Peace'; *VP*, 154), 'The Travail of Passion' (poem; *VP*, 172), and 'The Binding of the Hair' (story; *UP* I. 390–3) published in the *Savoy*, and 'Everlasting Voices' (poem; *VP*, 141) in the *New Review*. In the middle of the month WBY suffers severely from toothache and has several teeth extracted.
14	JBY calls on WBY but Symons tells him he is working hard in the British Museum Reading Room.
18	Spends some days with his family in Bedford Park.
19	Accompanies JBY to a meeting of the 'Calumets', a Bedford Park discussion club.
22	Attends a dinner at the New Lyric Club for contributors to the *Savoy* with Max Beerbohm; Aubrey and Mabel Beardsley, Arthur Symons, Leonard and Alice Smithers also present.

February
Late this month WBY moves from the Temple to rooms at 18 Woburn Buildings to further his relationship with OS. He also starts work on a novel, *The Speckled Bird*.

March
1	(Sun) Dines with the Gosses.
7	'William Carleton' (review; *UP* I. 394–7) published in the *Bookman*. 'O'Sullivan the Red to Mary Lavell' (two poems, later 'He tells of the Perfect Beauty' and 'A Poet to his Beloved'; *VP*, 164, 157) published in the *Senate*.
13	Sees W. T. Horton in afternoon and borrows Thomas Lake Harris's *God's Breath in Man*.
21	Horton initiated into the GD, WBY probably acting as Hiereus, and sponsoring him through the ritual. In the evening goes to the ILS.

April
c.3	(Fri) AE, in London for a few days; sees WBY, who takes him to tea with OS at Porchester Square.
4	'Rosa Alchemica' (story; *Myth*, 267–92), 'A Cradle Song' (poem, later 'The Unappeasable Host'; *VP*, 146–7), 'The Valley of the Black Pig' (poem; *VP*, 161), and 'Verlaine in 1894' (article; *UP* I.

397–9) published in the *Savoy*. 'The Vision of O'Sullivan the Red' (story, heavily revised later as 'Hanrahan's Vision'; *Myth*, 246–52) published in the *New Review*, and 'William Blake' (review; *UP* I. 400–3) in the *Bookman*.

*c.*18–21   Stays for a few days with his family in Bedford Park; he has been ill, but is now is busy furnishing his new rooms and arranging a commission for his novel, *The Speckled Bird*, with Lawrence and Bullen.

24   Sees Horton at Woburn Buildings and goes on to Westminster.

25   Dines with the Gosses.

May

2   (Sat) 'An Irish Patriot' (review; *UP* I. 403–6) published in the *Bookman*.

8   Horton calls at 11.30 am and has breakfast with WBY.

28   Symons calls on WBY in the late evening and tells him that his article for the *Savoy*, 'William Blake and his Illustrations to the Divine Comedy I', must be done by 1 June.

June

3   (Wed) Receives £4 from Elkin Mathews as advance on royalties for *The Wind Among the Reeds*. Invites Richard Le Gallienne to dinner before going on to the ILS where Gosse takes the chair at Herbert Trench's lecture on Aubrey de Vere, to which WBY replies.

4   Attends the GD's Corpus Christi Ceremony in the Vault of the Adepts.

6   'The New Irish Library' (review; *UP* I. 406–8) published in the *Bookman*.

*c.*9   Arranges for the photographing of Linnell's Blake designs for his *Savoy* article.

13   Visits Horton in Brighton and stays until 15 June.

22   Invites the novelist 'George Egerton' to his 'At Home' to meet Havelock Ellis and Symons.

July

4   (Sat) 'O'Sullivan Rua to Mary Lavell' (poem, later 'He remembers Forgotten Beauty'; *VP*, 155–6) and 'William Blake and his Illustrations to the Divine Comedy I' (article; *E & I*, 116–28) published in the *Savoy*.

5   Meets the Danish critic Georg Brandes at Gosse's house.

16   Visits JBY at Bedford Park who lends him 2*s*. 6*d*.

20   Returns Lake Harris's *The Apocalypse* and *Songs of Fairyland*, and extracts from Jules Bois' 'Le satanisme et la magie' to Horton.

25   Arrives in Dublin from London with Symons.

26   They call on Edward Dowden in Killiney.

27   WBY and Symons travel from Dublin to stay with Edward Martyn at Tillyra Castle, Co. Galway, and they go to visit the French novelist Paul Bourget, who is a guest of the Comte de Basterot's at Duras House.

August

1   (Sat) 'William Blake and his Illustrations to the Divine Comedy II' (article; *E & I*, 128–40) published in the *Savoy*.

5   WBY, Symons, Martyn, and Martin Morris sail to the Aran Islands in a hooker and visit Inishmore and Inishman, but are unable to land on Inisheer. WBY reads Fiona Macleod's 'The Washer of the Ford' on the way over.

7   WBY and his companions return to Tillyra from Aran.

*c.*10   Martyn takes WBY to visit AG at Coole.

15   WBY has a vision of an Archer at Tillyra.

*c.*29   WBY and Symons arrive in Sligo from Tillyra. ECY is already there and Jack Yeats and his wife arrive soon afterwards.

September

5   (Sat) 'William Blake and his Illustrations to the Divine Comedy III' (article; *E & I*, 140–5) and 'O'Sullivan Rua to the Secret Rose' (poem, later 'The Secret Rose'; *VP*, 169–70) published in the *Savoy*.

*c.*11   WBY and Symons spend 3 days in a cabin at Glencar on the slopes of Ben Bulben.

*c.*18   WBY and Symons leave Sligo to stay with Hyde at Frenchpark.

*c.*22   WBY and Symons go to Dublin where WBY probably stays with AE at 3 Upper Ely Place.

October

3   (Sat) 'Greek Folk Poetry' (review; *UP* I. 409–12) in the *Bookman*.

*c.*6   Sees the Fenian Patrick Gregan in Dublin.

*c.*11   Returns to London.

*c.*13   Calls on Mark Ryan thinking JO'L is there.

21   'Where There Is Nothing, There Is God' (story; *Myth*, 184–90) published in the *Sketch*.

November

1   (Sun) Dines at Edmund Gosse's with Arthur Anstruther, Arthur Symons and Edward Marsh, and gives an account of visions he has had in Ireland.

2   'O'Sullivan Rua to the Curlew' (poem, later 'He reproves the Curlew'; *VP*, 155), 'Out of the Old Days' (poem, later 'To his Heart, bidding it have no Fear'; *VP*, 158), and 'The Tables of the Law' (story; *Myth*, 293–307)) published in the *Savoy*. 'The Cradles of Gold' (story; *UP* I. 413–18) published in the *Senate*, and 'The Well at the World's End' (review; *UP* I. 418–20) published in the *Bookman*.

4	Meets G. A. Greene to discuss a Gaelic metrical charm.
6	Sees W. T. Horton at 4.30.
c.20	Aubrey Beardsley begins drawings for a proposed edition of *The Shadowy Waters* to be published by Leonard Smithers.
22	SMY leaves Hyère for London.
26	WBY addresses members of the GD at Mark Mason's Hall.
28	Posts Smithers an extract from *The Shadowy Waters* for Beardsley.

December

c.2	(Wed) Goes to Paris to work at *The Speckled Bird* and *The Shadowy Waters*.
5	'Miss Fiona Macleod as a Poet' (review; *UP* I. 421–4) published in the *Bookman*, and 'The Death of O'Sullivan the Red' (story, later 'The Death of Hanrahan'; *Myth*, 253–61) in the *New Review*. 'Costello the Proud, Oona Macdermott, and the Bitter Tongue' (story, later 'Proud Costello, MacDermot's Daughter, and the Bitter Tongue'; *Myth*, 196–210) published in the *Pageant*.
12	Accompanies Symons to performance of Alfred Jarry's contentious play, *Ubu Roi*.
17	WBY and Symons working to finish articles are unable to meet Henry Davray until 6 pm when they take hashish before dinner and meet followers of the French occultist Louis de Saint-Martin.
21	First meeting with John Synge at the Hotel Corneille.
23	A formal Agreement between WBY and Lawrence and Bullen for *The Speckled Bird*.

1897

January

1	(Fri) Accompanies Synge to the inaugural meeting of MG's *L'Association Irlandaise*, the Paris branch of the Young Ireland Society.
2	'Young Ireland' (review; *UP* II. 33–5) published in the *Bookman*.
9	'The Valley of Lovers' (poem, later 'He tells of a Valley full of Lovers'; *VP*, 163) published in the *Saturday Review*.
14	Meets Synge at a social gathering in Paris.
15	Invites several friends, including Synge, to tea.
c.17	Returns to London from Paris.
22	Sees Horton.
31	Probably writes 'The Song of Wandering Aengus'.

February

6	(Sat) 'Mr. John O'Leary' (review; *UP* II. 35–7) published in the *Bookman*. Early in the month is deep in *The Speckled Bird* which goes slowly.

14	AG invites WBY to dinner with Barry O'Brien, Sir Harry and Lady Johnston, Sophie Lyall, Alfred Cole and Sir Arthur Clay. WBY praises Goethe.
16	Attends a meeting of the London Young Ireland Society which resolves itself into a Committee to celebrate the centenary of the 1798 Irish Rebellion. WBY is elected chairman.
22	Accompanies Ernest Rhys to a Welsh society, the 'Cymru Fydd'.
23	To tea with AG and Sir Alfred Lyall and tells her of his plans for a 'Celtic Theatre'.
28	To dinner at AG's but Henry James cannot come.

March

2	(Tue) Chairs a meeting of the Young Ireland Society.
c.3	WBY and Frank Hugh O'Donnell cross to Dublin as the London delegates to a meeting of the '98 Committee.
4	Attends a large meeting of the '98 Committee in the Dublin City Hall, but feels the absurdity of this undertaking.
6	Calls on T. W. Rolleston and complains about the intrigues in the '98 Committees.
7	In the evening goes to T. W. Rolleston's with John McGrath to discuss a new nationalist paper that McGrath is to edit. They stay until after 1 am.
8	Attends W. A. Henderson's lecture on 'The Stage Literature of Ireland' at the NLS and speaks afterwards.
c.13	Returns to London with O'Donnell and on the boat tells him that *United Ireland* has promised their faction of the IRB a weekly column.
14	Dines with the Gosses.
16–22	Reading widely in the works of Robert Bridges, especially the plays.
21	Dinner at AG's with Barry O'Brien and Horace Plunkett followed by a long discussion of current Irish politics.
24–27	Writing a ballad, 'The Blessed', for the *Yellow Book*.
27	Spends the weekend with the Robert Bridges at Yattenden near Newbury.
28	Bad weather keeps WBY and the Bridges indoors all day and WBY gets them to see visions with the help of Tattwa symbols.
29	After a walk with Robert Bridges, WBY returns to London.
31	Writes to the Parisian Irish Society, the Société de Sainte-Patrice, to repudiate Charles Teeling's denunciation of MG as an English spy.

April

2	(Fri) Has Horton to tea.
3	'Mr. Arthur Symons's New Book' (review; *UP* II. 38–42) published in the *Bookman*, and 'The Blessed' (poem; *VP*, 166–8) in the

Yellow Book. Chairs a meeting of the London '98 Committee, where O'Donnell's tendentious account of the recent Dublin meeting leads to friction with the Dublin Committee.

5   Publication of *The Secret Rose*.

11   To dinner at AG's with George Moore, Nevill Geary, Barry O'Brien and Milly Childers.

12   Consults Barry O'Brien about the quarrel between the London and Dublin '98 Committees and is advised not to write to the papers.

28   'Miss Fiona Macleod' (review; *UP* II. 42–5) published in the *Sketch*. Late this month WBY experiments with the drug mescal (mescaline), provided by Havelock Ellis.

May

*c.*5   (Wed) Crosses from London to Dublin, where he stays with Standish O'Grady.

10   Spends the evening at T. W. Rolleston's with AE, Lyster and J. E. Healy.

14   Goes to Sligo to stay with George Pollexfen and adopts a strict routine so as to get on with *The Speckled Bird*, poems and reviews.

June

5   (Sat) 'Mr. Robert Bridges' (review, later *The Return of Ulysses*; *E & I*, 198–202) published in the *Bookman*, and 'The Desire of Man and of Woman' (poem, later 'He mourns for the Change that has come upon him and his Beloved'; *VP*, 153) in the *Dome*. Later this month Bullen publishes *The Tables of the Law and The Adoration of the Magi* in a limited private edition.

16   Goes from Sligo to Tillyra Castle to stay with Edward Martyn.

19   'William Blake' (article, later 'William Blake and the Imagination'; *E & I*, 111–15) published in the *Academy*.

20   Goes to Dublin and is present at MG's anti-Jubilee speech to James Connolly's Socialist meeting in College Green.

21   Attends an Executive Meeting of the Dublin '98 Committee with MG; afterwards they attend an anti-Jubilee parade organized by Connolly in Foster Place. In the afternoon WBY calls to see T. W. Rolleston and tells him that MG is planning a riot the following day.

22   Attends a '98 Convention in Dublin City Hall, which lasts from 6 to 11 pm, with JO'L in the chair. WBY proposes the resolution that 'this Convention ... declares its belief in the right of Ireland to freedom'. After the meeting WBY and MG go to the National Club in Rutland Square where the police baton a large crowd. WBY locks MG in the Club for her protection and goes round to newspaper offices to take responsibility for this action. These events reawaken his love for MG.

25   Returns to Tillyra from Dublin where AG visits and finds him haggard and voiceless. Later this month WBY, AG and Martyn make plans for a Dublin-based 'Celtic Theatre' during a visit to de Basterot at Duras and set about raising subscriptions for the venture.

July

3   (Sat) 'The Treasure of the Humble' (review; *UP* I. 45–7) published in the *Bookman*. WBY remains at Tillyra until 17 July, writing lyrics including 'Maid Quiet', for *The Wind Among the Reeds*.

14   'Bards of the Gael and Gall' (review; *YA5*, 203–11) published in the *Illustrated London News*.

17   Leaves Tillyra to stay with George Pollexfen at Rosses Point, where AE joins him and they go in quest of new gods.

24   'Song' (poem, later 'The Lover pleads with his Friend for Old Friends'; *VP*, 172–3) published in the *Saturday Review*.

26   WBY and AE travel from Rosses Point to stay with AG at Coole. AE leaves after a few days, but WBY stays on for two months, collecting folklore with AG. William Sharp, Hyde and Dr. Moritz Bonn also pay visits during this time.

27   AG takes WBY and AE to the Burren hills at Corcomroe.

August

4   (Wed) 'A Mad Song' (poem, later 'The Song of Wandering Aengus'; *VP*, 149–50) published in the *Sketch*.

7   'Mr. Standish O'Grady's "Flight of the Eagle"' (review; *UP* I. 47–51) published in the *Bookman*, and 'O'Sullivan the Red upon his Wanderings' (poem, later 'Maid Quiet'; *VP*, 171) in the *New Review*.

September

4   (Sat) 'Aglavaine and Selysette' (review; *UP* I. 51–4) published in the *Bookman*.

6–9   Stays with Lord Castletown at Doneraile.

9   Returns to Coole where Standish O'Grady is staying for a short visit.

10   Horace Plunkett visits Coole for a meeting of the Irish Agricultural Organisation Society (IAOS) in Gort, and dines with AG, WBY and Martyn.

21   Consecration of the GD's new premises at 36 Blythe Road.

28   WBY re-elected *in absentia* as president of the London Young Ireland Society.

October

3   (Sun) Accompanies MG to Manchester to address long and exhausting '98 political meetings. Between sessions he and MG go to see the Rossetti pictures in the City Art Gallery.

4	WBY and MG speak on behalf of '98 Committee at Hanley, Staffordshire.
5	Returns to London and spends the evening with Symons.
c.7	Returns to Dublin, probably with MG.
13	In the West of Ireland, probably staying with George Pollexfen.
17	MG sails for the USA to lecture on behalf of '98 Movement and Amnesty.
c.30	WBY arrives back in Dublin.
31	Sees AE.

November

1	(Mon) WBY and Martyn go to the Contemporary Club to discuss the Celtic Theatre and find the members enthusiastic. Receives food hamper from AG.
3	Speaks at a dinner for Dairy Co-operators during the Annual Conference of the IAOS. At 9 pm he sees J. P. Quinn with Martyn about recovering his furniture and pictures and to discuss the theatre movement. Spends most of this month in Dublin helping Martyn with arrangements for the Celtic Theatre.
4	Organizing subscriptions for the Celtic Theatre.
6	'The Tribes of Danu' (article; *UP* II. 54–70) published in the *New Review*.
8	Spends the evening with Synge and AE, who sketches him for AG.
9	Trying to resolve difficulties about a venue and licence for the Celtic Theatre, and inspecting possible halls with Martyn.
14	Hears of W. E. Henley's dismissal from editorship of the *New Review*, which will not now take his article, 'The Tribes of Danu'.
17	Horace Plunkett promises to take up the question of a patent for the Celtic Theatre with the authorities.
18	Martyn leaves Dublin for London, but WBY remains to retrieve his pictures and books from store. Recommends AE to Horace Plunkett as IAOS organizer and sees Valentine Grace, actor and manager, about the Celtic Theatre.
19	Plunkett offers AE a post in the IAOS; WBY brings the Dublin theosophists to AE to assure him that they will hold together while he is away in the country.
22	Crosses by evening boat from Dublin to England.
23	Sees Martyn, FF and William Sharp at Woburn Buildings in the afternoon. In the evening he dines at AG's with Frederic Harrison and Edward Clodd.
24	'Three Irish Poets' (review; *UP* II. 70–3) published in *A Celtic Christmas*.
24–8	Trouble over WBY's objection to Sharp taking the chair at his forthcoming lecture on 'The Celtic Movement'.

28   AG invites Sharp to dine with her, WBY, the Leckys, Martyn,
            and Sophie Lyall, so smoothing the friction between him and
            WBY over the lecture.

December

1   (Wed) Chairs a meeting of the London Executive of the '98
            Centenary Association.
3   Stays with the Hunters in Chiswick to work on the divinations
            and rituals for his proposed Celtic Mystical Order, a plan he
            shared with MG of establishing a Castle of Heroes, 'an Irish
            Eleusis or Samothrace' (*Aut*), at Castle Rock, Lough Key.
4   Lectures on 'The Celtic Movement' at the Society of Arts, John
            Street, with Alfred Nutt in the chair. Afterwards AG holds a
            'fiesta' for him at the Metropole, attended by JBY, the Sharps,
            FF, Symons and Norma Borthwick.
5   Makes a long speech about proxy voting at the Young Ireland
            Society.
8   Sketched by JBY.
10   Spends an industrious day writing letters and measures his
            windows so that AG can have curtains made for him. Sees
            Horton at 1 pm to discusses his new drawings.
11   Accompanies AG to dinner at the Birches with the Comyns
            Carrs, Lady Edmund Fitzmaurice and Sir Bartle Frere. He dis-
            cusses visions and spiritualism after dinner, and the party does
            not break up until nearly midnight, when WBY walks home
            with Sir Bartle Frere and continues the discussion in his rooms.
12   JBY does sketch of WBY, who is expecting a visit from a priest
            who wants to discuss visions and magic.
13   JBY makes another sketch of WBY at Woburn Buildings.
14   JBY at Woburn Buildings doing portrait of WBY. In the after-
            noon AG calls to measure a window for curtains. WBY tries to
            see JBY off to Ireland, but he misses two trains at Euston. In the
            evening WBY dines with AG on his way to a '98 Committee
            Meeting and he talks at length about his unhappiness over MG.
16   Dines at AG's with Flora Shaw, William Peel, Sir Allen
            Johnson (Lionel Johnson's uncle) and Philip Comyns Carr
            among other guests.
18   WBY and FF dine with AG.
19   AG takes WBY to lunch at Lady Dorothy Nevill's where they see
            Sir Francis Jeune, the Francis Hollands, and Sir Arthur and Una
            Birch. They go on to interview an old Irish woman in Chiswick
            about folklore and then call into 3 Blenheim Road for tea with
            his sisters before returning to dinner at AG's rooms.
20   AG leaves London for Coole.

24	Buys presents for his sisters and goes to 3 Blenheim Road for Christmas, staying until 27 December. Receives a Christmas hamper from AG.
27	Returns to Woburn Buildings and spends some days writing articles for the *Nineteenth Century*.
28	Calls on Barry O'Brien to discuss '98 matters with him, Michael Davitt and others. Also tries to discuss the Celtic Theatre with O'Brien.
29	Meets the Hunters, Mary Briggs and Ada Waters at 8 pm to work on the Celtic Mystical Order.

1898

January

1	(Sat) 'The Prisoners of the Gods' (article; *UP* II. 74–87) published in the *Nineteenth Century*. At 7.30 pm WBY attends meeting of the Celtic Mystical Order at the Hunters.
2	Dines at the Gosses with Rothenstein, George Moore and Symons.
3	7.30 pm Dorothea Hunter and her husband call on WBY to discuss Celtic mysticism. Later, other 'Monday Evening' guests arrive, including Osman Edwards, Sarojini Chattopâdhyây, FF, Laurence Alma Tadema and Symons. WBY remains preoccupied with Celtic mysticism for the rest of the month.
4	Attends tea-party at Symons's rooms in the Temple to meet the Belgian symbolist poet, Émile Verhaeren. MG arrives in Queenstown (Cobh) on her return from her American tour.
9	Sends a second folklore article to the *Nineteenth Century*.
11	Reading the Finnish epic, *The Kalevala*, at the British Museum. In the evening Symons calls to read him his hostile review of Stephen Phillips' poems and WBY gives him raspberry vinegar.
14	Engaged on '98 Centenary politics.
15	The Dublin commercial theatres issue a public notice forbidding amateur theatricals in Dublin under an eighteenth-century Patent Act.
16	Speaks at a '98 Meeting in Holborn attended by Mark Ryan, Anthony MacBride and Alice Milligan.
20	MG arrives in London and WBY spends all one day and part of another seeing her about '98 work and visiting the Rossetti exhibition at the New Gallery.
22	Synge lunches with WBY at the British Museum and they go on to the New Gallery. Pheasants sent to WBY by AG arrive. WBY worried by AE's despondency in his new IAOS job.
26	Dines with Gosse, Henry James and Arthur Conan Doyle at the National Club.

29	At a meeting of the London '98 Executive to draft a reply to the National League's claims about the previous March's public meeting.
30	Meets Edward Clodd at the Shorters, and discusses folklore, the '98 Centenary and Verlaine.

February

5	(Sat) 'Mr. Lionel Johnson's Poems' (review; *UP* I. 88–91) published in the *Bookman*. WBY desperately busy for several days on 'The Celtic Element in Literature', an article for *Cosmopolis*.
9	'Aodh to Dectora' (poem, later 'He wishes his Beloved were Dead'; *VP*, 175–6) published in the *Sketch*.
10	Finishes 'The Celtic Element in Literature'.
c.12	The *Nineteenth Century* returns WBY's second folklore article complaining that it is too like the first.
13	AG returns to London from Coole and dines with WBY and Enid Layard. After Lady Layard's departure WBY tells AG of the disagreements in the '98 Committees and AG impresses him with her denunciation of MG's inciting Kerry famine victims to violence.
14	MG arrives from Paris to accompany WBY to Dublin, but they remain in London to register their complaints at the irregularities in the conduct of the London '98 Committee.
15	Sees the Irish MP William Field, who promises to bring in a Bill to widen the law on Dublin theatrical patents.
16	Attends a meeting of the '98 Centenary Committee in St James's Hall, Piccadilly.
19	Accompanies MG to Liverpool to speak at '98 celebrations.
20	Chairs a meeting of the '98 Executive Committee in Liverpool, and then speaks to a large demonstration at the Adelphi Theatre there, after which he confers with the delegates from 7.30 pm until a late hour.
21	Returns to London from Liverpool. Dines at AG's with Horace Plunkett and they discuss the agricultural movement and Parnell.
22	Attends a reception at Mrs Craigie's ('John Oliver Hobbes').
26	Dines with AG and they go on to the ILS for A. P. Graves' disappointing lecture on James Clarence Mangan. Rolleston, Taylor and McDermott speak to the paper, and WBY makes an impromptu speech praising Mangan's aestheticism. He introduces AG to Rolleston and returns home with her and reads Mangan's poem 'The Dark Rosaleen' to her before leaving.
27	WBY talks over theatrical matters with Rolleston.
28	Accompanies AG to a 'Literary Evening' at the Sesame Club.

March

1   (Tue) Dines with AG and tells her anecdotes about Rolleston, Moore, Symons and W. T. Stead. Later this month Horton's *A Book of Images* with his Preface is published.

2   Dines with Stopford Brooke who finds a great improvement in him.

6   Dines with AG and complains of the interruption to his work caused by his committees, politics and lack of money.

7   WBY's 'Monday Evening' attended by AG, Sharp, Johnson, Norah Hopper and Althea Gyles. Reads out poems by Norah Hopper and afterwards walks home with AG to tell her of MG's complaints about the intrigues in the Dublin '98 Committee.

9   Dines with AG who accompanies him to Euston Station where he catches the boat-train for Ireland.

10   WBY and MG investigate '98 Committee affairs in Dublin. In the evening they dine with AE and go on to a meeting at JO'L's house.

11   Lunches with AE.

12   WBY and Frank Hugh O'Donnell attend a Convention of the '98 Executive Committee in Dublin as the representatives of Great Britain.

13   Makes a speech from the Connaught platform at a '98 demonstration in Phoenix Park and catches a bad cold.

14–17   Spends his time trying to reconcile incompatible factions in the '98 Movement and discussing ways of circumventing the Dublin theatrical patent laws.

17   Leaves Dublin for London, arriving on 18 March.

19   WBY and Martyn dine with AG, and they all go on to an 'Original Evening' at the ILS. The evening is dull and AG, WBY and A. P. Graves take refuge in another room.

20   Goes to Blenheim Road to see George Pollexfen who is on a visit to London. FF is also invited to meet Pollexfen.

22   In London with George Pollexfen.

23   Probably attends the GD Neophyte Ceremony at Mark Masons' Hall with George Pollexfen.

24   George Pollexfen returns to Sligo. WBY dines with Moore and Symons.

25   Sees Horton in the morning. Buys Goblet d'Alviella's *The Migration of Symbols* and O'Curry's *Manuscript Materials* and *Manners and Customs* to help with his Celtic Mysteries.

27   Lunches with Lady Dorothy Nevill.

28   Althea Gyles attends WBY's 'Monday Evening'.

31   AG dines with WBY, and AE, who is in London for one day to give evidence on money-lending to a House of Lords committee, calls in afterwards.

April

1   (Fri) Meets Wilfrid Blunt for the first time, but the visit goes
           badly when WBY tries to make him see visions. 'Fiona Macleod'
           (review; *UP* II. 108–10) published in *L'Irlande Libre* (Paris).

2   'Mr. Rhys' Welsh Ballads' (review; *UP* II. 91–4) published in the
           Bookman, and 'The Broken Gates of Death' (article; *UP* II.
           94–108) in the *Fortnightly Review*.

4   Edward Clodd visits Woburn Buildings and he and WBY have
           long talk about folklore. AG returns to Coole.

6   Writes a review of AE's *The Earth Breath*.

11   Attends a Committee Meeting of the ILS.

13   Presides at the inaugural banquet of the London '98 Committee
           at the Holborn Restaurant and delivers a speech, 'The Union of
           the Gael'.

14   Sees William Rothenstein about sitting to him for a drawing.

15   Threatens to resign from the Committee of the ILS over the
           inadequate auditing of the Society's finances.

19   '"AE's" Poems' (review; *UP* II. 111–13) published in the *Sketch*.

23   Writes to the *Outlook* defending his folklore and arguing that
           the Irish peasantry has reconciled Christianity and Paganism.
           Leaves for Paris to stay with the Mathers and work on the Celtic
           Mystical Order. He cycles in the Bois de Boulogne, but finds MG
           ill with bronchitis.

26   MG visits WBY at the Mathers' to see visions, but has a row
           with Mathers which WBY is unable to reconcile.

May

7   (Sat) 'Aodh to Dectora. Three Songs' (3 poems, later 'He hears
           the Cry of the Sedge', 'The Lover mourns for the Loss of Love',
           and 'He thinks of those who have Spoken Evil of his Beloved';
           VP, 165, 152, 166) published in the *Dome*.

15   Returns to London from Paris prematurely, summoned by
           Martyn to see politicians about a proposed amendment to the
           Local Government Bill giving the power of theatrical licensing
           to the new Dublin County Council.

16   Goes to Houses of Parliament to lobby numerous MPs about the
           theatrical amendment to the Local Government Bill.

17   Writes to John Dillon, Tim Healy, John Redmond and Horace
           Plunkett about the theatrical amendment to the Local
           Government Bill. Sees Rothenstein who suggests designing a
           bronze medal of him.

18   Returns to the Houses of Parliament to lobby more MPs about
           theatrical amendment to the Local Government Bill.

20   Sees T. P. Gill about the crisis over the ownership of the Dublin
           Daily Express.

27	Attends George Savage Armstrong's lecture 'The Two Irelands' at the ILS, and attacks Armstrong's views.

June

1	(Wed) 'M. John O'Leary' (article; *UP* II. 113–15) published in *L'Irlande Libre* (Paris).
c.3	Sees MG in London and gives her talismans.
4	'The Celtic Element in Literature' (article; *E & I*, 173–88) published in *Cosmopolis*.
8	Arrives in Dublin from London.
9	Dines at the Rollestons with JO'L. AE marries Violet North.
12	Sketched by JBY. MG, thrown from a carriage, breaks her arm.
13	Sketched by JBY. Hears of MG's accident, postpones his visit to Coole, and goes to see her. Hears with misgivings of AE's marriage.
14–17	Moves to lodgings in AE's house at 10 Grove Terrace, Rathmines. Reads Moore's *Evelyn Innes* to the invalided MG and writes political letters for her.
17	Sees people all morning. MG is better and has caused consternation in '98 Committee by asking for a statement of expenditure and receipts.
20	Arrives in Coole, bringing his father's sketches of Hyde and AE. Recommences regular work on *The Speckled Bird*. Uses the symbol of the cauldron to evoke visions during this week and other symbols for divination throughout the month of July.
26	AG begins to teach WBY Irish and to read *War and Peace* to him.
27	Sees MG in a trance. Synge arrives at Coole from the Aran Islands.
28	WBY and Synge visit Martyn at Tillyra Castle.
29	Writing a folklore article for *Blackwood's Magazine*. Synge leaves Coole for Dublin.

July

4	(Mon) Sees a vision of MG while in a trance-like state.
9	Evokes a vision of wood-cutters.
10	Sleeping on his back, he passes through a nightmare to a beatific trance in which he sees books containing lost Blake poems and marvellous pictures.
11	An amendment to the Local Government (Ireland) Bill, giving the Lord Lieutenant power to grant occasional licences for theatrical performances in any approved building, paves the way for the ILT. Later this month WBY experiences a number of visions and dreams arising out of his sense of dependence upon the divine will.

August

6	(Sat) Travels from Coole to London for the '98 Celebrations, arriving on 7 August. Is writing his poem 'The Fish'.

9   Takes the chair and speaks at a 'National Banquet' at Frascati's Restaurant in Oxford Street. Lionel Johnson proposes the toast.
10   Seeing oculist about eye-trouble. Takes chair at '98 Celebration at St Martin's Town Hall and proposes resolution welcoming the French delegates.
13   Leaves London with MG and Amilcare Cipriani, arriving at Kingstown (Dun Laoighaire) by the afternoon boat to be met by the Dublin delegates and a large crowd. They travel to Westland Row Station where they are greeted by another large crowd.
14   Attends a reception for the overseas delegates to the '98 Celebrations at 116 Grafton Street.
15   Takes part in the procession to lay the foundation stone of the Wolfe Tone Monument. This starts from Rutland Square at 2.25 pm, with WBY, MG and Cipriani in the 3rd carriage, and reaches St Stephen's Green after a roundabout journey. JO'L presides and WBY makes a speech. In the evening he attends the Lord Mayor's Banquet.
17   Returns to Coole from Dublin. Angry at O'Donnell's attacks on Davitt.
c.24   Divination with cards produces a too general symbolism.
27   'Mr. Lionel Johnson and Certain Irish Poets' (article; *UP* II. 115–18) published in the Dublin *Daily Express*.

September
1   (Thu) Accompanies AG to the Galway Feis.
3   'The Poetry of "AE"' (article; *UP* II. 121–4) published in the Dublin *Daily Express*, and 'Celtic Beliefs about the Soul' (review; *UP* II. 118–21) in the *Bookman*.
7   MG sends him bottles of water from the Boyne and a sacred well, and earth from New Grange, which he uses for divination on the following 3 nights. This evening he has a spontaneous visionary experience; between sleeping and waking the words pass through his mind: 'They make an image of him who sleeps and this image is like him but is not him and it is called Emmanuel' (*Aut*).
8   Invokes the Celtic God Dagda and understands that he is the measure and number of things.
9   Experiences a vision of woodcutters and trees. Also has nightmare.
10   Evokes again after taking mescal and has a vision of patterns of painted gold leaves, and wheels like whetstones.
15   WBY and AG dine with Martyn at Tillyra Castle where Horace Plunkett and Lady Daisy Fingall are staying. At night WBY takes mescal, but not enough to produce any effect. On the following evenings he evokes the Celtic gods Aengus, Dagda and Lug and is rewarded with 'a great mystical inspiration' ('Vision Notebooks').

16	Drafting a new scenario for *The Countess Cathleen*. Plunkett and Lady Fingall visit Coole and WBY and Plunkett go boating on the lake.
17	WBY and Plunkett speak at a meeting of the Beagh and Kiltartan Co-operative Societies.
18	WBY and AG again dine with Martyn, Horace Plunkett and Lady Fingall at Tillyra.
*c.*20	AE visits Coole and he, AG and WBY wander the countryside seeing visions and arguing over symbols.
24	AG leaves Coole for London on her way to Venice. WBY and AE move to Tillyra where they remain until *c.*3 October, WBY working hard at *The Speckled Bird*, and comparing numerous visions with AE, who draws them. 'The Poems and Stories of Miss Nora Hopper' (review; *UP* II. 124–8) published in the Dublin *Daily Express*.

October

1	(Sat) 'Song of Mongan' (poem, later 'He thinks of his Past Greatness when a Part of the Constellations of Heaven'; *VP*, 177) published in the *Dome*.
*c.*3	Travels from Tillyra to stay with George Pollexfen at Rosses Point. A bad cold keeps him in bed for several days, doing hardly any work, and an ensuing depression with symptoms of morbidity lasts for a month, during which he conducts psychic experiments with Pollexfen.
*c.*17	WBY and Pollexfen move from Rosses Point to Sligo, where WBY remains until *c.*24 November and recommences work on *The Speckled Bird*.
19	Transcribes Mary Battle's vision of Queen Maeve into his 'Visions Notebook'.
23	Tells Pollexfen that they are being attacked by lunar powers and must evoke the sun.
24	Begins a quarrel by post with Elkin Mathews over the proposed design and materials for *The Wind Among the Reeds*.
29	'John Eglinton and Spiritual Art' (article; *UP* II. 128–32) published in the Dublin *Daily Express*.

November

3	(Thu) Hisses a Stage-Irish song at a Masonic Concert in Sligo.
8	Writes an unpublished article attacking John Eglinton's aesthetics.
13	Reads Barry O'Brien's *Life of Parnell* sent to him by AG.
*c.*24	Goes to Dublin from Sligo and stays at the Crown Hotel. Sees a good deal of MG and is embroiled in a whirl of social and administrative activities.
25	Attends a meeting of the Loan Picture Committee at Walter Osborne's studio, 5 Castlewood Avenue.

December

2	(Fri) Attends a meeting of the Pan Celtic Committee at the Mansion House.
3	'The Autumn of the Flesh' (article, later 'The Autumn of the Body'; *E & I*, 189–94) published in the Dublin *Daily Express*, 'A Symbolic Artist and the Coming of Symbolic Art' (review; *UP* II. 132–7) and 'Aodh Pleads with the Elemental Powers' (poem, later 'The Poet pleads with the Elemental Powers'; *VP*, 174–5) in the *Dome*, and 'Bressel the Fisherman' (poem, later 'The Fish'; *VP*, 146) in the *Cornish Magazine*.
6	Argues with John Eglinton at the National Library and reads Morris's *The Wood Beyond The World*. Dreams that MG kisses him.
7	Tells MG that he dreamed she had kissed him. They visit the old Fenian leader, James Stephens, and have tea with John Hughes, the sculptor. That evening MG kisses him on the lips for the first time and begins to tell him the story of her life.
8	Attends a public meeting of the Loan Picture Committee at the Metropolitan School of Art. Later MG tells him that she regrets having kissed him, that she can never be his wife, and gives him a full account of her life: her pact with the Devil over her father's death, her affair with Millevoye, and the birth of their children. This puts him into an emotional turmoil in which he feels 'like a very battered ship with the masts broken off at the stump' (to AG).
9–13	During a series of meetings, MG and WBY experiment with talismans and MG sees visions and visits him in dream.
11	At an 'At Home' at George Sigerson's where Bessie Sigerson goes into a trance while reading WBY's hand, telling him that his work is to bring a nearer relation between man and the spiritual powers than any one in the modern world had done and that he must pay even more attention to dreams and visions.
12	Moves from the Crown Hotel to lodgings at 6 Castlewood Avenue.
13	MG leaves Dublin to investigate evictions on Lord Clanricarde's estate at Woodford, near Loughrea.
14	Martyn arrives in Dublin from Tillyra and he and WBY engage the Antient Concert Rooms as the venue for the ILT's May 1899 season. AG arrives in London after spending the Autumn in Venice.
c.16	MG returns to Dublin from Loughrea.
17	WBY and MG invoke the Celtic god of love, Aengus, who tells them they were one in the prenatal life, and Lug, who invites them to take the Initiation of the Spear.
18	AG meets WBY in Dublin and they lunch with T. P. Gill and Rolleston. Dines with AG in evening; MG calls and AG is aghast at how ill she looks.

19	Takes AG to meet John Hughes the sculptor and then to see a portrait of Parnell recently acquired by the National Gallery. She invites WBY, AE and John Eglinton to dinner. MG leaves Dublin for Paris.
20	AG leaves for Coole. WBY dines with Margaret Stokes who shows him plans for *tableaux vivants* based on *The Countess Cathleen* to be performed under Lady Betty Balfour's aegis at the Viceregal Lodge.
22	Writes to ask AG to collaborate with him in compiling *Visions and Beliefs*. In the afternoon goes to see Lady Fingall about the *tableaux vivants* for Lady Balfour.
23	Travels from Dublin to Sligo to stay with George Pollexfen.
25	Has vision of a man with a tongue too large for his mouth and later smells a scent he associates with MG.
26	Tarot card divinations with George Pollexfen evoke Aengus.
27	Takes pellet of hashish and invokes Midir and Aengus. Has vision of the 'White Fool'.
29	Invokes the Celtic god Aengus again with talismans.

1899

January

1	(Sun) Experiences a vision of locked garden when thinking of MG.
7	Has visions of marriage ceremonies and flowers with George Pollexfen and Mary Battle.
8	Travels from Sligo to Dublin.
9	Announces the forthcoming ILT productions at a meeting of the NLS. Visits AE in the evening with a new theory about the Formorians.
12	Publishes letter in the Dublin press announcing the ILT.
13	Attends a Pan Celtic Committee Meeting, Lord Castletown in the chair. Goes to the *Daily Express* office to see Gill and then on to the Coffeys' to meet Eva Gore-Booth.
14	Attends Margaret Stokes' NLS lecture 'The High Crosses of Ireland' in the Leinster Lecture Hall and removes the special chairs provided for the Vice-Regal party. 'The Irish Literary Theatre' (article; *UP* II. 139–42) published in the Dublin *Daily Express*.
16	WBY and Martyn attend a meeting of the NLS and succeed in gaining the Society's sponsorship for the ILT; a sub-committee is set up comprising WBY, Martyn, Sigerson, Henderson and Mrs Coffey. Martyn indemnifies the Society against any losses incurred by the Theatre.
17	Attends a special Council Meeting of the NLS to consider arrangements for the ILT.

18	Returns to London.
24	Sees JBY and his sisters about hanging some of JBY's pictures in Jack Yeats's coming exhibition. The *tableaux vivants* from *The Countess Cathleen* are performed at the Chief Secretary's Lodge in Phoenix Park, Dublin, and are repeated on the following day.
27	Writes to the *Daily Chronicle*, contributing to a controversy about modern drama between George Moore and William Archer.
28	Introduces George Moore to FF. 'High Crosses of Ireland' (review of Margaret Stokes' lecture; *UP* II. 142–5) published in the Dublin *Daily Express*. Sketched by JBY for the frontispiece of *Poems* (1899).
31	Goes to Paris to propose to MG and stays with the Mathers. Receives royalties of £4 from Elkin Mathews.

February

1	(Wed) Has a bad time in Paris early this month, suffering from a cold and headache. Is trying to prepare the copy for a new edition of *Poems*, and to persuade Unwin to use Althea Gyles' design for the cover.
9	Lectures at a private house in Paris.
10	Synge meets WBY in the Bois de Boulogne.
12	Spends the day with Synge.
13	Meets Henry Davray, who has influenza, and is divorcing his wife.
16	Synge sees WBY off for London from the St Lazare station.
17	Dines with AG; has cough and lingering influenza and is depressed by his lack of success with MG in Paris. Goes on to a meeting of the ILS where he makes critical remarks about Thomas Davis.
19	WBY, Martyn, Horace Plunkett, FF and Alice Dugdale dine with AG and WBY reads poems from Hyde's *Love Songs of Connacht*.
20	Delivers the bulk of the copy for *Poems* (1899) to Unwin's office, and asks for special proofs of *The Countess Cathleen* to use as prompt copies during the ILT rehearsals. FF and Henry Davray attend WBY's 'Monday Evening'.
21	Sends Unwin another batch of copy for *Poems* (1899).
22	Down to his last 2*s.* 6*d.* WBY, AG, Martyn, Moore, Florence Burke, Bernard Holland, Lord Lytton and Lady Betty Balfour dine at Horace Plunkett's as part of his project to promote co-operation between practical men and the Irish literary movement. Going to Plunkett's, WBY is obliged to spend 6*d.* on a hansom cab because the servant tidying his room makes him late in dressing.
23	Sends more copy for *Poems* (1899) to Unwin. Staying in to save money, but speaks after Eleanor Hull's lecture on 'The Red Branch' at the ILS.

24	Finishes the Preface for *Poems* (1899).
25	Raises a loan of £7 from George Pollexfen. Dines with AG.
26	Sends remaining copy for *Poems* (1899) to Unwin. Dines with AG.
27	AG, Martyn, FF, Moore, Sarah Purser and John Todhunter at WBY's 'Monday Evening'.

March

1	(Wed) Speaks on 'The Celtic Renaissance' at a dinner of the City Socialist Circle at the Albion Hotel. 'Notes on Traditions and Superstitions' (article; *UP* II. 145–7) published in *Folk-Lore*.
2	Visits AG at 4.30 pm to show her his article, 'The Academic Class and the Agrarian Revolution', attacking Robert Atkinson of TCD for his denunciation of the Irish language, literature and folklore before the Commission for Intermediate Education. Has decided to write short articles until he has straightened out his finances. Goes on to dine with Moore.
3	Dines with AG and they go on to see Hubert O'Grady's melodrama, *The Fenian*, at the Imperial Theatre.
5	WBY dines at AG's with Martyn and Moore, who upset him by attacking FF's stage management of the ILT. WBY, reading *Endymion*, is full of Keats and Shelley and their philosophy.
6	AG, Martyn, Ernest and Grace Rhys, Althea Gyles, and J. T. Grein at WBY's 'Monday Evening'. Later MG and her sister, Mrs Pilcher, come in.
8	Dines with AG and discusses his relationship with MG.
10	WBY, Plunkett and Martyn go to AG's for lunch, where JBY is sketching William Peel.
11	'The Academic Class and the Agrarian Revolution' (article; *UP* II. 148–52) published in the Dublin *Daily Express*.
12	AG and WBY have tea with his family and later dine together.
15	Sees Moore and learns that AG is ill.
16	Dines with the Podmores and meets the journalist Henry Nevinson.
19	Dines at AG's and discusses Parnell with Barry O'Brien and Sir Wilfrid Lawson.
21	AG dines with WBY; as she is leaving, they find a letter from Martyn saying that he intends to withdraw from the ILT because of doubts about the orthodoxy of *The Countess Cathleen*. WBY walks AG part of the way home and then goes to call on George Pollexfen, who is visiting London.
22	Lunches with Moore at AG's to discuss Martyn's withdrawal from the ILT. T. P. Gill calls, and advises them to go on with the venture.
24	Visits Moore and writes to Fr William Barry about Martyn's scruples over *The Countess Cathleen*.

25	Sends a copy of *The Countess Cathleen* to the Irish Jesuit, Fr Finlay, for his opinion on its orthodoxy. Returns proofs of *Poems* (1899) to Unwin.
26	Fr Barry writes to say that *The Countess Cathleen* is theologically sound.
27	Oldmeadow, editor of the *Dome*, visits to discuss WBY's article on 'The Theatre'.
30	Martyn informs WBY that he has received such an offensive letter from Moore that he is quite determined to withdraw from the ILT.
31	WBY and FF go to Dublin to finalize arrangements for the ILT productions.

April

1	(Sat) 'The Theatre' (article; *E & I*, 165–72) published in the *Dome*. WBY and FF are extremely busy in Dublin with theatrical affairs. Frank Hugh O'Donnell denounces *The Countess Cathleen* as immoral and anti-national in a letter to the *Freeman's Journal*.
5	WBY sees the editor of the *Freeman's Journal*. Martyn and Moore are friends again and Fr Finlay has suggested only a few slight changes to *The Countess Cathleen*.
7	Returns to London on the morning boat.
8	Sees Moore who laments his lost controversy with Martyn as he planned to write an article on 'Edward Martyn and his Soul'.
10	Busy rehearsing ILT plays and preparing *Beltaine* for the press. JBY, FF and Lionel Johnson at WBY's 'Monday Evening'.
15	Rehearsing *The Countess Cathleen* and the cast are working well together. *The Wind Among the Reeds* is published.
*c.*17	Moore causes ructions at the ILT rehearsals by firing practically the whole cast that Valentine Grace has assembled.
18	At Moore's and Martyn's insistence WBY replaces Dorothy Paget in the role of the Countess Cathleen with May Whitty.
22	Too busy to attend rehearsals for some days. Lectures on 'The Ideal Theatre' (*UP* II. 153–8) to the ILS, with Edmund Gosse in chair and JBY and SMY in the audience.
23	Goes to dinner at Gosse's where he meets Eddie Marsh and walks home with him in the rain, discussing AE and George Moore.
25	Sees Symons every day until he leaves for Dublin.
*c.*26	Frank Hugh O'Donnell publishes his attack on *The Countess Cathleen* in pamphlet form as *Souls for Gold!*
27	WBY receives an advance copy of *Poems* (1899) and thinks it the best looking book he has yet published. Attends rehearsals of the ILT plays again.

May

1	(Mon) Ernest and Grace Rhys at WBY's 'Monday Evening'.
3	Leaves London for Dublin with FF.
4	They arrive in Dublin and rehearse the minor characters. WBY takes a paragraph publicizing the plays and Jack Yeats's forthcoming exhibition to all the Dublin papers.
c.5	*Poems* (1899) published.
6	Lectures on 'Dramatic Ideals and the Irish Literary Theatre' to the NLS at the Royal Society of Antiquities, with AG, and Jack and Cottie Yeats in the audience; afterwards they go on to a garden party at the Coffeys' to advertise the ILT. 'The Irish Literary Theatre' (article; *UP* II. 162–4) published in *Literature*.
c.7	Publication of *Beltaine*, the occasional journal of the ILT, edited by WBY and to which he contributes 'Plans and Methods'.
8	*The Countess Cathleen* produced by the ILT at the Antient Concert Rooms. Despite some barracking by a claque of students over its supposed anti-Irishism, the performance is a success. *Poems* (1899) published.
9	Attends private view of Jack Yeats's exhibition, 'Sketches of Life in the West of Ireland', at the Leinster Hall. The ILT produces Martyn's *The Heather Field*.
10	Cardinal Logue denounces the theology of *The Countess Cathleen* in the Dublin press.
11	Attends a dinner given in honour of the ILT by Gill and Plunkett of the Dublin *Daily Express*.
13	Contributes to the controversy over Cardinal Logue's condemnation of *The Countess Cathleen* with a letter to the London *Morning Leader*.
c.21	Goes to Coole where he remains, apart from short trips to Dublin and Belfast, until November. He renegotiates his contract with Unwin, insisting on higher royalties, and writes to Alice Milligan about a scheme to translate contemporary writers into Irish.
27	The prospect of staging *The Shadowy Waters* in London prompts him to try to finish it. Seeks advice from Clement Shorter about the renegotiation of his Unwin contract.
30	Goes to Dublin to chair a debate at the TCD Historical Society 'That any attempt to further an Irish Literary Movement would result in provincialism'. The motion is defeated almost unanimously and WBY's speech reported in the Dublin press on 1 June.

June

1	(Thu) Visits Edward Dowden.
c.3	Returns to Coole from Dublin and recommences work on *The Shadowy Waters*, trying to give it a grave ecstasy. *Literary Ideals in Ireland* published early this month.

11   Urges Methuen to reissue *A Book of Irish Verse.*
16   Speaks at a meeting to establish a Kiltartan branch of the Gaelic
            League and announces that he is learning Irish. In the middle of
            the month he suffers a rheumatic attack in his foot and knee.
*c.*20   Meets the Irish novelist Emily Lawless on her visit to Coole and
            has many arguments with her. He is re-reading Shelley.

July

1   (Sat) 'The Dominion of Dreams' (review; *UP* II. 164–6) published
            in the *Bookman*. During this month WBY works at Coole on *The
            Shadowy Waters*, composes an article on 'The Irish Literary
            Movement' for the *North American Review*, and writes to the
            guarantors of the ILT asking them to renew their subscriptions
            for 1900. In this period he uses apple blossom as an evocation
            and has visions of the Last Day and Tir na nOg. Fears that MG
            is about to sacrifice herself needlessly.
*c.*11–14   Goes with AG to stay with her niece in a shooting lodge at
            Chevey Chase. Beginning work on his essay 'The Philosophy of
            Shelley's Poetry'.
*c.*25   Hyde, his wife and John Eglinton begin a visit to Coole.
27   Replies to Hyde's lecture, 'The Irish Language Movement' deliv-
            ered at the Gort Court House.

August

*c.*11   (Fri) A payment of £40 from the *North American Review* for 'The
            Irish Literary Movement' enables WBY to pay all his debts for
            the first time in his life, and he sends JBY £5.
16   Sends the copy for new edition of *A Book of Irish Verse* to Methuen.
*c.*19–26   AE at Coole and conducts psychic experiments with WBY.
24   Has visions of the Sun and Moon.

September

2   (Sat) 'Ireland Bewitched' (article, *UP* II. 167–83) published in the
            Contemporary Review. Begins to paint in pastels.
14   Meets MG in Dublin.
18   Accompanies MG to Belfast.
*c.*20–25   In Belfast he meets the Fenian, Robert Johnston, a number of
            Gaelic Leaguers, and Standish O'Grady.
24   WBY's and MG's proposed visit to the Giant's Causeway aban-
            doned because of rain, and they climb Cave Hill instead.
25   Returns to Dublin. Sees AE and John Eglinton, with whom he
            argues about Individualism.
26   WBY and MG go to see AE.
27–30   Helping MG with preparations for a public meeting to
            denounce the imminent war in South Africa.

29	Visits the Dublin *Daily Express* office with AE to consult the staff about an attempted take-over.
30	Sees T. P. Gill about the situation at the *Daily Express*. In the evening he dines with Rolleston and Stopford Brooke at the Shelbourne Hotel.

October

1	(Sun) Shares the platform with MG and JO'L at a meeting about the South African situation held in front of the Custom House, Dublin.
2	'Dust Hath Closed Helen's Eye' (article; *Myth*, 22–30) published in the *Dome*. WBY returns to Coole.
*c.*10	Moves from Coole to Tillyra to begin his collaboration with Moore on *Diarmuid and Grania*, and they complete a scenario. Moore also begins to rewrite Martyn's play *The Tale of a Town*.
14	Visits AG at Coole to discuss their appeal to ILT guarantors.
16	Dreams of Grania.
28	Speaks at an IAOS meeting in Galway.
*c.*30	George Pollexfen's illness prevents WBY going to Sligo from Tillyra and so he returns to Coole.

November

2	(Thu) Writes to congratulate Michael Davitt on his resignation from Parliament in protest at the Boer War. During the early part of the month he continues to help Moore re-write *The Tale of a Town* and to draft *Diarmuid and Grania*.
15	Goes to Dublin from Coole, where he consults T. P. Gill about the situation at the *Daily Express*. He also meets AE and finds him disillusioned with Mrs Katherine Tingley, leader of one faction of the Theosophical Society. Sees MG who is waging an anti-enlistment campaign in Dublin.
17	Crosses to London with MG, who goes on at once to Paris.
19	Althea Gyles visits WBY to tell him that the bailiffs are being put into her rooms and bringing him books to look after.
20	Visits his father and sisters in Blenheim Road. Over the next week he sees a good deal of Moore, and continues to help him rewrite *The Tale of a Town*.
*c.*24	Attends Althea Gyles' 'At Home' and is disgusted by her familiarity with her new lover, the publisher Leonard Smithers.
27	Despite WBY's ban, Althea Gyles brings Smithers to WBY's 'Monday Evening' and he writes to repeat the prohibition.
28	Visits Moore to discuss his rewriting of *The Tale of a Town* and moderates his irritation with Martyn. Goes on to dinner with Mrs Kate Lee, a collector and singer of folksongs, whose portrait JBY is painting.

December

1	(Fri) 'The Literary Movement in Ireland' (article; *UP* II. 184–96) published in the *North American Review*. WBY spends most of this month working hard to finish *The Shadowy Waters*.
5	Dines with the artists Charles Ricketts and Charles Shannon.
*c.*15	Sends MG a public letter, hoping for a Boer victory.
22	AG sends him port wine and a draft of her article on the Gaelic poet Raftery.
23	Reads *The Shadowy Waters* to Moore, Gosse and William Barry.
24	Goes to Blenheim Road for an extended visit to his family.
30	Dines with Moore, Symons and JBY and reads them *The Shadowy Waters*.

1900

January

1	(Mon) 'The Irish Literary Theatre, 1900' (article; *UP* II. 198–200) is published in the *Dome* and a letter on 'The Irish Literary Theatre' in the *Irish Literary Society Gazette* (*UP* II. 196–7).
2	Calls to Blenheim Road, where he is being painted by JBY, and stays overnight.
3	WBY's mother dies and he takes charge of the funeral and other arrangements to remove the burden from his father.
6	Attends Susan Yeats's funeral at Acton Cemetery.
12	The Second Order of the GD refuses to admit Aleister Crowley to membership despite Mathers' instructions.
17	WBY spends day on theatre business.
19	Awarded a prize of 25 guineas by the *Academy* for *The Wind Among the Reeds*, as the best book of poems in 1899. Works in the morning on *Diarmuid and Grania*. AG arrives in London and WBY visits her for tea and dinner, before returning to Woburn Buildings for a committee meeting of the GD which discusses Mathers' autocratic behaviour.
20	Attends ILT rehearsals at the Comedy Theatre, and later dines with AG.
22	AG, Alice Milligan and Moore attend WBY's 'Monday Evening', where a row breaks out between Miss Milligan and Moore over his wish to rewrite her play, and between Moore and WBY over ILT parts for FF.
23	WBY, Barry O'Brien, Moore and Martyn dine with AG and discuss England's decadence.
*c.*24	WBY and Moore rewrite the 3rd act of *The Tale of a Town* (now called *The Bending of the Bough*).
25	Dines with AG and reads her the new version of *The Shadowy Waters*, revised with the help of Moore.

26	WBY, AG, Moore and Martyn attend a rehearsal of *The Bending of the Bough* from 12.00 to 3.30 pm.
27	Dines with AG and they quarrel over Moore's rewriting of Martyn's play and about *Beltaine*. WBY gives her Annie Besants' *The Ancient Wisdom*. They go on to the ILS, where WBY makes a speech about the ILT. Later in the evening WBY visits Moore to suggest further revisions to *The Bending of the Bough*.
30	The Irish Parliamentary Party reunifies under the leadership of John Redmond.
31	Attends Alice Milligan's illustrated lecture 'In the Gaelic Speaking Country' at the Bloomsbury Hall, London, and seconds the vote of thanks.

February

1	(Thu) Dines with AG and reads her his and Moore's essays for second number of *Beltaine*. At this time he is plagued by uncontrollable mystical dreams.
2	William Sharp, visiting Woburn Buildings, tells WBY that Fiona Macleod detects great powers of evil ranged against him.
5	WBY, AG and Martyn at a rehearsal of Martyn's *Maeve*. WBY and AG have tea with Geraldine Beauchamp.
6	AG buys sandwiches for a picnic lunch with WBY who is ill in his rooms.
7	Dines at AG's with Martyn, Albert Ball and Philip Comyns Carr; conversation centres mostly on the theatre.
9	Telegraphs AG that he has a cold and cannot come to see her. Takes Moore to see JBY in Blenheim Road and returns to Moore's rooms until 5 pm when he goes home, buying himself a hotwater bottle on the way.
10	AG visits WBY, finds him coughing badly, and makes him breakfast. In the evening Symons dines with WBY and they discuss whether men of self-respect could wear galoshes.
11	AG visits WBY and makes his fire and breakfast, returning in the evening with provisions for supper.
12	WBY, AG, Moore and Una Birch at a rehearsal of *The Bending of the Bough* at Terry's Theatre and have tea afterwards.
15	Dines with AG; they are both depressed about *The Bending of the Bough*.
16	WBY and AG attend a delayed and disappointing rehearsal of *The Bending of the Bough* which continues until 7 pm.
17	WBY, AG, and Moore leave London for Dublin by the 8.30 am train for the second season of the ILT. In Dublin WBY dines at AG's lodgings and they go on to an NLS reception where WBY makes a speech about the ILT.

18	'Plans and Methods' and '"Maive" and Certain Irish Beliefs' (articles; *UP* II. 201–4, 204–7) published in *Beltaine*. WBY and AG attend a preview of Jack Yeats's exhibition in the Leinster Hall. WBY calls on AG at 9.20 pm on his way round to newspaper offices to publicize the ILT plays.
19	WBY, AG and Jack Yeats at the Leinster Hall to arrange the pictures and prepare for AG's 'At Home' to open Jack Yeats's exhibition at 4 pm. WBY dines with AG and they go to the Gaiety Theatre to see Alice Milligan's *The Last Feast of the Fianna* and Martyn's *Maeve*, both of which are successful.
20	WBY and AG meet Jack Yeats at his exhibition in the morning and afternoon. WBY dines with AG and they go on to the Gaiety Theatre to see *The Bending of the Bough*.
21	WBY, AG and Moore attend a poor matinée of *The Bending of the Bough*, followed by tea at AG's lodgings. They dine at the Shelbourne and then attend another performance of *The Last Feast of the Fianna* and *Maeve* before a very small audience.
22	Attends the NLS luncheon for the ILT at the Gresham Hotel and delivers a speech advocating the teaching of Irish and denouncing TCD provincialism. Afterwards has tea at AG's lodgings, and in the evening they go to a performance of *The Bending of the Bough* which is so well received that it is decided to put it on again the following day.
23	WBY and AG attend the extra performance of *The Bending of the Bough* with AE and Hyde, but the audience is not as good as expected, despite the presence of the Lord Mayor of Dublin. WBY and AG attend a late supper at the Coffeys.
24	In the morning WBY and AG visit Jack Yeats's exhibition and then lunch with the T. P. Gills. In evening they attend a further performance of *The Bending of the Bough* and WBY makes a speech from his box. They have a late supper at the Gills where WBY and Moore abuse Martyn, who is threatening to withdraw from the ILT unless his plays are performed. Martyn comes in and they discuss his resignation from the Lord Lieutenantship of Galway.
25	Calls on AG in the morning and they agree that although the plays have made a financial loss, they have enhanced the reputation of the ILT. Dines with AG and sees her off to England from Westland Row Station. He has commissioned Shaw to write a play for the ILT.
27	Returns to London from Dublin and dines with AG; both are tired after their efforts in Dublin.
28	Receives £6 6s. from Elkin Mathews as part of the royalties on the first and second editions of *The Wind Among the Reeds*. The new edition of *A Book of Irish Verse* is published.

March

2   (Fri) AG brings sandwiches to WBY's for lunch and helps him hang his pictures.

3   Attends a secret meeting with FF, the Hunters, Bullock and Blackden to consider Mathers' allegation that Westcott, co-founder of the GD, had never been in communication with Fräulein Sprengel, its supposed authority.

4   Dines at AG's to meet Samuel Clemens (Mark Twain) and his wife. Moore calls in after dinner, and WBY reads out AG's and Hyde's translations from the Irish, staying on until after midnight.

6   WBY and AG attend a performance of Benson's uncut *Hamlet* which lasts from 3.30 to 6.30 pm and then from 8.00 to 10.30 pm. WBY receives a postal order for 10s. 6d. from Elkin Mathews for royalties.

7   WBY, AG and Jack Yeats dine at the Clemens's.

9   WBY and FF dine with AG and meet the Clays and Charles Hallé, Director of the New Gallery. WBY argues with Lady Clay but gets on well with Hallé.

10   Debates with Shaw at 'The Fellowship of the Three Kings' and tries to prove him reactionary.

11   Moore calls on WBY.

12   Sees Shaw, who talks of a play for the ILT on the contrast between the Irish and English character (this becomes *John Bull's Other Island*).

13   Visits AG in the late afternoon with his article 'The Way of Wisdom' and discusses methods of protesting against the Queen's forthcoming visit to Ireland.

14   To tea with AG and they call on the Clemenses.

15   AG visits WBY and they go together to Mudie's to have some of her books bound.

16   WBY, Moore and Philip Comyns Carr dine with AG and go on to the New Gallery to see Isadora Duncan's *Dance Idylls* after which they look round the pictures.

17   WBY, AG and Symons dine at Moore's and discuss a draft of WBY's letter denouncing Queen Victoria's proposed visit to Ireland.

18   AG types WBY's letter to the press about the Queen's visit and they dine together before her departure for Italy.

20   WBY's letter attacking the Queen's Irish visit is published in the Dublin nationalist papers. Later that day he interviews Westcott on behalf of the secret committee of the GD about Mathers' allegations that he forged the Sprengel letters authorizing the foundation of the Order. AG and Robert Gregory leave London for Italy.

22	Attends a committee of the GD to discuss Mathers' allegations about Westcott's forgeries. They decide to telegraph Mathers in Paris requesting his presence at a GD meeting on 24 March.
24	Attends a committee meeting of the GD at 4 pm. Mathers fails to turn up and the committee confirms its membership (WBY, FF, the Hunters, Blackden, Bullock and Jones) and suspends all GD business until it has reported on the quarrel with Mathers.
25–29	Writing his essay 'The Symbolism of Poetry', and reading Symons' *The Symbolist Movement in Literature*, finding it vague in its philosophy.
29	Finishes 'The Symbolism of Poetry' and attends a GD committee meeting at which it is reported that Westcott believes the Sprengel letters to be genuine.

April

2	(Mon) 'The Symbolism of Poetry' (article; *E & I*, 153–64) published in the *Dome*. The third and final number of *Beltaine* contains an article by WBY (*UP* II. 209–10). The Irish Party adopts WBY's resolution on the Queen's visit and he tries unsuccessfully to persuade Harrington to resign his seat in favour of John MacBride.
3	Sends a further letter to the Dublin press opposing the Queen's visit.
*c.*4–7	Has influenza, which leaves him with indigestion.
9	Sees MG on her way through London to Ireland.
10	After an intimate talk with WBY, MG leaves London for Dublin.
14	'The Way of Wisdom' (article, later 'The Pathway'; *CW* VIII. 189–96) published in the *Speaker*.
15	Does a tarot reading for himself and MG.
17	Aleister Crowley, acting for Mathers, seizes the GD headquarters at Blythe Road.
19	WBY and Edmund Hunter go to Blythe Road and persuade the landlord to change the locks. Crowley turns up in full highland dress and a black mask but is refused admission by WBY and Hunter. He calls a policeman who tells him to leave, which he does, saying he will consult a lawyer. WBY attends a GD committee meeting in the afternoon which suspends Dr. Berridge and Elaine Simpson, Crowley's accomplices, from membership.
21	Attends a meeting of 22 members of the GD at 116 Netherwood Road which suspends Mathers from the Order and withholds recognition of Crowley. WBY gives a history of the Order and eleven resolutions are passed, radically altering its constitution, with WBY being appointed instructor in Mystical Philosophy. 'Noble and Ignoble Loyalties' (article; *UP* II. 122–13) published in the *United Irishman*.

c.22–28	Busy seeing lawyers to counter Crowley's suit against the GD and guarding the Blythe Street headquarters against him, getting no more than four and a half hours sleep on some nights. Through the influence of Stephen Gwynn, Macmillan consider making an offer for WBY's books, but decide against it.
c.25	Sees the dentist, Baly, who tells him that he needs extensive and expensive dental treatment.
28	The GD win the case against Crowley, who is fined £5. Henrietta Paget does tarot readings for WBY and consults her spirit guide on his behalf.
29	Sees Fiona Macleod's play, *The Sons of Usna*, produced by the Stage Society at the Globe Theatre.
30	William Sharp visits WBY and prophesies MG's destruction.

May

1	(Tue) *The Shadowy Waters* (play; *VP*, 746–69) published in the *North American Review*.
3	AG arrives back in London from the Continent and WBY invites her and Moore to dinner.
4	AG has tea at WBY's to meet the Irish composer O'Brien Butler who, at WBY's suggestion, is writing an opera with Nora Hopper. WBY returns to dine with AG.
5	WBY and AG see Benson's production of *Richard III* and go on to the Fellowship of the Three Kings, where WBY lectures.
7	WBY and Moore dine with AG. Nora Hopper arrives after dinner and they work on her libretto for O'Brien Butler's opera, then WBY walks AG, who is returning to Ireland, to the train.
14	MG arrives in London from Ireland to enlist WBY's help in countering Frank Hugh O'Donnell's libels against her. WBY consults Barry O'Brien about this.
16	In the evening MG and her sister call on WBY and they evoke a druid for help on the rites for the Celtic Mystical Order.
c.19	Moore invites WBY to accompany him on a lecturing tour to the USA.
20	WBY renews contact with OS when he writes to commiserate with her on the death of her mother.
21	Responds to J. W. Brodie-Innes' lecture on 'Mystical Beliefs of the Western Highlands' at a meeting of the Sette of Odd Volumes at Limners Hotel, where he sees Clodd and Andrew Lang.
22	Begins a course of dental treatment which continues until the end of June.
26	Attends J. L. Garvin's ILS lecture, 'A Hundred Years of Irish Journalism'. Late this month he sees a good deal of Mrs Kathleen Pilcher, MG's sister, and calls for moderation in a

dispute in the ILS over Lord Russell's attack on the Irish language movement. He returns to writing *The Speckled Bird*.

28   Meets Kathleen Pilcher at tea party given by Mrs Antrobus.

30   Dines with the Podmores where he meets the Dutch man of letters
Frederik van Eeden and discusses the *anima mundi* with him.

June
c.3   (Sun) Informs Moore that he will not go on an American tour
with him.

4   O'Brien Butler calls on WBY in the evening.

6   Meets Westcott by chance in a bookshop and finds him defen-
sive on the subject of Mathers and the origin of the GD.

12   Measured for partial set of false teeth. He is making arrangements to transfer his literary affairs to the agent A. P. Watt.

21   Fitted with an upper set of false teeth but the lower set are a
failure. Sees MG who is in London.

23   Crosses from London to Dublin.

25   Meets MG and W. J. Stanton Pyper at the Nassau Hotel to
discuss the suppression of the *United Irishman* and the activities
of Frank Hugh O'Donnell.

26   Asks the Irish politician John Dillon to help MG's campaign
against the treachery of Frank Hugh O'Donnell.

28   Tries to call on Michael Davitt to enlist his help against
O'Donnell.

29   Leaves Dublin for Coole.

July
1   (Sun) Jack and Cottie Yeats arrive in Coole.

2   'The Philosophy of Shelley's Poetry' (article; *E & I*, 65–78) published in the *Dome*.

7   Writes to the *Speaker* denouncing the confiscation of the *United
Irishman* by the British authorities.

14   'Irish Fairy Beliefs' (review; *UP* II. 216–18) published in the *Speaker*.

17   AE, his wife and their new baby arrive in Coole for a holiday.
AE sketches with WBY and argues about poetry and mysticism.

24   WBY and AE sketch a tree at Raheen.

26   WBY and AE sketch together. In evening they tease each other
about mystical matters.

31   WBY and AE quarrel in Coole woods over the symbolic
significance of the sword but make it up in the evening. WBY
finishes his poem, 'Echtge of Streams'.

August
13   (Mon) Sends John Lane 'Echtge of Streams' for publication in
the *Anglo-Saxon* but it is in fact published in the *Speaker*.

c.20	Hyde and his wife are at Coole.
23	WBY, AG, Hyde and Robert Gregory attend the Feis in Galway, returning home late.
24	Attends a cricket match at Coole between Gort and Ennistymon.
25	'Echtge of Streams' (poem, later 'The Withering of the Boughs'; VP, 203–4) published in the Speaker.
26	WBY, AG and Hyde go to Killeenan where they meet Martyn for the dedication of a headstone at the grave of the Gaelic poet Raftery. Addresses of welcome are delivered to each of them at a public meeting.

September

1	(Sat) 'Irish Witch Doctors' (article; UP II. 219–36) published in the Fortnightly Review. WBY welcomes the first number of D. P. Moran's weekly, the Leader, in a long open letter.
3	The Hydes leave Coole. WBY rows AG across the lake for tea at Inchy where he composes part of his poem 'Under the Moon', AG supplying him with a rhyme.
6	Writes to Unwin about renegotiating his contract for Poems.
7	WBY and AG go to Duras to say farewell to the Comte de Basterot. WBY has all but finished 'Under the Moon'.
8	Finishes 'Under the Moon'.
11	WBY and AG go to Chevy Chase for the day. WBY takes The Shadowy Waters which he is altering, and they hear local superstitions and beliefs about the Boer War.
c.15	Moore arrives in Coole to recommence collaboration with WBY on Diarmuid and Grania. He promises £100 for the Theatre and goes to Tillyra where Martyn receives him cordially but refuses to give any more money to the ILT.
17	Moore returns to Dublin but remains in contact with WBY about Diarmuid and Grania by letter and telegram.
20	Martyn comes to dine at Coole; AG tries to change his mind about funding the ILT but he is resolute.
22	WBY works on the 2nd act of Diarmuid and Grania through the week with AG's secretarial assistance.
26	Moore writes that the 1st act of Diarmuid and Grania is too thin and that he is going to make the Fenians more turbulent.
27	Moore writes that the Fenians in Diarmuid and Grania are to be endowed with all the virtues.
28	AG telegraphs Moore to return to Coole so that he and WBY can work on the play together.
29	Moore arrives at Coole from Dublin.
30	Diarmuid and Grania is being radically revised. WBY urges Moore to publish his books in Dublin with Sealy, Bryers & Walker.

October

2   (Tue) AG and WBY tease Moore about his use of language in the play and he loses his temper.

3   WBY and Moore continue to write *Diarmuid and Grania*. Una Birch arrives in Coole and in the evening they read Hyde's *The Twisting of the Rope*. WBY sounds Moore out about taking a seat in Parliament.

5   Moore and Una Birch leave Coole; WBY remains, working on *Diarmuid and Grania*.

9   Leaves for Dublin where he continues working with Moore on the 3rd Act of *Diarmuid and Grania*.

10   Moore leaves Dublin. WBY reads the first two acts of *Diarmuid and Grania* to MG who listens with excitement and afterwards he accompanies her to a meeting of the pro-Boer Transvaal Committee.

11   Meets Horace Plunkett, depressed by his defeat in the South Dublin election. In the evening WBY makes a long speech in favour of the teaching of Irish at public meeting of the Gaelic League in the Rotunda.

12   Dines with MG and Sarah Purser.

13   Begins his essay 'Magic'.

17   Lectures to the Central Branch of the Gaelic League.

21   AG writes from London to request WBY's essay for her compilation *Ideals in Ireland*.

*c.*24   Crosses from Dublin to London.

25   Lunches with AG and stays to tea, at which Moore and others are present. Reads AG the 3rd act of *Diarmuid and Grania* and she finds Moore's inept expressions amusing.

26   Works on *Diarmuid and Grania* with Moore and accompanies him to Frank Harris's play *Mr and Mrs Davantry* at the Royalty Theatre, starring Mrs Patrick Campbell. Afterwards he sees Mrs Campbell in her dressing room and she urges him to let her read *Diarmuid and Grania*.

27   Works all afternoon on *Diarmuid and Grania* at Moore's. Dines with AG and they go on to the ILS to hear Stephen Gwynn's lecture on Irish Humour with Gosse in the chair and JBY in the audience. WBY responds to the paper and asserts that Swift's humour was Irish, a speech which causes Henn Collins to resign the vice-presidency of the Society.

29   Accompanies AG to Oxford for an exhibition of Jack Yeats's paintings. On their way home through Victoria a woman celebrating the return of Volunteers from the Boer War rushes at WBY and tickles his face with a feather.

November

2   (Fri) AG visits WBY to show him her translation of Hyde's essay for *Ideals in Ireland*. Together they have it typed at an agency and take it on to Oldmeadow at the Unicorn Press.

3   WBY, SMY and AG visit William Gibson and his wife at Moorhurst; other guests, including Viscount St Cyres, are also there. Gibson wears old Irish costume and they talk in the evening about original sin and heredity.

5   Ill with a bad cold, WBY wants to put off John Masefield, a new admirer, but AG persuades him to keep the dinner invitation open and goes to Woburn Buildings to help entertain. This is WBY's first meeting with Masefield.

6–9   His cold and asthma are worse and AG visits him every day to look after him. Towards the end of the week he rallies and writes a postscript to his essay in *Ideals in Ireland*.

11   Moore calls on WBY and is irritated to find him altering the text of *Diarmuid and Grania*.

15   Attends a GD committee meeting. AG meets Moore who denounces WBY's dictatorial behaviour over the revisions to *Diarmuid and Grania*. WBY dines with AG.

16   Lectures on 'The Theatre' at the Fellowship of the Three Kings, where he seeks Symons's advice in his dispute with Moore over the style of *Diarmuid and Grania*. Visits Unwin to renew his attempt to renegotiate his contract.

17   Visits AG with two letters from Moore complaining of his revisions to *Diarmuid and Grania*, to which he replies, insisting that he must be responsible for the style of the play. He sends Moore's letters to Symons, asking him to adjudicate on the disputed passages.

18   Dines with AG and shows her another wild letter from Moore about *Diarmuid and Grania*. Proofs of *The Shadowy Waters* have arrived, but WBY has broken his eyeglass and can do nothing without it.

19   Has tea with AG; is refusing to see Moore until arrangements about *Diarmuid and Grania* have been put in writing. She reads him proofs of *The Shadowy Waters* and he dictates a letter to Unwin about a new contract. Symons sees Moore about the quarrel over *Diarmuid and Grania* and finds him reasonable.

20   Dines with AG and tells her that Symons has seen Moore.

21   Visits Moore and they amicably rewrite the disputed passage in *Diarmuid and Grania*. Dines with AG and they go on to the Coronet Theatre, Notting Hill Gate, to see Forbes-Robertson in Shaw's *The Devil's Disciple*.

22	AG dines at Woburn Buildings with WBY.
23	AG calls on WBY prior to her departure for Ireland. In the evening WBY speaks at a dinner of the Chaucer Society at the Whitefriars Club to mark Chaucer's quincentenary.
25	Moore makes another fuss about revisions to Act 1 of *Diarmuid and Grania* but finally passes them.
28	WBY and Moore make revisions to Act II of *Diarmuid and Grania*.

December

1	(Sat) 'Postscript to a forthcoming Book of Essays by Irish Writers' (article; *UP* II. 244–6) published in the *All Ireland Review*. 'Introduction to a Dramatic Poem' (poem; *VP*, 217–19) published in the *Speaker*.
2	WBY and Moore have passed Act II of *Diarmuid and Grania* and Moore is negotiating with the actor-manager George Alexander to produce the play.
3	WBY and Moore meet to go through Act III of *Diarmuid and Grania*. They make further revisions to the whole play throughout the week.
8	Oldmeadow of the Unicorn Press informs WBY that his suspect political reputation is making the Press unpopular. In the evening WBY and FF give their first public demonstration of chanting at the ILS with renditions of 'The Lake Isle of Innisfree' and a lyric from *The Countess Cathleen*.
9	Sees Althea Gyles in the afternoon and later calls on Moore who shows him a new scene for Act I of *Diarmuid and Grania*.
10	WBY and Moore finish *Diarmuid and Grania*. FF demonstrates the art of chanting at WBY's 'Monday Evening'.
11	In the morning WBY goes through his letters and papers. In the afternoon he and Moore formally pass the whole of *Diarmuid and Grania*, and Moore takes it to read to Forbes-Robertson. WBY sees Althea Gyles who reads him Cecil French's poetry. Becomes embroiled in a quarrel at an ILS committee meeting when Barry O'Brien threatens to blackball Moore's application for election, so that WBY is obliged to withdraw his name until the General Meeting in March 1901.
12	Begins revising *The Countess Cathleen*. In the evening Tony Watts-Russell calls to see him.
13	Moore calls on WBY to tell him he has read *Diarmuid and Grania* to Mrs Patrick Campbell who seemed to like it. They decide to revise Act II, and do so over the following days. In the afternoon WBY discusses Althea Gyles' strained finances with Cyril French.
c.18	Takes JBY to see Stephen Phillips' *Herod*.

19	Working on his essay 'Magic', and the revisions to *The Countess Cathleen*. Goes to see Barry O'Brien, who is being sketched by JBY, about his blackballing of Moore.
20	*The Shadowy Waters* published. Sees Annie Horniman (AEFH) who is looking after Althea Gyles' health and interests. Agrees terms with Unwin over a new contract, except for American rights. Sees Sir Charles Russell about the ILS blackballing of Moore.
22	Sees Moore and learns that Mrs Pat Campbell proposes to produce *Diarmuid and Grania* in London in June 1901 and has offered an advance for the rights.
23	Dines at the Clement Shorters, where he is reintroduced to Violet Hunt.
24	Sees Mrs Campbell about her proposed production of *Diarmuid and Grania* and she offers to stage the play in London within six months, leaving him and Moore free to produce it in Dublin when they liked. AEFH has offered to guarantee the ILT.
25	Gives ECY Matthew Arnold's *Poems Narrative, Elegiac and Lyrical* for Christmas. Sees Moore who proposes asking Mrs Campbell to produce *Diarmuid and Grania* in London and Dublin in September.
29	Laid up with influenza, rheumatism and neuralgic headaches, which last into the new year.
30	Moore calls on WBY to tell him he has withdrawn *Diarmuid and Grania* from Mrs Campbell because of a supposed slight by her manager.

1901

January

4	(Fri) Moore calls to say that he will wait until *Diarmuid and Grania* has been produced before selling the American rights. WBY is still ill with influenza and neuralgia but during this time writes a new scene for the beginning of Act III of *The Countess Cathleen* (*VPl*, 81–93) and retouches *Diarmuid and Grania*. He also reads Laurence Binyon's poem 'Tristram' and Thomas Sturge Moore's play *Aphrodite Against Artemis*.
7	Conducts negotiations with Mrs Pat Campbell's manager over her possible production of *Diarmuid and Grania*.
8	Agrees with Unwin on American rights for new edition of *Poems*.
21	Tea with Sturge Moore at which they discuss Shelley. Writes to Mrs Pat Campbell's manager to hurry negotiations over *Diarmuid and Grania*.

22	Queen Victoria dies.
23	*Ideals in Ireland* published. Benson agrees to produce *Diarmuid and Grania* in Dublin.
25	Goes to see Sturge Moore.
	Late in this month WBY quarrels with George Moore over their collaboration on *Diarmuid and Grania*.
31	At the British Museum Library checking editions of Blake for Mark Perugini.

February

1	(Fri) Attends a contentious Council Meeting of the GD.
2	Writes letter to the Twelve Seniors of the GD, complaining about resolutions brought forward at the meeting on the previous day. Sends Unwin the MS of the new edition of *Poems*.
3	Sends Unwin the corrected agreement for *Poems*.
4	Sturge Moore, Binyon and Masefield to dinner.
5	Dines with George Moore and AG, who has just arrived from Ireland.
8–16	Working on his essay 'Magic' at the British Museum, where he sees a lot of AG.
9	With AG to Emery Walker's at 7 pm for tableaux vivants; afterwards AG reads him her essay on folk ballads.
10	AG reads to him from drafts of *Cuchulain of Muirthemne*.
c.13	Accompanies AG to Benson's production of *Coriolanus*.
16	Lectures on the psaltery at the Fellowship of the Three Kings, with Florence Farr and Anna Mather chanting. Afterwards WBY and Jack Yeats dine with AG.
19	Tea with Sturge Moore, Binyon and Wilfred Gibson in a Holborn teashop where they discuss Tolstoy's 'What is Art?'.
21	Liverish attack; stays at home correcting proofs.
26	Attends General Meeting of the GD to discuss a new constitution.
27	WBY, AEFH and Brodie-Innes resign their offices in the GD.

March

16	(Sat) Resigns from the committee of the ILS over the black-balling of George Moore. AG gives up her London apartment.
17	Dines at the Shorters with George Moore.
30	Attends a matinée of Gordon Craig's production of Purcell's *Dido and Aeneas* and *The Masque of Love*.

April

1	(Mon) Resumes serious work on *The Speckled Bird*. Receives a royalty cheque for £4. 0s. 10d. from Elkin Mathews for *The Wind Among the Reeds*. Early this month WBY distributes his

	pamphlet *Is the Order of the R.R. & A.C. to remain a Magical Order?* to the Adepti of the Golden Dawn.
2	At Euston Station seeing off Moore who is moving to Dublin. Declines Frank Harris's invitation to join the staff of his new weekly, *The Candid Friend.*
7	Visits Masefield in Walthamstow.
8	Craig to dinner to discuss stage scenery.
*c.*10	*Poems* (1901) published.
11	Visits the Rhyses.
12	Dines with Symons and his new wife, Rhoda.
19	Dines with AG on her return from a European tour; she gives him a Montenegran lute.
20	Accompanies AG to Henry Irving's production of *Coriolanus* at the Lyceum Theatre.
23–8	At Stratford-on-Avon to write about Shakespeare and Benson's productions for the *Speaker.*
29	Henry Newbolt to dinner and stays on for WBY's 'Monday Evening'; Sturge Moore and Christopher Wilson come in later.

May

4	(Sat) Writes *A Postscript to Essay called 'Is the Order of the R.R. & A.C. to remain a Magical Order?'* and distributes it to the Adepti of the Golden Dawn.
6	*The Land of Heart's Desire* produced at the Knickerbocker Theatre, New York, prior to an American tour.
7	Puts his publishing affairs into the hands of the agent A. P. Watt.
9	Crosses to Dublin and stays with Moore in Upper Ely Place, where they work on Act II of *Diarmuid and Grania.*
11	'At Stratford-on-Avon' (first part of an article; *UP* II. 247–52) published in the *Speaker.*
18	Unexpectedly meets Bullen in Dublin and finds him amazed at the hostility of Irish booksellers towards WBY. 'At Stratford-on-Avon' (second part of an article; *E & I*, 96–110) published in the *Speaker.*
19	Dines with Bullen who gets drunk.
20	Leaves Dublin to stay with George Pollexfen in Sligo, where he revises his book of Blake selections, collects folklore, and works slowly on *The Speckled Bird.*

June

1	(Sat) 'The Fool of Faery' (article, later 'The Queen and the Fool'; *Myth,* 112–16) published in the *Kensington.*
3	Repays £3 to JBY out of his payment from the *Speaker.*
15	'Under the Moon' (poem; *VP,* 209–10) published in the *Speaker.*

20	Goes to Dublin from Sligo.
*c.*21	Shown over Sandymount Castle, once the home of his great-uncle Robert Corbet.
23	Goes with Sarah Purser to enlist George Coffey's continuing support for the ILT. Later this month he leaves Dublin for Coole, where he remains until October.

July

1	(Mon) Spends the month at Coole, working on 'Baile and Aillinn', one of a planned series of poems on the Irish heroic age.
3	Moore sends WBY a five-part scenario which WBY subsequently uses as the basis of his play *Where There Is Nothing*.
13	'By the Roadside' (article; *Myth*, 138–40) published in *An Claideamh Soluis*.
25	Has nearly finished 'Baile and Aillinn' and is having his portrait painted by Alice Kinkead.
27	Gives a speech at the Galway Feis.

August

8	(Thu) Has literary conversations with Violet Martin ('Martin Ross'), who is visiting Coole with her mother.
9	More literary conversation and wandering in the garden with Violet Martin.
11	Finishes 'Baile and Aillinn' and begins writing *On Baile's Strand*.
20–3	Attends a Pan Celtic Congress in Dublin.
21	Speaks at the Pan Celtic Congress on the revolutionary impact of the language movement.
22	Advocates Celtic evening dress at a Pan Celtic Congress discussion.
23	Attends Kuno Meyer's lecture, 'The Present State of Celtic Studies', at the Pan Celtic Congress and in the evening gives an address at the closing Ceilidh on 'Ireland and the Arts'.
26–7	Is much excited by the Fay Company's productions of Alice Milligan's historical plays.
29	Travels from Dublin to attend the Galway Feis.
31	'Ireland and the Arts' (article; *E & I*, 203–10) published in the *United Irishman*.

September

2	(Mon) 'Magic' (article; *E & I*, 28–52) published in the *Monthly Review*. In the course of the month Jack and Cottie Yeats also visit Coole.

October

9	(Wed) Writes 'A Spinning Song'.
*c.*15	Goes to Dublin to attend Benson's rehearsals of *Diarmuid and Grania*. Contributes 'Windlestraws' (article; *Expl*, 73–84) to the first number of *Samhain*.

21	Makes a curtain speech at the first night of Benson's production of *Diarmuid and Grania* at the Gaiety Theatre, and attends the remaining performances on the following two nights.
23	Attends the opening of JBY's and Nathaniel Hone's Dublin exhibition.
25	Attends the opening of Jack Yeats's Dublin exhibition, 'Sketches of Life in the West of Ireland'.

November

1	(Fri) Speaks on nationality and art at AG's 'At Home' to publicize Jack Yeats's pictures and the ILT.
4	WBY has a cold but dines at the Hydes' with AG.
9	'John Eglinton' (review; *UP* II. 255–62) published in the *United Irishman*.
14	Returns to London from Dublin. Dissociates himself in a letter to the *Freeman's Journal* from George Moore's proposals for clerical censorship of the theatre.
16	Attends FF's Egyptian plays at the Victoria Hall.
18	At his 'Monday Evening' gives Masefield and FF an account of the production of *Diarmuid and Grania* in Dublin, and of Elgar's music for it.
19	Sees Mrs Pat Campbell's production of Bjornson's *Beyond Human Power* at the Royalty Theatre. Late this month he continues writing *On Baile's Strand* in the British Museum and sorts out his folklore notes for a new edition of *The Celtic Twilight*.
26	Calls on Mrs Pat Campbell to discuss her possible production of *Diarmuid and Grania*.

December

2	(Mon) Binyon attends WBY's 'Monday Evening'. Early this month WBY works with Arnold Dolmetsch on chanting and writes new essays for the revised *Celtic Twilight*.
7	'Literature and the Conscience' (article; *UP* II. 262–4) published in the *United Irishman*. Contributes to a symposium, 'Favourite Books of 1901', in the *Academy* (*UP* II. 264–5).
11	Visits the Shorters.
13	Sees John Murray about the publication of AG's *Cuchulain of Muirthemne*. In the evening attends a Johnson Club supper at the Cheshire Cheese as a guest of Unwin's.
20	Bumps into W. H. Nevinson in late evening.
25	Breakfast with John Masefield at Woburn Buildings.
28	First letter to the New York lawyer John Quinn inaugurates an important friendship.
29–30	Working at *On Baile's Strand*.
31	Stays up until 5 am working on mystical matters and evokes himself into a good frame of mind.

1902

January

1   (Wed) 'The Blood Bond' (poem; *VP*, 769–70) and 'Spinning Song' (poem, later 'There are Seven that pull the thread'; *VP*, 770–1) published in *A Broad Sheet*. WBY in fairly good spirits after a gloomy time.

2   Working on the rites for the Celtic Mystical Order.

5   Meets S. A. and Eugénie Strong who praise his essay 'Magic'.

7   Dines with Bullen.

9   AG sends him £10 on account for his as yet unwritten Preface to *Cuchulain of Muirthemne*.

11   'The Folly of Being Comforted' (poem; *VP*, 199–200) published in the *Speaker*. In the middle of this month WBY works on the new edition of *The Celtic Twilight* and on the Celtic Mystical Order.

18   'Enchanted Woods' (article; *Myth*, 60–4) published in the *Speaker*.

20   Masefield calls prior to moving to the country.

21   Sees FF's and OS's Egyptian plays again.

22   Visits Watt, Bullen and British Museum; attends a committee meeting of the ILS. Is in process of accepting a commission for a selected *Poems of Spenser*.

22–6   Weekend guest at Moorhouse, Holmwood, the Surrey home of the Hon. William Gibson, secretary of the ILS.

23   'Egyptian Plays' (review; *UP* II. 265–7) published in the *Star*.

26   Dines with AG on her return to London. Finally accedes to AE's request that the Fays produce *Cathleen ni Houlihan*, because Martyn's prevarications over the future of the ILT is putting the future of the Irish dramatic movement into doubt.

27   Lunches with AG and she later attends his 'Monday Evening' to hear FF chant; Newbolt also present.

29   Occupied with his mystical work.

February

2   (Sun) Sends his essay, 'Speaking to the Psaltery', to the *Monthly Review*.

c.5   Laid up with influenza until c.15 Feb; AG brings him bread and milk.

15   'Happy and Unhappy Theologians' (article; *Myth*, 42–6) published in the *Speaker*. Is reading Gautier's *Madamoiselle de Maupin*.

17   Joseph Nunan, Irish lawyer and colonial administrator, attends WBY's 'Monday Evening'.

24   Lady Margaret Sackville, Violet Hunt, Stephen Gwynn, Standish James O'Grady and H. W. Nevinson at WBY's 'Monday Evening', where FF chants.

25   At the British Museum.

27   Lectures to a group of mystics, probably at 'The Fellowship of the Three Kings'.

March

1   (Sat) 'What is "Popular Poetry"?' (article; *E & I*, 3–12) published in the *Cornhill Magazine*.

*c.*10   Attends the Purcell Society's productions of *Dido and Aeneas* and *The Masque of Love*, designed by Craig.

14   Attends an Omar Khayyam Club dinner at Frascati's Restaurant.

15   'The Old Town', 'War', and 'Earth, Fire and Water' (articles; *Myth*, 81–2, 110–11, 80) published in the *Speaker*.

17   Symons reads WBY his essay 'The New Art of the Stage', and they go on to the opening matinée of the Elizabethan Stage Society's production of *Everyman* at St George's Hall, Langham Place, and then to the Great Queen Street Theatre to introduce Symons to Gordon Craig.

22   Meets Nevinson and FF for dinner at the Comedy Restaurant, Haymarket, where the conversation turns on Purcell, WBY's mystical marriage to MG, politics, stories of his Pollexfen grandfather, Ireland, drama and gossip.

23   Helping to correct proofs of AG's *Cuchulain of Muirthemne*. Briefly thinks of becoming an actor to learn dramaturgy.

24   Complains to AG about her bowdlerizing in *Cuchulain of Muirthemne*. Dolmetsch calls at Woburn Buildings, enthusiastic about the chanting experiments.

25   Goes to AG's apartment to look for proofs of *Cuchulain of Muirthemne* sent there in error.

26   Crosses to Dublin.

April

1   (Tue) 'Away' (article; *UP* II. 267–82) published in the *Fortnightly Review*.

2–5   AE's *Deirdre* and WBY's *Cathleen ni Houlihan* produced to great acclaim by the Fays' Irish National Dramatic Company at St Teresa's Hall, Dublin, MG playing the title role in WBY's play.

3   Dictates a version of new 2nd Act of *Diarmuid and Grania* to Moore, who is to work on it in Paris. In the evening Padraic Colum reads him a version of his play, *Broken Soil*.

5   Moore helps him to simplify *On Baile's Strand*. He meets O'Grady in the morning; later attends a meeting at the Contemporary Club with AE, Martyn, the Fays and James Cousins to discuss setting up a National Theatre. Describes the action of *Cathleen ni Houlihan* in a note to the *United Irishman* (*UP* II. 283–4).

8   Returns to London.

c.9	Amends and returns the manuscript of a story by JBY.
12	Defends the INT productions in a letter to the *United Irishman*, 'The Acting at St Teresa's Hall'.
18	Planning *The Hour-Glass* and *The Pot of Broth* and dictating substantial parts of *The Speckled Bird* to a typist.
19	'A Voice', 'The Swine of the Gods', 'The Devil', 'And Fair Fierce Women' and 'Mortal Help' (articles; *Myth*, 68–9, 67, 41, 57–9, 9–10) published in the *Speaker*.
22	Sees FF's Egyptian play, *The Shrine of the Golden Hawk*, again.
24	Calls at John Murray's to find out the date of the publication of *Cuchulain of Muirthemne*. Goes on to work in the British Museum.
25	Meets AG and Robert Gregory on their return from Italy and accompanies them to the theatre.
26	Dines with AG and Blunt, and they go with him to the ILS, where he takes the chair for a lecture on 'An Old Irish Rath' by John Campbell, nationalist MP for Armagh. Defends the recent INT productions in a further letter to the *United Irishman*. 'Aristotle of the Books', 'Miraculous Creatures' and 'An Enduring Heart' (articles; *Myth*, 66, 65, 34–6) published in the *Speaker*.
c.28	Publication of AG's *Cuchulain of Muirthemne* with WBY's Preface.
30	Dines with Dolmetsch and FF; they arrange for six more psalteries to be made.

May

1	(Thu) 'Speaking to the Psaltery' (article; *E & I*, 13–27) published in the *Monthly Review*. WBY suffers from eye trouble which persists throughout the summer.
2	Attacked for neo-Paganism in the *Freeman's Journal*.
c.12	Lectures on 'The Theatre' to the Pioneer Club.
14	In the afternoon calls on Sturge Moore and complains about argumentative women.
15	WBY and FF give a private Demonstration Lecture on the psaltery at Clifford's Inn for critics.
16	Sturge Moore and William Sharp at WBY's.
17	Goes to Oxford, stays with Eric Maclagan at Christ Church, and sees Robert Gregory.
18	Lectures in the evening on 'The Theatre' to an open and well-attended meeting of the St John's College Essay Society; discussion lasts until 10.50 pm.
19	Lunches with Robert Gregory in Oxford before returning to London.
22	Visits oculist, who prescribes new glasses for distant objects.
25	Meets Sydney Cockerell at Emery Walker's and discusses his sisters' plans for setting up a printing press in Ireland.

27	Preparing *Cathleen ni Houlihan* for publication but has still not decided on the title. Writes a letter to the *TLS* criticizing Churton Collins for an attack on Blake's 'The Tiger'. Sees Symons who is engaged in a newspaper controversy over Stephen Phillips.

June

3	(Tue) Calls on Bullen. Is writing 'The Players ask for a Blessing on the Psaltery and on Themselves'. Early in the month quarrels with Althea Gyles.
6	Receives royalties of £1 11s. 3d. from Unwin. WBY and Sturge Moore dine at the Michael Fields's.
7	Consults Eric Maclagan about ecclesiastical embroidery for SMY.
10	Delivers a well-attended lecture on 'Speaking to Musical Notes' at Clifford's Inn, illustrated by FF's first public performance on the psaltery, with Dolmetsch in the chair.
13	Finishes a draft of *The Hour-Glass*, the scenario of which has delighted Gordon Craig. Lets his London rooms prior to leaving for Ireland.
14–16	Spends the weekend at Blunt's 'Poets Party' (apparently to celebrate WBY's 37th birthday) at Newbuildings, with Cockerell, Neville Lytton, Eddie Marsh and Lord Alfred Douglas and his wife, Olive.
15	Sits up until midnight with Douglas and Cockerell discussing poetry, recitation and philosophy.
16	Surprised that he has been suggested as one of the 3 directors of the *United Irishman*. Maclagan discusses embroidery with SMY at WBY's 'Monday Evening'.
18	In the evening visits Dolmetsch and discovers that his poems are made to actual tunes.
19	Attends a private performance of Lugné Poe's production of Maeterlinck's *Monna Vanna* (in French).
20	Signs an open letter to the London press protesting at the censorship of *Monna Vanna*. Sees Sarah Bernhardt's production of Racine's *Phèdre* in French at the Garrick Theatre.
21	Crosses to Dublin and stays with Moore.
22	Visits Tara with Moore and Hyde to investigate unauthorized excavations.
23	Joins Hyde and Moore in letter to *The Times* (published 27 June) protesting against the excavations at Tara. Moore arranges a dinner party for him in the evening.
24	Travels by the 9.15 am train to Coole, where he attends the celebrations for Robert Gregory's Coming of Age, and devotes himself to finishing *Ideas of Good and Evil*.

July
1   (Tue) 'Baile and Aillinn' (poem; *VP*, 188–97) published in the
           Monthly Review. Spends most of month writing *The Hour-Glass*
           and *The Pot of Broth*; his eyes still troubling him. Early in the
           month he publishes the revised and enlarged edition of *The
           Celtic Twilight*.

*c.*24   Sends the Fays *The Hour-Glass* and *The Pot of Broth*, and makes
           suggestions about casting.

August
8   (Fri) The Fay Company moves into the Camden Street Hall as its
           permanent home and begins rehearsals.

9   The Irish National Theatre Society (INTS) formally founded, and
           appoints a committee with officers: WBY as President; AE, MG
           and Hyde as Vice-Presidents; and Frederick Ryan as Secretary.

*c.*15   Meets the American critic, Cornelius Weygandt, who is visit-
           ing Coole. Writing 'In the Seven Woods'.

20   Attends the Connacht Feis in Galway, where he sees Hyde's and
           AG's *An Posadh* (*The Marriage*). AG, Padraic Pearse and Martyn
           also there, and the Hydes stay on at Coole. Late this month he
           writes 'The Old Age of Queen Maeve'; the American actress
           Mabel Taliaferro visits Coole and WBY persuades her to act *The
           Land of Heart's Desire* for him.

c. 27   Sends the Fays the MS of *The Countess Cathleen*.

31   Speaks in Craughwell at the Killeenan Feis, in memory of the
           Gaelic poet Raftery, accompanied by AG, Jack Yeats, and John
           Quinn, whom he is meeting for the first time.

September
1   (Mon) Quinn suggests that WBY should undertake an American
           lecture tour.

7   Changes the title of *The Beggarman* to *A Pot of Broth* and dis-
           cusses with Frank Fay the costumes, make-up, wigs, astrological
           allusions and Latin words in *The Hour-Glass*.

15   Writes to Frank Fay about the production of *The Hour-Glass*. In
           the middle of the month he drafts a new passage for *The Hour-
           Glass* and Quinn sends him a copy of Tille's translation of
           Nietzsche's *Thus Spake Zarathustra*. Later in the month a quarrel
           with Moore over the rights in a scenario provokes him to write
           Where There Is Nothing at great speed.

28   Supports John Shawe-Taylor's call for an all-party conference on
           the Land Question.

October
3   (Fri) Goes to Dublin until 7 October to watch INTS rehearsals
           and to arrange for the publication of *Where There Is Nothing* in

	the *United Irishman*. Early this month the Caradoc Press publish *Cathleen ni Houlihan* in an edition of which WBY disapproves.
4	Death of Lionel Johnson.
5	Attends MG's talk on 'Emer' to the *Inghinidhe na nEireann*.
7	Returns to Coole from Dublin. Correcting proofs for *Samhain* (1902).
8	Synge visits Coole until 13 October.
c.19	Arranges with Bullen for *Plays for an Irish Theatre*; drafting the Introduction to his selections from Spenser.
21	Quinn offers to arrange an American copyright edition of *Where There Is Nothing*.
27	FF in Dublin demonstrates chanting with explanations by WBY as part of the opening night programme of the INTS in the Antient Concert Rooms.
29	Attends all the INTS Samhain week productions, which continue until 1 November at the Antient Concert Rooms. Edits and contributes notes and *Cathleen ni Houlihan* to *Samhain* (1902).
30	*Where There Is Nothing* appears in the *United Irishman* (dated 1 November) and takes Moore by surprise. Quinn publishes an American copyright edition simultaneously.

November

1	(Sat) In the afternoon WBY and FF lecture on 'Speaking to Musical Notes', and attend the INTS performances in the evening. 'The Freedom of the Theatre' (article; *UP* II. 295–9) published in the *United Irishman*. Early this month WBY has his first meeting with James Joyce who tells him he has met him too late.
3	AG invites Joyce to dine with herself, WBY and JBY at the Nassau Hotel. WBY is revising *Where There Is Nothing*.
c.14	Returns to London from Dublin and continues rewriting *Where There Is Nothing*.
15	Sees Watt about the publication of *Where There Is Nothing*.
16	Reads the revised *Where There Is Nothing* to Symons.
17	Sees Unwin about becoming co-publisher of AG's *Poets and Dreamers*. In the evening Pixie Smith, AEFH, Sturge Moore and Duncombe-Jewell at WBY's 'Monday Evening'.
18	Reads the revised *Where There Is Nothing* to Bullen.
19	Dines with the Rhyses at the Shorters.
21	Auditions Mary Price-Owen for chanting to the psaltery.
24	The Dun Emer printing press arrives at Gurteen Dhas. Late this month WBY's eye trouble recurs but he manages to read allegories at the British Museum in preparation for his selection from Edmund Spenser.
26	Reads the revised *Where There Is Nothing* to Binyon, Sturge Moore, Rhys and others.

27   Has an inspiration for a new fantastic opening to Act IV of *Where There Is Nothing*.

December

1   (Mon) 'Adam's Curse' (poem; *VP*, 204–6) published in the *Monthly Review*. Pixie Smith attends WBY's 'Monday Evening' and shows him the designs for a proposed Stage Society production of *Where There Is Nothing*.

2   Looks after Joyce on his way through London to Paris, entertaining him to breakfast, lunch and dinner, and introducing him to Symons and the editors of various journals.

4   Visits Watt, and later Charlotte and G. B. Shaw to discuss staging of *Where There Is Nothing*.

6   Contributes to a symposium in the *Academy* on 'Favourite Books of 1902'.

c.8   Sturge Moore executes stage designs for *The Hour-Glass*.

9   Visits the *Academy* office to persuade them to commission contributions from Joyce. Goes on to Edith Craig's to meet members of the Stage Society.

10   Calls to see Cockerell at Clifford's Inn.

14   Reads *Where There Is Nothing* to the actor Harry Irving.

15   Reads *The Hour-Glass* and *The Pot of Broth* to Edith Craig, Pixie Smith and others.

16   Finishing his essay on Spenser

17   Sees Laurence Housman's nativity play *Bethlehem*, designed by Craig. Meets Ellen Terry and Edith Craig, who shows him the lighting secrets of the production. In the middle of this month he reads Nietzsche intensely, finding him 'a strong enchanter' (to AG).

26   Receives £5 from Bullen.

29   Sees W. G. Fay in London and discusses future INTS programmes.

31   Dictates the last of the Spenser MS to a typist and takes Masefield to see Cockerell at Clifford's Inn.

1903

January

1   (Thu) 'The Old Men Admiring Themselves in the Water' (poem; *VP*, 208) published in the *Pall Mall Gazette*. Early this month Mme Laura Troncy draws two sketches of WBY.

2   Sends Colum a volume of Ibsen's early plays and posts the Spenser introduction to publishers.

5   At WBY's suggestion, Sturge Moore proposes that Craig and Ricketts should stage *The Countess Cathleen*. WBY angered by FF's bad performance of chanting at his 'Monday Evening'.

7	WBY sees Watt and Bullen about the publication of his Irish plays.
8	Visits Sturge Moore. Engages in an angry correspondence with FF over her bad performance on the psaltery.
9	Consults Cockerell about the printing of the Dun Emer edition of *In the Seven Woods*, the Press's first publication.
12	WBY dines with Stephen Gwynn to discuss a visit of the INTS to London. Synge attends WBY's 'Monday Evening' with Sturge Moore, Cockerell, MG, AEFH, Pixie Smith and others.
15	WBY's newly acquired gas stove is at last in working order; he is writing new passages for *On Baile's Strand* and correcting proofs of *Ideas of Good and Evil*.
17	In the afternoon attends a meeting at Clifford's Inn with Cockerell, Margaret Sackville, Katharine Horner and Emery Walker to discuss a proposed magazine, the *Celt*.
18–22	WBY introduces Joyce to various London editors with a view to finding him journalistic work.
19	Synge spends the evening with WBY.
20	WBY hears Synge read *Riders to the Sea* at AG's.
21	Spends the morning with Synge.
23	Calls on Cockerell to discuss the *Celt* and the Dun Emer Press.
25	Sees the Stage Society's production of Ibsen's *When We Dead Awaken*.
26	Synge attends WBY's 'Monday Evening'.

February

1	(Sun) The Irish National Theatre Society formally founded, with WBY as President.
2	Synge at WBY's and reads *Riders to the Sea* to MG and Chesterton.
3	WBY with Synge at a psaltery recital by FF.
5	Dines with Cockerell, FF, Lady Margaret Sackville and Katharine Horner; they go on to Forbes-Robertson's production of *Othello* at the Lyric Theatre and WBY has supper with Cockerell at Gatti's afterwards.
6	Sends Quinn the revised version of *Where There Is Nothing*.
7	Lectures on 'The Future of Irish Drama' to an Irish cultural club, Na Geadhna Fiadaine (The Wild Geese) at the Bijou Theatre.
8–10	Writes a series of agonized letters to MG, begging her not to join the Catholic Church and not to marry John MacBride. Mathews issues the 4th edition of *The Wind Among the Reeds*.
9	Reads *On Baile's Strand* at his 'Monday Evening', which is attended by AG, Synge, Sturge Moore, Cockerell, Binyon, Strang, Pixie Smith, Jack Yeats, Edie Craig and Masefield among others.
10	Synge dines with AG and WBY.
14	WBY has tea with Lady Margaret Sackville, Katharine Horner and Cockerell and they discusses the theatre until nearly 7 pm.

17	MG received into the Catholic Church.
19	WBY lectures on 'The Irish Faery Kingdom' at the Cory Hall in Cardiff.
20	Lectures on the Irish Intellectual Revival to the Welsh Society at University College, Cardiff.
21	MG marries Major John MacBride in Paris.
26	The 'big wind' devastates Coole and the West of Ireland.

March

2	(Mon) 'The Happiest of the Poets' (article on William Morris; *E & I*, 53–64) published in the *Fortnightly Review* and 'Poets and Dreamers' (article, later 'The Galway Plains'; *E & I*, 211–14) in the *New Liberal Review*. Synge dines with WBY.
3	Hears Synge read his two comedies at AG's.
7	WBY lectures in London.
11	At the Chiswick Press, where he discovers that the printing of *Where There Is Nothing* has been delayed by the lack of paper and the order to begin. Meets Elkin Mathews by chance.
12	Writes a lament for use in the Craigs' production of Ibsen's *The Vikings of Helgeland*. That evening he crosses to Dublin.
13	Attends the dress rehearsal of *The Hour-Glass* at the Molesworth Hall.
14	Lectures on 'The Reform of the Theatre' between performances of *The Hour-Glass* and AG's *Twenty-Five* at the Molesworth Hall.
c.15	Travels from Dublin to Coole.
17	Announces the setting up of the London Masquers Theatrical Society.
25	Writing 'The Happy Townland'.
27	Visits his sisters at Dun Emer Industries during a short trip to Dublin.

April

1	(Wed) 'The Old Age of Queen Maeve' (poem; *VP*, 180–7) published in the *Fortnightly Review*, and 'Red Hanrahan's Song about Ireland' (poem; *VP*, 206–8) in *A Broad Sheet*. Joins protests against Edward VII's visit to Ireland.
4	'The Reform of the Theatre' (article; *Expl*, 107–10) published in the *United Irishman*.
11	'Emotion of Multitude' (article; *E & I*, 215–16) published in the *All Ireland Review*.
12	Attends INTS performance at Loughrea.
13	Dines with the Revd Jeremiah O'Donovan, administrator of St Brendan's Cathedral, Loughrea.
c.25	Returns to Dublin from Coole and upbraids Joyce for his bad behaviour towards London editors. Remains at the Contemporary Club until 4.00 am discussing the theatrical movement.

28	Leaves Dublin for London.
29	Calls on Cockerell for advice about the ecclesiastical banners being executed by the Dun Emer Industries.
30	Sees the Craig–Terry production of Ibsen's *The Vikings of Helgeland*.

May

1	(Fri) 'A Canonical Book' (review of AG's *Poets and Dreamers*; *UP* II. 299–303) published in the *Bookman*.
2	Attends the matinée and evening INTS performances at the Queen's Gate Hall. This, the first visit by the Society to London, is a resounding success.
4	MG calls for two hours and confesses that her marriage is unhappy. WBY reads *The King's Threshold* and *The Travelling Man* to Granville Barker, AEFH and other guests at his 'Monday Evening'.
5	*Ideas of Good and Evil* published. WBY dines at Sir Henry Lawrence's before going on to lecture with FF on 'Recording the Music of Speech' at Clifford's Inn Hall.
12	Lectures with FF on 'Heroic Folk Literature' at Clifford's Inn Hall.
13	William Sharp calls on WBY.
15	WBY lectures with FF and Mary Price-Owen on 'What the Theatre Might Be' at Caxton Hall.
16	Lectures with FF on 'Chanting' at the ILS. Supports the Irish National Council's protest against the Royal Visit to Ireland.
17	Travels to Manchester with FF.
18	Lectures on the psaltery with FF at Owens College, Manchester.
19	WBY and FF return to London.
23–5	Spends weekend at Gilbert Murray's.
25	Visits Cockerell at Clifford's Inn.
26	Calls again on Cockerell at Clifford's Inn.
29	Lectures with FF on 'Poetry and the Living Voice' at Clifford's Inn Hall. Later this month *Where There Is Nothing* is published as Vol. 1 of 'Plays for an Irish Theatre'.

June

1	(Mon) A revised version of *The Land of Heart's Desire* published in the *Bibelot* (Portland, Maine).
c.1	WBY goes to Dublin.
3	Sketched by JBY.
3–4	The New York Irish Literary Society stages WBY's plays at the Carnegie Lyceum.
4	'The Happy Townland' (poem; *VP*, 213–16) published in the *Weekly Critical Review*.
8	WBY arrives with AG to stay with Hyde in Roscommon.
9	WBY, AG and Hyde visit Ráth Cruacháin, Rosnaree and Rátha.

11	AG leaves Frenchpark.
12	WBY spends the day talking to Hyde.
13	Leaves Frenchpark and goes to stay with George Pollexfen at Rosses Point, Sligo.
c.21	Goes from Rosses Point to Coole.

July

3	(Fri) Leaves Coole for London, seeing AE and the Fays on his way through Dublin.
6	Attends a business meeting of the Masquers Society in Clifford's Inn.
9	Returns to Coole. Writing 'O Do Not Love Too Long'.
12	Finishes the poem 'O Do Not Love Too Long'.
13	Writes to the *Freeman's Journal* protesting against Edward VII's visit to Ireland.
c.18	Sees Fr Jeremiah O'Donovan in Loughrea and discusses the Dun Emer banners for the Cathedral there.
c.19–21	Stays at Ballydonelan Castle, Loughrea, and then returns to Coole.

August

1	(Sat) Writes to the *United Irishman* protesting against the reception of the King at Maynooth.
15	Goes to Dublin from Coole to cast *The King's Threshold*.
c.16	Returns to Coole.
24	Receives royalties of £13 17*s*. 11*d*. from Unwin.
25	*In the Seven Woods* published. Late this month he writes the play *Heads or Harps* with AG.

September

1	(Tue) *The Hour-Glass* (play; *VPl*, 576–647) published in the *North American Review* and *The Pot of Broth* (play; *VPl*, 236–55) in the *Gael* (NY). Early this month he writes a Masque, 'The Marriage of Sun and Moon', for the opening ceremony of the Masquers Society.
7	The Hydes leave Coole after a visit.
9	'A Prologue' (to *The King's Threshold*; *VPl*, 313–14) published in the *United Irishman*.
19	Goes from Coole to Dublin to help with rehearsals of forthcoming INTS plays. Returns to Coole later this month.
c.26	MG, Hyde, Digges and Maire Quinn withdraw from the INTS in protest against the production of Synge's *In the Shadow of the Glen*. *Samhain* (1903) published.

October

| 3 | (Sat) WBY goes to Dublin from Coole. |
| 8 | Speaks from the stage after the INTS production of *The King's Threshold*, *In the Shadow of the Glen* and *Cathleen ni Houlihan* |

at the Molesworth Hall. Writes to the *Irish Times*, protesting against the censorship of Flaubert at the Irish National Library.

9	Attends the INTS productions again.
10	Writes to the *United Irishman* to defend artistic and dramatic freedom in Ireland. Attends the INTS plays with AG and Synge.
14	Corrects the MS of *The King's Threshold* to send to Quinn for American copyright publication.
17	Writes a further letter to the *United Irishman* to defend artistic and dramatic freedom in Ireland.
*c.*19	Crosses to London from Dublin.
20	WBY has tea at AG's with Robert Gregory, Cockerell and Frank Fay, who is in London to see a performance by Duse.
24	Speaks after a lecture on Daniel O'Connell at the ILS. Writes a third letter to the *United Irishman* to defend artistic and dramatic freedom in Ireland.
30	Elkin Mathews calls to see WBY to discuss the publication of a revised version of *The Tables of the Law*, and the termination of WBY's agreement with John Lane for *The Wind Among the Reeds*.

November

4	(Wed) Leaves from Liverpool on the *Oceanic* for an extended tour of the USA.
11	Arrives in New York and is met by a crowd of reporters; stays at the Plaza Hotel.
12	Meets William Bourke Cockran and Judge Martin Keogh. The Masquers Society is dissolved in London.
15	WBY moves from the Plaza Hotel to Quinn's apartment. In the evening he and Quinn are dinner guests of John D. Crimmins.
16	Lunches with Quinn and Judge Keogh. Gives his first American lecture ('The Intellectual Revival in Ireland') at Yale.
17	Lectures to the New Haven Irish Literary Society on 'The Heroic Literature of Ireland', followed by a reception.
18	Lectures at Smith College ('Heroic Literature') and later at Mount Holyoke College ('The Theatre and What It Might Be').
19	Lectures ('The Theatre') at Amherst College.
20	Lectures ('Heroic Literature') at Trinity College, Hartford.
22	Returns to New York.
23	Travels to Philadelphia, and lectures ('The Intellectual Revival') at the University of Pennsylvania.
24	Dines with the Shakespearean scholar Dr Howard Furness.

25	Returns to New York where he meets Archbishop Ireland and lectures at the City College ('The Intellectual Revival') followed by supper with Irish-American writers and journalists.
26	Sees George Bryan about contributing to a multi-volume Irish anthology, *Irish Literature*; he later gives an interview to the *Critic* and meets the critic Horatio Krans.
27	Revises the proofs of *The King's Threshold*, after which he is photographed for the newspapers and leaves for Boston on an overnight train.
28	Lectures ('The Intellectual Revival') at Wellesley College, followed by a reception.
30	Second lecture ('Heroic Literature') at Wellesley College.

December

1	(Tue) 'Red Hanrahan' (story; *Myth*, 213–24) published in the *Independent Review*. Lectures at Harvard on 'Poetry in the Old Time and in the New' and meets William James.
2	Returns briefly to New York.
3	Lectures at Bryn Mawr on 'The Intellectual Revival'.
4	Lectures at Vassar College on 'The Intellectual Revival'.
5	Lectures ('The Intellectual Revival') to the Long Island Historical Society, Brooklyn, followed by reception at the Hamilton Club.
6	Attends a private dinner in Brooklyn with Quinn from 6 to 10 pm.
7	Delivers a further lecture ('Heroic Literature') at Bryn Mawr.
8	Lectures ('The Theatre') to the Contemporary Club, Philadelphia, and stays with Joshua Lippincott.
8–20	Writes the poem 'Old Memory'.
9	Returns to New York.
10	Lectures ('The Theatre') at the Cosmopolitan Building, New York.
15	Travels to Germantown, Pennsylvania, where he lectures to the Science and Art Club, and stays with Cornelius Weygandt's father.
16	Returns to New York and goes from there to Canada.
17	Lectures at McGill University, Montreal, on 'Heroic Literature'.
18	Returns to New York.
20	Given a dinner in New York by the Sligo Men's Association.
22	Photographed by Alice Boughton at her studio on Madison Avenue.
*c.*23	Stays with Francis DeLacey Hyde at Plainfield, New Jersey.
24–5	Dictates new versions of his lectures to T. J. Curtin, Quinn's stenographer.
26	Attends a reception in his honour at the Hamilton Club.
28	Lunches with President Theodore Roosevelt and his family in Washington and discusses Irish fairies.

29	Speaks at a Press Club reception and luncheon in New York.
30	Lectures on 'Poetry' to the New York Arts Club and dines with Julia Ellsworth Ford and her husband. The INTS is registered under the Friendly Societies Act in Dublin.
31	Speaks on the laboriousness and necessity of style at a reception at the Authors' Club, New York.

1904

January

1	(Fri) Works on his Carnegie Hall lecture and writes to George Brett of Macmillan (New York) about the terms on which that firm would become his American publisher.
2	Rehearses his lecture at the Carnegie Hall; in the evening lectures at the Brooklyn Institute.
3	Delivers a major public lecture on 'The Intellectual Revival in Ireland' at the Carnegie Hall; afterwards John Devoy brings a deputation from the Clan-na-Gael to meet him.
4	Leaves New York for St Louis and arrives 5 hours late.
5	Lectures on 'Heroic Literature' to a large audience at the St Louis Society of Pedagogy.
6	Lectures ('The Theatre') to the Wednesday Club of St Louis.
7	Sees representatives of the Irish concession at the St Louis World Fair.
8	Leaves St Louis for Indianapolis.
9	Lunches with James Whitcomb Riley in Indianapolis; in the evening lectures ('The Theatre') to the Athenaeum Club at Butler University.
10	Given a banquet luncheon by the Emmet Club of Indianapolis.
11	Leaves Indianapolis for Lafayette.
12	Lectures ('The Intellectual Revival') at Purdue University.
13	Leaves Lafayette for Chicago where he lectures ('The Intellectual Revival') to the Twentieth Century Club at Harriet Pullman's house.
14	Lectures to the Chicago Women's Club, followed by luncheon; in the evening attends a performance of *The Land of Heart's Desire* by the Chicago University Dramatic Club.
15	Lectures ('Poetry') at the University of Notre Dame and in the evening ('The Theatre') at St Mary's College.
16	Lectures ('Heroic Poetry') at St Mary's College and in the afternoon talks to a literary class at Notre Dame. In the evening he lectures on 'The Intellectual Revival' and sits up talking with the priests afterwards.
17	Returns to Chicago from Notre Dame.

18	Leaves Chicago at 8.30 am to deliver a lecture at Indiana University, Bloomington, returning to Chicago by overnight train.
20	Leaves Chicago for St Paul on an overnight train.
21	Dines with Archbishop Ireland and the Knights of Columbus before lecturing ('The Intellectual Revival') at the St Paul Seminary.
22	Meets the bibliophile and land-speculator James Carleton Young in Minneapolis before leaving for San Francisco.
26	MG's son, Sean MacBride, born in Paris.
27	WBY arrives in San Francisco. He lectures on 'The Theatre' in the afternoon at Berkeley, and in the evening on 'The Intellectual Revival' for the League of the Cross at the Alhambra Theatre.
28	Interviewed by the *San Francisco Examiner* and is later driven to the ocean by James Phelan to dine with his friends. WBY meets the poet Agnes Tobin.
29	Lectures ('Heroic Literature') at Stanford in the afternoon and at Santa Clara College ('The Intellectual Revival') in the evening; he then tours the printing-works of the *Daily Mercury*, and spends the night in San Jose.
30	Lectures ('The Theatre') at the Alhambra Theatre, San Francisco. AEFH is thinking of funding a Dublin Theatre.
*c.*31	Publication of AG's *Gods and Fighting Men* with a Preface by WBY.

February

1	(Mon) Probably lectures to St Ignatius College. Dines with Phelan and local literary people at the Bohemian Club, San Francisco.
2	Lectures to the College of the Sacred Heart.
3	Lectures ('The Intellectual Revival') to the Tuesday Club, Sacramento.
4	Leaves Sacramento for Chicago.
7	Arrives in Chicago from California.
8	Lectures at the social settlement, Hull House, Chicago.
9	Lectures ('The Theatre') at the University of Wisconsin.
10	Delivers a second lecture ('Heroic Literature') at the University of Wisconsin in the afternoon; in the evening he lectures at Beloit College.
11	Lectures at Mrs Coonley Ward's in Chicago in the morning, after which he leaves for Canada.
12	Lectures ('Poetry') at Queen's University, Kingston, Ontario, and later leaves for Toronto by a midnight train.
13	Lectures ('Poetry') at the University of Toronto.
14	Returns to New York from Toronto, arriving at about 11 pm.
15	Leaves New York for Baltimore, where he lectures in the afternoon.
17	Leaves Baltimore for New York.
18	Lectures ('Heroic Literature') to the Fenelon Reading Circle, Brooklyn.

19	Lectures at Wells College.
21	Lectures ('The Intellectual Revival') at the Catholic University in Washington.
24	Lectures ('The Intellectual Revival') at Wallace Hall, Newark.
25	May have lectured at Bridgeport, Connecticut.
26	May have lectured at Paterson, New Jersey.
28	Gives a major lecture on Robert Emmet to the Clan-na-Gael at the Musical Academy, New York.

March

1	(Tue) Calls with Quinn at the Macmillan (NY) office and they discuss with Herbert Williams (Brett being away) the possibility of the firm becoming WBY's American publisher and issuing a Collected Edition of his work. Writes poem 'Never Give all the Heart'.
4	WBY meets the poet and journalist Witter Bynner.
5	WBY given a dinner at Metropolitan Club. 'Emmet the Apostle of Irish Liberty' (the lecture of 28 Feb; *UP* II. 310–27) published in the *Gaelic American*.
6	Guest of honour at a reception given by the Irish Literary Society of New York.
8	Lectures at Dobbs Ferry. Writes to Brett about the American publication of his works.
9	Quinn gives a farewell dinner for WBY, who afterwards sails for England on the *Oceanic*.
9–16	Sketched by William Strang on the *Oceanic*. *The King's Threshold: and On Baile's Strand* published at this time.
16	Arrives in Liverpool after a good crossing.
17	Returns to London.
18	Discusses Irish participation in the St Louis World Fair with Horace Plunkett at AG's; sees George Brett about Macmillan (NY) becoming his American publisher.
20	AG gives a dinner party for WBY, Ricketts, Shannon and Hugh Lane.
22	Attends a performance of *The Land of Heart's Desire* by the Chelsea Mummers.
25	Lunches with the INTS company at Restaurant Roche, Old Compton Street, on their second London visit.
26	The INTS performs with great success to a distinguished audience at the Royalty Theatre, London, in the course of which WBY receives a curtain call. AG entertains WBY and Company to tea at the Criterion after the matinée to meet people interested in the plays.
29	WBY leaves London for Coole.
31	Receives royalties of £16 6s. 9d, from Unwin.

April

2	(Sat) Returns proofs of *The Tables of the Law and The Adoration of the Magi* to Elkin Mathews. WBY and AG resisting attempts to recruit a company from the INTS to play at the St Louis Exhibition.
6	P. J. Kelly expelled from the INTS for contracting to act in St Louis.
7	Goes to Dublin from Coole. In the evening he sees James Reardon to discuss terms on which he would permit his plays to be performed in St Louis. *The Hour-Glass* produced at the Garrick Theatre, New York.
8	AEFH formally offers to buy the Mechanics Institute and convert it into a theatre for the INTS.
9	WBY sees Sir Anthony MacDonnell, Under-Secretary for Ireland, about securing a Patent for the new theatre.
11	The theatregoer and architect Joseph Holloway meets WBY for the first time when AEFH brings him to inspect the Mechanics Institute at 3.30 pm. The manager denounces them as land-grabbers and orders them off the premises. WBY and AEFH go on to visit the Hibernian Academy.
15	WBY conducts rehearsals of *The King's Threshold* at the Camden Street Theatre, and revises it while doing so.
16	Gives Whitney & Moore, the INTS's solicitors, a draft petition for the Abbey Theatre patent; in the evening leaves Dublin for London.
23	WBY introduces Synge to Ricketts and Shannon.
25	Receives a satisfactory contract from Macmillan (NY). Crosses to Dublin.
26	The INTS mount private performances of *The King's Threshold* and *The Shadowy Waters* at a special *conversazione* for WBY and Stephen Gwynn.
27	Returns to London.
28	Sees AG for lunch.
29	American productions of *The Land of Heart's Desire* and *The Hour-Glass* by Margaret Wycherly at the Alcazar Theatre, New York.
30	WBY and AG attend an abridged version of Aeschylus' Oresteian Trilogy at Stratford-upon-Avon.

May

10	(Tue) Dines with AG, Robert Gregory, Gilbert Murray and Blunt.
11	WBY and the rest of the INTS write formally to accept AEFH's offer of a theatre on the terms she has stipulated.
16	Shannon, AG and Archie Russell dine at WBY's before attending his 'Monday Evening'.
20	Dines *chez* Ricketts and Shannon with Rothenstein and they discuss artistic talent and achievement.

26   Attends Gilbert Murray's version of Euripides' *Hippolytus* at the Lyric Theatre, with FF leader of the chorus.

28   Meets the Irish playwright William Boyle at the ILS to discuss revisions to his play *The Building Fund*.

June

1   (Wed) George Moore snubs WBY at the Symons's house. Later this month *Poems* (1904) appears.

2   WBY consults Granville Barker about the cast for the Stage Society's forthcoming performance of *Where There Is Nothing* and then goes to Cambridge to lecture on 'The Heroic Poetry of Ireland'.

3   Lunches with James Phelan and afterwards accompanies AG to the last performance of *Hippolytus*.

4   Speaks after the Chelsea Mummers' performance of *The Land of Heart's Desire* and *The Poorhouse* at the Passmore Edwards Settlement.

6   Maclagan, Nevinson and Gordon Bottomley at WBY's 'Monday Evening'.

13   Pamela Colman Smith at WBY's 'Monday Evening'.

c.21   Attends an informal meeting to discuss Hugh Lane's proposal for a Dublin Exhibition of Contemporary French paintings.

c.25   Attends a rehearsal of *Where There Is Nothing* with MG, JBY, Mrs Pilcher and Mrs Victor Plarr.

26   WBY dines before the performance with AEFH, Shannon, Ricketts, FF, JBY and Robert Gregory. At the performance he shares a box with AEFH and Arthur and Rhoda Symons.

26–9   Attends the Stage Society's performances of *Where There Is Nothing*, which plays to large houses at the Royal Court Theatre.

28   AG introduces WBY to the Countess of Cromartie at a performance of *Where There Is Nothing*.

29   Goes to tea with the Countess of Cromartie at Stafford House, the residence of her aunt, the Duchess of Sutherland, and meets the Duchess and Queen Alexandra there.

30   Visits the artist Walford Robertson.

July

1   (Fri) Accompanies FF to the Bernhardt-Campbell production of Maeterlinck's *Pelléas et Mélisande*; in the evening he calls on Ricketts and Shannon to discuss the failure of *Where There Is Nothing*.

4   Publication of Hyde's *Love Songs of Connacht*, with a Preface by WBY.

5   WBY attends Violet Hunt's 'At Home'.

11   Goes to Coole from London.

12   Begins work on his play *Deirdre*, which he continues to write slowly throughout the summer. Later this month Synge and AE visit Coole; WBY is run-down after a series of colds and his eyes give him great trouble.

August

*c.*2   (Tue) Goes to Dublin to prepare for the Abbey Theatre patent application. While in Dublin he attends rehearsals of Synge's *The Well of the Saints*.

3   Lunches with Plunkett, who is helping with the Abbey patent.

4   WBY testifies at the Abbey Theatre patent hearing; afterwards he inspects the building work at the Theatre.

5   Sees Dr Charles Fitzgerald, his oculist, who recommends new glasses.

*c.*9   Returns to Coole.

17   Accompanies AG to the Great Connaught Feis in Galway, but they leave early when they discover that Hyde's play *The Lost Saint* has been withdrawn.

19   AEFH staying at Coole.

20   WBY takes AEFH out fishing on Coole Lake. In Dublin a restrictive clause is added to the Abbey patent.

September

1   (Thu) Spends the month working on *Deirdre*.

*c.*10   Shaw sends him the MS of *John Bull's Other Island* for production at the Abbey Theatre. Later this month Elinor Monsell and Frank Fay stay at Coole.

October

2   (Sun) Returns Joyce's translations of plays by Hauptmann as unsuitable for the Abbey.

5   Writes to Shaw, suggesting cuts in *John Bull's Other Island*.

*c.*14   Goes to Dublin from Coole.

24   Chairs a meeting which radically revises the rules of the INTS Reading Committee.

25   Quinn arrives in Dublin at 6.30 am and WBY takes him to breakfast in JBY's studio, and then to lunch with Colum and JBY; in the evening he, with AG, Hyde and O'Grady, attends a reception and dinner at which Quinn meets the INTS actors.

26   Breakfasts with Quinn and they go to JBY's studio and later all lunch together with O'Grady. In the evening he has dinner with Quinn and AG and afterwards they sit in on a rehearsal while WBY attends a meeting of the INTS Reading Committee.

27	Breakfast with Quinn; then to JBY's studio; lunch with W. F. Bailey at the University Club and dinner with AG and Quinn.
28	Breakfasts with Quinn at JBY's studio and has tea at AG's with Quinn, the Hydes and Martyn; in the evening he attends a meeting of the INTS with Synge, Colum and AE, at which he announces that henceforward W. G. Fay is to be paid a salary.
29	Dinner with Quinn, AG, the Fays and Stephen Gwynn.
30	Dinner with AG and Quinn; afterwards he dictates part of the 1904 *Samhain*.
31	Sees James Starkey (Seamus O'Sullivan) to discuss the MS of his book of poems, *The Twilight People*; afterwards he, AG and Quinn attend the first rehearsal held in the Abbey Theatre.

November

2	(Wed) Attends a dinner at the Shelbourne Hotel in honour of John Quinn with AG, the Fays, Synge, JBY, SMY and ECY, and others.
c.3	Crosses to London and appears before an Income Tax board of enquiry to appeal against his excessive assessment. Early this month he sees and dislikes Beerbohm Tree's production of *The Tempest* at His Majesty's Theatre.
4	Accompanies Quinn and Robert Gregory on a visit to Ricketts and Shannon.
c.5	Sees *John Bull's Other Island* with Quinn at the Court Theatre.
6	Takes Quinn out to FF's to hear her chant to the psaltery.
7	Entertains Quinn, FF and Jeremiah O'Donovan to dinner.
12	Sees Ricketts and Shannon at AG's. Hugh Lane's exhibition of French pictures opens in Dublin.
c.17	Examines Japanese prints at the British Museum to get ideas for Abbey scenery.
c.18	Returns to Dublin to attend rehearsals for the opening of the Abbey Theatre.
20	Inspects Con Markiewicz's paintings to see if she is capable of designing scenes for the Abbey Theatre and stays on to lunch.
22	Attends a Committee Meeting of the INTS with the Fays and Fred Ryan.
23	At rehearsals with Synge.
26	Bayard Veiller and Margaret Wycherly produce *Cathleen ni Houlihan*, *The Hour-Glass* and *The Land of Heart's Desire* in Boston for a season of 7 weeks.

December

1	(Thu) Attends a Committee Meeting of the INTS.
3	Calls on Moore, who asks him to arbitrate in a quarrel with Pearl Craigie over the authorship of a play.

7	AEFH arrives in Dublin for the opening of the Abbey.
8	WBY proposes the vote of thanks at Moore's lecture 'Personal Reminiscences of Modern Painters' at the Royal Hibernian Academy.
10	Attends a Committee Meeting of the INTS.
14	Attends a private view of the Abbey Theatre, and also the first meeting of Lane's Pictures Committee at Kilworth House, where he announces that the ILT will give a benefit performance in aid of the fund.
16	Attends the first dress rehearsal at the Abbey.
17	Attends another dress rehearsal at the Abbey.
27	Attends the opening productions at the Abbey Theatre: *On Baile's Strand, Spreading the News,* and *Kathleen ni Houlihan,* which are a great success. Edits and contributes to *Samhain* (1904).
28	Attends the second night of the Abbey Theatre.
29	Speaks in reply to his father's Royal Hibernian Academy lecture, 'The Art Instinct'.
31	AG, recovering from illness, comes up to Dublin to attend the Abbey plays and sees in the New Year with WBY.

1905

January

1	(Sun) Meets the Australian dramatist Louis Esson at AE's house.
c.4	Returns to London where he sees Laurence Housman's play *Prunella* and Carr's production of *The Knight of the Burning Pestle.*
9	Learns that MG is seeking a divorce.
11	Shocked by Mrs Clay's account of MG's marital problems, and in the evening discusses the divorce with Barry O'Brien.
15	Lunches with D. S. MacColl to enlist his support for Lane's purchase of pictures for a Dublin gallery.
16	Returns to Dublin to oversee the scenery for Synge's *The Well of the Saints.*
21	Publication of WBY's selection of Lionel Johnson's *Twenty One Poems.* Late this month he rewrites *On Baile's Strand* and *The King's Threshold* and becomes involved in a press controversy over Synge's *In the Shadow of the Glen.*
27	Writes 'Mr. Synge and his Plays', later the Introduction to *The Well of the Saints.*

February

1	(Wed) Attends a meeting of the INTS Reading Committee.
4	Attends the first night of Synge's *The Well of the Saints.*
12	Colum reads part of *The Land* to WBY.
18	MG begins divorce proceedings against MacBride in Paris.

21	AE tells WBY he has suggested arbitration in the MacBride divorce.
23	WBY reads Fay a new version of *On Baile's Strand*.
24	Quarrels with AE over drama and MG's divorce; later discusses the divorce with Henry Dixon.
28	*The Pot of Broth* begins a series of matinées in London.

March

1	(Wed) 'Red Hanrahan's Vision' (story; *Myth*, 246–52) published in *McClure's Magazine*. Early this month WBY crosses to London, where he is disgusted with the production of *The Pot of Broth* at the Court Theatre; visits the Whistler Exhibition and sees Bullen about publishing projects.
13	Attends a Stage Society production of Brieux's *The Three Daughters of M. Dupont*; in the evening Maclagan is among those attending WBY's 'Monday Evening'.
15	Meets the Irish musician Herbert Hughes.
*c.*20	Leaves London for Dublin.
24	Attends a dress rehearsal of AG's *Kincora*.
25	At the first production of *Kincora* at the Abbey. Late this month he revises *The King's Threshold*.
30	*The Hour-Glass* produced in Chicago by Anna Morgan.

April

1	(Sat) 'America and the Arts' (article, *UP* II, 338–42) published in the *Metropolitan Magazine*. WBY attends the last performance of *Kincora*, and AG's party afterwards.
7	Gogarty calls on WBY and AEFH at the Nassau Hotel.
8	WBY replies to Cruise O'Brien's paper at University College, Dublin, and defends Synge and modern literature.
*c.*10	Accompanies Colum to Coole, where he advises him on playwriting and resumes work on *Deirdre*.
*c.*20	Returns to Dublin from Coole.
24	Attends a revival of *Kincora* at the Abbey with AG and Synge and meets Boyle there.
26	Attends a performance of *Kincora* and at party afterwards tells Maurice Joy and Holloway that he had Parnell in mind when writing *On Baile's Strand*.
28	Attends another performance of *Kincora*, followed by tea with AG.

May

1	(Mon) Early this month he accompanies AG on a folklore expedition beyond Dundrum.
*c.*10	Crosses to London from Dublin.
11	Sees Irving in Tennyson's *Becket* at the Theatre Royal.
*c.*12	At Philip Carr's production of Jonson's *The Silent Woman*.

13	Attends the first production in England of Wilde's *Salomé*. In the middle of this month WBY advises George Roberts and Joseph Hone on establishing the Maunsel Press.
16	*Stories of Red Hanrahan* published.
c.18	Sends Hone to seek Bullen's advice on setting up the Maunsel Press. Writing 'The Ragged Wood'.
21	Attends the first performance of Shaw's *Man and Superman*.
23	Stays with Bullen in Stratford, where he purchases a 40-vol. edition of Balzac and discusses the publication of the *Collected Works* and other books.
26	Returns to London from Stratford.
c.28	Sees Carr's production of W. S. Gilbert's *The Palace of Truth* at the Great Queen Street Theatre.

June

3	(Sat) Symons calls on WBY.
8	Sees Coquelin's French production of Molière's *Les Precieuses Ridicules* at the Shaftesbury Theatre.
9	Travels by the day boat with AG to Dublin, where they see Colum's *The Land* that evening.
10	WBY sits up to the small hours discussing theatrical matters with W. G. Fay.
13	Friends give WBY a copy of the Kelmscott *Chaucer* for his 40th birthday.
18	Attends a General Meeting of the INTS.
19	Catches the morning boat to England and dines with FF that evening.
20	Dines with FF after a rehearsal of *The Shadowy Waters* and attends several more rehearsals of it in the following days.
24	Dines with Masefield at Woburn Buildings and afterwards speaks at the Lyceum Club, where he denounces domesticity.
29	Accompanies FF to Pinero's *The Cabinet Minister* at the Haymarket Theatre.
30	Calls to see Ricketts in the evening and talks discouragingly about Ireland and disparagingly about Maxim Gorki.

July

1	(Sat) WBY takes Frank Fay to a rehearsal of *The Shadowy Waters*.
8	Loathes FF's production of *The Shadowy Waters* at the Annual Congress of the Theosophical Society.
10	FF recites to the psaltery at WBY's 'Monday Evening'.
c.11	Leaves London for Coole, where the radical rewriting of *The Shadowy Waters* occupies him for the next five weeks.
19	Dines with Martyn at Tyllira.

August

9   (Wed) MG granted a legal separation from John MacBride. During the first half of this month WBY corresponds with AE about the reorganization of the INTS. In mid-August the Countess of Cromartie and Lady Margaret Sackville visit Coole.

19   AG takes WBY to Recess in Connemara for a few days.

25   WBY's selection of *Some Essays and Passages* by John Eglinton published.

27   WBY and AG attend a General Meeting of the INTS in Dublin at which it is agreed that some of the actors should be paid.

September

2   (Sat) 'Queen Edaine' (poem, later 'The Entrance of Deirdre'; *VP*, 771–3) published in *McClure's Magazine*.

15   Jack and Cottie Yeats leave Coole after a fortnight's visit.

16   WBY, AG and Synge hold a policy meeting at Coole to plan the reorganization of the INTS.

*c.*17   AEFH arrives in Coole.

20   WBY, Synge and AEFH travel to Dublin from Coole.

21   WBY consults AEFH and AE about the reorganization of the INTS and afterwards visits Jack Yeats's Exhibition.

22   Attends a General Meeting of the INTS, which votes to turn the Society into a limited liability company.

23   Attends a meeting of the Contemporary Club and discusses Oscar Wilde with Robert Sherard, Wilde's biographer. AE, Synge and JO'L also present.

24   Sherard calls in during the morning.

25   Discusses details of the reorganization of the INTS with AE, Synge and Ryan.

29   Discusses the reorganization of the INTS with AE. In the evening attends rehearsals of *The Building Fund* and *The Land* at the Abbey, accompanied by AEFH and Synge.

30   Catches a bad cold at the Abbey and is indisposed for several days.

October

2   (Mon) Sees productions of *The Building Fund* and *The Land* at the opening night of the Abbey's new season. Edits and contributes to *Samhain* (1905). Early this month AG types a prose scenario of *Deirdre* for him as well as his changes in *The King's Threshold*.

7   'Do Not Love Too Long' (poem; *VP*, 211–12) published in the *Acorn*.

9   Attends a General Meeting of the National Theatre Society.

13   Gives evidence at Leinster House to a Parliamentary Committee enquiring into the running of the Dublin art schools and later attends a rehearsal at the Abbey.

24	Dismisses George Roberts from role of Conchobar in *On Baile's Strand*. The new National Theatre Society is formally registered as a limited company.
25	Discusses arrangements for the Abbey's forthcoming London tour and attends a rehearsal of AG's *The White Cockade*.
28	Accompanies AG and Martyn to a performance of Dinneen's Irish play *Creideamh agus Gorta* (*Faith and Famine*) given by the Keating Branch of the Gaelic League at the Abbey Theatre.
29	Reads his new version of *The Shadowy Waters* to members of the Abbey Company at the Nassau Hotel.
31	Accompanies AG to the Cumman na nGaedheal plays at the Molesworth Hall, where they see Hyde's *Teach an mBocht* and the first production of Martyn's *The Tale of a Town*. Major John MacBride is also in the audience.

November

1	(Wed) Leaves Dublin for London in the morning.
2	Consults Mathews about future publication of *The Wind Among the Reeds* and in the evening sees Bouchier's production of *The Merchant of Venice*.
3	Calls on Ricketts and Shannon and is much impressed with Ricketts' new paintings.
5	Reads a new version of *The Shadowy Waters* to FF and, later, to Symons.
7	Calls on Shaw and persuades him to publish an early story, 'The Miraculous Revenge', in the *Shanachie*.
8	Calls on AEFH and finds her ill.
9	Goes with Jeremiah O'Donovan to Cambridge, where he lunches with the Professor of Arabic, and makes a speech at Newnham College to prepare for the Abbey's visit.
10	Consults John Murray on the republication of AG's books, and then calls on AEFH; in the evening he meets Hughes, an Irish musician, at FF's.
*c.*14	Sees Ernest Rhys's *Guinevere* at the Coronet Theatre.
22	Travels with Synge to Oxford, where he lectures to an undergraduate society.
23	Attends the Abbey performances at Oxford, after which he and the company are entertained to supper by the Senior Tutor of St John's College.
24	Accompanies the Abbey Company on their visit to Cambridge.
26	Addresses the Dramatic Debaters at Frascati's on 'The Drama as it is and What it Might Be', with J. T. Grein in the chair.
27	Publication of his selection of *Sixteen Poems* by William Allingham.
27–8	Attends the Abbey Company's performances at St George's Hall, London.

December

1	(Fri) Dines with Synge at Ricketts' and Shannon's house, and the journalist Charles Hind calls in later.
2	'Never Give All The Heart' (poem; *VP*, 202) published in *McClure's Magazine*. J. M. Synge's *The Well of the Saints* with WBY's Introduction appears early this month.
3	Calls on Gosse and discusses Ibsen.
4	Denounces the tyranny of a written culture at an 'Original Evening' at the ILS.
*c.*4	Leaves London for Dublin.
14	Lectures on 'What is National Literature' to the Literary and Scientific Society in Cork.
16	Sees AE who warns him of serious dissension in the new NTS.
20	Goes to Dundrum to persuade Maire Walker to sign an acting contract with the NTS and discusses her hesitations with Fay and Synge in evening.
21	Goes through the Abbey accounts with Ryan to apportion shares for the costumes, and later sees Maire Walker.
22	Has two long interviews with Maire Walker and dines with Tom Kettle in the evening.
23	Maire Walker signs contract.
*c.*27	WBY returns to London and begins writing the lyrical part of the revised *On Baile's Strand*.
30	Learns that Maire Walker is backing out of her contract and threatens her with legal action.

1906

January

1	(Mon) Dines with Vera Esposito in London and offers her an acting job at the Abbey. Masefield reads WBY his play, *The Campden Wonder*.
3	The controversy over WBY's prosecution of Maire Walker continues, earning him deep opprobrium in Dublin.
4	Decides to drop threat to prosecute Maire Walker, but the quarrel brings to a head disagreements with AE which lead to their estrangement for seven years.
6	Hears that the seceders from the NTS have formed a rival theatre group, the Theatre of Ireland, and are rehearsing Colum's *The Land*.
7	Goes to Edinburgh as guest of the Scots Celtic scholar Alexander Carmichael.
10	Lectures on 'Irish Heroic Poetry' to the Celtic Union in the Hall of the Philosophic Institution, Edinburgh, with Carmichael presiding.

11	Lectures in Dundee on 'Literature and the Living Voice'.
12	Lectures to the Aberdeen University Literature Society on 'Literature and the Living Voice', and is entertained to supper in the University Union afterwards.
13	Leaves Aberdeen by a 10.05 am train for Strathpeffer, were he is the guest of the Countess of Cromartie and her husband at Leod Castle, and where he remains until 19 January, working at *On Baile's Strand*.
20	Arrives back in Dublin and undertakes a number of informal lectures.
23	Discusses the inadequate heating at the Abbey Theatre with the architect, Holloway.
25	Lectures on the work of the artist George Frederick Watts at Royal Hibernian Academy under the title 'The Ideal in Art'.

February

1	(Thu) Speaks in a discussion after AE's lecture, 'Art and Literature' at the Royal Hibernian Academy.
2	At an Abbey rehearsal of AG's *Hyacinth Halvey* and his *Cathleen ni Houlihan*.
5	Speaks to an NLS paper by George Sigerson, 'The Irish Theatre and the Peasant', deploring Irish enslavement to History.
6	Travels to Coole to devote two weeks to drafting *The Player Queen*. Has begun eastern meditations in hope of finding a dynamic and substantializing force.
c.17	Returns to Dublin.
18	Synge gives him further information about their rivals, the Theatre of Ireland; visits JBY's studio.
c.19	Returns to London where he dines out a great deal.

March

3	(Sat) Stays with Lord Howard de Walden until 5 March.
8	Reads Robert Gregory the additions to *On Baile's Strand*.
10	Stays with the American hostess Mrs Emily Ladenburg at Melton Mowbray until 12 March.
14	Lectures on 'Poetry and the Living Voice' at the Leeds Arts Club.
15	Lectures in Liverpool on 'Poetry and the Living Voice'.
16	Returns to London from Liverpool.
18	Accompanies AG and Robert Gregory to Charles Shannon's studio to view his portrait of Robert. Later this month WBY rewrites his introduction to *The Poems of Spenser* and further revises *On Baile's Strand* as well as dining with T. P. O'Connor and meeting Prince Christian.
28	Sees Pinero's new 4-Act play, *His House in Order*, at the St James's Theatre but does not like it.

29	Has tea with Mrs Albert Montgomery and afterwards attends a production of Gilbert Murray's version of Euripides' *Hippolytus* at the Court Theatre.
30	Finishes dictating the new version of his Spenser introduction; sees a play in the afternoon and Stephen Phillips' 4-act poetic spectacular, *Nero*, in the evening.

April

1	(Sun) Calls on Cockerell at Richmond, and afterwards goes to the King's Hall, Covent Garden, to see Sturge Moore's play, *Aphrodite against Artemis*, which he pronounces a failure.
2	Sturge Moore at WBY's 'Monday Evening'.
3	Accompanies AEFH to F. Anstey's comedy *The Man from Blankeys* at the Haymarket Theatre.
4	In the afternoon collects two theatre wigs from Clarksons and in the evening crosses to Dublin.
6	Attends a rehearsal of *On Baile's Strand* at the Abbey.
7	Reading Shaw's plays for possible production at the Abbey.
11	Attends a dress rehearsal of the revised *On Baile's Strand* and AG's version of Molière's *The Doctor in Spite of Himself* at the Abbey.
13	Attends the final dress rehearsal of the two plays.
14	Present at the first night of AG's version of *The Doctor in Spite of Himself* and the revised *On Baile's Strand*.
17	Discusses Molière and the revised *On Baile's Strand* with Holloway at the Abbey, praising AG's translation and the acting.
23	Attends the Abbey Company's performances at the Midland Hall, Manchester, where he remains until 24 April.
29	WBY goes to Coole, where he remains until *c*.20 May, working on his play, *Deirdre*.

May

24	(Thu) Attends the AGM of the National Theatre Society at the Abbey Theatre.
26	The Abbey Company, managed by Alfred Wareing, begins an extended tour to Cardiff, Glasgow, Aberdeen, Newcastle, Edinburgh and Hull, which lasts until 9 July.
27	With the Abbey Company at the Theatre Royal, Cardiff.
30	Addresses a luncheon at the Royal Hotel, Cardiff, on the Celtic Revival and the desirability of National Theatres. Late this month 'Against Witchcraft' and 'The Praise of Deirdre' (poems; *VP*, 775–6, 771–3) are published in *The Shanachie*.

June

1	(Fri) Back in London, he accompanies Rothenstein on a visit to Ricketts and Shannon and they discuss the theatre. He is writing a series of short essays later published as 'Discoveries'.

7	In Edinburgh with the Abbey Company, remaining there until *c*.12 June, giving two lectures and spending much time looking at Mrs Phoebe Traquair's paintings.
8	Dispatched to Glasgow by AEFH to sort out a dispute between W. G. Fay and J. J. Bell over theatre make-up.
15	Back in London, he calls on Ricketts with Charles Hind.
18	Sees the Literary Theatre Club's productions of Wilde's *Salome* and *A Florentine Tragedy* at the King's Hall, Covent Garden. In the middle of this month Swinburne attacks WBY in the preface of the new edition of his *William Blake*.
25	WBY sees Bullen to discuss the publication of 'Discoveries', in the *Gentleman's Magazine*.
30	WBY spends a pleasant weekend at Katharine Horner's manor house at Mells in Somerset, with Sydney Cockerell, Lady Cromartie, Lady Margaret Sackville and Raymond Asquith.

July

1	(Sun) Reads Agnes Tobin's translations of Petrarch to Miss Horner's house party. In the evening he talks of ghosts and reincarnation. Corrects proofs of *The Poetical Works*.
3	Calls on Agnes Tobin in London in the late afternoon.
8	Consults Alfred Wareing about hiring a manager for the Abbey Theatre.
10	Crosses to Dublin in the morning and in the afternoon has a long talk with Frank Fay about the Company's unruly behaviour on the recent tour.
11	Sees W. G. Fay and Synge about the bad behaviour on the recent Abbey tour.
12	Accompanies the Abbey Company on its visit to Longford, where he remains until 13 July.
14	WBY at Coole for a series of Abbey Directors' meetings to discuss the reorganization of the Company; W. G. Fay is also present.
17	Synge joins AG, WBY and W. G. Fay at Coole, and together they put the Abbey Company on a new footing. Later in the month WBY corrects the proofs of the New York edition of his poems, condenses his selection from Spenser, and flirts with Dorothy Carleton, Wilfrid Blunt's mistress, who is visiting Coole.
27	Karel Musek, the Czech theatre director, visits Coole and stays until 31 July.
29	WBY spends the day going through a second Dun Emer selection of AE's poems, and subsequently sends an imperious letter to ECY demanding that the book be postponed.

August

1   (Wed) The actress Letitia Darragh arrives at Coole to see if she would make a suitable Deirdre and a dispute with the Fays ensues over whether she or Sara Allgood should play the heroines in *The Shadowy Waters* and *Deirdre*. In the middle of the month WBY quarrels with ECY over the selection of books for the Dun Emer Press, and resigns as literary advisor. He continues work on *Deirdre* and 'Discoveries'.

September

6   (Thu) W. G. Fay visits Coole. For the rest of the month WBY reads Jonson, Donne and the Jacobean dramatists, works on 'Discoveries' and is absorbed in writing *Deirdre*. His edition of *The Poems of Spenser* appears towards the end of the month.

15   'My Thoughts and My Second Thoughts' (essays; *E & I*, 261–70) published in the *Gentleman's Magazine* (238–46).

October

1   (Mon) 'Literature and the Living Voice' (article, *Expl*, 202–21) published in the *Contemporary Review*. WBY sets out his terms for continuing to act as editor and advisor to the Cuala Press but these are not finally accepted by ECY until late November. W. A. Henderson takes up duties as secretary to the Abbey Theatre.

8   Goes to Dublin for the opening of Jack Yeats's exhibition 'Sketches of Life in the West of Ireland'.

9   Attends rehearsals at the Abbey with AG, before returning to Coole.

13   Travels from Coole for the Abbey's 'At Home', and makes a speech on the achievements and plans of the Irish Dramatic Movement. 'My Thoughts and My Second Thoughts' (essays; *E & I*, 270–81) published in the *Gentleman's Magazine* (358–66).

14   Before returning to Coole, he leaves copy for the theatrical periodical the *The Arrow* with W. G. Fay.

19   Attends a dress rehearsal of *The Mineral Workers* and *The Gaol Gate* at the Abbey.

20   Attends the productions of Boyle's *The Mineral Workers* and AG's *Gaol Gate* and *Spreading the News* at the Abbey. 1000 copies of the occasional theatrical periodical, the *The Arrow*, edited and largely written by WBY, are posted to Abbey subscribers.

23   Attends rehearsals at the Abbey and has a long talk on theatre business with Synge. Late this month *Poems 1899–1905* published.

November

2	(Fri) Meets Synge at the Abbey Theatre, and dines with him and AG in evening.
3	At the Abbey's packed revival of *The Doctor in Spite of Himself*, *Hyacinth Halvey*, and *Riders to the Sea*.
13	Synge reads *The Playboy of the Western World* to WBY and AG.
16	At the Abbey with AG for a rehearsal of his *Deirdre*.
17	'My Thoughts and My Second Thoughts' (essays; *E & I*, 281–90) published in the *Gentleman's Magazine* (494–501).
23	At a rehearsal of *Deirdre* and discusses the play with Holloway.
24	Attends the first night of *Deirdre*, with Letitia Darragh in the title role. Edits and contributes to the second number of *The Arrow*.
27	Vol. 1 of *The Poetical Works of William B. Yeats* published by the Macmillan Co., New York.
29	WBY and AG at a sparsely attended performance of *Deirdre*.

December

1	(Sat) ECY accedes to WBY's right of veto over Cuala books and their illustrations. First ever matinée performance at the Abbey inaugurates a regular practice.
2	Writes a memo calling for changes in the NTS, particularly the injection of more capital, a larger company, more foreign plays, guest actresses, and a managing director to take administrative chores off W. G. Fay's shoulders.
3	Begins a selection of KT's poems for the Cuala Press.
7	Attends the Theatre of Ireland's first productions at the Molesworth Hall.
8	At the Abbey for the first production of the revised *Shadowy Waters* (with Letitia Darragh playing Dectora) and AG's *The Canavans*. Edits and contributes to *Samhain* (1906).
9	Gives an interview (published on 10 December) to the *Freeman's Journal* on the proposed reform of the Hibernian Academy.
10	Speaks after an NLS lecture by Padriac Colum on the need for Irish actors in Irish plays.
15	Meets Synge and AG at the Abbey to discuss the reorganization of the Company.
16	Crosses to London.
17	Dines with AEFH.
20	Lunches with Frank Sidgewick, and hears that 800 copies of *Poems 1899–1905* have been sold, the quickest sale he has ever had.
21	Sees FF in the evening.
22	Making revisions and correcting proofs for Vol. II of *The Poetical Works* (NY). Late this month he confers by letter with AG, AEFH

and Synge about the management and reorganization of the Abbey Company and the difficulties caused by the position and personality of W. G. Fay.

1907

January

1   (Tue) Reads *Deirdre* to FF.

3   Writes to AG telling her of AEFH's objections to W. G. Fay, and that he must not be left in charge of the Abbey Company.

7   Consults J. E. Vedrenne about a new manager for the Abbey.

8   Attends the first night of Masefield's play *The Campden Wonder*, which horrifies the audience.

10   Sees Sir Charles Holroyd, Director of the National Gallery, London, about Lane's plans for a Municipal Gallery in Dublin.

*c.*12   Sees Mrs William Sharp, lately widowed, who confirms his long-held suspicion that her husband was 'Fiona Macleod', and gives him full details of that relationship.

14   Again seeks Vedrenne's advice about a new manager for the Abbey; in the evening discusses the shocked reception of *The Campden Wonder* with Masefield.

15   Lunches with the journalist Ella Hepworth Dixon at the Lyceum.

16   Writes to invite Ben Iden Payne to become manager of the Abbey.

18   FF leaves for a lecturing tour in the USA; in the evening WBY goes to see Ricketts and discusses Letitia Darragh's acting.

21   Despite a bad cold goes to see Sidgwick at Bullen's about the price of a proposed collected edition of his work.

22   Sees AEFH, just back from Algeria.

23   Visits AEFH again; in the late evening goes to a party at Miss Stone's.

25   Lectures in Aberdeen on 'The Heroic Poetry of Ireland' under the auspices of the Franco-Scottish Society.

26   Remains in Aberdeen until 27 January as the guest of H. J. C. Grierson. In Dublin the first performance of *The Playboy of the Western World* breaks up in a riot at the word 'shift'. Disturbances continue over the following week.

29   WBY, back in Dublin, makes a speech in front of the Abbey curtain inviting the protesters to a discussion about *The Playboy* on 4 February. Police present in the theatre and students from TCD shout for the play.

30   In the morning WBY attends trials of Patrick Columb and Piaras Beaslai for rioting at the Abbey; in the evening present at a further performance of *The Playboy*.

February

1   (Fri) WBY attends the trial of Patrick Hughes and John Duane for rioting at the Abbey; in the evening goes again to *The Playboy* where there are more arrests.

2   Calls at the *Leader* office to get a copy of the Christmas issue which attacked Boyle. Attends the matinée and evening performance of *The Playboy*.

4   Arranges and speaks at a public debate at the Abbey on 'The Freedom of the Theatre', to discuss the dispute over *The Playboy*.

6   Goes to Wexford, where Ben Iden Payne is on tour, to discuss his new duties at the Abbey; remains there until 7 February.

9   Visits Synge at his mother's house in Glenageary, but Synge is too ill to see him; in the evening is given a curtain-call at the Abbey after a performance of *Cathleen ni Houlihan*.

16   Calls again to see Synge, who is still too ill to see him.

23   Edits and contributes to the third number of *The Arrow*.

25   Present at George Sigerson's NLS lecture, 'The Peasants of the West'.

*c.*28   Leaves Dublin for London.

March

1   (Fri) Sees Shaw who refuses permission for the Abbey to produce *John Bull's Other Island*, and visits AEFH in afternoon; in the evening he discusses with Agnes Tobin the possibility of impresario Charles Frohman arranging an American tour for the Abbey Company.

2   Sees Cecil French in afternoon and hears news of Althea Gyles.

6   Consults Watt about the transfer of his books to Bullen in preparation for the *Collected Works*; sees Frohman about possible American tour for the Abbey; takes the revised *Deirdre* to be copied for the American edition; and in the evening hears Norrys Connell read his play *The Piper* at AEFH's apartment.

8   Receives the MS of Lionel Johnson's *Essays*, and sees AEFH about the Abbey's coming British tour.

12   AG arrives in London and WBY reads *The Piper* to her.

13   WBY and AG see Bullen at the Euston Hotel and exult over the downfall of the publisher Oldmeadow.

14   WBY crosses to Dublin, lending Bullen his London rooms while he is away.

16   Death of JO'L. In the evening WBY attends performances of *On Baile's Strand*, Maeterlink's *Interior* and *Cathleen ni Houlihan* at the Abbey.

19   WBY chooses not to attend JO'L's funeral. That evening he makes a speech at the Bohemians Club, giving his reminiscences of Oscar Wilde, and revealing that the Abbey would produce four new plays next season.

21	Accompanies AG and a number of the Abbey Company to performances of the Theatre of Ireland at the Rotunda.
*c.*22	Goes to London for a few days to see Aeschylus' *The Persians*, designed by Charles Ricketts, at Terry's Theatre and stays at the Euston Hotel because Bullen is using his rooms.
30	Back in Dublin, attends performances of *The Pagans* and *The Turn of the Road* given by the Ulster Literary Theatre at the Abbey.
31	Visits Synge who is recuperating at Glendalough House.

April

1	(Mon) Attends Abbey performances of his revised *Deirdre* and Winifred Letts' *The Eyes of the Blind*. Charles Frohman is also there, accompanied by J. M. Barrie.
2	Consults with AG and Ben Iden Payne at the Abbey. Addresses the Company to steel their nerve for the production of *The Playboy* in England.
3	Accompanies AG to performances of *The Poorhouse*, *Gaol Gate*, *Deirdre* and *The Jackdaw* at the Abbey, where he talks to Atkins, a journalist on the Dublin *Evening Mail*.
5	Sees Synge and AG at the Nassau Hotel.
6	At the Abbey with AG to see Maeterlinck's *Interior*, *The Poorhouse*, *The Rising of the Moon* and *The Jackdaw*.
*c.*7	Returns to London.
10	Leaves London to join AG and Robert Gregory in Florence.

May

3	(Fri) WBY and the Gregorys visit Rimini.
5	WBY and the Gregorys visit San Marino, where WBY overcomes an intense desire to throw himself from a cliff.
11	Abbey Company begins tour to Glasgow, Cambridge, Birmingham, Oxford and London. In the middle of the month WBY and the Gregorys travel to Venice, driving in carriages through the Apennines, and by Urbino to Ravenna, to approach the city by sea.
22	Summoned back from Venice by a telegram from AEFH telling him that the Lord Chamberlain might refuse to license *The Playboy* for performance in Britain.
23	Arrives in Cambridge (where the Abbey is performing) with AG and AEFH.
27	Invites Holbrook Jackson and A. R. Orage to his 'Monday Evening' to discuss performances of *The Playboy* on the Abbey's British tour.
*c.*28	Visits Birmingham with the Abbey Company and remains there until 1 June.
31	Consults W. G. Fay about the Abbey Company's lack of discipline on their British tour.

June

1	(Sat) Edits and contributes to the fourth number of *The Arrow*.
3	In Oxford with the Abbey Company, staying with George Mair at Christ Church, where he remains until 5 June.
7	Temporarily resigns as Director of the Abbey following a dispute with AEFH.
9	With Ben Iden Payne attends a matinée of the Stage Society's production of Charles McEvoy's *David Ballard*.
10	Present at the opening production of the Abbey Company at the Great Queen Street Theatre, London, and afterwards dines with Synge, Lord Dunraven and Annette Meakin.
11	Attends a rehearsal of *The Shadowy Waters* at the Great Queen Street Theatre, with AG and Synge. In the evening sees performances of *Riders to the Sea*, *The Jackdaw*, *Spreading the News* and *The Shadowy Waters*.
12	Again attends rehearsals at the Great Queen Street Theatre with AG and Synge. In the evening he is present at performances of *The Hour-Glass* and *The Playboy*, and talks to Shaw in the interval.
14	Present at a minor disturbance during the performance of *The Playboy* at the Great Queen Street Theatre.
15	Receives a special curtain call after the last performance of the Abbey's London tour.
16	Discusses with AEFH and Payne the possibility of her setting up another theatrical initiative, using Dublin as a base.
17	Sees AEFH, who tells him that she is abandoning Dublin altogether, and invites him to join her new theatrical venture in Manchester; she also announces that she is withdrawing as patron of the Abbey Theatre, but will continue her subsidy until the end of 1910.
19	Consults AG and W. G. Fay about AEFH's decision to withdraw from the Abbey; in the evening he goes to see AEFH to discuss the Abbey's finances.
22	Ben Iden Payne formally resigns his managership of the Abbey.
25	WBY, W. G. Fay and Payne decide at a morning meeting to fire W. A. Henderson and put the actor Ernest Vaughan into his place as Abbey secretary; they also plan an Advent tour to Glasgow, Edinburgh and Manchester.
26	Dines with Mrs Eveleen Myers to meet the Revd R. J. Campbell, author of *The New Theology*.

July

1	(Mon) Leaves London for Coole, where he begins to prepare the copy text for the *Collected Works* (*CW*), to write *The Golden Helmet*, and, with AG's help, to turn *Where There Is Nothing* into

The Unicorn from the Stars. Feeling unwell and close to a nervous breakdown.

5   Works until the end of the month finishing his essays for *Discoveries*.

8   Vol. II of *The Poetical Works of William B. Yeats* published by the Macmillan Co., New York.

10   Sends Bullen a rewritten version of 'Maid Quiet'.

24   Calls to see Martyn at Tillyra.

28   Sends Bullen a corrected version of 'The Hollow Wood', with an improved rhyme scheme.

August

4   (Sun) Finishes *The Golden Helmet*. Spends most of the month at Coole, continuing work on the *Collected Works*.

6   Publication of his selection of KT's *Twenty One Poems*.

c.18 *Deirdre* published. Later this month he declines a romantic liaison with American poet Agnes Tobin. His rage at the appointment of George Plunkett to the Directorship of the Irish National Museum in preference to Hugh Lane provokes him to begin his poem 'An Appointment'.

c.30 Sees W. G. Fay while in Dublin on his way to London from Coole.

September

c.1   (Sun) In London he visits the dentist and sees Agnes Tobin and Granville Barker.

4   Attends a performance of Binyon's play, *Attila*, with FF.

6   Returns to Dublin from London.

7   Travels to Coole, where he returns to revisions for *CW*, reads North's *Plutarch*, and is sketched by Augustus John.

13   Synge in the Elphis nursing home for an operation on his neck glands; remains there until 26 September.

23   Augustus John leaves Coole after sketching WBY.

26   Robert Gregory marries Margaret Graham Parry in London.

October

1   (Tue) 'Discoveries' (essays; *E & I*, 290–96) published in the *Shanachie* (II. 127–31).

3   Leaves Coole for Dublin to attend the first production of George Fitzmaurice's *The Country Dressmaker* at the Abbey.

4   Meets the Italian painter Antonio Mancini and is delighted with him; in the evening he sees Forbes-Robertson's production of Shaw's *Caesar and Cleopatra*.

5   Visits Synge who is recuperating after the operation on his neck. In the evening sees another performance of *The Country Dressmaker*.

6	Mancini paints a portrait of him in pastels.
10	Attends a Directors' Meeting at the Abbey Theatre with AG and Synge.
11	Present at a special Abbey matinée for the Beerbohm Tree and Forbes-Robertson Companies who are performing in Dublin.
17	Stays with Lord Dunraven at Ardare Manor, remaining there until his return to Dublin on 19 September.
19	Attends Abbey with AG to see a revival of Colum's *The Land*.
24	Present at a dinner at the United Arts Club in honour of Mrs Pat Campbell, and pays tribute to her genius as an actress.
25	Finishes his poem 'An Appointment'. Attends a special Abbey matinée in honour of Mrs Pat Campbell's Company. Mrs Campbell moves him deeply by offering to take the title role in his *Deirdre* at the Abbey in November 1908.
26	Sees Mrs Campbell's production of Sudermann's *Magda* and she delights him by describing him in a speech from the stage as 'my dear friend and your great poet'.
29	Signs a public protest against stage censorship.
31	Attends the first production of AG's *Dervorgilla* at the Abbey.

November

2	(Sat) At the Abbey for another performance of *Dervorgilla*, and holds a meeting with AG and Synge there afterwards.
*c.*7	Visits the Irish International Exhibition in Ballsbridge.
9	At the Abbey Theatre.
10	Sees Ella Young to discuss astrology and dines later with the actor-manager Martin Harvey.
13	Dines with Lawrence Binyon at the Arts Club and afterwards attends a discussion there on Modernism in the Catholic Church, introduced by William Gibson.
14	Attends a lecture by John Martin Harvey at the Theatre Royal, Dublin, to inaugurate the Dublin Branch of the British Empire Shakespearean Society. In the evening speaks on behalf of an Irish Catholic University at a dinner arranged by the Corinthian Club at the Gresham Hotel in honour (although WBY did not know this in advance) of Lady Aberdeen, wife of the Lord Lieutenant.
15	Present at a special Abbey matinée for the Martin Harvey and Frank Benson Companies who are performing in Dublin.
19	Dines with Synge, AG and the actor and producer William Poel. He later addresses the inaugural meeting of the TCD Gaelic Society.
20	At AEFH's behest he calls on the manager of the Theatre Royal, Dublin, to make sure that no Abbey actors were involved in a demonstration against Forbes-Robertson's production of

Rosamund Langbridge's *The Spell*. Later he accompanies AG to a performance of Shaw's *John Bull's Other Island* at the same Theatre.

21   In the afternoon present at the Abbey for a lecture by William Poel on the Elizabethan Playhouse, and in the evening attends the first production of *The Unicorn from the Stars*. Writes to the *Leader* to defend his presence at the Corinthian Club dinner of 14 November.

24   Talks with the amateur theologian Edward Evans. The Abbey Company begins an Advent tour to Manchester, Glasgow and Edinburgh which lasts until 15 December and intensifies the antagonism between the Company and W. G. Fay.

30   Present at the Contemporary Club for a discussion about Shaw's *John Bull's Other Island*.

December

2   (Mon) Sees AG and Synge; casts Synge's horoscope and hears of his proposal to write *Deirdre of the Sorrows*. WBY's portrait is being painted by JBY on a commission from Quinn.

4   WBY, AG and Synge hold a long meeting in Dublin to discuss W. G. Fay's troublesome behaviour on the current Abbey tour; in the evening WBY and Synge attend a debate at the Arts Club.

5   Sits for JBY.

6   Sits for JBY.

7   Leaves Dublin for London, where he meets a very bad-tempered AEFH in the evening.

8   Sees FF.

9   Sees a much subdued AEFH and FF also calls. Orage drops in later and they discuss clairvoyant experiences.

13   Attends a lecture at the New Gallery and hears Rothenstein praise Mancini's portrait of Hugh Lane; in the evening dines with the astrologer, Ralph Shirley.

14   Works in the British Museum Library.

15   *Discoveries* published by the Dun Emer Press; WBY goes to Ralph Shirley for a lesson in astrology. Correspondence between the Abbey directors about W. G. Fay's position in the Company continues until the end of the month.

16   Receives two etched portraits of himself from Augustus John which he shows to AEFH, who dislikes them.

19   Dines with Norreys Connell to discuss the proposed production of his play *The Piper*.

20   Calls on Ricketts and Shannon to discuss arrangements for Shannon's portrait of him.

21   JBY and SMY sail on the *Carmania* for a short trip to New York, but JBY is destined to remain there for the rest of his life.

1908

January

6	(Mon) WBY enlists Masefield's support for Hugh Lane's Dublin gallery.
7	Charles Shannon does a preliminary sketch of WBY for a full portrait.
8	Visits Shannon for the first sitting for his portrait.
10	Leaves London for Dublin.
11	A meeting between WBY, AG and Synge about W. G. Fay and Abbey affairs goes on all afternoon.
13	W. G. Fay, his wife, the actress Brigit O'Dempsey, and his brother, Frank, resign from the Abbey Company.
14	WBY, AG and Synge meet to discuss the Fays' resignation.
16	In the absence of W. G. Fay, WBY and Synge pay the Company's salaries at the Abbey; afterwards they see journalists to explain the circumstances of the Fays' resignations.
18	Goes through Abbey papers with Synge.
20	Attends the official opening of Hugh Lane's Municipal Gallery of Modern Art at 17 Harcourt Street, Dublin.
21	Present at a dinner to honour Hugh Lane at the Nassau Hotel.
22	Writes the poem 'Words' under its original title 'Consolation'. Discusses the Fays' departure from the Abbey with D. J. O'Donoghue.
23	Revises 'Words'.
25	Sees Holloway about the Abbey's heating system.

February

1	(Sat) Discusses the repainting of the Abbey Theatre with Holloway. In the evening attends part of a discussion on 'Tragedy in its relation to Life' at the Contemporary Club.
3	Henderson invited back as secretary to the Abbey as a consequence of the Fays' resignations.
*c.*4	WBY goes to Coole to correct proofs of *The Unicorn from the Stars*. W. G. Fay wires for permission to produce *The Pot of Broth* in the USA, and WBY reluctantly gives his assent.
8	Returns to Dublin and dines at the Arts Club with Norreys Connell, the Duncans and John O'Connell. Speaks there with Mme Markiewicz. The Fays leave for an American tour.
10	Discusses the Fays' American contract with Holloway. Attends a dress rehearsal at the Abbey, after which he speaks on 'art for art's sake' after a lecture at the NLS.
11	Absent-mindedly eats two dinners at the same sitting at the Arts Club.

13	Attends performances of *The Piper* and W. F. Casey's *The Man Who Missed the Tide* at the Abbey, and goes on to an impromptu dinner at the Arts Club. *The Piper* causes some controversy both in the audience and in the Dublin press.
14	Meets Holloway at the Abbey and discusses the current productions.
15	Speaks from the stage before *The Piper* to explain its meaning to the audience.
18	Suffers from a bad attack of influenza, which continues until 26 February.
20	Holloway chats with an ill-looking WBY at the Abbey.
26	WBY sees the actor Ambrose Power at the Nassau Hotel to discuss the Fays' behaviour in the USA.
27	In the morning takes a rehearsal at the Abbey for the first time since his attack of 'flu. Sees a paragraph in a theatre magazine which suggests that the Fays are passing themselves off in America as the Abbey Company.
28	Takes a rehearsal for two hours and is exhausted. Reading Balzac's *The Chouans*.

March

2	(Mon) Wires to tell the Fays that they cannot borrow the Abbey actor Joseph O'Rourke for America. Attends to Abbey business.
3	Writes to Quinn, asking for his advice and help over the Fays' behaviour in America. Also writes to the New York press pointing out that Fays are not the Irish National Theatre Company, and that the plays they are performing are not representative of the Abbey Theatre. In the evening he attends a discussion on the theatre at the Arts Club.
4	Writes to W. G. Fay and Frohman complaining of their misrepresentations. Instructs Bullen about the portraits to be used in *CW*. In the evening he rehearses *The Rogueries of Scapin* and *The Workhouse Ward* at the Abbey.
6	Receives an unsatisfactory reply from Frohman's manager about the Fays' misuse of the Abbey name in America and decides to withdraw their right to produce *The Pot of Broth* there. Attends a dress rehearsal of *The Hour-Glass*.
7	Attends performances at the Abbey and afterwards discusses with Holloway the acting since the departure of the Fays.
8	Receives a copy of Alvin Langdon Coburn's photograph of him.
9	Works all afternoon on a new number of *Samhain*. Attends the Abbey in the evening and talks with Henderson and Holloway about the Fays' misuse of the Abbey name in the USA
11	AG arrives from Coole. WBY again ill with influenza.

12	Begins a dispute with Bullen over the placing of the portraits in *CW*.
14	At the Abbey Theatre to chair a meeting of the 'Consultations Committee', made up of representatives of the actors and the management.
15	Has recovered from influenza and is teaching verse-speaking every day.
16	Discusses fire precautions at the Abbey with Holloway.
17	Sees Holloway and Maire Walker at the Abbey and, later, William Poel. With Synge, attends crowded performances of *Cathleen ni Houlihan*, *The Hour-Glass*, *The Rising of the Moon* and *In the Shadow of the Glen* there.
18	Attends a dress rehearsal of *The Golden Helmet*, and later a committee meeting of the NTS which suspends the Fays' membership. At about this time WBY meets the Irish writer Lord Edward Dunsany for the first time.
19	At 4 pm Synge reads him two acts of his *Deirdre of the Sorrows*. In the evening WBY takes a curtain-call at the Abbey after the first production of *The Golden Helmet*, which is presented with George Fitzmaurice's *The Pie-Dish* and AG's translation of Sudermann's *Teja*.
20	Attends to Abbey business and rehearsals of AG's adaptation of Molière's *The Rogueries of Scapin*.
21	Chairs a meeting of the 'Consultations Committee' at the Abbey.
25	Calls on Synge who has a cold. Returns proofs of *The Golden Helmet* to Bullen.
27	John Singer Sargent, who is to draw him for *CW*, telegraphs to arrange a sitting for the following week.
28	Attends the General Meeting of the NTS, followed by performances at the Abbey, after which he goes to the Arts Club and argues with Countess Markiewicz for an hour.
29	Begins a relationship with the physiotherapist Mabel Dickinson.
30	Meets Mabel Dickinson in the late afternoon. Crosses to London by the night boat.
31	Lunches with AG at Woburn Buildings.

April

1	(Wed) Sargent makes a preliminary sketch of him.
2	Sargent makes another fine sketch of WBY, but is not satisfied with it.
7	Sits for Sargent from 1 pm until dusk.
8	Sits for Sargent from 11 am until dusk.
10	Sargent finishes his third drawing, which WBY thinks a fine thing. WBY is also sitting intermittently for Shannon's portrait.
11–13	Visits Bullen in Stratford-upon-Avon and is delighted with a sample volume but finds that Vol. IV of *CW* is too short by 40 pages.

13	Sits to Kathleen Bruce for a bronze mask.
14	Sits to Shannon all day and goes to the theatre in the evening.
15	Sits to Shannon in the morning; corrects proofs for *CW* in the afternoon and tries in vain to get music for the psaltery copied professionally in Regent Street for *CW*.
16	Tries to get the extra copy for 'The Irish Dramatic Movement' section of Vol. IV typed but finds the office closed for Easter. In the evening attends a performance of Edwin Royle's *The White Man* at the Lyric Theatre.
17	Goes to Hampstead to get music for the psaltery copied professionally for *CW*.
20	Calls on Ricketts who agrees to design Synge's *The Well of the Saints* as a matter of urgency.
21	Visits Stratford-upon-Avon to see Sara Allgood play Isabella in William Poel's production of *Measure for Measure*.
22	Leaves Stratford for London.
24	*CW* now finished except for the proofs.
25–9	Arranges his papers and letters prior to returning to creative work.
26	Worried by apparent irregularities in the Abbey accounts; goes through the latest audit and finds anomalies. He visits AEFH, who has also noticed irregularities, and they enlist the help of a Manchester accountant who is visiting her. WBY promises to go to Dublin to sort things out.
27	In the morning the scenario for *The Player Queen* suddenly resolves itself. Later, he sits for Kathleen Bruce.
28	Dines with Masefield and hears a new version of the first act of his play, *Pompey the Great*.
29	Sits for Kathleen Bruce. In the afternoon his Sargent portrait arrives. MG visits him and tells him that under French law she has practically no chance of a divorce.
30	Takes the Sargent portrait to Emery Walker to make a block of it for *CW*. Attending to Abbey audit. Learns that he must return to Dublin to take charge of the Abbey because Synge needs an operation. Dines with Masefield and hears the rest of *Pompey the Great*.

May

1	(Fri) Calls on FF who has just returned to London.
2	Gives Shannon the last sitting for his portrait.
3	Last sitting for Kathleen Bruce.
5	Crosses to Dublin, taking his psaltery. Surgeons operating on Synge discover an incurable tumour, although Synge is not told of this.
6–14	Visits Synge in hospital and oversees rehearsals of his *The Well of the Saints*. Synge's grave illness makes death a reality to WBY for the first time in his life. He continues to correct proofs of *CW*.

9	Chairs a meeting of the 'Consultations Committee' at the Abbey.
13	*The Unicorn from the Stars and Other Plays* published by the Macmillan Co., New York.
14	Attends revival of Synge's *The Well of the Saints* at the Abbey.
16	Chairs a meeting of the 'Consultations Committee' at the Abbey.
23	Chairs a meeting of the 'Consultations Committee' at the Abbey.
24	Writes to the Dublin press refuting the Fays' charges that the Abbey Directors discouraged the work of young writers.
28	Elected a member of the Dublin Arts Club.
29	Chairs a meeting of the 'Consultations Committee' at the Abbey. In the evening he sees the Abbey productions of AG's *Dervorgilla* and Sheridan's *The Scheming Lieutenant* (*St Patrick's Day*).
30	Attends the final performances of the season at the Abbey.

June

1	(Mon) Chairs a meeting of the 'Consultations Committee' at the Abbey.
c.5	Leaves Dublin for London.
8	Spends the evening with Mrs Patrick Campbell, tells her the plot of *The Player Queen*, and reads *Deirdre* to her.
9	Sees Masefield's *The Tragedy of Nan* at the Haymarket Theatre where he sits in Masefield's box. Quinn issues an American copyright edition of *The Golden Helmet*.
12	Calls upon Symons to borrow a book.
17	Goes to Paris to see MG, and stays at the Grand Hotel de Passy.
17–23	In Paris, spends much time in the Louvre and visits the Gustave Moreau Museum, finding that he now admires David and Ingres more than the Symbolist painters. Takes his meals with MG and they talk over old things. Has long talks with Iseult Gonne and sees Sarah Purser.
23	Leaves Paris for London.
c.25	Crosses to Dublin. Collects financial details of the last Abbey London tour for Granville Barker, sees the convalescent Synge and Mabel Dickinson. *Poems* (1908) published late this month.

July

2	(Thu) Goes from Dublin to Coole.
3	Writes the poem 'His Dream' after dreaming of an elaborate ship.
4	Starts work again on *The Player Queen*.
c.7	Dines with Martyn at Tillyra and learns he has resigned from the Sinn Fein movement.
11	Goes with AG, Robert Gregory and his wife to their summer house in the Burren where he dictates a scenario of *The Player Queen* and writes more 'Discoveries'. He is doing physical exercises prescribed by Mabel Dickinson daily. 'His Dream' (poem; *VP*, 253–4) published in the *Nation* (London).

13	William Poel arrives in Dublin for two weeks to coach the Abbey Company in verse speaking, and rehearse them in Calderon's *Life is a Dream* (*La Vida es Sueno*).
17	AEFH reiterates her intention to withdraw from the Abbey after the expiry of the Patent in December 1910.
23	WBY invites Norrys Connell to manage an Abbey autumn tour to England.
25	WBY and MG believe that they are in astral contact. Late in the month WBY and AG cross Galway Bay by boat to visit John Shawe Taylor and inspect a hall he wants to use for an Abbey visit to the Galway Feis in September. WBY is working hard at *The Player Queen* and they pass Lennox Robinson's (LR's) rewritten *The Clancy Name* for production.

August

1	(Sat) Returns from the Burren to Coole.
3–8	Learns that Boyle is demanding exorbitant terms for returning his plays to the Abbey and goes to Dublin to sort things out. Arranges the Abbey's late Summer and Autumn programme, hears *Life is a Dream* and AG's *Hyacinth Halvey* with new casts, and discovers from Synge's fiancée, Molly Allgood, that the recent operation was not a success.
5	Has a long talk with Synge, who is recuperating at his sister's house in Kingstown (Dun Laoighaire).
8	Returns to Coole and continues writing *The Player Queen*. His nerves are in a wild state and his work goes slowly. Probably writes a draft of 'At Galway Races'.
23	W. F. Casey is at Coole finishing his play *The Suburban Groove*; Jack and Cottie Yeats also visit, as does Evan Wentz, who is collecting folklore.
29	WBY finishes a prose version of *The Player Queen*.
31	Begins to turn the prose *Player Queen* into verse.

September

3	(Thu) Goes to Dublin to attend a meeting of the British Association.
4	Delegates to the British Association attend a special matinée at the Abbey at which WBY delivers an address on 'The Theatre'.
5	Synge meets WBY and AG in Dublin.
7	Attends an Abbey production of *The Well of the Saints*.
9	Discusses Synge's poems with him.
10	Returns to Coole. About this time writes the poem 'Reconciliation' (*VP*, 257).
12	Makes the invocation of the Union in connection with the rites of the Celtic Mystical Order.
13	Repeats the invocation of the Union.

15	Writes his poem 'All Things can Tempt Me'.
16	Attends the Abbey performances at the Galway Feis.
17	Attends further Abbey performances at the Galway Feis as well as the presentation immediately afterwards of medals to foreign delegates attending the Industrial Exhibition.
18	Lectures on 'The National Theatre of Ireland' to the delegates to the Industrial Exhibition in Galway. At night he has a visionary dream involving MG. Writing 'At Galway Races'.
19	Attack on WBY in *Sinn Fein* over his running of the Abbey.
c.20	Vols I and II of *CW* published.
23	In the morning experiences a mystical union with MG and feels the old ecstasy.
30	Goes to Dublin from Coole.

October

1	(Thu) Attends the first production of Casey's *The Suburban Groove* at the Abbey and sounds Holloway out over the possibility of Boyle returning his plays to the Abbey.
2	Synge gives him the MS of his poems. WBY again at the Abbey plays and has a long talk with Shaw who is in the audience.
4	Visits ECY at Dundrum to arrange the publication of Synge's poems by the Cuala Press.
5	Crosses to London.
c.10	Sees MG but finds no change in their relationship.
13	Hears that Symons has suffered a severe mental breakdown and that Sara Allgood has asked AEFH for a job at the Gaiety Theatre, Manchester.
14	Leaves London for Dublin. Reads most of Balzac's novels over the coming months.
15	Attends an Abbey production of Thomas MacDonagh's *When the Dawn Is Come* and AG's adaptation of Molière's *The Rogueries of Scapin*. MG is in Dublin, staying with Ella Young.
16	Discusses the deficiency of language in *When the Dawn Is Come* with MacDonagh. MG and Ella Young go to tea with WBY and in the evening he attends a second performance of *When the Dawn Is Come*.
17	WBY, at third performance of *When the Dawn Is Come*, sits with MG and Ella Young. He is revising *The Golden Helmet*.
18	Sees Sara Allgood to discuss her future plans. In the evening he leaves Dublin for Liverpool to see Mrs Patrick Campbell.
19	Arrives in Liverpool. Sees Pinero's *The Thunderbolt*, reads *Deirdre* to Mrs Patrick Campbell in her dressing room, and has supper with her and FF.
20	Has lunch with FF, Mrs Campbell and her son and daughter; in the evening Mrs Campbell shows him the dress she intends to wear as Deirdre. Vols III and IV of *CW* published.

21	Sees Mrs Campbell in her production of Hugo von Hofmannsthal's *Elektra*.
22	Returns to Dublin from Liverpool and attends an Abbey performance of AG's *The Jackdaw* and the revised version of Casey's *The Man Who Missed the Tide*.
23	Sara Allgood agrees to stay on at the Abbey for 10s. a week extra.
26	Chairs a meeting of the 'Consultations Committee' at the Abbey.

November

2	(Mon) WBY and AG attend Mrs Campbell's rehearsals of *Deirdre* until 8 November.
4	WBY and AG see Mrs Campbell's production of *Elektra* at the Theatre Royal, Dublin.
5	At a rehearsal of *Deirdre* with Mrs Campbell in the morning; in the evening attends a performance of AG's *Kincora*. Much troubled by sexual desire.
7	Goes through a ceremony of spiritual union with MG.
c.8	Edits and contributes to *Samhain* (1908).
9	Attends the first performance of Mrs Campbell's production of *Deirdre* at the Abbey.
10	Attends the second performance of *Deirdre* with Mrs Campbell in the title role and afterwards speaks at a public dinner for her at the Gresham Hotel.
11	While seeing Mrs Campbell about business arrangements for *Deirdre*, WBY has an altercation with Casimir Markiewicz over the financial arrangements at the time of the 1906 split in the INTS.
12	Sees James Duncan about his dispute with Markiewicz, who is contemplating an action against WBY for slander. Chairs a meeting of the 'Consultations Committee' at the Abbey.
14	Attends the final performance of Mrs Campbell's *Deirdre*.
c.17	Vols V and VI of *CW* published.
22	Crosses to London in storm; tips the steward a half-sovereign in mistake for a shilling but returns before the train leaves to retrieve it.
23	At Mrs Campbell's rehearsals of *Deirdre* all day.
24	At Mrs Campbell's rehearsals of *Deirdre*; in the evening dines with Norreys Connell and hears his play *Shakespeare's End*.
25	Inspects the scenery for Mrs Campbell's London production of *Deirdre* at the New Theatre.
26	At Mrs Campbell's rehearsals of *Deirdre* from 11 am to 6 pm, taking a lunch of sandwiches in the theatre.
27	Mrs Campbell's production of *Deirdre* performed in a matinée with *Elektra*. WBY is called several times before the curtain and the matinées continue intermittently until 1 December.

| 28 | In the morning writes to AG about the reception of *Deirdre* and visits his dentist. Lunches with Annette Meakin and then calls on Mrs Campbell. In the evening he gathers a party to hear Connell read *Shakespeare's End* a second time. |
| 30 | Attends a further matinée performance of *Deirdre*. |

December

1	(Tue) Sees Mrs Campbell's lawyer about a contract for her production of *The Player Queen*. Publication of Vols VII and VIII of *CW* and of *Poetry and Ireland*.
2	Leaves London for Paris to write *The Player Queen* for Mrs Campbell, but loses his glasses at Victoria Station and can do nothing. Stays at the Hotel de Passy.
5	Receives a duplicate pair of glasses and begins work on *The Player Queen*.
6–28	Writes poem 'No Second Troy' (*VP*, 256–7). Works every morning on *The Player Queen* and after lunch writes letters and then walks to the other side of Paris for a French lesson. Continues to read Balzac. While in Paris he makes constant evocations with MG, mainly the Initiation of the Sword and Cauldron, and casts MG's horoscope.
10	Calls on the Irish sculptor John Hughes.
13	Looks though Vol. VII of *CW* and discovers what is wrong with *The Tables of the Law*.
c.14	Dines with John Hughes.
16	Meets a young man at MG's who is writing a thesis on him at the Sorbonne. Agnes Tobin arrives in London.
17	Sees a performance of Molière's *Scapin* at the Odeon.
19	Was to have met Rodin at lunch, but is ill with indigestion and cannot go.
23	Has finished a scenario for Act I of *The Player Queen* which is longer than the previous scenario for the whole play, and is starting on Act II. Buys exotic fruit for AG's Christmas present.
24	Works on the scenario for Act II of *The Player Queen*.
26	Sees MG and Ella Young, whose combination of stupidity and self-assurdedness irritates him; this leads to a quarrel with MG.
27	Lunches with MG.
28	Returns to London from Paris.
c.30	Is disturbed by his visit to Symons who seems completely mad.

1909

January

| 1 | (Fri) Dines with Agnes Tobin at Claridges and they write to Rhoda Symons. |

2	Goes to see AEFH in Manchester, where he suffers a severe rheumatic attack and takes to his bed.
6	Crosses to Dublin from Manchester to take rehearsals of AG's adaptation of Molière's *The Miser* and falls into a daily routine over the next fortnight, spending two hours dictating in the morning, rehearsing *The Miser* from 2–5 pm, studying French from 5.15–6.15 pm, and then, after writing letters and having dinner, more rehearsals from 8–10 pm
9	Dines with SMY.
10	Visits Dundrum to go through the family 'Ancestor Book' with SMY. Asks AG to send him Balzac's *Cousine Bette* or *Cousin Pons*.
11	Suffers another attack of rheumatism.
13	Attends a political debate at the Arts Club. Is seeking to escape from logic and obviousness through personality and mask.
14	Arranges for a young man to act as his typist every morning.
16	An agreement with Mrs Campbell gives her exclusive acting rights in *Deirdre*. SMY dines with WBY at the Nassau Hotel, and they examine the family 'Ancestor Book'.
17	Ill with some sort of nervous strain, which continues until 20 January.
21	Attends the first night of AG's adaptation of *The Miser* at the Abbey.
22	Rewrites his poem 'Words'; talks to one of AE's group whom he finds depressingly typical of the new class now growing up in Ireland.
23	Revises 'Words' and writes the quatrain 'My dear is angry that of late'. Chairs a meeting of the 'Consultations Committee' at the Abbey and in the evening sees *The Miser* again and speaks to Holloway about retrieving Boyle's plays for the Theatre. Meets Birrell and discusses wealth, power and the fine life.
24	Muses upon the attenuated nature of modern poetry. Begins a brief visit to Coole where he remains until *c*.28 January.
29	Back in Dublin, he consults Molly Allgood about visiting Synge.
30	Visits Synge; finds him ill, and meditates upon the prospect of his death.

February

1	(Mon) Sees a rehearsal of AG's *Kincora* at the Abbey.
3	Sees Sara Allgood at 5.30 pm at the Abbey on theatre matters and later talks at the Arts Club on 'The Ideas of the Young'.
4	Learns that AG is seriously ill at Coole and begins to write the poem 'A Friend's Illness' (*VP*, 267), which he sends to her on 8 February.

6	'On a Recent Government Appointment in Ireland', 'At Galway Races', and 'Distraction' (later 'All Things can Tempt me'), (poems; *VP*, 317–18, 266, 267) published in the *English Review*.
7	Walks in the Dublin mountains with Edward Evans and discusses religion.
8	Sees George Roberts about Maunsel's publication of AG's books.
9	Speaks at the Annual Conversazione of the Ladies Committee of the Feis Ceoil Association at the Abbey Theatre and confesses he knows nothing about music.
10	Attends the dress rehearsal of the revised *Kincora* from 8 pm until after midnight.
11	Attends a production of the revised *Kincora* at the Abbey.
13	Has a long discussion with Seamus O'Connell, Secretary of the Theatre of Ireland, about their using the Abbey again, and writes to AEFH recommending this.
14	Goes to Coole until *c.*20 February.
20	Returns to Dublin, where he meets Hugh Lane at the Arts Club and learns that he is threatening Dublin Corporation with the withdrawal of his pictures.
22	Sees Martyn at the Abbey about a production of *The Heather Field*. Loses his temper with the actor Arthur Sinclair over his bad behaviour in Manchester. Reads Coventry Patmore's poems to Edward Evans.
23	Dreams of walking along a path by a precipice with AG, and of a book containing the secret of MG, but in writing too small to read.
24	At the Abbey from 11.15–1.00 pm; from 1.30–4.45 pm writes letters and reads plays for the Abbey and at 5.00 pm attends an Arts Club committee meeting.
25	From 11.30 to 1.30 pm sees Beatrice Elvery about Abbey scenery and Henderson on theatre business. Reads plays for the Abbey from 2–3.30 pm, and writes letters from 3.30–4.50 pm.
26	At the Abbey from 11 to 12 noon, after which he writes letters and mystical notes. From 1.30 to 2.40 pm he pays visits and spends the rest of the afternoon writing more letters. He copies out a version of his poem 'Reconciliation' in his notebook.
27	After a bad night he breakfasts at 10.45 am and writes letters and revises scripts for the Abbey from 11 am to 1.10 pm. From 2.30 to 3.40 pm attends a matinée at the Abbey and writes letters from 4 to 7 pm. In the evening he attends a performance at the Abbey.
28	Spends the late morning and early afternoon writing letters. He thinks of ways of improving the constitution of the Arts Club, and later visits Mrs Napier, who is staying with General Monro.

March

1 (Mon) Present at James Duncan's play *A Gallant of Galway* at the Abbey, where he speaks to O'Connell about the Theatre of Ireland and sees Synge and Hyde.

2 Idles in the morning; works on *The Player Queen* from 1–1.45 pm, and reads plays and writes letters from 2.30 to 5 pm

3 Two hours idleness before doing astrology and then spends an hour on *The Player Queen*. In the afternoon he attends an Arts Club committee meeting.

4 Manages to resolve difficulties in *The Player Queen* and finishes Act I. Sara Allgood asks permission to sing at Lady Lyttelton's military charity concert. Getting *The King's Threshold* typed and reading Coventry Patmore with great excitement. At the Abbey in the evening he discovers that Sara Allgood has already signed a contract for Lady Lyttelton's concert.

6 Works at *The Player Queen* and becomes abundant and cheerful because he has some philosophy in his mind. At the Abbey he sees Mrs Napier and hears that Arthur Sinclair has been unpunctual at rehearsals. In the evening he copies out some of the revised *Golden Helmet*.

7 Does a good morning's work on *The Player Queen*; then copies and revises *The Golden Helmet*, and writes a note on class hatred. Lunches at Lady Lyttelton's with Judge Ross, W. F. Bailey, Sarah Harrison and Mrs Napier.

8 Henderson visits WBY at the Nassau Hotel to arrange the Abbey tour to Cork and to complain about Sara Allgood's flirtations with Sinclair and Kerrigan. WBY works on *The Player Queen* and *The Golden Helmet*. Reading Coventry Patmore and prefers the Odes to *The Angel in the House*. In the evening he goes to the Abbey to check lighting for Winifred Letts' *Stephen Grey*.

9 In morning he sees Beatrice Elvery about designs for *Time* and *The King's Threshold* and they discuss Binyon's *Painting of the Far East*. In the afternoon he goes to the Abbey to see *Stephen Grey* through for the first time. Writes a number of notes in his diary and has dinner at the Arts Club with Mabel Dickinson.

10 Works at *The Golden Helmet*, sees Henderson on theatre business and attends an Arts Club committee meeting where he recommends that the Club should register under the Friendly Societies Act. Has volunteered to spend the night in a haunted house. Sees rehearsal of *Stephen Grey* and thinks it thin.

11 Meets Lady Lyttelton who tells him that the national anthem is to be played at her concert and so Sara Allgood must withdraw from it. Sees Beatrice Elvery about theatre designs and goes on to the Abbey where Connell's *Time* is being read. Takes over the

direction of *The King' Threshold*.Thomas MacDonagh and then SMY call on him. He goes to the Abbey for Professor Maurice Gerothwohl's lecture on Molière and for performances of *Stephen Grey* and AG's adaptation of *The Rogueries of Scapin*.

c.13–19   Goes to Coole from Dublin and tries to work at *The Player Queen*.

19   Returns to Dublin.

20   Goes to the Abbey where Norreys Connell is rehearsing *Time*, and on to the Rotunda to see the Theatre of Ireland's production of Rutherford Mayne's *The Turn of the Road*. He walks with John Eglinton to George Moore's, but refuses to go in. Calls at the Abbey again, where he hears a disturbing report of Synge's health from Molly Allgood.

21   Reads J. F. Taylor's *Owen Roe O'Neill* and reflects on the differences between Catholic and Protestant Ireland. Writes his poem 'The Coming of Wisdom with Time'.

22   In the morning takes rehearsal of LR's *The Cross Roads*, helped by Norreys Connell. Attends a rehearsal of Connell's *Time* in the afternoon and then takes Connell to the Royal Irish Academy. Meets Molly Allgood in the street; she informs him that Synge is much weaker. He dines off sandwiches and then goes out to Pearse's school, St Enda's, to see Hyde's *The Lost Saint* and Standish O'Grady's *The Coming of Finn*. Hears that the Irish Party is unlikely to help the Corporation fulfil their promise of providing a gallery for Lane's pictures.

23   Spends the morning at the Abbey. Lunches with Lord Dunsany and sketches out a scenario based on one of his stories. From 3 to 5 pm rehearses LR's *The Cross Roads* and sees LR from 5 to 7 pm, after which MacDonagh calls. After dinner Molly Allgood calls to say that Synge wants to see him. Later in the evening goes to the Kildare Street Club to see Dunsany about his play *The Glittering Gate*.

24   Synge dies in the early morning. WBY sees Molly Allgood in great grief. In afternoon he goes to the Elphis Hospital to see Synge's brother-in-law, Harry Stephens, about Synge's literary remains. Performances at the Abbey are cancelled, and WBY spends much time arranging notices in the Dublin papers. In the evening he gives an impromptu tribute to Synge at the Arts Club.

25   Busy all day about Synge's affairs. Goes to Kingstown (Dun Laoighaire) to try to get a death mask made, but the coffin has already been closed. Orders wreaths. Dunsany calls and reads a story and revisions to *The Glittering Gate*.

26   Attends Synge's funeral.

28   Hears an account of Synge's death from Harry Stephens. Looks through Synge's poems and reflects bitterly upon the reception of poets in Ireland.

31   At an Abbey business meeting all afternoon and attends long dress rehearsals of *Time* and *The Cross Roads* in the evening.

April

1   (Thu) Sees Stephens about Synge's will but learns nothing. Spends all afternoon trying to write a new paragraph in his Preface for Synge's *Poems and Translations*. In the evening he attends Abbey productions of LR's *The Cross Roads* and Norreys Connell's *Time*.

2   Feeling very tired; Molly Allgood tells him that Synge knew for a year that he was dying. In the evening George Moore visits him at the Nassau Hotel and praises *The Cross Roads* and *Time*.

3   Working on his Synge Preface. Entertains Norreys Connell and his wife for tea and they stay until 6 pm, discussing Connell's terms for managing the Abbey.

4   Finishes his Preface, 'J. M. Synge'.

5   Visits his sisters in Dundrum and walks home with John Eglinton.

6   In the morning sees Connell about the scenery for Dunsany's plays. At 1 pm leaves Dublin for London.

7   Sees AEFH who approves Connell's appointment as an Abbey Director.

8   Writes to inform Connell that AEFH agrees to his appointment as Managing Director of the Abbey. Sees Mrs Patrick Campbell, FF, Elkin Mathews and Shannon.

9   Dines with Ricketts and Shannon.

10   Goes to Stratford-upon-Avon to see Bullen. Swinburne dies.

13   Leaves Stratford for Dublin, arriving in the evening.

14   At the Abbey, tries to telephone Stephens about Synge's *Deirdre of the Sorrows*, and sees Dunsany. Gets a resolution transforming the Arts Club's constitution (including the resignation of the Committee) passed unanimously by its Committee. Meets SMY and tells her that, with the death of Swinburne, he is 'King of the cats'.

15   Attends a revival of Martyn's *The Heather Field* at the Abbey. AG is also there, the first time she has been to the Theatre since her illness.

18   Lunches with Lady and General Lyttelton and discusses modern armies.

18–24   WBY and AG remain in Dublin while the Abbey Company is on tour in Cork, conducting difficult negotiations with the Synge family over his literary effects.

19   Public announcement of Connell's appointment as a Director of the Abbey. AG and Molly Allgood see Stephens about Synge's *Deirdre of the Sorrows*.

21	Sees Gogarty who speaks of Synge's death. In the evening Mabel Dickinson informs him that several members of the Arts Club will protest against an invitation to the Lord Lieutenant; WBY has already registered his protest in the minutes.
22	Desires open air and quiet. Late at night Stephens at last sends the MS of Synge's *Deirdre of the Sorrows*, but it is a bad version.
23	Writes the poem 'To a Poet, who would have me Praise certain Bad Poets, Imitators of his and Mine' (*VP*, 262).
25	Goes to AE's 'Sunday Night' and is dispirited by the conventionality of the gathering.
26	WBY, AG and Connell agree that it is too late to produce *Deirdre of the Sorrows* for the Abbey's London tour.
27–30	Goes to stay with Dunsany at Dunsany Castle, Co. Meath, but comes up to Dublin daily.
28	Sees Molly Allgood who shows him a good MS of *Deirdre of the Sorrows*. Is writing a lecture for the Arts Club.
29	Dunsany sends WBY into Dublin in his car to deliver a lecture on 'Contemporary Lyric Poetry' to a large audience at the Arts Club. In the evening WBY attends the first production of Dunsany's *The Glittering Gate* at the Abbey.
30	Returns to Dublin from Dunsany Castle to help Molly Allgood with the MS of *Deirdre of the Sorrows*. Gogarty, MacDonagh, Colum and others nominate WBY for the Chair of English at the National University.

May

3	(Mon) Leaves Dublin for London, where MG is staying.
5–6	Clearing off his backlog of letters at the typists.
6	Hears he has not been appointed to the Chair of English at the National University. Sees MG prior to her departure for Ireland.
7	Takes Dunsany to meet Ricketts and Shannon.
8	Sees AG in London at 5 pm on her way to Venice and they have dinner at 7 pm.
10	Ezra Pound at WBY's 'Monday Evening' with the Italian man-of-letters Antonio Cippio, FF and others.
12	AG leaves London for Venice.
13	Receives a letter Synge wrote to him before his 1908 operation, sent on by Edward Stephens.
14–23	Still recovering from his Dublin trip; has a very bad week, but he starts creative work *c*.23rd, rewriting *The Golden Helmet*.
19	Visits Symons, who is quite happy and full of affection.
23	Goes to Brooke House asylum to see Symons with MG; Agnes Tobin is there and she and MG strike up a surprising friendship.
24	A great many people at WBY's 'Monday Evening', including Lord Dunsany, very excited at meeting Mabel Beardsley.

25	Evokes a vision of his own horoscope, which warns him of an impending shock, tells him of a new influence coming to him, and advises him to abandon *The Player Queen* for five years.
27	MG leaves London for France.
28	Has a confused dream about a ghost and wonders if it is a manifestation of MG.
*c.*30	Visits Symons again.

June

2	(Wed) Reads *Deirdre of the Sorrows* to Ricketts and Shannon and other friends.
3	Consults the occultist Mrs Harriet Felkin, who evokes a dark woman and Egyptian mummies, while Dr R. W. Felkin tells him of seeing a Dervish dancing a horoscope.
6	Calls on AG at about 12.30 pm for lunch. Consults Ethel Felkin, who psychometricizes a letter from MG.
7	The Abbey opens its London Tour at the Royal Court Theatre; WBY and AG go there at midday to help and attend performances in the evening with FF.
8	At 11 am WBY and AG rehearse *Dervorgilla* at Tedworth Gardens as it is down for a matinée on 9 June.
9	Meets AG and Blunt at the Court Theatre for a half-empty matinée of *Dervorgilla* and *The Playboy*, and in the interval tells Blunt that he is writing a play in rhyming alexandrines. In the evening WBY arrives in middle of the second play and briefly meets Mrs Philips.
19	Has a discussion with AEFH about turning the Abbey Theatre into a limited company after the expiry of the patent. In the evening he reads Basil Valentinus on the marriage of the Sun and Moon, which results in a dream of his flying and asking dream figures about the future of his relationship with MG.
23	Learns that Herbert Trench is trying to poach Molly Allgood for the Haymarket Theatre. Mrs Patrick Campbell gives a dinner for WBY and the Abbey Company on their London tour.
24	Sees Shaw about the Abbey Appeal for funds to buy out AEFH.
28	In the morning writes letters. At 3 pm sees Allan Wade at the Court Theatre to find out how the Abbey has done financially on the London tour, and then visits Una Birch.
29	Gives the artist Gerald Kelly two sittings.

July

| 1 | (Thu) AEFH demands an apology from him, AG and all concerned because Sara Allgood performed at a suffragette meeting organized by Edith Lyttelton in London, so breaking AEFH's 'no politics' rule governing the Abbey. |

2	Norreys Connell resigns his Abbey directorship on receipt of an abusive letter from AEFH.
3	WBY leaves London for Dublin.
5	Publication of Synge's *Poems and Translations* with a Preface by WBY. WBY sees Edward Synge, and Edward Evans comes to his 'Monday Evening' and discusses his visions at New Grange.
6	Goes to Coole, where he writes to Connell to try to dissuade him from resigning from the Abbey.
8	A dream gives him the theme for his poem 'When Helen Lived'.
9–31	At Coole writing, and arranging for the Abbey production of Shaw's *The Shewing up of Blanco Posnet*, banned in England.
29	Dreams of water, which he interprets as the rise of physical desire.
30	Again dreams of water.

August

1	(Sun) Exhausted by unrequited physical desire.
7	At Coole writes 'Upon a House Shaken by the Land Agitation'.
10	A 'most evil day': hears of trouble over the Castle authorities' attempt to ban *The Shewing up of Blanco Posnet*, and, from MG, that Quinn is deeply offended about his attempt to seduce his mistress, Dorothy Coates.
12	AG wires WBY from Dublin to come up to help defend the Abbey against the Castle censorship.
13	Goes up to Dublin by the first train. He arrives at 2 pm and he and AG call on Whitney and Moore to discuss the legal aspect of the censorship and then see the Under Secretary who threatens that the Abbey's patent may be cancelled if they do not withdraw *Blanco Posnet*.
14	WBY and AG go to Dublin Castle to explain their attitude to Shaw's play. They call on the Under Secretary at his house in Phoenix Park and are told that the Viceroy Lord Aberdeen will settle the matter on his return to Dublin on 17 August.
15	Spends from 4 to 5.30 pm at a typing office, dictating a letter to AEFH about the *Blanco Posnet* dispute. In the evening he tries unsuccessfully to see Quinn, who is visiting Dublin.
16	At 11 am calls on Quinn and discusses the Dorothy Coates affair with him; this leads to a rupture in their friendship which lasts until 1914. AG is ill and returns to Coole.
17	WBY leaves Dublin for Coole.
20	WBY and AG return to Dublin to take up the dispute with the Castle over *Blanco Posnet*. They spend all day at the rehearsal of the play, and receive a letter from Lord Aberdeen threatening legal action.
21	Meeting of the Abbey Directors to consider their strategy in the *Blanco Posnet* dispute. They issue a first press release on the matter.

22	They issue a second press release about the *Blanco Posnet* dispute.
24	Gives an interview about the *Blanco Posnet* dispute to the *Irish Independent*. In the evening he and AG attend the Abbey's revival of *The Playboy* and *The Rising of the Moon*.
25	The Abbey produces Shaw's *The Shewing up of Blanco Posnet* despite Castle threats. Mrs Shaw is in the audience and the play is received enthusiastically. WBY is again interviewed about the play by the *Irish Independent*. He edits and contributes an article, 'The Religion of Blanco Posnet', to the fifth number of *The Arrow*.
26	He and AG issue a third press release about *Blanco Posnet*.
*c.*27	WBY and AG return to Coole.
28	Dreams of Madame Blavatsky and two heaps of plovers' eggs.

September

	Early in the month he drafts a prose version of his poem 'The Fascination of What's Difficult' (*VP*, 260).
8	(Wed) A bad morning because a letter from AEFH uses up his emotional power. Is ill with 'head queer' and the 'sensation of last spring' (*Mem*).
16	Head still not good, but he manages to write a verse squib about Augustine Birrell (*Mem*, 230–1) and to rewrite 'His Dream'.
20	Has a new idea for Act III of *The Player Queen*.
21	Finishes rereading Symons' translation of D'Annunzio's *Francesca di Rimini*. Trying to get into Act III of *The Player Queen* the thought that life is a perpetual preparation for what never happens.

October

*c.*3	(Sun) Remains in Coole working on *The Player Queen*, preparing Synge's MSS for publication and negotiating with Boyle for the return of his plays to the Abbey. He is exhausted by unrequited physical desire.
7	Receives £32 from Unwin as annual royalties for *Poems*.
9	In the evening WBY reads Act I of *The Player Queen* to Robert and Margaret Gregory, and, realizing it is wordy and far-fetched, starts the play afresh.
10	After a sleepless night caused by excitement at seeing how to recast *The Player Queen*, he delays beginning the rewriting until the following day, but gets a new MS book for the purpose.
11	Starts a new version of *The Player Queen*. Has nearly finished reading through Balzac, with only 4 of the 40 volumes left to read.
12	Despite eye trouble he manages to write a lot of letters and pay some bills. Receives an invitation to lecture in America in the Autumn of 1910.
15	Goes to Dublin from Coole, and attends a dinner for the actor-manager Martin Harvey.

17	William Boyle agrees to return his plays to the Abbey.
20	Performs the Ritual of Union.
21	Attends a special Abbey matinée in honour of the Martin Harveys and accompanies AG and Robert Gregory to *Riders to the Sea* and *The Miser* in the evening.
22	Attends Abbey performances in the evening.
23	Sees Martin Harvey's production of *Hamlet* at the Theatre Royal in Dublin.
24	Stays at Fairfield, Glasnevin, working on *The Player Queen*.
27	Studies drawings of Venetian costumes in Craig's magazine the *Mask* for possible use at the Abbey.
28	At the Abbey with AG, MG, Lord Dunsany and Lady Middleton and party to see *The Shewing up of Blanco Posnet*, *The Jackdaw*, and *The Gittering Gate*.
29	Proposes asking E. Lyall Swete to take charge at the Abbey, but AG wants an Irishman, and WBY writes a poem about this (*Mem*, 234–5). In the evening, at the Abbey with AG. That night he dreams of MG.

November

3	(Wed) Goes from Dublin to Cork for a psaltery recital with FF, staying with Professor William Stockley.
4	WBY and FF in Cork. Boyle's *The Building Fund* revived at the Abbey, the first of his plays to be produced there since the furore over *The Playboy of the Western World*.
8	Attends the dress rehearsal of AG's *The Image* at the Abbey, and on the way home has an urge to throw his ring into the canal.
9	Rewrites part of his poem 'The Arrow', and contemplates an ideal of love. Rewrites a passage in *Deirdre*.
11	Attends first production of *The Image* at the Abbey.
c.20	Crosses from Dublin to London.
21	Arrives at Mrs Campbell's at 1.15 pm to read her *The Player Queen* but the interrupted reading goes on until after midnight.
24	In the evening dines at the Gosses' with the Prime Minister, Lord Cromer, the Lord Chief Justice, Alfred East, Anthony Hope and Austin Dobson.
25	Goes to see a very bad production of Synge's *The Tinker's Wedding* at His Majesty's Theatre, but walks out in disgust. Sees a good deal of General Ian Hamilton over the coming days.
27	Consults Frederick Whelan about an Abbey tour to London.
28	The Abbey Company arrives in London and WBY attends a rehearsal of *Blanco Posnet*; Shaw also sits in and improves the actors' performances.

29	Calls at the Stage Society offices with Henderson and O'Rourke to discuss the production of *Blanco Posnet* for the Society.
30	Attends a rehearsal of the Abbey Company.

December

1	(Wed) Goes to Cambridge to see a production of Aristophanes' *The Wasps*, and orders Jebb's translation of Sophocles' *Oedipus*, with a view to adapting it for the Abbey.
*c.*4	Leaves the MS of *The Player Queen* in a London taxi and applies to Scotland Yard for its return.
4	Visits Scotland Yard about the missing MS; afterwards shops, sees friends and goes to a rehearsal.
5	The Abbey Company produces *Blanco Posnet*, *Cathleen ni Houlihan* and *The Workhouse Ward* for the Stage Society at the Aldwych Theatre. The performances repeated on 6 December.
7	Writes the poem 'King and No King' (*VP*, 258).
8	Agnes Tobin and Mrs Meiking take him to Mrs Campbell's production of Maeterlinck's *The Blue Bird*, which he dislikes. Gets the MS of *The Player Queen* back from Scotland Yard.
9	Agnes Tobin informs him that Gosse is trying to arrange a Civil List pension for him. Sees AEFH about her terms for transferring the Abbey Theatre and thinks her unusually mad. Sees Perceval Landon's melodramatic problem play *The House Opposite* at the Queen's Theatre and likes it.
10	Meets Ezra Pound again and is impressed with him. An agent, recommended by Shaw, is reading WBY's plays with a view to German and Hungarian performances.
12	Has a serious talk with Agnes Tobin about a Civil List pension.
13	Visits the Birches and discusses ways of buying the Abbey Theatre from AEFH.
16	Lunches with Gosse at the House of Lords to discuss a Civil List pension, but the presence of Agnes Tobin and Rhys inhibits confidential conversation.
17	Discusses AEFH's obstructive behaviour over the Abbey with Shaw, and later with Una Birch.
21	Busy revising *The Golden Helmet*; in the evening he sees Murray Carson about producing *Oedipus* in Dublin, with Carson in title role.
*c.*22	Dines with Gosse who also invites the artist Walter Sickert.
26	Is making a final copy of *The Golden Helmet*; dines with Craig who demonstrates his stage screens.
27	Works in the British Museum Library.
31	Finishes *The Golden Helmet* and starts to write lectures.

1910

January

3   (Mon) Suffering from a cold. Has a dream of a trireme and wonders if this is a symbol of the Abbey's need for capital.

4   Dreams he is a ghost teaching children to pray.

7   Craig and Binyon dine with WBY, and Craig tells him more about his stage screens.

8   Improves Emer's song in *The Golden Helmet* (now retitled *The Green Helmet*). Reads Swinburne's poetry in the British Museum, finding it mere rhetoric.

10   Has a strange dream of a slow barge manned by two lovers.

11   Leaves London for Dublin, where he stays with Lord Dunsany at Fairfield, Glasnevin.

13   Present at the Abbey for the first production of Synge's *Deirdre of the Sorrows*.

14   Sees Thomas MacDonagh at the Abbey. WBY is rehearsing Maeterlinck's *Interior* and hopes to start writing *Oedipus* after that.

15   Sees *Deirdre of the Sorrows* again, and finds Maire O'Neill's performance in the title role improved.

16   Returns MacDonagh's poems with his comments. In the afternoon Padraic Colum reads him his new play, *Thomas Muskerry*.

17   The Abbey Theatre is valued for purchase from AEFH.

20   At the Abbey for productions of *Interior* and *The Canavans*; meets and talks to Nancy Maude there.

21   The valuation of the Abbey Theatre arrives and is disappointingly low.

23   Hears Moore read the Shelbourne Dinner chapter from *Ave*.

24   Consults the Abbey solicitors, Whitney and Moore, about the valuation of the Theatre.

25   Sees Whitney and Moore again about the financial arrangements at the Abbey. Attends an Abbey rehearsal of *Mirandolina* and, in evening, of his *The Green Helmet*.

26   In the morning attends an Abbey rehearsal of his *Deirdre*. Reads through Goldoni's plays at the National Library looking for possible pieces for the Abbey.

27   Sees Keohler at Whitney and Moore, who have drafted a purchase proposal for the Abbey, and he later consults the auditor Buckley about this.

28   Sees Whitney and Moore about the Abbey purchase and, at 12 noon, Buckley. Wires and writes to AG, asking her to approve the purchase proposal.

| 29 | Sees Whitney and Moore at 12 noon about the Abbey purchase and is irritated by Shaw's interference in the matter. Rehearsing *Mirandolina* with Abbey Company. |

February

1	(Tue) Craig's model stage with his screens arrives and WBY is delighted with it.
3	Attends a production of the revised version of LR's *The Cross Roads* at the Abbey.
4	Works for $2\frac{1}{2}$ hours with Craig's model, mainly on scenes for *On Baile's Strand* and *The Land of Heart's Desire*. Resigns from Committee of the Shakespeare Memorial Theatre.
5	Takes photographs of Craig's model. Rehearses in the evening at the Abbey and tries to adjudicate squabbles between Sara Allgood and Sinclair. Weir Johnston offers to become a Director of the Abbey. Dreams of the theme for 'The Grey Rock'.
7	WBY and Henderson go over Buckley's financial statement about the Abbey, but find it hard to understand.
8	Rehearses for four hours. His lecture at the Dublin Arts Club on 'The Tragic Theatre' starts an hour late at 9 pm with Dunsany in the chair and Padraic Pearse giving a vote of thanks.
9	Rehearses his *Deirdre* and attends the dress rehearsal of *The Green Helmet*.
10	Attends the first production of *The Green Helmet*, played in a double bill with Synge's *The Playboy of the Western World*.
11	Attends special 'professional' matinée of *The Green Helmet*, put on at 2.30 pm for the Benson Company which is on tour in Dublin.
13	Lectures to the NLS, ostensibly on 'Ireland and the Arts', but in fact on the Rhymers' Club.
15	Goes to a party at his sisters' house in Dundrum and stays the night.
17	Writes 'A Drinking Song' (*VP*, 261). Sees Whitney and Moore about the Abbey purchase and learns that AEFH will sell the Theatre and adjoining shop for £1,000.
22	Sees Keohler about the Abbey purchase.
23	Dictates the first draft of his planned London lectures on the Theatre.
24	Attends the first production of *Mirandolina*, AG's version of Goldoni's *La Locandiera*, at the Abbey.
26	AG arrives in Dublin from Coole and attends a performance of *Mirandolina* with WBY and Lord Dunsany.

March

| 1 | (Tue) Arrives in London from Dublin and has breakfast and a bath at the Euston Hotel. Since he has let 18 Woburn |

Buildings, he stays at the Edward's Hotel. Probably sees performances of Galsworthy's *Justice* in the afternoon and Giovanni Grasso's Sicilian Players' production of G. Polver's three-act play *Omerto*, translated into Sicilian dialect by S. Arcidiacone, at the Lyric Theatre that evening. *Poems: Second Series* published by Bullen.

2   Goes to a matinée of Justin Huntly McCarthy's *The O'Flynn* at His Majesty's Theatre, with W. G. Fay in the cast. Returns to Dublin that night.

3   Lectures on 'The Theatre and Ireland' at the Central Branch of the Gaelic League, with Hyde presiding and Padraic Pearse giving a vote of thanks. MacDonagh, Colum, Maguire and Dunsany also speak.

4   At the Abbey for a performance of AG's *The Image*, attended by Lady Lyttelton.

c.5   Returns to London from Dublin.

7   Revises poem 'The Ragged Wood' (*VP*, 210–11). Lectures on 'The Theatre' at the Adelphi Club.

9   Lectures on 'Friends of my Youth' at the Adelphi Club, with Gosse in the chair and William Carlos Williams and Pound in the audience.

11   Lectures on 'The Contemporary Irish Theatre' at the Adelphi Club, with Shaw in the chair.

15   Leaves London for Dublin by an 8.30 am train. In the evening he replies to E. J. Gwynn's Centennial lecture on Samuel Ferguson at Trinity College; Mahaffy and Hyde also speak.

16   At the Abbey, where LR distributes parts for Colum's new play, *The Magnate* (later *Thomas Muskerry*). Dines with LR in the evening.

17   LR's first day in sole charge of the Abbey.

18   Attends rehearsal taken by LR, and approves. Sees AE.

20   WBY is staying at Dunsany Castle; revises 'The Fascination of What's Difficult'.

21   Begins his Introduction to Synge's *Collected Works*.

23   Leaves Dunsany Castle for Dublin by 9.30 am train and meets AG at the Abbey.

25   Attends the Annual General Meeting of the NTS at the Abbey.

•28   At the Abbey with AG and LR.

29   Sees his *Deirdre*, revived at the Abbey with Sara Allgood in the title role, in a double bill with AG's *The Workhouse Ward*.

30   Oversees business and rehearsals at the Abbey and in the evening attends another performance of *Deirdre*.

31   At Abbey attending to business and writing a lecture on the theatre which Sara Allgood is to give in Manchester.

April

1   (Fri) Sees the Abbey production of Boyle's *The Eloquent Dempsy*, of which he disapproves, and then catches the night boat to England.

2   With Ricketts, sees *Otello*, an Italian translation of Shakespeare's *Othello*, the last performance of Giovanni Grasso's Sicilian Players at the Lyric Theatre, London. Develops a bad cold.

4   Gertrude Kingston shows him over her recently built Little Theatre in the Adelphi, with a view to the Abbey leasing it for London tours.

5   Finishes 'On those that hated "The Playboy of the Western World", 1907' (*VP*, 294) and begins 'A Woman Homer Sung' (*VP*, 254–5).

6   Given a second tour of the Little Theatre by Gertrude Kingston.

*c.*9   Goes to Stratford-upon-Avon to consult Bullen about the publication of his books; stays until 11 April.

12   Gosse invites him to join an English Academy of Letters. Attends a tea-party at Hugh Lane's.

15   Entertains Gertrude Kingston to dinner at Woburn Buildings to meet John Masefield. Finishes 'A Woman Homer Sung'.

17   Sees Gosse about setting up an Academic Committee under the aegis of the Royal Literary Society. Replies to the toast of 'The Repertory Theatre' at the annual dinner of the Incorporated Stage Society.

19   Goes by evening train to Manchester, where the Abbey Company is on tour.

20   Attends a matinée of the Abbey Company's performance of *The Canavans* in Manchester.

22   Goes from Manchester to Birmingham to see a production of *Measure for Measure* by John Drinkwater's Pilgrim Players.

23   WBY and AEFH are guests of honour at the Birmingham Dramatic Literary Club's Shakespeare Commemoration Banquet at the Grand Hotel.

*c.*24   Returns to London.

25   Henderson calls to discuss the plays to be performed by the Abbey in London. Masefield dines with WBY at Woburn Buildings, and Maclagan arrives as he is leaving.

28   WBY goes to Normandy to stay with MG.

29   In Normandy, works mainly on his essay 'Synge and the Ireland of his Time'; he also reads extracts from Milton's prose and writes lyrics.

May

3   (Tue) Goes to Caen to meet Iseult Gonne, and look at the churches. Talks through the political parts of his Synge essay with MG. Writes the poems 'Peace' (*VP*, 258–9) and 'These are the Clouds' (*VP*, 265) during this month.

7	LR fails to close the Abbey Theatre on the announcement of King Edward VII's death, a telegram to AG having been delayed, thus precipitating a terminal quarrel between the Abbey Directors and AEFH.
11	WBY and the MacBrides rise at 4 am to go to Mont St Michel for two days. Writes the poem 'Against Unworthy Praise' (*VP*, 259–60).
12	AG writes to warn WBY that AEFH is on the warpath.
16	WBY returns to London from Normandy to find a mass of telegrams and letters about the dispute over the Abbey and the King's death.
17	Writes to AEFH to complain about her intemperate responses in the dispute over the Abbey's remaining open.
*c.*18	Leaves London for Dublin.
19	Consults Keohler about the legal implications of the dispute between AEFH and the Abbey Theatre. Also sees Maire O'Neill, AE and Colum. In the evening attends the Abbey productions of *The Green Helmet* and LR's *Harvest*, but has to leave in the middle.
20	Leaves Dublin for London by the morning boat.
21	Joins a weekend party given by Lady Katherine Somerset at Reigate Priory with the Duchess of Bedford and General Sir Ian Hamilton.
23	Returns to London.
24	Goes to Cambridge where the Abbey is on tour and stays with the Burkitts. Sees AG's *The Image* and Fitzmaurice's *The Pie-Dish* and is interviewed by the *Cambridge Daily News*.
26	Returns to London from Cambridge.
29	Lunches with AG at Queen Anne Mansions.
30	The Abbey Company performs at the Court Theatre, London, and remains there until 25 June, with WBY in regular attendance.

June

1	(Wed) Dines out, but returns to the Court Theatre for the Abbey plays and meets Rider Haggard.
5	WBY and AG visit Blunt in Sussex and stay overnight.
*c.*8	Elected an Honorary Fellow of the Royal Society of Literature and a member of the Academic Committee.
7	Accompanies AG to tea with Teddy and Mrs Roosevelt at Arthur Lees'.
10	WBY and Lord MacDonald are guests at the annual dinner of the Oxford University St Patrick's Club.
12	Proposes the toast 'The Drama' at the sixty-fifth dinner of the Royal General Theatrical Fund, held in the Whitehall Rooms of the Hotel Metropole, with Martin Harvey presiding.

14	WBY and AG launch an Appeal in the London press for funds for the Abbey Theatre.
16	'The Art of the Theatre' (contribution to a symposium; *UP* II. 382–4) published in the *New Age*.
19	Interviewed in the *Observer* about the Abbey Appeal and the Irish theatre.
24	Attends AG's meeting to raise funds for the Abbey at Hugh Lane's house, 100 Cheyne Walk; the Abbey Company perform *Gaol Gate* and the guests are addressed by Ford Madox Hueffer (later Ford Madox Ford), WBY and Shaw.
25	Jack Yeats sells his cottage in Devon and he and his wife move to Ireland.
27	*Cathleen ni Houlihan* produced at Eton College. Frederick A. King attends WBY's 'Monday Evening'.

July

1	(Fri) Begins to rewrite sections of *The Green Helmet*.
2	Spends the morning altering *The Green Helmet*. In the afternoon sees Alice Stopford Green about Lord Dunraven's proposed new journal.
5	Publication of Synge's *Deirdre of the Sorrows* with a Preface by WBY. WBY begins negotiations through Watt and Chappell for the use of his plays as libretti for operas. Rewriting his lecture 'The Tragic Theatre' as a preface to the new edition of his plays.
9	Interviewed in the London *Daily News* about *The Player Queen* and Craig's screens.
10	Sees Una Birch and discusses his plays.
13	Consults Gosse in the Library of the House of Lords about the first meeting of the new Academic Committee. At night WBY crosses over from London to Dublin.
14	Sees Holloway about lowering the Abbey stage at a cost of £14.
15	Goes to the Abbey, where the levelling of the stage has begun, to consult Henderson and arrange a new curtain. In the evening discusses Maire Walker's acting with Moore.
16	Leaves Dublin for London.
17	Sara Allgood wires that she is leaving the Abbey Company on 1 August.
19	Attends the first meeting of the Academic Committee.
*c.*20	Crosses from London to Ireland and stays with AG in the Burren.
22	In the Burren, carries on a dispute by letter with Sara Allgood over the terms of her contract.
24	AG and WBY go to Coole from the Burren. WBY disappoints AG by failing to support her in her quarrel with Gosse over the application for WBY's Civil List Pension. He remains at Coole until 18 September, mainly working on *The Player Queen*, finishing his

essays on 'The Tragic Theatre' and 'Synge and the Ireland of his Time', and reading the novels of Alexandre Dumas.

August
9   (Tue) Hears from the Prime Minister's Secretary that he has been awarded a Civil List Pension of £150 a year. In the middle of the month Shaw and his wife visit Coole and remain there until *c*.7 September. At this time begins writing his poem 'The Mask' (*VP*, 263).

September
15   (Thu) Hears from SMY that his uncle, George Pollexfen, is dying in Sligo.

19   Travels to Dublin from Coole and meets LR in the evening.

20   Attempts to persuade Martyn to become the lessee of the Abbey, but Martyn refuses because he disapproved of the production of Shaw's *Blanco Posnet*. WBY dictates 'Synge and the Ireland of his Time' to a typist; in the evening he discusses plays with LR.

21   Still seeking a lessee for the Abbey, he tries to see Sir Philip Hanson, but he is not in his office. Meets AE and goes on to Whitney and Moore to suggest that Dr Moore should become the lessee. Moves on to the Abbey and discusses the financial position of the Theatre with the whole Company in the Green Room. Interviews Maire O'Neill, Sara Allgood (about her contract), Fred O'Donovan and Seaghan Barlow (about setting up the Craig screens). In the evening calls to see ECY and finds Jack and Cottie Yeats there.

22   Sees Jacob Geoghegan who declines to become the lessee of the Abbey. Meets Roberts of the Maunsel Press, who confesses to publishing Synge's journalistic essays against WBY's express instructions. Arrives at the Abbey between Acts 2 and 3 of *The Well of the Saints* and goes off afterwards with George Moore.

23   Chairs a meeting of the 'Consultations Committee' at the Abbey, which draws up rules for discipline and time-keeping.

24   Returns to Coole from Dublin and finds a letter from SMY telling him that George Pollexfen is very near death.

25   George Pollexfen dies in Sligo.

27   WBY goes to Sligo from Coole for George Pollexfen's funeral. Stays at the Imperial Hotel for the night and sees SMY and Arthur Jackson.

28   Attends George Pollexfen's funeral; SMY and Jack Yeats also present.

29   Travels to Dublin from Sligo. LR introduces him to Mrs Day, Bourke Cockran's sister, and they discuss Abbey finances. Complains to Dominick Spring-Rice of Roberts's duplicity over

publication of Synge's articles. In the evening attends the first production of Ray's *The Casting Out of Martin Welan* at the Abbey.

30 Consults Hanson about Abbey affairs, and also meets with several people about his prospects of becoming Professor of English at TCD if Edward Dowden resigns.

October

c.1 (Sat) Travels to Coole from Dublin. 'The Tragic Theatre' (article; *UP* II. 384–92 and *E & I*, 238–45) published in the *Mask* (Florence).

3 Writes to Hone to complain of Roberts's deception over the Synge articles. Learns that George Pollexfen has left one-ninth of his real and personal estate to be divided between him and his siblings.

14 WBY goes to Dublin and consults Keohler about the Abbey patent, and later meets Bailey, Hanson and Robert Gregory. Goes to the Abbey in the evening to see *Thomas Muskerry* and *A Pot of Broth*.

15 Has a violent row with Roberts over the publication of Synge's articles. At the Abbey again in the evening.

c.16 Crosses to London from Dublin.

17 Sees FF and Darrell Figgis.

18 Spends the morning going over George Pollexfen's papers and books.

c.19 Sees a dramatization of Conan Doyle's *The Speckled Band*.

c.20 Sees Somerset Maugham's play, *Grace*.

21 Calls on Charles Ricketts to show him Craig's theatrical designs.

22 Meets the dramatist St John Ervine for the first time.

26 Travels from London to Dublin by the 1 pm train and stays at the Nassau Hotel.

27 Attends a meeting at Pembroke House, Dublin, to raise money for the Abbey Theatre; AG, Birrell and Judge Ross also speak. Attends the first production of T. C. Murray's *Birthright* at the Abbey.

28 At a Professional Matinée at the Abbey, and speaks to T. C. Murray and Moore.

29 Leaves Dublin for Manchester.

31 In Manchester staying with his friends, the Dreys. Gives the first of a series of three lectures in the Memorial Hall, on 'Contemporary Poetry'.

November

1 (Tue) Lectures at Leeds University on 'The Dramatic Movement in Ireland'.

5 Goes to Stratford-upon-Avon to see Bullen and reads him *The Green Helmet*.

7 Travels from Stratford to Manchester for his second lecture, on 'The Theatre'.

8 Sees Montagu of the *Manchester Guardian* about Abbey affairs.

10	Goes to London and sees Miss Block about costumes for the Abbey.
11	Lunches with the Shakespears; Nancy Maude also there.
12	Leaves London for Manchester on an early afternoon train.
13	In Manchester the Dreys give him dinner parties every night and inform him he has made £89 on his lectures there.
14	Consults Mair about the Abbey Appeal and in the evening gives the last of his Manchester lectures, on 'The Intellectual Movement in Ireland'.
15	Lectures to the Liverpool Playgoers' Society on 'The Irish Dramatic Movement'.
16	Lectures on 'The Theatre' at the Kursaal Theatre, Harrogate.
17	Returns to Dublin direct from Harrogate. Spends the next fortnight working at the Craig scenery and seeing lawyers about the new Abbey patent.
18	At the Abbey, sees *Riders to the Sea*, *Mirandolina* and *The Full Moon*.
21	Attends an afternoon entertainment at the Abbey in aid of the Abbey Appeal: the Company put on *Hyacinth Halvey* and WBY speaks about Abbey finances.
23	The first application for the transfer of the Abbey patent is heard by the Solicitor General for Ireland.
24	Attends the first Abbey production of Seamus O'Kelly's *The Shuiler's Child*.
25	Dines with AG and Professor Tyrrell of TCD; they discuss the possibility of WBY succeeding to Dowden's Chair of English.
26	The Solicitor General for Ireland hears an application from AG and WBY in the Library of Dublin Castle for a new Abbey patent.
30	AG formally takes over the patent of the Abbey Theatre from AEFH for 21 years.

December

2	(Fri) WBY chairs a meeting of the 'Consultations Committee' at the Abbey Theatre, which discusses a profit-sharing scheme.
3	WBY returns to London from Dublin. Reads a selection of his poems at an ILS 'Original Night'. 'Youth and Age' (poem, later 'The Coming of Wisdom with Time'; *VP*, 261), and 'To a Certain Country House in Time of Change' (poem, later 'To a House Shaken by the Land Agitation'; *VP*, 264) published in *McClure's Magazine*.
5	Sees Herbert Trench who tells him he hopes to play *Oedipus* at the Haymarket sometime next spring.
6	Lectures to the 'Tuesday Club' on Contemporary Poetry.
10	Working on *The Player Queen* and reading Chaucer and Gower at British Museum; this plan of work continues until the end of the month. Consults Bailey about the Abbey Company and the

difficulties with the Allgoods. Sends the proceeds of his Liverpool lecture to the Abbey Endowment Fund.

13   In the evening sees the actor and playwright Murray Carson about theatrical matters. *The Green Helmet and Other Poems* published in the middle of this month.

18   In evening sees Murray Carson who tells him that Tree is also planning a production of *Oedipus*.

19   Works with Ervine on his play *Mixed Marriage* from 6 pm until guests arrive for his 'Monday Evening'.

23   Hears from Henderson that AEFH is demanding her £1,000 from the Abbey immediately.

31   Sees Chinese players at Gertrude Kingston's Little Theatre for the second time.

1911

January

1   (Sun) Writing the poem 'Friends'. Returns corrected copy for *Plays for an Irish Theatre* to Bullen.

2   Has theatrical masks sent to Craig for his advice.

6   Sees Curtis Brown about Abbey tours and other theatrical matters.

7   Leaves London for Dublin and is furious to discover that Henderson has returned Sara Allgood's contract to her, even though she had threatened to tear it up.

8   Sees Hyde's *The Nativity*, on the same bill at the Abbey as *The Rogueries of Scapin*. Consults LR about rearranging the Abbey programme in case Allgood has to be suspended.

9   Allgood has not returned her contract and so WBY dismisses Henderson; he interviews Allgood, who refuses to return the contract until she has seen AG. WBY rehearses *The Hour-Glass*.

10   Consults Keohler about Abbey affairs.

*c.*12   Returns to London from Dublin.

16   FF reading Chrétien de Troyes to WBY. Begins a quarrel with Heys, business manager of the Gaiety Theatre, Manchester, over the selection of plays for the Abbey's Manchester tour.

17   Enlists Gosse's help on hearing that the Vigilance Society are threatening to prosecute the *English Review* over its publication of Sturge Moore's story, 'A Platonic Marriage'.

19   Has nearly finished his poem 'Friends'.

21   Invites FF to act as First Musician in the revival of his *Deirdre* at the Abbey. Finishes 'Friends' and goes to Hampstead Heath to relax.

23   Having 'Synge and the Ireland of his Time' typed, prior to sending it to Cuala and is reading about Chaucer and his age. Has a long telephone conversation with Harrison, editor of the

English Review, about the Vigilance Society. He is interviewed about his forthcoming lectures, and consults Drey about alternative Manchester theatres since he is still in dispute with Heys.

25   Heys backs down in his dispute with the Abbey.

26   WBY crosses to Dublin with FF by night boat.

27   Meets Dunsany who is pleased with the success of his play. Takes Maire O'Neill twice through *Deirdre*. Visits the Post-Impressionist Exhibition at the Dublin Arts Club and in the evening sees Dunsany's *King Argimenes and the Unknown Warrior* at the Abbey.

28   Consults Jack Yeats about JBY's return to Dublin from New York and they each send him £5. Consults O'Rourke about the Abbey players' financial grievances. AEFH's solicitors demand the proceeds from the sale of the Abbey, which should have taken place by 1 December 1910. In the evening WBY sees *King Argimenes* for the second time and learns from Mair that C. P. Scott has offered to arbitrate in the dispute between AEFH and the Abbey over the payment of her final subsidy.

30   Spends three hours dictating statements about the dispute with AEFH for Scott. In the evening attends rehearsals of *Deirdre*.

31   Attends rehearsals of *Deirdre* in the morning and afternoon. In the evening he and LR add more to the statements for Scott.

February

1   (Wed) Seeks W.F Bailey's advice about the letter from AEFH's solicitors. Is impressed with Maire O'Neill's acting at a dress rehearsal of *Deirdre*. In the evening writes to Scott, with a covering letter to Mair.

2   In the morning attends a Committee Meeting at the Abbey which approves the Manchester programme, and proposes a committee of 3 actors to discuss the Company's financial grievances. In the evening WBY attends a production of *Deirdre* (revived with LR's *Cross Roads* and AG's *Coats*) and afterwards goes on to a party in Bailey's rooms.

3   Meets a depressed Lord Castletown in the street. Gogarty phones that Dowden is resigning his Chair at TCD and that Mahaffy, the Provost, is now eager that WBY should succeed him. WBY sees *Deirdre* again.

6   Instructs Whitney and Moore to inform AEFH's solicitors that the Abbey Directors accept Scott's offer of arbitration. Attends a meeting of players which rejects the plan to elect three representatives to discuss salaries, but unanimously urges a system of teaching. In the evening WBY crosses to London.

8   Spends all day writing letters. Reading Fielding's *Tom Jones*.

9   Working on *The Player Queen*.

14–15   Working on his lecture.

16	Lectures on 'The Irish Intellectual Movement' at The Little Theatre.
17	Working on *The Player Queen*.
18	Travels to Manchester by an early train; has lunch there with Mair and his friends, and goes on to Dublin to see the first Abbey production of *The Land of Heart's Desire*.
19	Returns to Manchester from Dublin via Holyhead.
20	Conducts a lighting rehearsal in Manchester, where he stays with the Dreys.
21	Leaves Manchester for Norwich, where he sees Nugent Monck's production of *The Countess Cathleen* and stays overnight.
22	Returns to Manchester for a successful production of his *Deirdre*.
25	Goes to see Mair and probably meets Scott. In the evening attends a performance of *The Playboy*.
26	Leaves Manchester for London, where he dines with Gosse to discuss Academic Committee business.
28	Feeling languid after the excitement of many plays.

March

2	(Thu) Making changes in the first half of *Deirdre*. Dines with Clive Bell.
4–6	Weekend guest of Lady Katherine Somerset at Reigate Priory, where he meets Winston Churchill. During this stay he visits Mrs Watts's Potteries.
6	Signs the arbitration document and sends it to AG for forwarding to the solicitors and to Scott.
7	Doing about an hour a day on *The Player Queen*.
9	Lunches with Sara Allgood at the Brices to discuss her future at the Abbey. In the evening goes to the Trevelyans.
c.10	Sees Masefield's play, *The Witch*, and admires its power.
13	Invites Masefield to dinner to meet Eric Maclagan.
14	Working on a statement denouncing Roberts's publication of Synge's articles. The INTS incorporated under the Companies Consolidation Act (1908) thus acquiring the Abbey Theatre from AEFH. In the evening WBY goes to see Sara Allgood, O'Donovan and Fay in Johanna Redmond's *Falsely True* at the Palace Theatre.
19	Writes to protest against an attempt to blackball MG at the Dublin Arts Club.
23	Goes to Norwich to see Nugent Monck's production of *The Book of Job* and stays overnight.
25	Attends a luncheon party given by Lady Desborough, where he meets and likes Arthur Balfour.
27	Sends AG his commentary on AEFH's statement about the Abbey subsidy. Is feeling out of sorts, diagnosed as nervous indigestion.

28   Goes to Dublin to sort out the legal problems connected with the Abbey.

31   Chairs a meeting at the Abbey to discuss the duties of the 'Consultations Committee' and the dissolution of the INTS.

April

6   (Thu) Returns proofs of the new version of *Deirdre* to Bullen.

7   In the afternoon attends a memorial address for the classicist S. H. Butcher given by Gilbert Murray for the Academic Committee, with Haldane in the chair.

8   AG takes WBY to Paris to work on *Visions and Beliefs* and to help him recover from nervous indigestion. While there he writes 'At the Abbey Theatre'.

9   Transfers 9 shares in the NTS to Philip Hanson.

26   Calls on Davray in Paris.

29   Scott decides in favour of the Abbey Directors in their dispute with AEFH over the witholding of her last subsidy.

May

1   (Mon) Returns to London from Paris. In the evening sees Franco Leoni about setting *The Countess Cathleen* to music, with Clara Butt singing the leading role.

2   Goes to Stratford-upon-Avon to see the Abbey produce his *Deirdre* there.

4   Returns to London and writes a conciliatory letter to AEFH, telling her that the Abbey will not accept the money awarded by Scott.

5   AEFH sends a bitter telegram, refusing conciliation: 'repentance must come first'.

8   AG calls on WBY before leaving for Ireland. He has started a new lyric.

9   Sends AG the Deed of Dissolution of the NTS.

11   Leoni calls and tells WBY that he hopes to get *The Countess Cathleen* done at Covent Garden. Stormy meeting of the Academic Committee over WBY's proposal of Shaw for membership. Still working at his lyric, probably 'Brown Penny' (*VP*, 268).

15   At work every day on his lyric, which 'may not be very good'.

21   Has finished his lyric. Gosse tells him that Shaw headed the first poll in the election to the Academic Committee.

23   Sees LR.

27   In the evening sees James Roche, acting for George Tyler of Liebner & Co, and Gaston Mayer, about an Abbey tour of the USA in the autumn.

29   Sees Curtis Brown to discuss an American tour for the Abbey Company.

30	Goes to Oxford to see the Abbey Company on tour there.
31	Returns to London to ensure Shaw's election to the Academic Committee on the second ballot. Writes Aleel's lyric 'Lift up the white knee ...' for the new second scene of *The Countess Cathleen* (*VPl*, 57–9), inspired by seeing the Russian ballet.

June

2	(Fri) Calls on Shaw to discuss the Academic Committee and the Abbey taking *Blanco Posnet* to America.
3	'The Folly of Argument' (Diary; *UP* II. 394–6) published in the *Manchester Playgoer*. WBY Stays with Ethel Sands until 5 June.
5	The Abbey Company opens a three-week season at the Court Theatre, London. WBY attends most of the performances.
9	Interview with WBY in the *Pall Mall Gazette*.
13	Meets the agent who is arranging the American tour at Hugh Lane's.
*c.*21	Stays with Eva Fowler in Brasted, Kent, to work on material for Leoni.
24	Returns to London to see AG's new version of *The Image* and goes on to Ethel Sands for the weekend.

July

2	(Sun) 'John Shawe-Taylor' (obituary; *E & I*, 343–5) published in the *Observer*.
10	Craig dines with WBY at 7.00 pm.
15	Goes every afternoon to Cheyne Walk where AG is staying to plan the American tour and an Abbey School of Acting that will constitute a second company in Dublin while the main company is away.
16	Attends a public dinner at the Café Royal to celebrate Gordon Craig's return to England, but declines to take the chair to avoid proposing the King's health.
17	Lunches with Mrs Asquith in Downing Street.
19	Leaves London for Dublin.
20	Gives his cousin Ruth Pollexfen away at her marriage to Charles Lane-Poole in St Columba's College Chapel.
21	Goes to Coole, where he spends the mornings rewriting *The Countess Cathleen* and the afternoons on theatrical correspondence and reading plays submitted to the Abbey.
22	Appoints Nugent Monck to run the proposed Abbey Acting School.
*c.*25	Receives a copy of René Francis's translation of Flaubert's *Temptation of St. Anthony*, and reads it over the following days.
26	*Synge and the Ireland of his Time* published.

August

23	(Wed) Leaves Coole for London.
24	Dines with Monck, who is anxious to produce *Oedipus*.
25	Meets Gaston Mayer for an hour in the morning, settling details of the Abbey's American tour. Later sees Curtis Brown.
26	Leaves London for Dublin.
27	Dictates to his typist, Raven Byrne.
28	Has satisfactory interview with Fred O'Donovan about his future at the Abbey. Dines with Gogarty in the evening.
29	Stays with the Dunsanys in Meath until 1 September. Works in his room each day until the late afternoon.
30	Rewriting the Abbey Appeal and revising *The Countess Cathleen*.

September

1	(Fri) Returns to Dublin from Dunsany Castle in the evening.
2	Continues rewriting *The Countess Cathleen*. Discusses with LR his future as business manager of the Abbey Company.
3	Finishes the new version of *The Countess Cathleen*.
4	In the evening attends the W. A. Henderson Benefit Performance at the Abbey, consisting of musical turns and two one-act pieces.
5	Lunches with LR and Bailey to discuss Abbey affairs. Attends a rehearsal of *Deirdre* and alters the stage management at the beginning of the play. Sends a copy of an Abbey profit sharing agreement to AG.
6	Meets Edward Synge and Gogarty. Sees his *Deirdre* performed at the Abbey, where Maire O'Neill informs him that her doctor forbids her going to America.
7	Finds Cathleen Nesbitt disappointing in the first act of the *Playboy*.
c.9	Goes to Coole.
13	Arrives in Queenstown (Cobh) ready to embark on the *S. S. Zeeland* with the Abbey Players for their first American tour. During the voyage he makes a selection from Lord Dunsany's work for Cuala.
21	Rehearses the Company on arrival in Boston, and gives interviews and dictates articles.
23	The first ever American performance of the Abbey Company takes place at the newly-opened Plymouth Theatre, where they present *In the Shadow of the Glen*, *Birthright*, and *Hyacinth Halvey*. WBY makes a speech about the Abbey's work.
26	Attends Abbey performances of *The Well of the Saints* and *The Workhouse Ward*.
28	Lectures on the Irish National Theatre Movement to the Boston Drama League.

| 29 | AG arrives in Boston. |
| 30 | First attack on the Abbey Players in the Catholic periodical *America*. |

October

2	(Mon) Lectures with AG at the College Club, Boston.
3	Violent attack on the Abbey Players by Dr J. T. Gallagher in a letter to the *Boston Post*.
4	With LR a guest of honour at a lunch in Boston.
5	Writes to the Boston and New York papers defending the Abbey against charges of paganism. At 4.00 pm he lectures at Harvard University on 'The Theatre of Beauty'.
6	Speaks after a lunch given by the John Boyle O'Reilly Club.
7	Speaks after a lunch given by the Twentieth Century Club.
9	Lunches with the President of Wellesley College and in the afternoon lectures there on the Irish Theatre.
10	Lectures to the Browning Society with AG. Leaves for New York.
11	Interviewed by the New York press at the Waldorf-Astoria. In the evening he dines with JBY and his friends at Petipas, the pension at 14 West 29th Street where JBY lodges. AG granted a patent for the Abbey Theatre for 21 years, running from 1 December 1910.
12	Lectures at Bryn Mawr College on the Irish Theatre.
*c.*14	Returns to Boston.
15	With AG and members of the Company attends an evening reception given by Mrs Marie Curley in Roxbury.
16	The Abbey Players' first American production of *The Playboy of the Western World* receives a fairly peaceful reception at the Plymouth Theatre.
17	Attends a professional matinée given by the Abbey Company for Boston actors. Leaves Boston for New York.
18	Sails from New York on the *Lusitania*.
23	Arrives in Liverpool and returns to London that evening.
24	Dines with Craig to propose that he should give Tyler the rights in his screens for WBY's plays, and that he should produce four of WBY's plays for Dublin and the USA.
26	Leaves for Dublin to help Monck with the Acting School.
27	Reads first part of Moore's satirical memoir *Hail and Farewell*. Sees a rehearsal of the chorus of *Oedipus* at the Acting School.
30	Interviewed by the *Irish Times* about the Abbey's reception in America. In the evening sees a rehearsal of *The Interlude of Youth*, given by the Acting School.

November

| *c.*1 | (Wed) Begins rewriting *The Hour-Glass* in verse. |
| *c.*2 | Returns to London from Dublin. |

4	Sees James Roche who thinks W. H. Brayden, editor of the *Freeman's Journal*, is stirring up opposition to the Abbey Company in America.
6	Invites Craig and his wife to his 'Monday Evening'.
7	Lunches with Craig at the Rendezvous Restaurant in Dean Street.
8	Takes Monck's cottage in Norwich for a week to work at his plays undistracted.
11	'The Theatre of Beauty' (address; *UP* II. 397–401) published in *Harper's Weekly*.
15	Returns to Dublin.
16	Attends the Acting School's performances of *The Interlude of Youth*, *The Marriage*, and *The Shadow of the Glen* before an invited audience and makes a speech.
17	WBY and Monck meet Maire O'Neill at Bailey's to plan the future of the Acting School. WBY sees Martyn to find out if priests would support the Acting School if it specialized in religious drama.
21	Leaves Dublin for London.
25	Discusses the American reception of *The Playboy* with William Archer and also sees Shaw. Lays awake making a lyric, apparently the beginning of 'The Cold Heaven'.
26	Tries all morning to make more progress on 'The Cold Heaven', and continues to work at *The Player Queen*.
28	Sees reports in the London evening papers of the riot in New York over the Abbey's production of *The Playboy*. Sees Knoblock's *Kismet*, and remarks on its plagiarism from Colum's *The Desert*.
30	Crosses to Dublin and attends the Acting School's production of *The Second Shepherd's Play*, *Dervorgilla* and *The Workhouse Ward*.

December

2	(Sat) 'On Those Who Dislike the Playboy' (poem, *VP*, 294) published in the *Irish Review*. *Plays for an Irish Theatre* published by Bullen.
3	Attends Monck's rehearsal of the Acting School from 5.00 to 11.00 pm.
4	Attends a first dress rehearsal of the Acting School.
5	Attends a second dress rehearsal of the Acting School.
6	Attends a rehearsal of two acts of *The Countess Cathleen* by the Acting School. Goes to St Saviour's Priory to consult Fr D'Alton about the Acting School producing religious plays with clerical sanction.
7	Attends the Acting School's production of Rutherford Mayne's *Red Turf* and AG's *Dervorgilla*.

14–16	Attends all the performances of the Abbey School's productions of *The Second Shepherd's Play* and the revised version of *The Countess Cathleen*.
15	Attends the copyright performance of AG's *MacDaragh's* (later *McDonough's*) *Wife* at the Abbey.
18	Spends the day at the Abbey with Monck and Miss Moore, the dressmaker, demonstrating Craig's screens and hires a projectionist to help these experiments.
19	Leaves Dublin for London.
21	Sees Curtis Brown about a Music Hall project for the Abbey Company.
25	Sees Masefield in the morning and dines with Gosse in the evening.
26	Still at work on *The Countess Cathleen*, making changes suggested by the recent Dublin performance.

1912

January

2	(Tue) Has visits from Tennyson of the *TLS* and Miss Moore, the costume maker, and later sees Bailey who is on his way to the West Indies.
4	Prostrated for two days by a violent attack of indigestion.
5	Crosses to Dublin.
6	Dictates his revisions to Jebb's *Oedipus* to Monck and attends performances by the Acting School in the afternoon and evening.
10	Promoted to Theoricus Adeptus Minor, second stage of the $6°=5°$ grade, in the Stella Matutina after examination. Attends a dress rehearsal of AG's *MacDaragh's Wife*.
11	Attends the Acting School's performances of *MacDaragh's Wife*, *The Workhouse Ward*, *The Marriage* and *Red Turf*, which continue for a week. Deep in a lyric, possibly 'The Cold Heaven'.
12	Lectures on Ghosts and Apparitions to the Arts Club. Talks afterwards to Joseph Campbell and his wife.
13	Goes to London.
15	Attends a meeting of the Academic Committee.
17	Returns to Dublin.
18	Finishes the lyric he has been working on for seven or eight days. Is also writing *Oedipus* and attending rehearsals of the Acting School, which produces *The Building Fund*, *The Rising of the Moon* and *Dervorgilla* for a week. The Abbey Company is arrested in Philadelphia for presenting 'immoral or indecent plays', but is defended by Quinn and acquitted on 22 January.
20	St John Ervine and his wife Leonora dine with WBY.

21	Monck goes to England for a week and WBY takes over rehearsals and an elocution class. Revising *The Land of Heart's Desire*.
24	Leaves Dublin for London.
25	Lectures on Psychical Research to a large audience.
26	Goes to Ricketts', where he admires his design for a Japanese *King Lear*.
27–31	Working on his lecture to the Ghost Society, about which he is very nervous.
30	Receives royalties of £30 4s. 9d. from Unwin for *Poems*.

February

1	(Thu) Lectures very successfully to the Ghost Society on Psychic phenomena.
2	Returns to Dublin.
3	Sees the Acting School's production of *The Goal Gate* and the last act of *The Country Dressmaker*.
4	'The Story of the Irish Players' (article; *UP* II. 402–4) published in the Chicago *Sunday Record-Herald*.
5	Monck ill with a cold and so WBY takes some of the Acting School rehearsals. Quarrels again with Heys of the Gaiety Theatre over the selection of plays for the Abbey's planned tour to Manchester.
8	Sees *The Countess Cathleen* and *Spreading the News* at the Abbey.
12	In the evening sees rehearsals of *The Canavans* and of the new version of his *The Land of Heart's Desire*, which he believes he has purged of sentimentality.
14	Attends an Acting School performance of *The Canavans* and *The Tinker and the Fairy*, and meets the Duchess of Sutherland there.
15	Finishes the dialogue for *Oedipus*.
c.22	Out of sorts with indigestion and takes a short break in Margate, staying with the Tuckers. Has finished his version of *Oedipus* except for the chorus.
24	Returns to Dublin and sees another performance of the revised *Land of Heart's Desire*.
25	Urges Gosse to lead an Academic Committee deputation to the Home Secretary to protest against censorship.
29	The Acting School puts on *The Worlde and the Childe*.

March

1	(Fri) Early this month WBY rewrites *The Hour-Glass*, making a prose sketch and then working it over.
12	The Abbey Company returns from America. The School of Acting is dissolved and reconstituted as the Abbey's Second Company.
14	The First Abbey Company re-opens with *In the Shadow of the Glen*, *Birthright* and *The Workhouse Ward* but WBY is angered by

the bad acting habits that Arthur Sinclair seems to have picked up in America.

18   Attends a rehearsal of *The Mineral Workers* and *A Pot of Broth* and discusses a proposed agreement about the players' salaries with LR.

19   Attends the Second Company's performance of *A Pot of Broth* and *The Mineral Workers*.

21   In the morning addresses the assembled Abbey Company about the financial situation and informs them that salaries cannot be raised. In the evening leaves Dublin for Wales.

22   Lectures in Wales.

26   Returns to Dublin.

28   Attends the First Company's production of Boyle's *Family Failing*.

April

3   (Wed) Writes the poem 'On hearing that the Students ...'.

*c.*4   Leaves Dublin for London.

9   Sees Curtis Brown's representative, Maire Tempest, about contractual arrangements for Abbey plays and players to appear at the Coliseum and in other English music halls. Is trying to weave lyrical passages into *The Hour-Glass*. Depressed by a performance of *The Workhouse Ward* at the Prince of Wales Theatre.

10   Wires to Cathleen Nesbitt to come as replacement for Miss Weldon at the Prince of Wales Theatre.

11   Discusses terms for the production of *The Workhouse Ward* at the Prince of Wales Theatre with Curtis Brown's representative.

13   Receives and signs a new agreement for the production of Abbey plays and players at the Coliseum.

14   Working on revisions to *The Hour-Glass*.

22   Sees W. T. Horton in the evening.

May

2   (Thu) Dines at Eva Fowler's with Arthur Galton, OS and Aimée Lowther, who makes a vehement attack on him.

3   Reading Dryden to understand his use of rhyme on the stage.

4   Suffers another violent attack of indigestion and cannot work.

7   Sees the impresario Anning about the production of Abbey plays in London.

12   Gossips about politics with Mair of the *Manchester Guardian* and gives him the correspondence with Heys about the choice of Abbey plays for the Manchester tour.

14   Dines with Mair and his new wife Maire O'Neill. Continuing to rewrite *The Hour-Glass* in verse.

16   Working well: rising at 8.30 am each morning and devoting three hours to writing poetry. Farrell Pelly calls about the production of *The Workhouse Ward* at the Prince of Wales Theatre.

20	Attends a meeting of the Academic Committee.
21	Consults Percy Withers about the campaign to get a Civil List Pension for A. H. Bullen.
22	At Earl's Court to see *The Merchant of Venice* in a replica of the Globe Theatre.
23	Long conversation with Mrs Stewart, a London spiritualist, about dream experiences.
24	Spends £2 on second-hand books, mainly 17th century, on psychic subjects. Leaves London to stay with Eva Fowler in Brasted, Kent.
*c.*27	Returns to London.

June

2	(Sun) WBY and Newbolt go to Max Gate, Dorchester, to present Thomas Hardy with the Gold Medal of the Academic Committee in honour of his 72nd birthday. The presentation is made at dinner and they stay overnight.
3	Returns to London.
4	Sleeps 14 hours and wakes feeling well.
7	Sees OS.
8	Sees Gordon Craig.
12	Calls on the Shakespears for tea and praises Pound's poems 'The Return' and 'Apparuit' recently published in the *English Review*.
14	Sees Nathan of the Coliseum about the production of Abbey plays and players there.
*c.*15	Revised versions of *The Countess Cathleen* and *The Land of Heart's Desire* published by Unwin.
16	Lunches with Miss Amhurst at 23 Queens Gate Gardens. Goes on to see AG at Lane's Lindsey House in Cheyne Walk.
17	Sees the manager of the Coliseum.
22	Inscribes the new edition of *The Land of Heart's Desire* for Mabel Dickinson, with whom he is still having an affair.
23	At Gosse's with Walter Sickert, Robert Ross and Freya Stark.
26	Séance with the medium Mrs Thompson.
27	Meets AG at Lindsey House at 5.00 pm for discussions about the Theatre. At 7.30 pm dines with William Rothenstein to meet the Bengali poet Rabindranath Tagore.
28	Meets Walter Rummel at tea at the Shakespears; they discuss music for *The Countess Cathleen* and WBY sings a song. In the evening WBY attends a large séance at Cambridge House with Miss E. K. Harper as the medium.
29	Dines with FF and they go on to see Boyle's *Family Failing* at the Court Theatre.

July

7	(Sun) Reads from Tagore's *Gitanjali* at a soirée at Rothenstein's. Spends the week revising the translations of Tagore's poems.
10	Chairs an Indian Society Dinner for Tagore at the Trocadero Restaurant attended by 70 people, including MG, H. G. Wells and the composer Vaughan Williams.
11	Attends the Abbey's production of the revised *Countess Cathleen* at the Court Theatre.
14	James Joyce calls on WBY with his son Giorgio and has tea. WBY tells him that he has rewritten *The Countess Cathleen*.
15	Ervine and his wife at WBY's 'Monday Evening'.
18	Lunches at 1.00 pm with Tagore at the Hotel Gwalia and they go on to Woburn Buildings to discuss the translations of his poems. In the evening attends FF's final public performance on the psaltery at the Clavier Hall.
28	WBY spends the weekend at Ethel Sands' with George Moore.
*c.*30	Discusses the arrangements for an Abbey tour to America with Curtis Brown and Fred O'Donovan.

August

1	(Thu) Sees Pond's representative about an American lecture tour.
2	Arrives in Normandy to stay with MG. Works on his selection of Dunsany's work for Cuala.
7	A revised edition of vol. II of *The Poetical Works* (NY) published.
8	Thinks the recently written poems 'The Mountain Tomb' and 'To a Child Dancing' good. Has sent his preface for the Dunsany selection to Cuala and has written the introduction for *The Cutting of an Agate*. Is reading Stokes' *The Celtic Church*.
10	Finds that the regular country life in Normandy has cured his indigestion.
11	Starts his third lyric, 'Love and the Bird' ('A Memory of Youth'), and is continuing Stokes' *The Celtic Church*.
13	Has finished 'A Memory of Youth' (*VP*, 313–14) and thinks it one of his best poems. Accompanies MG in a violent storm to meet James and Margaret Cousins, who are to stay with her.
16	Leaves Normandy for London.
17	A violent attack of indigestion forces him to take to his bed and adopt a milk diet.
20	Leaves London by night train for Ireland and goes directly on to Coole where he works on Tagore's poems and his Introduction to *Gitanjali*, to be published by the India Society.

September

4	(Wed) Writes to the press to denounce Martin Harvey for surrendering to Irish groups by withdrawing *The Playboy* from his provincial tour. Continues working on Tagore's *Gitanjali*.
5	FF leaves permanently for Ceylon (Sri Lanka).
6	Sends Tagore his revised version of the poems in *Gitanjali*.
8	Falls into a daily routine at Coole, reading from 10 to 11 am, writing from 11 until lunch at 2 pm; after lunch reads until 3.30 pm, then walks in the woods or fishes until 5 pm. Thereafter writes letters or works until 7 pm when he goes out for an hour before dinner. Writing 'To a Squirrel at Kyle-na-no'.
10	Sends Rothenstein his Introduction to *Gitanjali*.
*c.*28	Goes to Dublin from Coole. *Poems* (1912) published late this month.

October

2	(Wed) Leaves Dublin for London, where he sees Craig about a possible production of the new version of *The Hour-Glass*.
*c.*3	*Selections from the Writings of Lord Dunsany*, with an Introduction by WBY, published.
*c.*4	Goes to stay with the Tuckers in Lynton, North Devon; OS and Dorothy Shakespear also there.
9	WBY, the Tuckers and the Shakespears return to London.
*c.*10	Goes to stay with Eva Fowler in Kent, and meets Elizabeth Radcliffe who produces automatic writing for him.
15	Lunches with Rothenstein and Tagore.
17	Sees Tagore about Abbey productions of his plays.
18	Goes to Dublin by morning boat; discovers that the production of Ervine's *The Magnanimous Lover* at the Abbey on 17 October has caused a short-lived controversy.
19	Travels to Coole by morning train. Sends 'At the Abbey Theatre' to the *Irish Review*.
21	Sends Pound a group of poems for *Poetry* (Chicago). Is writing 'The Grey Rock'.
23	The American edition of *The Green Helmet and Other Poems* published.
*c.*25	Leaves Coole for Dublin.
28	Lunches with Casimir Markiewicz who informs him that a Warsaw producer wants to put on Irish plays. Sees a rehearsal of the new *Hour-Glass*.
31	Crosses to London. About this time he receives H. J. C. Grierson's edition of Donne's poetry and understands Donne for the first time.

November

2	(Sat) Sees Curtis Brown about the dates of the next Abbey tour to America.

3	Trying to start a lyric without much success. The Nassau Hotel, WBY's and AG's Dublin base over the previous decade, closes down.
4	Collapses with violent indigestion and spends two days on his sofa eating nothing but bread and milk.
6	Cancels an appointment with Craig at 7.45 pm because of indigestion. Pound comes to help him, but they quarrel over Pound's rewriting of his poems for *Poetry*.
8	The indigestion attack continues, causing pains in his stomach and legs.
9	Reading the poetry of Wordsworth and Bridges; Wordsworth enrages him but he cries over Bridges.
10	Improving health allows him to return to a meat diet.
11	Crosses to Dublin.
12	Arrives in Coole by the morning train.
13	*The Cutting of an Agate* published by the Macmillan Company, New York.
14	Reading Tagore's plays. Annoyed that Pound has implicated him in a misunderstanding with Rothenstein over copies of Tagore's poems. Has finished 120 lines of a narrative poem ('The Grey Rock'). Is trying to get Tagore elected to the Academic Committee.
21	Urges JBY to write his autobiography.
30	Contracts with Maurice Browne of the Little Theatre, Chicago, for the production there of *On Baile's Strand* and *The Shadowy Waters*.

December

5	(Thu) Returns to Dublin from Coole by an evening train and begins poem 'The New Faces' (*VP*, 435).
7	Finishes 'The New Faces'. Sees the accountant Harris about a new financial scheme for the Abbey and wins approval for it. In the evening crosses to London. 'At the Abbey Theatre' (poem; *VP*, 264–5) published in the *Irish Review*. 'The Realists', 'The Mountain Tomb', 'To a Child dancing in the Wind', 'A Memory of Youth' and 'Fallen Majesty' (poems; *VP*, 309, 311, 312, 313, 314–15) published in *Poetry* (Chicago).
11	His doctor puts him on a sour milk cure for his indigestion attacks. An interview for *Great Thoughts* takes an hour and a half.
12	Interviewed by the *Daily News*. Works with LR on proposals for the Acting School and Second Company, and on plans for the production of a Strindberg play. Sees Masefield in the evening. Has a poem in his head which becomes 'On a Wealthy Man ...'.
c.13	Sees Ricketts.

14	Spends part of day in the British Museum looking up facts for his poem 'On a Wealthy Man', but work on it is interrupted by the proofs for his Tauchnitz selected poems.
15	Masefield dines with WBY.
16	Rothenstein and K. Ghose, a teacher at Tagore's school, call.
17	Wires O'Donovan about the Music Hall contracts.
18	Begins French lessons. Attends Mrs Annette Meakin's wedding. AG and Abbey Company depart for the second American tour.
21	Pound calls at 4.00 pm and stays until 2 am, going home by taxi. They discuss poetry and the Georgian Anthology; WBY is feeling gloomy about his work.
22	Correcting Tauchnitz proofs, particularly those of *The Countess Cathleen*. Sends a new version of *The Hour-Glass* to the typist to be copied. Calls to see AEFH who has been knocked down by a taxi. Hears that Mabel Beardsley is dying of cancer.
25	Finishes 'To a Wealthy Man' and returns to the revision of 'The Two Kings'. Dines with Masefield.
c.26	Interview with WBY in *Hearth and Home*.
30	Sturge Moore goes though WBY's new poems with him.
31	Reads his new poems to Pound and tells him his criticism is far more valuable than Sturge Moore's.

1913

January

1	(Wed) Sends Lane a copy of 'The Gift' ('To a Wealthy Man'). Revising 'The Two Kings' to get rid of Miltonic generalization. Meets Letitia Darragh at 5 pm to discuss plans for a Repertory Theatre in London.
4	Sees Letitia Darragh again and they decide to launch the Repertory Theatre.
5	Lunches with Lane and urges him to buy the land for a Dublin picture gallery himself. Goes afterwards to visit Mabel Beardsley, now in hospital; that night he begins to plan 'Her Courtesy', the first of a series of poems about her.
6	Revising the proofs for the Tauchnitz edition of his poems. Dines with Hone and persuades him to publish 'The Gift' in the *Irish Times* and to write an accompanying article.
7	Dines with Pound and gives him a copy of 'The Gift' for *Poetry* (Chicago).
8	Invites Dunsany to contribute a play to the opening night of the proposed London Repertory Theatre.
9	SMY sends him a copy of Jack Yeats's *Life in the West of Ireland*.

11	'The Gift' (poem, later 'To a Wealthy Man ...'; *VP*, 287–8) published in the *Irish Times*, with Hone's article in support of Lane's Gallery. WBY is still suffering intermittent bouts of indigestion and consulting his doctor, who puts him on a strict diet to lose 14lb.
13	Stephen Gwynn sends £5 for the Gallery, inspired by reading 'To a Wealthy Man'. Ervine comes in after dinner and WBY dissuades him from taking a libel action against the *Freeman's Journal*.
15	Visits a medium near Bond Street at 5 pm, after which he attends a French class. Dines with Hone and Joseph Campbell at 7.30 pm.
16	A. H. Bullen, who owes him £400, calls to tell him that Chapman and Hall are remaindering half of the 250 sets of *CW* they took. WBY suggests adding an extra volume of new work, so making Bullen's remaining 500 sets the only complete edition. Drinkwater also calls, seeking permission to produce AG's *The White Cockade* at his new Birmingham Repertory Theatre. In the evening WBY sees W. F. Bailey to discuss Abbey affairs and learns that O'Donovan has not shown him the Music Hall contract.
17	Lunches with Herbert Asquith, the Prime Minister, with AE, Walter de la Mare and Eddie Marsh.
18	Finishes 'Her Courtesy', his first poem about Mabel Beardsley, and begins 'Certain Artists bring her Dolls and Drawings', and others.
19	Visits Mabel Beardsley in hospital.
20	Has Ervine and his wife to dinner.
21	Has now written 3 lyrics on Mabel Beardsley and plans a fourth. Attends a lecture by Pound at 3.30 pm, sees one of his mystics at 5 pm and from 6 to 7 pm attends a Berlitz French class. At 8 pm has Pound to dinner; he also invites Rupert Brooke.
22	Sends Bullen detailed suggestions for the revision and amplification of *CW*. Sees the Prime Minister's Secretary about a Civil List Pension for Bullen. Dines with Rupert Brooke and Eddie Marsh and they stay until nearly midnight discussing poetry.
23	Travels to Dublin and lets his London rooms to Robert Gregory. Sees G. Sidney Paternoster's *The Dean of St. Patrick's* performed by the Abbey's Second Company and meets the author afterwards at the Arts Club.
24	WBY speaks at a crowded meeting of the Protestant Home Rule Association.
c.27	Returns to London.
28	Attends a meeting of the Academic Committee.
30	Dines at 7.30 pm at the House of Commons with Gwynn and meets the Irish MPs Lardner, Hazleton and Devlin.

February

2	(Sun) Visits Mabel Beardsley in hospital and has now written five poems about her. In the evening he sees Lane and learns that he has been informally offered a Gallery in London. They compose telegrams setting out Lane's conditions for a Dublin Gallery. Later this month Tauchnitz publish *A Selection from the Poetry of W. B. Yeats* in Leipzig.
3	Sends Mabel Beardsley his series of poems about her.
6	Dines with the artist and Blake expert W. Graham Robertson.
7	Deep in his 7th lyric about Mabel Beardsley. Receives a letter from O'Donovan giving details of an offer for an Abbey visit to Chicago.
9	Visits Mabel Beardsley in hospital.
13	Dines with Eva Fowler and the painter Sargent.
16	Sees Mabel Beardsley in hospital. In the evening goes to the Stage Society with a party of friends and has supper with them.
18	Sends FF his 'last' Mabel Beardsley poem, 'Her Race'. Has Stephen MacKenna and his wife to dinner.
23	Visits Mabel Beardsley in hospital, staying until 7 pm, and goes on to dine with Lane and Hone and his wife.
27	Reads with Wilfrid Gibson at Harold Monro's Poetry Bookshop.
28	Meets Bullen, who is full of publishing projects.

March

*c.*1	(Sat) Goes to see Ibsen's *The Pretenders*.
2	Dines at the Ervines' with Rupert Brooke and Eddie Marsh, who walk back into town with him.
3	Horton attends WBY's 'Monday Evening'; Rupert Brooke and Craig also there.
5	Finishes 'The Three Hermits' (*VP*, 298–9) and plans to write 'The Three Beggars'. Planning a project for poetic drama with Craig. Finishes his thirtieth French lesson and pays for 50 more.
7	Hears from Monck that he wants to resign as manager of the Abbey Company. Lunches with Craig to discuss the scheme for poetic drama. Dines with Ricketts and they go on to the Russian Ballet, which WBY finds exquisite and profound.
8	WBY takes Chair at Edith Roth Wheeler's ILS lecture, 'Romance in Irish Poetry and Drama' and speaks in defence of Synge.
10	W. Graham Robertson comes to dinner.
11	Attends a meeting of the Academic Committee to plan a reception for Tagore and goes on to a dinner at Raymond Buildings to celebrate Rupert Brooke's Fellowship at King's College, Cambridge, with Eddie Marsh, Mrs Churchill, Helen Asquith, Cynthia Asquith and others.
13	Meets Lane at a dinner party, who speaks of abandoning his plans for a Dublin Gallery.

15	Endures a stormy passage on his way from London to Dublin, where he is bored by a production of John Guinan's *The Cuckoo's Nest*.
16	Spends the morning with LR deciding on the Abbey programme for the remainder of the season. Sends AG a copy of 'The Three Hermits' and continues writing 'The Three Beggars'.
17	Goes through all the correspondence about the Lane Gallery and writes to the *Irish Times* in support of Edwin Lutyens' design of a building on a bridge over the Liffey. Sees the last half of Fitzmaurice's *The Country Dressmaker* and finds it surprisingly good.
18	Lectures on Craig at the Dublin Craig Exhibition.
19	Sees the accountant Harris about the financial reorganization of the Abbey.
23	Lectures on Tagore in Dublin.
24	Returns to London and finds that Dublin has upset his digestion again.
25	Pound and Ghose dine with WBY at Woburn Buildings. *Stories of Red Hanrahan: The Secret Rose: Rosa Alchemica* published by Bullen later this month.

April

2	(Wed) Sees Letitia Darragh, who tells him that Charles Cochran is prepared to finance the London Repertory Theatre. Also meets Granville-Barker.
3	Leaves for Birmingham at 2 pm to see Drinkwater's production of *The Countess Cathleen*, which he finds feeble. He stays with Drinkwater and finishes 'The Three Beggars', but decides that its metre is wrong and starts it again.
4	Edward Dowden's death renews WBY's interest in Chair of English at TCD.
5	Leaves Birmingham for Dublin to manage the Abbey for a week and give LR a break. 'The Grey Rock' (poem; *VP*, 270–6) published in the *British Review* and *Poetry* (Chicago).
6	Approves of the production of Hauptmann's *Hannele* at Abbey.
13	Finishes a week of Abbey rehearsals; has also been attending French lessons.
14	Irritated by an inaccurate interview in *TP's Weekly*.
15	Returns to London.
21	Visits Mabel Beardsley in hospital.
*c.*22–4	Has an attack of illness.
25	Sends ECY corrected proofs for the Cuala selection from his love poetry and suggests she should publish an edition of JBY's letters.
28	Visits the White Star office to find out when the Abbey Company returns from America.

29	Sets out for Stratford-upon-Avon to see Masefield's *Pompey* and on the way catches a violent cold which brings on indigestion.
30	Sees *Pompey* at Stratford. The First Abbey Company land at Queenstown (Cobh) after their American tour.

May

1	(Thu) Attends the crowning of the May Queen at Stratford and discusses his publishing affairs with Bullen. Owing to his illness, he returns to London instead of going on to Dublin as planned.
2	Still weak with cold and indigestion; he is to be X-rayed for gallstones and has lost nearly 28lb.
7	Finishes poem 'The Three Beggars' and writes another poem, probably 'Beggar to Beggar Cried' (*VP*, 299–300), in one sitting.
8	Sees his doctor who postpones the X-rays but insists upon a careful and precise routine.
9	Travels to Dublin by the morning boat to reply to a speech of the Lord Mayor in the evening.
10	Consults Louis Purser about the TCD Chair, and then Gogarty. Discusses Abbey affairs with Bailey and arranges the forthcoming London programme with LR. Sees and admires Lutyens' designs for a Gallery on the bridge site. Dines with Gogarty and J. E. Healy, editor of the *Irish Times*, before leaving by the night boat for England.
11	May have met George Hyde-Lees at lunch.
12	Attends at a disappointing 9.35 am séance at Cambridge House with the American medium Mrs Etta Wreidt.
13	A second 9.35 am séance with Mrs Wreidt is also a failure. Receives £249. 9s. 1d. from George Pollexfen's will. Tagore sends him poems to make a selection for a new book.
14	Makes a formal enquiry about the TCD Chair. Hears from Letitia Darragh that she has failed to raise the finance for the London Repertory Theatre.
15	Meets Elizabeth Radcliffe again at Eva Fowler's and becomes greatly excited by her facility for taking automatic script.
17	Spends the weekend at Lady Desborough's at Taplow Court with Lady Lyttelton and other congenial guests.
19	Returns to London from Taplow Court. Takes Elizabeth Radcliffe's automatic script to the British Museum to decipher the various languages in which it is written.
22	Arrives in Coole from London via Dublin. Is delighted with Tagore's new poems, which he is reading daily.
24	Has a symolic dream of the Middletons and their house at Rosses Point. Writes 'The Witch' (*VP*, 310).
30	Returns to Dublin from Coole.

June

3	(Tue) Attends a séance with Mrs Wreidt at Cambridge House.
7	Takes more of Elizabeth Radcliffe's automatic scripts to the British Museum.
9	The Abbey Company begins its London tour at the Court Theatre and WBY attends most of the performances in the following fortnight.
10	Presides at a lecture by T. W. Rolleston at University College, London, to celebrate the 21st anniversary of the foundation of the ILS.
11	Dines at Lady Hamilton's with Roger Fry, Charles Whibley and Eddie Marsh, to whom he talks after dinner, regaling him with accounts of his latest occult research and scandalous stories about George Moore.
12	Meets Elizabeth Radcliffe at the Abbey plays.
15	Extremely alarmed that he may have made Mabel Dickinson pregnant and that he will have to marry her.
18	Has symbolic dream of a black juggler; that evening WBY meets Audrey Locke for the first time when Horton brings her to dine; they get astral writing and discuss the Radcliffe scripts. Begins a row with ECY over the Cuala publication of Dowden's poems, of which he disapproves.
25	Insists that the Cuala Press issue a circular dissociating him from the publication of Dowden's poems.
26	Attends a séance at Cambridge House.
27	Ananda Coomaraswami, his wife and child, dine with WBY.
28	Sees Curtis Brown about Liebler's inability to pay dramatists' royalties for the recent American tour and agrees to a temporary compromise. Attends an Abbey matinée at the Court Theatre.
29	Horton and Audrey Locke dine with WBY and continue psychic experiments with a planchette, a form of ouija board; Sturge Moore, and perhaps George Hyde-Lees, also present.
30	Attends first night of *The Gombeen Man* and speaks to George Moore and Orpen.

July

1	(Tue) Greatly relieved to discover that Mabel Dickinson's 'pregnancy' is a false alarm. In the evening attends another Abbey performance of R. J. Ray's *The Gombeen Man* at the Court; meets Lane there and discusses possible financial support for the Abbey with him and Sheffield Neave.
2	Trying to arrange a special performance of Shaw's *Blanco Posnet* in aid of Lane's Dublin Gallery. Attends another performance of *The Gombeen Man* in the evening.
3	Consults Shaw about the special performance of *Blanco Posnet* and also sees Mrs Leslie and Lady Powerscourt about this. Goes

on to the Court Theatre to see a dress rehearsal of Tagore's *The Post Office* and later gives a poetry reading at Harold Monro's Poetry Bookshop to a packed audience.

5   Has a symbolic dream of being on board a ship. Sees an agent about an Abbey tour to America, starting in January 1914.

7   Sees LR at 1 pm and goes on to stay with Eva Fowler at Brasted, where he works on Elizabeth Radcliffe's automatic script, copying out the Greek and Latin.

12   Returns to London from Kent and sees an Abbey performance of Tagore's *The Post Office*.

14   At 3 pm attends a private performance of *Blanco Posnet* at the Court Theatre in aid of the Municipal Gallery and makes a speech. Immediately afterwards he returns to Eva Fowler's in Kent and conducts more experiments with Elizabeth Radcliffe and her automatic script.

15   Getting 'wonderful' results with Elizabeth Radcliffe's automatic writing, especially in the interpretation of symbols.

17   Returns to London from Kent and begins to check Elizabeth Radcliffe's script at the British Museum.

19   Lunches at Sir Ian and Lady Hamilton's with Eddie Marsh and tells them of his latest occult investigations.

20   Traces Anna Louise Karsch, John Mirehouse and Henry Larkin, three of the spirits in Elizabeth Radcliffe's script. Sees Tagore, who asks if Radcliffe will do automatic writing for him.

21   Spends the morning at the British Museum tracing the spirits mentioned in Elizabeth Radcliffe's script.

22   Takes Elizabeth Radcliffe's script to the Catalan, Coptic and Assyrian departments of the British Museum and obtains a copy of the will of John Mirehouse from Somerset House. Visits Sturge Moore and they compose a letter to the Royal Society of Literature advocating procedural rules and a revision of the terms relating to the award of the Polignac Prize.

23   Leoni calls to ask for the Italian rights to WBY's and AG's plays, and repeats his suggestion of turning some of them into operas. WBY continues his study of Radcliffe's scripts for the rest of the month.

25   *A Selection from the Love Poetry of William Butler Yeats* published.

27   Visits Norwich to discuss theatrical matters with Monck and remains there until 29 July, staying at the Maid's Head Hotel.

c.31   Visits Oxford to consult experts about the Radcliffe scripts.

August

1   (Fri) Sends ECY the MS of Tagore's *The Post Office* for publication at Cuala and again insists that Cuala issue a circular dissociating him from the publication of Dowden's poems.

*c.*3	Goes to Winchelsea to investigate Elizabeth Radcliffe's spirits.
5	Leaves London to consult Kathleen Pallister, a medium in Bath. Stays there until the 9th and writes the first version of 'Romance in Ireland' ('September 1913').
9	Back in London; sees Tagore and Iseult Gonne.
13	Receives information about Thomas Emerson, one of Elizabeth Radcliffe's spirits, from the Home Office through the influence of Mrs Raymond Asquith. George Hyde-Lees, later his wife, assists him in the identification of the German spirits.
16	Stays for ten days with Pound at The Prelude, Colmans Hatch, Sussex, a cottage belonging to Eva Fowler, where he finishes an essay for Coomaraswamy and continues writing 'September 1913'.
26	Filled with bitterness on learning from the *Morning Post* that Lane's Gallery project is at an end. Returns to London in the afternoon to attend a farewell dinner for Tagore.
28	Visits the Coliseum in the hope of seeing the manager about withdrawing O'Donovan from the music hall performances of *The Workhouse Ward*, but, after waiting an hour in vain, leaves.
29	Dines at the Hamiltons, with Lady Hamilton on one side and Katherine Lyttelton on the other.
30	Questions the actor Farrell Pelly about his performance in the Coliseum production of *The Workhouse Ward* and the reason for the play's failure.
31	Goes to Folkestone to see Edwin Ellis, who has suffered a severe stroke.

September

2	(Tue) Leaves London for Dublin, where he sees LR about theatrical affairs.
3	Travels to Coole by morning train; remains in Galway until late October, writing several poems and a long essay on the Elizabeth Radcliffe scripts.
6	'The Three Hermits' (poem; *VP*, 298–9) published in the *Smart Set*.
7	Finishes 'Romance in Ireland'.
8	'September 1913' (poem; *VP*, 289–90) published in the *Irish Times* under the title 'Romance in Ireland'.
16	Writes 'To a Friend whose Work has come to Nothing' and 'Paudeen' (*VP*, 290–1).
20	Writes 'Running to Paradise' (*VP*, 300–1) and begins 'When Helen Lived' (*VP*, 293), 'The Magi' and 'The Dolls' (*VP*, 319).
29	Finishes 'When Helen Lived'. Writes 'To a Shade' (*VP*, 292–3).

October

4	(Sat) 'The Two Kings' (poem; *VP*, 276–86) published in the *British Review* and *Poetry* (Chicago). *Poems Written in Discouragement* published later this month.

13	Has finished his essay on Elizabeth Radcliffe's scripts. LR resigns as manager of the Abbey, but stays on until April 1914.
18	Write to tell James Stephens that he has been awarded the Polignac Prize for 1913 for *The Crock of Gold*.
19	Writes 'The Hour before Dawn' (*VP*, 302–7).
*c.*24	Travels to Dublin from Coole to attend séances.
30	Lectures to the Dublin branch of the Psychical Research Society, giving an account of Elizabeth Radcliffe's automatic script.

November

1	(Sat) Writes to the *Irish Worker* denouncing the action of employers, police and the press in curtailing the civil liberties of the workers locked out in the bitter Dublin industrial dispute of 1913. This reconciles him to AE.
2	Crosses from Dublin to London.
4	Sees Lane about continuing the campaign for the Municipal Gallery. Lane tells him that he has made a new will, bequeathing his picture collection to London, but will make a new collection for Dublin.
7	Awarded a prize by *Poetry* (Chicago) for the best poem of 1913 ('The Grey Rock') but asks them to give most of it to Pound. Sees Pound in the evening and tells him he will use the remaining £10 to commission a book-plate from Sturge Moore.
8	Attends an Indian Society Dinner and makes a speech. Sits next to Alice Meynell.
10	Goes for the winter to Stone Cottage, Colman's Hatch, Sussex, with Pound as his secretary. They fence together in the evenings.
13	Beginning of a dispute with the Abbey players over distribution of money originally earned by them for the now abandoned Dublin Gallery.
15	'The Three Beggars' (poem; *VP*, 294–7) published in *Harper's Weekly*. WBY visits London and returns to Sussex.
17	Visits London for his 'Monday Evening', at which he is obliged to ask Marinetti to stop bawling out his poems because the neighbours are complaining of the noise. He also consults Sturge Moore about the design of his book-plate.
20	Rewriting his American lectures, in particular 'The Theatre of Beauty'.
22	Writes 'The Peacock'.
24	Goes to London and stays there until 29 November. Suffering from bad eye-sight.
25	Meets Lane at a performance of Shaw's *Great Catherine* at the Vaudeville Theatre.
27	Disturbances at Abbey production of *The Playboy* in Liverpool.

28	Presents the Polignac Prize to James Stephens at the Caxton Hall, London, on behalf of the Royal Society of Literature. Consults Shaw about the dispute with the Players over the rights to the money earned by performances in aid of Lane's now abandoned Gallery.
29	The Liverpool police ban a matinée of *The Playboy* for fear of demonstrations. WBY sees Shaw for advice and writes to *The Times* in protest. Returns to Sussex in the evening.

December

3	(Wed) Writes the poem 'Two Years Later' (*VP*, 312–13) and, at about this time, 'Pardon old fathers ...'.
4	The Abbey Company sends AG a joint letter insisting upon their right to the money earned for the abandoned Gallery scheme.
5	WBY visits London and meets Elizabeth Radcliffe at Eva Fowler's.
6	Goes to Oxford for the day to read his Radcliffe lecture to Professor Harold Hartley.
7	Back in London, consults AG about the dispute with the Abbey actors.
15	The Abbey players call on legal advice in their dispute over the Gallery money.
17	Despite a severe cold, WBY comes up from Sussex to attend a séance with the American medium Mrs Herbine.
18	Gives a lecture at OS's house in London.
20	Sees AG at 7.30 pm and stays up until late, reading to Pound.
23	Returns to Sussex from London.
24	Sends Professor Hartley the MS of the Radcliffe script.
30	Goes to London.
31	Returns to Stone Cottage.

1914

January

3	(Sat) Finishes poem 'Pardon old fathers ...' (*VP*, 269–70) and sends a copy to AG.
4	Advises AG on her dispute with George Moore over his accusations in *Hail and Farewell* that she had been a Protestant proselyter. Is writing a note on the Lane Pictures.
5	Working at the lecture he is to give at the City Temple.
6	Continues to work on his lecture. Pound and he are reading the Abbé de Villars' book of Rosicrucian magic, *Comte de Gabalis*.
7	Goes to London from Stone Cottage with Pound.
8	After dining with AG, WBY lectures at 8 pm at the City Temple with the Revd Campbell in the Chair.

9	Goes at 11 am to Mrs Fowler's London house to hear her 'Spirit MSS' and stays to lunch. In the evening has dinner with AG. Develops a violent cold.
11	Back in Colmans Hatch, he dictates 21 letters to Pound.
13	Writes 'While I, from that reed-throated whisperer'.
16	Leaves Stone Cottage with reluctance after an unusually creative winter.
17	Visits Mabel Beardsley in hospital in the afternoon and entertains Yone Noguchi, the Japanese poet and teacher, to dinner in the evening.
18	Motors to Sussex to pay formal tribute to Wilfrid Scawen Blunt with Pound, Plarr, Sturge Moore and others. They lunch off peacock at 12.30 pm, then present Blunt with a stone box containing poetic tributes. Pound reads his commendatory verses and WBY makes a speech. At 3.30 pm Belloc joins the party, and the poets leave at 5.00 pm in a motor hired by WBY from Harrods at a cost of £5.
19	Busy all day.
20	Leaves London at 1 pm for Dublin to sort out the trouble over the distribution of money raised for the Lane Gallery and finds the Company very bitter. Visits the Arts Club in the evening and stays at the Sackville Street Club.
21	Rehearses *The King's Threshold* and afterwards holds a meeting with the Abbey Company to discuss the dispute over the Gallery Fund and salaries in general.
22	Sees Bailey about the dispute with Company over the Gallery Fund.
23	Sees Arthur Sinclair about taking the Gallery Fund dispute to arbitration, and then accompanies Bailey and LR to see the lawyer, Stritch. In the evening LR suggests that, although giving up the managership of the Theatre, he should continue to act as a producer.
24	Sees *The King's Threshold* at the Abbey. The trouble over the Gallery Fund deepens when Arthur Sinclair refuses to sign his contract for the forthcoming American tour.
25	Inspects the new scenery for *The Canavans* at the Abbey, and crosses over to London by the night boat.
26	Dines with Pound before his 'Monday Evening'.
30	Sees a Miss Ward about joining the Abbey Company. Packs for America and dines with Eva Fowler in the evening.
31	Leaves for his American lecture tour, departing from Euston at 11.50 am for Liverpool where he joins the *Lusitania*. Meets Lily Carstairs on the boat.

February

1   (Sun) Very rough seas keep WBY to his bed for three days without eating.

4   Ventures from his cabin to meet his fellow passengers.

7   Arrives in New York in the morning, a day late because of the storms. Sees a great deal of his father. 'Notoriety' (poem; *VP*, 320–1) published in the *New Statesman*.

9   Lectures to the University Club, Brooklyn, on 'The Theatre of Beauty'.

10   Lecture on 'Contemporary Poetry' to a Poetry Society luncheon.

11   Lectures in the morning on 'The Theatre' for the League for Political Education, New York.

12   Lectures at 8.15 pm to the Montreal Arts Association on 'The Theatre of Beauty'.

13   Lectures to the Toronto Gaelic League on 'The Theatre of Beauty'.

14   Lectures on 'The Theatre of Beauty' at St Catherine's, Ontario, where he remains until 16 February as the guest of a hotel proprietor.

16   Lectures at 8.15 pm to the Twentieth Century Club, Buffalo, on 'Contemporary Poetry'.

17   Lectures to Wells College. The Abbey begins its Chicago tour.

18   At Rochester, New York, and calls on the Crangles in Buffalo.

19   Lectures to the Twentieth Century Club, Detroit, on 'The Theatre of Beauty'.

20   Lectures in Cleveland, Ohio.

21   Lectures in the afternoon at Kenyon College, Gambier, Ohio.

23   Lectures in the evening to the Twentieth Century Club, Chicago, on 'The Theatre of Beauty'.

24   Lectures in the afternoon to the Chicago University Lecture Association in the Fine Arts Theatre and, in the evening, to the Fortnightly Club, after which he attends the Abbey Company's production of *The King's Threshold*.

26   Lectures in the afternoon to the Chicago Fortnightly Club and in the evening to the Book and Play Club.

28   Lectures in the morning to the Chicago Teachers' Association and in the evening at Northwestern University, Evanston, on 'Synge and the Ireland of his Time'.

March

1   (Sun) Guest of honour at a supper given by *Poetry* (Chicago) at the Cliff Dwellers, Orchestra Hall, Chicago, where he speaks on 'Contemporary Poetry', and is thanked in a brief reply by Nicholas Vachel Lindsay.

2   Leaves Chicago.

3	In Memphis, Tennessee, where he has a heavy cold and finds everything except the climate detestable. Lectures at 3 pm to the Nineteenth Century Club and in the evening to the Goodwyn Institute on 'The Theatre of Beauty'.
4	Leaves Memphis for Cincinnati.
5	Lectures at 2.30 pm to the Woman's Club, Cincinnati, on 'The Theatre of Beauty' and attends a reception and dinner given in his honour by the Women's Club, the MacDowell Society and the Drama League.
6	Leaves Cincinnati for Pittsburgh.
7	Lectures in Pittsburgh in the afternoon and evening.
8	Writes from Pittsburgh to congratulate Pound on his engagement to Dorothy Shakespear.
10	Lectures in the evening to the Gaelic Society of Washington, DC on 'The Theatre of Beauty'.
11	Returns to New York, staying at the National Arts Club, Gramercy Park, but exhausted by a cold. Agrees to prolong his American tour at Pond's request. Delighted when Quinn writes to make up their quarrel, and tries to telephone him at once.
12	Meets Quinn for lunch before leaving for Washington, Connecticut.
13	Lectures in the evening at Amherst College, Massachusetts, on 'Synge and the Ireland of his Time'.
14	At Amherst, revises 'While I, from that reed-throated warbler'.
16	Lectures at Amherst College in evening on 'Contemporary Poetry'.
17	Lectures in the evening at Yale University, and stays with the bookseller E. Byrne Hackett. Makes more revisions to 'While I, from that reed-throated warbler' ('Notoriety').
18	Lectures in the afternoon to the Women's Club, Stanford, Connecticut on 'Contemporary Poetry'.
19	Lectures at 5.00 pm at Amherst College on 'The Theatre of Beauty', followed by a reception in the Faculty Club.
20	Leaves Amherst in the morning, arriving at Montclair, New Jersey, in the afternoon for an evening lecture.
21	Lectures in the evening at Orange, New Jersey, and returns to New York where he is reunited with Quinn.
22	Spends the day with Quinn in New York and also sees JBY, Mrs McGuinness and William Bourke Cockran.
23	Lectures to the Drama League of New York after lunch at the home of Mrs Benjamin Nicoll.
24	Lectures in the afternoon in Philadelphia.
25	Lectures in Brooklyn in the evening.
26	Lectures in the afternoon to the University of Pennsylvania. Returns to New York and goes with Quinn to visit JBY at his lodgings.

27	During his last week in New York WBY sees more of JBY, has dinner with the Hunekers and attends a luncheon given in his honour by Bourke Cockran.

April

1	(Wed) Quinn gives a farewell dinner for WBY at Delmonico's, after which he accompanies him to the boat.
2	WBY sails for England on the *Adriatic*.
10	Arrives in London.
14	Arrives in Dublin where he sees AG and attends a performance of her *Kincora* by the Abbey's Second Company.
18	Returns to London from Dublin and probably attends an afternoon party hosted by Hope Shakespear for his daughter and Ezra Pound.
19	Spends the morning listening to Eva Fowler and her sister denouncing Pound for his bad manners.
20	Acts as best man at Pound's marriage to Dorothy Shakespear.
22	Sends Macmillan his Preface for Tagore's *The Post Office*.
23	Delivers a lecture on 'Ghosts and Dreams' to the London Spiritualist Alliance at the Salon of the Royal Society of British Artists.
29	Trouble with the First Abbey Company who are returning from their American tour and accuse WBY and AG of using their profits to fund the Second Company. WBY has a bad cold.
30	Sees A. P. Wilson, the new Abbey manager, about the dispute with the First Company. Lunches at Eva Fowler's and tires himself out talking to a priest about ghosts.

May

1	(Fri) Goes to see Charles Ricketts with Binyon; they discuss spiritualism and WBY asks Ricketts to design costumes for *The King's Threshold*.
2	Twelve poems from *Responsibilities* published in *Poetry* (Chicago).
4	Sees his doctor, who tells him he is not to work for the present.
5	Sees the occultist Dr Robert Felkin and discusses Elizabeth Radcliffe's automatic script with him.
7	Sees his doctor again, who prescribes a tonic and a new diet. Corrects proofs of *The Post Office*.
8	Leaves for Paris with Everard Feilding to investigate a miracle at Mirabeau. He immediately arranges a séance in Paris with a musical medium.
9	Attends unsuccessful séances with Mme. Bisson, a famous materializing medium. 'Paudeen', 'To a Shade' and 'The Magi' (poems; *VP*, 291, 292–3, 318) published in the *New Statesman*.
10	Attends more disappointing séances with Mme. Bisson in Paris.

11	Travels to Mirabeau, near Poitiers, with Feilding and MG to investigate the 'miracle' of a bleeding oleograph.
12	Back in Paris, and staying in MG's house, WBY begins to write an account of the bleeding oleograph.
17	Hears that the Abbey Company lost over £500 on their American tour.
*c.*20	Has a successful séance in Paris with Mme Bisson, who produces ectoplasm.
25	Finishes 'On Woman' and starts another poem. *Responsibilities* published.
26	Has a final séance with Mme Bisson in the evening.
27	Returns to London from Paris.
29	Goes to see Ricketts and denounces the revengeful hypocrisy of the British public.
31	AG arrives in London from Ireland and she and WBY transact a great deal of theatre business.

June

3	(Wed) Invites James Pond to lunch to discuss a future American tour.
4	Writes 'The Fisherman'.
5	Goes to Cheltenham to stay with Ruth Lane Poole and to lecture.
6	Returns to London and attends a séance given by Mrs Etta Wreidt at Cambridge House from 7.10 to 10 pm with Sir Arthur Turner, Estella Stead and Miss Scatcherd.
13	Calls on Ricketts, who is out, and sees Charles Shannon.
14	Attends Abbey productions most evenings during their London tour.
20	First part of 'Art and Ideas' (essay; *E & I*, 346–50) published in the *New Weekly* (6–7). Writes poem 'The Dawn'.
27	Second part of 'Art and Ideas' (essay; *E & I*, 350–55) published in the *New Weekly* (38–40).
28	Sees Ricketts and discusses Swinburne.

July

3	(Fri) Attends a supper for Granville Barker at the Savoy Theatre. Shaw, Rupert Brooke, Chesterton, Barrie, Ricketts and Asquith are also present.
8	AG returns to Ireland. WBY begins to write his autobiography.
13	George Plank attends WBY's 'Monday Evening'.
14	Lunches with Lady Pembroke; F. E. Smith also present.
16	Lunches with the Asquiths.
19	Goes to see Mabel Beardsley.
20	W. T. Horton and Audrey Locke attend WBY's 'Monday Evening' and deliver a prophesy.
21	Lectures to his mystical group.

24	George Hyde-Lees formally admitted to the Order of the Golden Dawn at 56 Bassett Road, North Kensington, taking the motto 'Nemo Sciat' and sponsored by WBY.
25	WBY leaves London for Coole.
27	Publication of Tagore's *The Post Office* with a Preface by WBY.
28	Has almost finished the first draft of *Reveries over Childhood and Youth*. The Third Irish Home Rule Bill passed but immediately suspended because of the European situation.

August

4	(Tue) The First World War begins.
26	Returns to London from Coole to look up information for *Visions and Beliefs* in the British Museum.
28	Lunches with Stephen Gwynn, who makes gloomy political predictions.
30	Goes to see Mabel Beardsley and hears a great deal of war gossip from Romanian and French attachés who are also there.
31	Goes to Cunard to arrange a transatlantic crossing for AG.

September

| 1 | (Tue) Delays his departure for Ireland after leaving a bag of letters in a taxi cab. |
| 2 | Leaves London for Coole where he works for the rest of the month on the Introduction and Notes for *Visions and Beliefs*. Writes only one poem and none of his autobiography. |

October

1	(Thu) Goes to Dublin from Coole on Abbey business.
2	In the morning meets Lane at the Irish National Gallery. Spends the afternoon going over plays submitted to the Abbey, including Guinan's *The Plough Lifters*, and in the evening dines with his sisters at Dundrum.
3	In the afternoon again revises Guinan's play before leaving for England by the evening North Wall boat.
4	Arrives in London and in the afternoon visits Mabel Beardsley in hospital.
9	Goes to see OS and then to inspect Pound's gas stove. Has put himself on an eccentric diet for mental reasons.
12	Sees Gosse.
16	Undergoes the 6°=5° ritual of the Stella Matutina Temple as Postulant.
21	Reads scenarios of proposed plays by LR and Guinan. Is rewriting and expanding *Reveries over Childhood and Youth*. His evenings are a burden owing to his poor eyesight.
31	Reads T. C. Murray's play *The Briary Gap* and approves of it.

November

1	(Sun) Dines with Everard Feilding.
c.5	Crosses to Dublin.
c.7	Goes from Dublin to Coole, where he remains until 17 November.
9	Begins writing 'A Meditation in Time of War'.
17	Goes to Dublin to lecture at the Thomas Davis Centennial meeting of the TCD Gaelic Society, but it is banned by the College Board because Padraic Pearse is to speak at it.
18–19	Days filled with interviews about the banned meeting.
20	Speaks at the banned meeting, which now takes place at the Students National Literary Society.
c.21	Returns to London from Dublin.
23	Allan Wade attends WBY's 'Monday Evening'.

December

1	(Tue) Visit from Miss Alcock who wants to produce his plays in aid of the War effort. AG arrives in London.
3	Having great changes made at Woburn Buildings, including new bookshelves and furniture, and so goes to stay with the Tuckers (parents of his future wife, who is also there) and OS in Brighton, and takes the opportunity of having plays read to him.
10	Returns to London.
11	Sees Everard Feilding and discusses War news and Sir Roger Casement with him.
14	A violent cold interrupts his dictation of *Reveries over Childhood and Youth* over the following week. Mair, now involved with War propaganda, calls to see him and they discuss naval strategy.
20	Still weak from his cold, sleeps for most of the afternoon.
22	Leaves London for Coole.
25	Finishes *Reveries over Childhood and Youth*.
31	Goes from Coole to Dublin, where he stays at the Stephen's Green Club.

1915

January

1	(Fri) Busy in Dublin all day.
2	Reads *Reveries over Childhood and Youth* to SMY and probably leaves for London that night. AG leaves for American tour.
6	Goes to Stone Cottage, Sussex with Ezra and Dorothy Pound, remaining there for two months, revising *Reveries* and *The Player Queen*, writing notes for AG's *Visions and Beliefs*, reading nearly the whole of Wordsworth, as well as Doughty's *Arabia Deserta*, various Norse sagas and Browning's 'Sordello'. Writing 'His Phoenix'.

10	Writes 'The People'.
11	Sends a revised version of *Reveries over Childhood and Youth* to the typist. Goes up to London for his 'Monday Evening', and visits the New English art exhibition.
14	Hears that Sara Allgood will return to the Abbey Theatre on a limited contract.
18	Has finished Wordsworth's *Excursion* and is about to begin *The Prelude*.
20	Writing notes for AG's *Visions and Beliefs*.
23	The vicar of Colman's Hatch visits WBY at Stone Cottage. WBY interrupts his notes for *Visions and Beliefs* to make final revisions to *Reveries*.
27	Writes 'Her Praise'.
29	Has two of his rooms at Woburn Buildings scraped and repapered. Pound is reading Icelandic Sagas and Doughty's *Arabia Deserta* to him. With the help of Pound, he reduces *The Player Queen* to two manageable acts, and continues to work on it; he is also working on notes for *Visions and Beliefs*.

February

1	(Mon) In London for his 'Monday Evening'.
5	Applies for an overdraft for the Abbey Theatre.
6	Writes 'On being asked for a War Poem'.
8	In London for his 'Monday Evening', and also to see Allan Wade and Frederick Whelan about hiring a London theatre for an Abbey tour.
9	Dines at the Huth Jacksons' and sees the Pope-Hennessys.
12	Returns to Stone Cottage.
18	Visits London from Stone Cottage.

March

1	(Mon) Returns to London from Stone Cottage.
10	Goes to Dublin to see AG's *Shanwalla* at the Abbey but finds it has been put off for two weeks. Discovers the Abbey in a financial crisis having lost nearly £1,200, and thinks of closing it for the duration of the War. Attends a party given by Bailey and sees Gogarty and Hyde.
11	Sees Louis Purser about obtaining a reader's ticket for TCD Library, where he reads 17th-century Platonists.
12	Consults Harris about the Abbey's finances; he advises the purchase of the Mechanics Institute, which is acquired on 19 March for £1,200. Attends a rehearsal of *Shanwalla*.
20	Tires himself out reading Bram Stoker's *Dracula*. Is rehearsing plays at the Abbey and experimenting with an ouija board. Sees Lord Dunsany, just off to the War. Is writing 'The Scholars' (*VP*, 337).

April

5   (Mon) AG returns from her American lecture tour, and WBY dines with her, Horace Plunkett, Nathan and W. F. Bailey.

7   Spends the afternoon at the Irish National Gallery with AG and Hugh Lane.

8   Lunches with Horace Plunkett, Sarah Purser, AG and W. F. Bailey. In the evening, attends the first production of AG's *Shanwalla* at the Abbey.

9   Sends £100 to Quinn to help pay off JBY's debts.

*c.*11   Returns to London.

14   Dines with Allan Wade to discuss theatre matters.

*c.*18   Sees Ricketts about designing new costumes for *On Baile's Strand*.

19   Sees A. P. Wilson, who is in London seeking a theatre for the Abbey summer tour.

*c.*21   Attends a party at the Gosses'. Begins work on *The Player Queen* again but soon puts it aside.

26   Sees Wilson about the Abbey's London programme.

30   Dines with Ricketts to discuss his designing costumes for *The Well of the Saints* and *On Baile's Strand*.

May

2   (Sun) Attends the Pioneer Players' production of Claudel's *L'Echange* in an English version by Rowland Thurnam at the Little Theatre. Is writing 'To a Young Girl'.

3   Edmund Dulac and Eric Maclagan and his wife attend WBY's 'Monday Evening'.

4   Sees Mabel Beardsley, and reads her poems from Pound's *Cathay*.

7   Hugh Lane drowned when the *Lusitania* is torpedoed off the Irish coast.

9   AG arrives in London for the Abbey season at the Little Theatre.

13   WBY sees Elizabeth Radcliffe.

14   Attends a crisis meeting of the Abbey Company in London about the financial situation. The actors ask that there should be no vulgarization of their work and oppose proposals of the manager, Wilson.

18   Attends a rehearsal of *The Well of the Saints* with AG and Ricketts. Probably writing 'To a Young Girl' (*VP*, 336).

21   Sees Ricketts and Shannon and tells them of Lane's last moments. In late May visits Blunt in Sussex with AG.

31   Attends Synge's *Deirdre of the Sorrows*, performed with improvised costumes and scenery.

June

4   (Fri) The success in London of *On Baile's Strand*, with costumes by Ricketts, revives WBY's confidence in himself.

5	The Abbey's London season ends.
*c.*7	AG returns to Ireland.
10	Drops in to see Ricketts and discusses the zeppelin raids on London.
13	Consults Elizabeth Radcliffe about contacting Lane's spirit to discover whether he left a hidden will bequeathing his pictures to the Dublin Municipal Gallery.
14	Goes to the London Spiritualists Alliance to enquire about mediums, and returns there at 2.55 pm to meet Mrs Cannock, who tells him that a drowned man wishes to communicate with him.
15	At 5.00 pm goes by appointment for a séance with Mrs Cannock who puts him in touch with a spirit claiming to be Hugh Lane.
18	In the evening consults Ricketts about a replacement for Lane as Director of the National Gallery of Ireland; he suggests Binyon or Maclagan.
19	Spends a pleasant, talkative weekend visiting Robert Bridges in Oxford.
21	Trying to arrange an American Music Hall tour and a tour to Australia to save the Abbey from financial collapse.
22	Dictates notes on the spiritualistic search for Lane's will to a typist.
24	Sees Binyon and sounds him out about Directorship of the National Gallery of Ireland. Also meets Wilson and discusses redundancies at the Abbey.
25	Spends the evening at Ricketts and asks Sturge Moore to design the frontispiece of *Reveries*.
28	Has a tooth filled by his dentist. Receives a new offer for an Abbey tour to Australia. Accompanies Sturge Moore to a performance of Seumus O'Brien's play *Duty*, performed by a group of Abbey actors at the Coliseum.
29	Binyon declines to apply for the Directorship of the National Gallery, and so WBY sees Eric Maclagan who also refuses to stand.

July

*c.*1	(Thu) Much impressed by the work of the Serbian sculptor Ivan Mestrovic at the Victoria and Albert Museum.
2	Visits Ricketts to discuss the Directorship of the National Gallery of Ireland, and he suggests Robert Witt.
3	Goes to stay with Eva Fowler at Brasted, remaining there until 8 July.
5	Writes 'The Collar-Bone of a Hare'.
6	Writes to Gosse, proposing James Joyce for a grant from the Royal Literary Fund.
8	Attends a séance with Mrs Harris.

9	Does a good day's work.
10	Suffers a collapse.
12	Discusses American and Australian Abbey tours with Wilson and discovers that neither is possible without Sara Allgood.
13	In the evening dictates the final notes for *Visions and Beliefs* to a typist.
14	Meets Bailey and the second executor of Lane's will at the Reform Club and discusses the Directorship of National Gallery of Ireland and the legal status of Lane's will.
15	Informed by Dossy Wright that the Abbey Manager, Wilson, is trying to make a deal with American music halls behind the backs of the Directors, and telling the actors that the Abbey is finished. WBY goes to see the impresario W. A. Macleod, who tells him that the Australian tour may still be on. Also sees Richard Witt, and sounds him out about standing as Director of the National Gallery of Ireland. Witt advises him to ask D. S. MacColl to write the biography of Lane.
16	In a state of nervous exhaustion, but sees Dossy Wright at 11 pm.
17	Sees Dossy Wright again to discuss Abbey affairs, and to dismiss Wilson as Abbey manager.
18	Sees Bailey, who advises winding up the Abbey Company, and then consults Dossy Wright who advises him to keep it going.
19	Meets Dossy Wright to discuss Abbey affairs.
20	'Thomas Davis' (lecture) published in *New Ireland*. Sees Horton in the morning and in the afternoon meets Dossy Wright and Kerrigan about the Abbey crisis. Attends a séance at 7 pm with Mrs Wreidt.
22	Sturge Moore visits with Miss Scatcherd, who does automatic writing.
24	Sends Gosse letters and papers in support of Joyce's application for a grant from the Royal Literary Fund.
26	Sees Watt about the offer by Macmillan (NY) for *Reveries* and afterwards sets off for Ireland. Stays a few hours in Dublin before going on to Coole, where he continues *Reveries over Childhood* and works on *The Player Queen*.
29	Writes to the Royal Literary Fund on behalf of Joyce.

August

20	(Fri) Sends 'On Being asked for a War Poem' to Edith Wharton for her anthology for War Relief, *The Book of the Homeless (Le Livre des Sans-Foyer)*.

September

30	(Thu) Leaves Coole for Dublin. Sees Bailey about Abbey Theatre affairs.

October

2   (Sat) Sees Aldermen Kelly, Cosgrove and Sherlock about Dublin
           Corporation support for the campaign to get the Lane Pictures for
           Dublin. Asks Ellen Duncan to lobby William Martin Murphy.

4   Again sees Kelly, Cosgrave and Sherlock about support from
           Dublin Corporation for the Lane pictures. Trouble with the
           Abbey Company who are in London.

5   Addresses the Dublin Corporation Finance Committee about the
           Lane Pictures, and they give him a formal statement avowing their
           intention to go on with the Gallery.

c.8   Returns to London.

10   In the morning two Abbey actors, Sinclair and Morgan, dis-
           missed for refusing to sign new contracts, call upon WBY and
           ask to be reinstated; WBY says he cannot interfere.

12   Meets Witt and the artist Henry Tonks at MacColl's house to
           discuss the Lane Pictures. After Witt and Tonks have left, WBY
           asks MacColl to write Lane's biography.

13   Sees Ervine about his play *John Ferguson* and suggests he should
           become manager of the Abbey Company. Later WBY is caught in
           a zeppelin raid while dictating letters near the British Museum.

16   Visits Sir Charles Holroyd to discuss the Lane Pictures.

17   Writes 'A Deep-Sworn Vow'.

18   Dines with his new romantic interest Alick Schepeler before his
           'Monday Evening', to which Horton brings Audrey Locke.

19   Goes to see Sargent and gets a favourable statement about the
           Lane Pictures, which he sends to the Dublin Corporation.

c.22   Ervine accepts the management of the Abbey Theatre.

23–4   Writes 'Broken Dreams'.

29   Tells Ricketts that Sir Charles Holroyd intends proposing him as
           his successor as Director of the English National Gallery.

November

2   (Tue) Consults Thomas Beecham about musical versions of his
           plays. Is writing 'Presences' and 'A Thought from Propertius'.

6   Meets Beecham at Lady Cunard's and continues their discussion
           about musical productions.

8   Shows SMY's embroidery to a large and admiring gathering at
           his 'Monday Evening'.

9   Consults Lady Cunard about a proposed lecture in aid of the Abbey.

10   Dines at the Ritz with Lady Cunard, Lord Wimborne and the
           Master of the Horse and discusses the possibility of a Vice-Regal
           visit to the Abbey Theatre.

12   Ervine and Bailey wire, warning of official objections to the
           Abbey's production of Shaw's *O'Flaherty V. C.* WBY calls on
           Shaw, who writes letters of protest.

13	Ervine wires him to come to Dublin and he begins to pack but Bailey writes that his presence is not neccessary.
14	Wires Bailey about *O'Flaherty V. C.* Sees Mrs Shine to make extracts from cutting books about the Lane Pictures. Suffers an asthmatic attack and takes to his bed.
15	Despite the asthmatic attack and a cold, he gets up for his 'Monday Evening' where he discusses SMY's embroidery and the illustrations for *Reveries over Childhood and Youth*.
16	Still suffering from asthma.
18	Dines with Dorothea Hunter, and admires her Mancini paintings.
22	Probably meets George Hyde-Lees in the afternoon, and may have discussed marriage.
26	Takes Bailey to see Ricketts to discuss candidates for the Directorship of the Irish National Gallery.
27	Dines with Lady Cunard to meet Balfour; Sturge Moore also present. After dinner Lady Cunard tells him that he is to be offered a knighthood.
28	In the afternoon sees Maud Mann and the musician John Foulds with whom he practises chanting. Visits Gosse in the evening.
30	Goes to Dublin to see Ervine's *John Ferguson* and to consult with him and Bailey. Talks to Dermod O'Brien about the Directorship of the Irish National Gallery. Dines with ECY, SMY, Ervine and Bailey.

December

1	(Wed) Discusses a music hall scheme with Ervine.
2	Gives his 6 December lecture a trial run before a small audience at the Arts Club.
3	Returns to London. Writing 'Ego Dominus Tuus'.
4	Presides at a meeting of the ILS at which Émile Cammaerts speaks on Belgian poetry.
6	Lectures on 'The Irish Theatre and Other Matters' in aid of the Abbey Theatre at the Duchess of Marlborough's Sunderland House at 3.30 pm, and announces that the Abbey debt of £1,200 has been paid off. Later Maud Mann, Foulds, Horton and Audrey Locke come to his 'Monday Evening'.
9	Attends the Cuala Industries Sale at the ILS with OS to see SMY's and ECY's embroidery.
10	Lady Cunard again sounds him out about a knighthood, which he refuses.
12	Sees Alick Schepeler in the evening.
c.14	Dines with Lady Wimborne, wife of the Lord Lieutenant of Ireland.
20	Dines with the Lyttons. Jack Yeats has had a nervous breakdown.

21   Goes to Stone Cottage with Pound and his wife.
23   Reads a new version of *The Player Queen* to Pound. He remains
      with the Pounds at Stone Cottage over the Christmas holidays,
      writing 'Leo Africanus' and reading Savage Landor.

1916

January
1   (Sat) WBY remains at Stone Cottage with the Pounds until early
      March, revising *The Player Queen* and reading Landor.
10   Goes up to London to see Bailey and for his 'Monday
      Evening'.
23   Attends the Stage Society production of Sturge Moore's *Judith* at
      the Queen's Theatre.
31   Dines with Sturge Moore at Woburn Buildings.

February
4   (Fri) Pound and his wife are asked to report to the police
      because as alien nationals they are living in a prohibited area;
      WBY writes to the Home Office on their behalf. Begins writing
      At the Hawk's Well.
5   Publishes nine poems in *Poetry* (Chicago).
6   Another policeman calls to check on Pound for living in a pro-
      hibited area.
7   Returns to London from Stone Cottage for his 'Monday
      Evening'.
8   Calls to see AG, who has recently returned from America and is
      staying at Cheyne Walk. At 5.00 pm he sees Lady Cunard to
      discuss the production of *At the Hawk's Well*.
12   In London, working on *At the Hawk's Well* and his memoirs.
15   Sees Allan Wade in the evening to discuss the production of
      At the Hawk's Well.
16   Sees Elizabeth Radcliffe and raises the spirit of an Irish gov-
      erness drowned in Russia.
17   Reads *Three Sisters* by Elsa d'Esterre Keeling at the British Museum
      to corroborate Elizabeth Radcliffe's spiritualist messages.
c.18 Returns to Stone Cottage from London.
21   In London for his 'Monday Evening'.
22   Meets Ervine to discuss Abbey affairs and reads him *The Player
      Queen*.
23   Writing the lyrical parts of *At the Hawk's Well*. Proofs of *Visions
      and Beliefs* begin to arrive.
28   In London for his 'Monday Evening'.
29   Goes to Dulac's to inspect the masks for *At the Hawk's Well*.

March

5   (Sun) Attends a performance of *The Hour-Glass* in Chelsea.

6   Returns to London from Stone Cottage.

11   Transfers his books to Macmillan and Co.

*c.*12   Meets a representative of the Red Lion Charity and later sees Alick Schepeler.

12   Consults Harris and Ervine about Abbey policy and, later, Plunkett about the Carnegie Trust.

13   Sees Wade at his 'Monday Evening' and arranges rehearsals for *At the Hawk's Well*. Row with LR over his acceptance of a portrait of the actor Fred O'Donovan by Sleator for the Abbey Theatre. Is busy from now until late March rehearsing *At the Hawk's Well*.

17   Holds discussions with his new publisher, Macmillan, about a 'Collected Edition' of his work. Proof reading *Visions and Beliefs*.

20   *Reveries over Childhood and Youth* published.

22   Attends a morning rehearsal and later reads LR's new play, *The Whiteheaded Boy*.

*c.*24   In dispute over the pirating of his poems by *Form*.

26   Consults Dulac on appropriate gestures for the actor Henry Ainley.

31   First complete run-through of *At the Hawk's Well*, attended by OS and Eva Fowler.

April

2   (Sun) *At the Hawk's Well*, the first of WBY's Noh plays, produced at Lady Cunard's House, 20 Cavendish Square. Thomas Beecham present.

4   A second production of *At the Hawk's Well* staged at Lady Islington's house, 8 Chesterfield Gardens, with Queen Alexandra, Pound and T. S. Eliot in the audience.

5   Revises Tagore's *Fruit Gathering* and *A Lover's Gift* for Macmillan.

8   Discusses Rossetti at lunch with Lady Cunard, Lady Horner and Ricketts.

*c.*9   Consults Dulac, Ricketts and Beecham about taking the Aldwich Theatre for a season in 1917.

10   Begins to plan a play which becomes *The Only Jealousy of Emer*.

11   Recites poetry at Baroness D'Erlanger's house in aid of the Star and Garter Fund.

14   Returns his revised version of Tagore's *Fruit Gathering* to Macmillan and continues revising *A Lover's Gift*. In the middle of this month he rents two extra lower rooms at Woburn Buildings, but discovers that the lease of the house has only two more years to run.

17   Writing an introduction to Pound's edition of Noh plays for Cuala Press. Very short of money.

20	Goes to stay with Rothenstein, who executes drawings of him, arriving at Stroud, Gloucestershire, at 5.30 pm. Stays until 26 April with long sittings, and talk into the small hours.
24	The Easter Rising takes place in Dublin.
26	Returns to London and sleeps $10\frac{1}{2}$ hours.
27	Meets important staff member of *The Times* who gives him inaccurate information about the Easter Rising.
28	Calls on Ricketts and Shannon, much affected by the Rising.
30	Sends the MS of *Responsibilities* to Watt for transmission to Macmillan.

May

3	(Wed) Dulac and Maclagan at WBY's.
4	Hears from AG that she is safe and well. Continues to work on the proofs of *Visions and Beliefs*.
5	John MacBride executed for his part in the Easter Rising.
8	Death of Mabel Beardsley.
10	Sets out for Mabel Beardsley's funeral but is taken ill and returns home.
11	Trying to write a poem on the Easter Rising.
15	Sees Allan Wade.
16	Lectures to the Brotherhood of Arts, Crafts and Industries on 'The Theatre of Beauty' at the Temporary Hall, 19 Tavistock Square, London. Iseult Gonne arrives in London.
17	Lunches with Iseult Gonne, who tells him she wants him to return with her to France to look after MG. Invites Elizabeth Radcliffe and her mother to tea; she gives him psychic messages.
*c.*19	Takes Iseult Gonne to dine with Shaw.
20	Thinks of giving up his rooms in London to live permanently in Dublin.
21	Bullen sends crates of WBY's unbound books to Macmillan as part of the transfer.
22	Iseult Gonne and May Clay dine with WBY at Woburn Buildings to meet the Pounds.
24	Takes Iseult to Rothenstein's Private View. In the evening interviews the Irish actor, J. Augustus Keogh, with a view to hiring him for the Abbey.
25	Proposed for membership of the Savile Club by Albert Rutherston, seconded by Gosse, Logan Pearsall Smith and Sidney Colvin.
27	Ervine, in dispute with the Abbey actors, dismisses nearly the whole Company. Elizabeth Radcliffe and her mother call on WBY and he asks her to discover from her spirit guides whether he should marry MG.
29	Sees Horton and Sturge Moore.
31	Exchanges contracts with Macmillan for *Responsibilities* and *Reveries over Childhood and Youth*.

June

2	(Fri) Goes to Dublin to try to sort out tangled Abbey affairs.
8	Sees Bailey and the Theatre's solicitors about the unauthorized use of the Abbey name by seceding actors.
10	Returns to London.
11	Sees Iseult Gonne about the timing of his trip to France.
12	Meets Ellen Duncan who tells him of a dispute between the Irish National Gallery and the Municipal Gallery.
14	Auditions the Irish actor Basil Sydney, and hires him for the Abbey. Sees Robert Ross who tells him that Ricketts has refused the Directorship of the English National Gallery.
15	Lunches with Iseult Gonne.
16	Sees MacColl about a biography of Lane. In the evening calls on Ricketts and Shannon and discusses the Directorship of the Irish National Gallery.
17	Occupied in getting a passport for his visit to France.
19	Sees Allan Wade.
22	Consults Bailey about Abbey affairs, and they discuss the merits of Basil Sydney, J. Augustus Keogh and LR as possible managers after Ervine. Goes to an agency to arrange a lecture tour in November.
24	Goes to Paris and then to Normandy.

July

1	(Sat) Asks MG, widowed by MacBride's execution after the Easter Rising, to marry him; she refuses. In Normandy, writes his memoirs, flies kites with Sean MacBride, reads the modern French poets with Iseult Gonne and discusses marriage with her.
10	Watt exchanges contracts with Macmillan whereby they agree to take over WBY's *CW*.
14	Watt reminds Macmillan that £210 is due to WBY on the return of his contract.
c.15	WBY writes to the Home Secretary urging him to commute the death sentence passed on Roger Casement for high treason, and sends a copy of his letter to Asquith, the Prime Minister.
16	Writes to Ervine, dismissing him as manager of the Abbey.
17	Visits Bayeux with MG and Iseult.
18	Returns proofs of *Responsibilities* and *Reveries over Childhood and Youth* to Macmillan.
19	Returns the remainder of the proofs of *Responsibilities* to Macmillan. Writes 'Men improve with the Years'.

August

1	(Tue) Sends Quinn £40 for his father and finds himself in the worst financial situation for ten years. Keogh appointed Abbey manager.

10	Encourages Iseult Gonne to write a book on the new French Catholic poets, and begins to read Peguy, Jammes and Claudel in translation.
*c.*12	Proposes marriage to Iseult Gonne but is refused.
13	Iseult Gonne tells him that she is haunted by a voice accusing her of worthlessness.
18	Discusses with Quinn the possibility of an enquiry into the trial and conviction of Casement.
20	Writes to Eddie Marsh in support of Joyce's application for a pension from the Civil List.
22–4	Writes 'In Memory of Alfred Pollexfen'.
31	Returns to London from Normandy.

September

2	(Sat) Catches a violent cold trying to get a glimpse of a zepellin raid at 2.15 am
4	Horton, OS and Pound attend WBY's 'Monday Evening'.
*c.*6	Consults Ruth Shine about the Directorship of the Irish National Gallery.
7	Experiences material manifestations at a séance.
8	Hears that the London National Gallery has been promised money for a new wing, which will strengthen its claim to the Lane Pictures.
9	Warned that his Civil List pension may be suspended because he is suspected of being pro-German.
12	Sees Robert Langton Douglas about the Lane Pictures and the necessity of enlisting the help of the Irish Party in restoring them to Dublin. Also consults Bailey on this topic.
13	Meets John Squire at 1.30 pm to discuss the publication of his poems in the *London Mercury*.
14	Advises Macmillan to publish Iseult Gonne's translation of Peguy. Leaves London for Dublin.
15	Delivers a box of embroideries to SMY from Sturge Moore.
16	Leaves Dublin for Coole. *Certain Noble Plays of Japan* published with his Introduction.
25	Finishes 'Easter 1916'. Begins 'Lines Written in Dejection'.

October

2	(Mon) Begins negotiations for Thoor Ballylee, a Norman tower near Coole. Writing 'The Wild Swans at Coole'.
6	Returns to Dublin from Coole and goes to a performance at the Abbey.
8	Arrives back in London.
10	Macmillan publish an enlarged edition of *Responsibilities*.
13	Calls to see Ricketts and Shannon; Dulac is also there and they discuss the political situation in Ireland and the return of the Lane Pictures to Dublin.

15	Calls on AG at 4 pm to discuss agitation for the return of the Lane Pictures to Dublin. Spends much of the following weeks lobbying people and collecting names for a petition about the Pictures.
15–27	Revising *At the Hawk's Well* for periodical publication and writing an introductory essay.
26	Visits Dulac in the evening to go over stage directions for *At the Hawk's Well*.
27	Goes to see Ricketts and Shannon.
28	Lunches with OS and they go on to the Arts and Crafts exhibition.

November

*c.*3	(Fri) Travels from London to Dublin, enduring one of the roughest passages he has ever had. In the following month he does a great deal of Abbey business, reads numerous plays, and sets up an Abbey Lecture Committee.
4	Goes over the Abbey buildings with Harris, with a view to letting some of them; interviews the actor Kerrigan about his future relationship with the Abbey; sees Boyle's play *Nic* but finds it disappointing. He also consults the new Abbey manager, J. Augustus Keogh, the secretary Miss McConaghy and the actor O'Donovan.
6	Sees Harris again and also arranges the forthcoming Abbey programme with Keogh. Attends a performance of McNulty's *The Lord Mayor* at the Abbey.
7	Quizzes Henderson about the Irish Princess Dervorgilla for his new play, *The Dreaming of the Bones*. Sees *The Jackdaw* at the Abbey.
11	Bailey consults him about a Memorial from a number of Irish institutions calling for the Lane Pictures to be returned to Dublin. Sees *The Jackdaw* again at the Abbey.
13	Consults the Inspector at the Congested Districts Board about the purchase of Thoor Ballylee.
14	Sees *The Man Who Missed the Tide* at the Abbey.
20	Travels to Galway by a 9 am train to look over Thoor Ballylee with the Inspector from the Congested Districts Board.
*c.*25	Back in Dublin, sees Martyn, who offers him Dungory Castle if the purchase of Thoor Ballylee falls through.
26	Sees the Landed Estates Inspector about possible flooding at Thoor Ballylee and the architect Scott about refurbishing it. Returns to London that evening.
27	In London, confers with AG at Cheyne Walk over a letter to *The Times* about the Lane Pictures and later takes the letter in person to the editor.
28	Lunches with AG, and they go on to the House of Commons to see John Redmond, leader of the Irish Party.
30	Spends the evening at AG's with Shaw and Una Troubridge discussing psychic phenomena.

December

1	(Fri) Lunches with AG and the actress Lillah McCarthy at 10 Downing Street, as guests of the Prime Minister, Asquith.
2	Lunches with AG at Woburn Buildings to discuss the Lane Pictures.
3	In the afternoon accompanies AG to *The Times* offices to arrange for the publication of a letter about the Lane Pictures.
4	AG calls to tell him that *The Times* has refused her letter. He accompanies her to *The Times* offices, and arranges that the editor should call him at the Royal Societies Club at 5 pm. When he fails to do this, WBY phones the Irish journalist and politician T. P. O'Connor to make an appointment for AG. Alick Schepeler, Sturge Moore and Una Troubridge come to his 'Monday Evening'.
6	AG's letter appears in *The Times*, and she takes WBY to see other editors: Spender of the *Westminster Review*, Garvin of the *Observer*, and Johnson of the *Evening Standard*. They have lunch and then WBY calls on Howard Gray of the *Pall Mall Gazette*.
7	Calls on AG in the afternoon and finds Lady Margaret Sackville there. They discuss theatre business, and he recites 'Easter 1916'. In the evening he and AG begin an article on the Lane Pictures for the *Observer*.
8	WBY and AG are interviewed by a journalist from the *Observer* and afterwards they finish their article for the same paper.
9	Spends the afternoon with AG.
10	Dines with AG and sees her off for Ireland, but they fail to get a taxi for the station and she remains an extra day in London.
15	Meets AG at his club at 2.30 pm; they have a snack for lunch, and go on to a typing office to dictate letters about the Lane Pictures. WBY takes one to *The Times* offices at 5 pm, and then dines with AG and Ruth Shine at Woburn Buildings before AG leaves for Ireland.
16	Has dinner at Una Troubridge's.
17	The interview about the Lane Pictures appears in the *Observer*. WBY is now writing to the weeklies about the Lane Pictures and much occupied with the agitation.
18	His letter about the Lane Pictures appears in the *Morning Post*.
19	Sends Macmillan the revised copy for a new edition of *Responsibilities*.
23	The *Spectator* publishes his letter on the Lane Pictures.
24	The *Observer* publishes a long letter by him on the Lane Pictures.
27	Attends a séance with Mrs Leonard.
28	His letter about the Lane Pictures published by *The Times*.
30	Enlists the help of the painter John Lavery in organizing an artists' Memorial about the Lane Pictures; stays to lunch and meets the designer Robert Anning Bell.

1917

January

4   (Thu) Writes to the Congested Districts Board outlining his terms for the purchase of Thoor Ballylee. Dines with Lalla Vandervelde and meets Robbie Ross.

5   Holds a séance with the medium Vout Peters at Woburn Buildings at 8.30 pm. Early in the month WBY and AG quarrel with MacColl over his approach to the biography of Lane.

8   Sees Sturge Moore in the evening to discuss dramatic copyright. Begins working on a long letter to the *Observer* about the Lane pictures to sum up the controversy.

10   Consults Lord Plymouth about the Lane Pictures.

13   Sees Alec Martin, art dealer and friend of Lane.

*c.*16   Roger Fry advises WBY on the roofing of Thoor Ballylee.

17   Sees Alec Martin about the Lane Pictures and Lane's biography.

21   WBY's long letter on the Lane Pictures published in the *Observer*. Meets various people, including Shaw, Ross, Bailey and Mrs Hutchinson at Lalla Vandervelde's. Attends the Stage Society's production of Synge's *The Tinker's Wedding* and Shaw's *Augustus Does His Bit* at the Court Theatre.

22   Phones T. P. O'Connor to set up a meeting with him that afternoon to discuss the Lane pictures; O'Connor hints at the possibility of a breakfast with Lloyd George and arranges for WBY to see William Sutherland, Lloyd George's Private Secretary.

23   Sees Sutherland, who is sympathetic and sends him to the Irish Office to see Henry Duke, who is however in Ireland.

24   Consults Martin about the Lane pictures; also sees Sturge Moore, who approves of his letters in the controversy with MacColl. Late this month WBY works on a pamphlet about the Lane Pictures, and revises Tagore's *A Lover's Knot*.

26   Elected a member of the Savile Club, and has to pay £17 entrance fee as well as a first annual subscription.

29   Sees Lavery's secretary about the Lane Memorial. Maire O'Neill brings Lord Dunraven to WBY's 'Monday Evening'.

30   Visits David Wilson from 2 pm to midnight at St. Leonards-on-Sea to investigate his machine which is purported to register Odic forces and record psychic manifestations.

February

2   (Fri) Spends the morning writing a report on David Wilson's 'psychic machine'. Reads Joyce's *A Portrait of the Artist as a Young Man* early in the month, finding it 'remarkable' (to AG).

3   Goes to Mrs Troubridge's at 8.00 pm.

6	Sees T. P. O'Connor in the afternoon, and suggests a Lane Committee.
7	In the morning sees AG's niece Ruth Shine about a draft affidavit concerning the Lane Pictures.
8	Sees W. A. Macleod to arrange terms for the Abbey Company's appearance at the Coliseum. Goes to the House of Commons at 4.30 pm to lobby MPs about the Lane Pictures; remains there for two hours without meeting anyone of importance, but finally sees Richard Hazleton.
11	Writing his 'philosophic essay' 'The Alphabet'.
12	Pound gives WBY an MS copy of Joyce's *Exiles* at his 'Monday Evening'.
14	Sends Shorter corrected proofs of 7 poems (these were for a small, private edition which never appeared).
19	Dines with Alick Schepeler.
20	Sees Dulac and others about David Wilson's machine.
22	Calls at the War Office to enlist Gilbert Murray's help in retrieving Wilson's 'psychic machine' which the police have impounded.
23	Sees Gilbert Murray, who speaks with enthusiasm of AG doing the Lane biography.
24	WBY continues writing 'The Alphabet' (later *Per Amica Silentia Lunae*).
25	Finishes his essay 'Anima Hominis' for *Per Amica Silentia Lunae*.
26	Goes to 10 Downing Street to see William Sutherland about the Lane Pictures. Late this month he meets George Hyde-Lees in St James's Street and they go to a séance together.

March

1	(Thu) Worry over the purchase of Ballylee causes him a sleepless night. Takes the Lane pamphlet to the printers.
3	*At the Hawk's Well* (play; *VPl*, 398–419) published in *Harper's Bazaar*, with a Preface.
4	Dines at the Gosses'.
5	Pound and Dulac at WBY's 'Monday Evening'.
6	Reads *The Player Queen*, finished at last, to Mrs Campbell, who professes great enthusiasm for it. After she has gone to the Coliseum, WBY dines with her husband.
10	Dines with Horton.
c.11	At the Omega Club, talks to T. S. Eliot about psychical research. Hears that the police have returned the 'psychic machine' to Wilson.
12	Attends a meeting of the Lane Pictures Committee.
14	Goes to the House of Commons to see Hazleton about the Lane Pictures, and finds that he and Capt. Charles Craig are planning a Bill on the matter.

15	Sees Langton Douglas, now Director of the Irish National Gallery.
c.16	Lunches with Gilbert Murray at the Westminster Palace Hotel.
18	Calls on the Tuckers and George Hyde-Lees.
22	Spends the day at St Leonards in Sussex with Dulac and Denison Ross investigating David Wilson's psychic machine; he stays behind after they leave and gets a message from the machine.
27	Buys Thoor Ballylee from the Congested Districts Board.
28	Sends Shorter the MS of 'Easter 1916'.
30	Goes to Birmingham to see a good production of his revised *The Hour-Glass* by Drinkwater's Repertory Company.
31	Returns from Birmingham and calls on Horton three times without success to try to patch up a quarrel over his essay on Symbolism.

April

1	(Sun) Returns the corrected proof of 'Easter 1916' to Shorter. In the evening he sees Margaret Gregory about alterations to Ballylee.
2	Sees his banker, and finds his investments down.
3	Goes to the House of Commons to see Hazleton, but is kept waiting an hour without seeing him. Sends poems to Pound for the *Little Review*.
4	Sees Shaw in the morning about a government job for Dulac. Goes on to see Estella Stead about Wilson's psychic machine, which he discusses that evening at the Ghost Club.
6	Writes 'The Rose Tree' and sends AG a copy on the following day.
c.10	Gives Sturge Moore a copy of Joyce's *Exiles* for possible production by the Stage Society.
18	Goes to Dublin, where Keogh is refusing a new contract.
19	Attends a public meeting about the Lane Pictures at the Mansion House. O'Donovan appointed Abbey manager.
20	Attends a meeting of Abbey Lecture Committee.
21	Attends a Directors' Meeting at the Abbey Theatre which declines to reinstate Keogh as manager of the Abbey. Afterwards he leaves Dublin for Coole, where he remains until 21 May, revising *The Player Queen*, writing *Per Amica*, and discussing the renovation of Thoor Ballylee with the architect William A. Scott.

May

9	(Wed) Finishes his essay 'Anima Mundi' for *Per Amica*.
11	Writes the Prologue and Epilogue to *Per Amica*.
16	Thoor Ballylee formally handed over to WBY.
21	Leaves Coole for London.
23	Attends a meeting of the Lane Picture committee at 6.30 pm.

24	Goes to Edinburgh to lecture. Suggestion that he be given a permanent lectureship at Edinburgh.
28	Leaves Edinburgh for Birmingham.
29	Lectures in Birmingham on Synge and the Irish Theatre.
30	Returns to London. Dictates *Per Amica* to a typist every afternoon from 3.30 pm.

June

2	(Sat) Publishes seven poems in the *Little Review*.
5	Sees Horton and makes up their quarrel.
10	Moved by a performance of Claudel's *L'Annonce faite à Marie* played in English. Working on *The Dreaming of the Bones*.
13	Makes a classification of all JBY's letters to him.
16–18	Spends the weekend at Maidenhead.
18	Discusses the Lane Pictures with Charles Craig, who introduces him to Lord Lonsdale, the leader of the Irish Unionists. They advise a deputation of Irish MPs to the Prime Minister.
19	Sees Ellen Duncan in the morning and they call upon Duke at the Irish Office about the Lane Pictures; in the afternoon they call upon Irish MPs Devlin and Law.
21	Gives a poetry reading in aid of a War charity.
26	Sees Roger Fry about the purchase of a Titian for Dublin and tries to get Robert Ross on the phone on the same topic.
27	Sees Alec Martin to seek his opinion about the Titian. In a panic over his work and suffers a nightmare.
28	Finalizes the arrangements for a series of lectures in France.
29	Sends the MS of 'Easter 1916' to Clement Shorter and Dora Sigerson, but stipulates that it is not for general circulation in case it compromises the Lane Picture campaign. Writes to Margaret Gregory about the refurbishment of Thoor Ballylee.
30	Has recovered from his panic about his work. Sees his bank manager and arranges to pay £35 for Thoor Ballylee and finds that after spending £200 on the cottage he can still have an overdraft of £300. Feels he is over the financial crisis he has been in since the beginning of the War.

July

1	(Sun) Returns the signed agreement for Thoor Ballylee to the Congested Districts Board. Invites J. C. Squire to his 'Monday Evening' on the following night.
*c.*4	Leaves London for Dublin, where he stays at 15 Ely Place with Gogarty. While in Dublin he enjoys a whirl of excellent talk, and sees numerous people, including his sisters, James Stephens, AE, Hyde and Scott, the architect for Thoor Ballylee. On Gogarty's commission, Arthur Power makes a bust of him.

9	Travels from Dublin to Coole, where he works on his French lectures, oversees the beginning of building work on Thoor Ballylee, and walks in the hills to get the atmosphere for his play *The Dreaming of the Bones*.
17	Works on the Planisphere, sent on to him by Dulac.
26	Crosses to London, and sees Horton that evening at 8.30 pm, although they quarrel.

August

6	(Mon) Arrives in Paris where he is delayed for a day by passport difficulties, and where he reads *The Dreaming of the Bones* to Walter Rummel, who agrees to write music for it.
7	Arrives to stay with MG in Normandy, where he proposes to Iseult but is refused. Finishes *The Dreaming of the Bones*, and sends the copy for *Per Amica Silentia Lunae* to Macmillan via Watt. Writing 'The Living Beauty' (*VP*, 333–4).
11	'Upon a Dying Lady' (seven poems; *VP*, 362–7) published in the *New Statesman*.
13	Preparing his second French lecture on lyric poets and another on William Blake. Taking long walks with Iseult Gonne.
26	Moves from Colleville to Paris, where he stays at the Hotel Gavarni in Passy. Writes to tell Joyce that he cannot recommend *Exiles* for production at the Abbey. Writing 'A Song'.

September

17	(Mon) Returns to London, with Maud and Iseult Gonne, who are searched at Southampton as possible spies. Stays at the Arts Club in Dover Street and sees a good deal of the Gonnes over the coming days in his attempt to persuade the authorities to allow them to travel to Dublin.
18	Instructs Ervine to refuse Arthur Sinclair rights in his Abbey plays for his touring company because he insists on calling it 'The Irish Players'. Sees MG in the evening. A disturbed night as he ponders his emotional life and the possibility of asking George Hyde-Lees to marry him.
19	Discusses his planned proposal to George Hyde-Lees with Iseult Gonne and has lunch with her, MG and Horton. Writes to tell AG that he has resolved to ask George Hyde-Lees to marry him.
20	Invites Horton to lunch to meet Iseult and MG.
21	Sees Iseult Gonne and discusses his relationship with her if he marries George Hyde-Lees.
24	Goes to stay with Mrs Tucker and her daughter George Hyde-Lees in Crowborough, Sussex.
26	Proposes to George Hyde-Lees and is accepted. Stays in Sussex until 1 October.
27	Telegraphs AG to ask if he can come to see her in Coole.

29   'The Balloon of the Mind' and 'To a Squirrel at Kyle-na-no' (poems, *VP*, 358, 359) published in the *New Statesman*.

October

1   (Mon) Returns to London from Crowborough accompanied by George Hyde-Lees, who applies for a marriage licence at a Paddington registry office.

2   Introduces his new fiancée to Iseult and MG.

3   Leaves London for Dublin and has a stormy passage. Goes to the Abbey Theatre after dinner.

4   Goes to Coole on a 7.00 am train. AG, very pleased at his engagement, advises him to marry as soon as possible. In the evening he cannot write because of the dark and has to talk to dull visitors.

5   Stays in Coole, writing from 11 am to 2 pm and then again after 5 pm. In the afternoon he drives to Ballylee with AG to see how the building is progressing and to give directions to the workmen.

6   'Ego Dominus Tuus' (poem (*VP*, 367–71) published in *Poetry* (Chicago). Tries but fails to start an essay and a poem, and discusses Abbey business with AG.

8   Goes to Dublin from Coole

9   Leaves Dublin for London. Sees George Hyde-Lees and they set their wedding-date for 20 October.

10   With the wedding fixed, he falls into wild misery, fearing that he has acted out of the wrong impulses.

12   Spends the day with Iseult Gonne.

13   Calmer about his emotional state and now thinks his marriage promises happiness and tranquillity.

15   Writes to tell JBY of his coming marriage. Sees George Hyde-Lees in the evening and chaffs her about Machiavelli.

17   Sees George Hyde-Lees at 3.00 pm

19   Sets out to tell Ricketts of his impending marriage, but is driven back by a zeppelin raid to MG's house, where he is dining, and is apparently obliged to remain the night there, but may have visited George Hyde-Lees.

20   Marries George Hyde-Lees at Harrow Road Registry Office, Paddington, with Pound as best man. WBY has two days of feverish illness and they postpone their honeymoon.

22   The Yeatses begin their honeymoon in Forest Row, Ashdown Forest, Sussex. WBY still in an agitated emotional state, reflected in his poem 'The Lover Speaks', which he writes over the next few days.

24   Both the Yeatses in a state of deep unhappiness and cast hororaries.

25   At Ashdown Forest writing verse, while the new Mrs Yeats (GY) casts horoscopes.

27	Finishes 'The Lover Speaks' and writes 'The Heart Replies' (later 'Owen Aherne and his Dancers'). GY begins the automatic writing that is to form the basis of *A Vision* and turns WBY's misery to happiness.
28	They walk to an inn on the edge of Ashdown Forest.
29	They visit the Dulacs for a few days. Walter Rummel sends WBY the music for *The Dreaming of the Bones*.

November

2	(Fri) They return to London until *c*.20 Nov. WBY refuses Elizabeth Young permission to produce *The Shadowy Waters*.
3	Has begun *The Only Jealousy of Emer*, a new Cuchulain play.
5	GY records 4 pages of automatic script, probably in the afternoon, and they do more in the evening, with Thomas of Dorlowicz as 'communicator'.
6	More automatic writing.
7	Two sessions of automatic writing with Thomas of Dorlowicz.
8	Repeats to Joyce that the Abbey Theatre cannot produce *Exiles*. Moves from London to Stone Cottage with GY. In the evening GY does more automatic writing.
9	At 6.45 pm another automatic writing session, largely taken up with an analysis of Iseult Gonne.
10	The automatic writing produces 17 pages of script.
11	More automatic writing, largely on the question of 'dreaming back' and the soul's desire for freedom.
12	Automatic writing in the afternoon, followed by a long session beginning at 5.35 pm.
13	Invites Horton to meet his new wife.
17	*The Wild Swans at Coole* published.
20	Returns with GY to Stone Cottage, where WBY continues writing *The Only Jealousy of Emer*, and GY works on a translation of Pico della Mirandola. They recommence the automatic writing sessions.
21	Two sessions of automatic writing.
22	Long session of automatic writing in the afternoon.
23	Short session of automatic writing.
24	Two session of automatic writing, the first beginning at 5.30 pm, the second at 8.30 pm.
25	Session of automatic writing. Thomas of Dorlowicz informs them that he has finished what he came to tell them at this period, but will return later.
29	A session of automatic writing under the control of 'Marcus'.
30	Two long sessions of automatic writing; Thomas has returned temporarily to help WBY write an essay.

December

3	(Mon) Session of automatic writing with Marcus as control.
5	A session of automatic writing at 8 pm with Thomas as control.
6	Two sessions of automatic writing with Thomas.
7	Sessions of automatic writing with Thomas, who advises WBY to stop for a month, and assures him that Iseult is all right.
8	The Yeatses move from Stone Cottage to Woburn Buildings, where they see a good deal of MG and her family.
10	Horton comes in for the evening.
15	Iseult Gonne stays the night at Woburn Buildings. WBY stops work on *Per Amica* and returns to writing poems, including 'Sixteen Dead Men'.
17	LR has dinner at Woburn Buildings and they discuss his new play, *The Lost Leader*.
c.18	Psychic experiments with Professor William Barrett.
19	A zeppelin raid on WBY's district of London lasts three hours, during which he and GY sit on the stairs.
20	The Yeatses move to Ashdown Cottage, Forest Row, to escape the zeppelin raids on London.
21	Two sessions of automatic writing, the second, beginning at 8.00 pm being particularly concerned with WBY's Cuchulain plays.
22	Session of automatic writing.
23	Session of automatic writing.
24	Iseult Gonne comes to spend Christmas with the Yeatses.
25	Very brief session of automatic writing.
c.26	The Yeatses stay with the Dulacs for a few days.
29	A session of automatic writing centres on an unsuccessful attempt to obtain information about Lane's will.
c.30	The Yeatses return to London, where WBY contracts influenza. They decide to live in Oxford and postpone their proposed trip to Ireland until the spring.
31	Session of automatic writing.

1918

January

1	(Tue) Session of automatic writing.
2	The Yeatses move to 45 Broad Street, Oxford. In a session of automatic writing, WBY tries to ascertain MG's appropriate phase.
3	Session of automatic writing.
4	Session of automatic writing, beginning at 5.00 pm.
5	Session of automatic writing, beginning at 8.35 pm.

6	Long session of automatic writing, with 'Thomas', 'Leaf' and 'Fish' as controls.
7	Two sessions of automatic writing with 'Leaf' as control.
10	Receives £15 for contributions to the *Little Review*.
13	Discusses his new dramatic projects at Gilbert Murray's house.
14	Finishes *The Only Jealousy of Emer*, and begins to think out *Calvary*.
17	A severe cold prevents any work for the following 8 days.
18	*Per Amica Silentia Lunae* published.
23	Robert Gregory killed by friendly fire in Italy.
29	WBY sends a batch of poems to Shorter. Because of ill-health, he does not attend a big Lane Picture Meeting in Dublin.
30	Writes to the *Observer* about the Lane Pictures.

February

6	(Wed) Finishes a Cuchulain poem, probably for *Only Jealousy*.
7	WBY and GY working every day in the Bodleian and in the evening on the increasingly subtle *Vision* system.
9	Asks Iseult Gonne for Thora Pilcher's horoscope. Is getting the encyclicals of Leo XIII and Pius X for MG, and suggests she studies Catholic economics.
16	Writes 'Tom O'Roughley'.
17	'Major Robert Gregory' (obituary appreciation; *UP* II. 429–31) published in the *Observer*.
22	Trying to write an elegy on Robert Gregory and has found a house at 4 Broad Street, Oxford, which he and GY will take from September.

March

4	(Mon) At a session of automatic writing the spirit of Anne Hyde, Countess of Ossory, suggests that WBY and GY should have a child.
5	Session of automatic writing.
8	The Yeatses abandon plans to stay in London on their way to Ireland and go directly from Oxford by way of Chester.
9	Arrive in Dublin, where they stay at the Royal Hibernian Hotel. Session of automatic writing.
10	WBY introduces GY to SMY, ECY, and probably Jack and Cottie Yeats at a family supper at Dundrum. Writing 'Under the Round Tower' (*VP*, 331–2) at this time.
11	Brief session of automatic writing.
12	Discusses with O'Donovan an Abbey revival of *The King's Threshold*, as the current hunger strikes give it topicality. Sees Gogarty's *Blight* and is disappointed. WBY and GY meet his sisters at the Abbey and GY is introduced to the Company in the Green Room after the plays.

13	The Yeatses leave Dublin for the Royal Hotel, Glendalough, where the sessions of automatic writing continue daily, and they read numerous plays submitted for production at the Abbey.
20	Finishes 'Shepherd and Goatherd', his first elegy for Robert Gregory.
22	Goes to Dublin for a meeting of the Lane Picture Committee.
24	Returns to Glendalough from Dublin.
26	Subscribes to the Coffey Memorial Fund.
28	The Yeatses leave Glendalough for Glenmalure. Begins writing 'The Double Vision of Michael Robartes' (*VP*, 382–4).
30	Session of automatic writing.

April

3	(Wed) The Yeatses move from Glenmalure to the Gresham Hotel in Dublin, where they invite James Stephens and his wife to dinner.
6	They leave Dublin for Coole.
8	Finishes 'Solomon to Sheba' (*VP*, 332–3).
13	WBY goes up to Dublin with GY.
14	Lectures on Blake at the Abbey on behalf of Lane Pictures.
15	The Yeatses return to Coole.
17	WBY argues with Margaret Gregory over dinner. The Yeatses stop using contraception. Writing 'A Prayer on Going into My House'.
20	The Yeatses leave Coole for Galway, where they stay c/o Mrs Little, The Crescent.

May

2	(Thu) The Yeatses move from Galway to Ballinamantane House, near Coole, where they conduct regular sessions of automatic writing. WBY is reading Catholic economics.
8	WBY goes to see AG about the threat of conscription in Ireland, and they think of closing the Abbey at the end of May.
13	Cancels a proposed lecture in Dublin on Modern Poetry because of the disturbed state of the country.
17	MG is arrested in Dublin on suspicion of being involved in a pro-German plot and, although never charged, is taken to England and imprisoned in London.
24	Is writing 'In Memory of Major Robert Gregory' and discussing it with AG.
25	Publishes a letter in the *Nation*, protesting against the plan to extend conscription to Ireland.
27	GY in Dublin. WBY visits Coole and inspects the refurbishment of Ballylee with Leslie Edmunds. Has finished reading medieval history and intends to turn to Spinoza.

June

1   (Sat) Spends the month at Ballinamantane House writing poems, continuing with the sessions of automatic writing, and keeping an eye on the workmen repairing Ballylee. He and GY cancel a proposed trip to London to attend to Iseult Gonne's and Sean MacBride's affairs on discovering that their difficulties have been resolved.

2   GY returns to Galway from Dublin.

14   Finishes 'In Memory of Major Robert Gregory'.

30   Writes a version of 'An Irish Airman Foresees his Death'.

July

6   (Sat) Visits Lough Cultra Castle with the architect Scott. Is writing 'The Phases of the Moon'.

13   Arranges for a copy of Aquinas's *Summa* to be sent to MG in Holloway prison, and is reading Joyce's *Ulysses* as it appears in the *Little Review*.

c.14–17   GY spends a brief holiday at Lahinch on the coast of Co. Clare.

22   Dines at Coole with Sean MacBride, who is staying with the Yeatses in Ballinamantane House.

Late July The Yeatses pay a visit to Gogarty and his wife at Renvyle House in Connamara.

August

3   (Sat) 'In Memory of Robert Gregory' (poem; *VP*, 323–8) published in the *English Review*.

c.10   WBY and GY go to London to save Iseult Gonne from the clutches of Iris Barry, and move her from her flat to Woburn Buildings. They see Pound there.

16   Accompanied by Iseult Gonne, WBY consults Ricketts about furniture for Ballylee and afterwards dines with Iseult.

17   WBY returns alone to Dublin from London.

20   Returns to Galway; Sean MacBride also there. Late this month WBY writes a Preface for a new edition of *The Wild Swans at Coole*.

September

2   (Mon) Sean MacBride leaves Ballinamantane House.

12   The Yeatses move into the cottage at Ballylee, although the Castle is still unfinished.

13   Discusses the future of the Abbey with AG and writes to LR with their proposals.

20   Writes 'Two Songs of a Fool' (*VP*, 380–1).

24   Goes to Dublin from Galway with GY to look for a house to rent and to see various people about the campaign for the

return of the Lane Pictures. Sees Maurice Dalton's *Sable and Gold* at the Abbey.

25   WBY, GY and SMY see over MG's house at 73 Stephen's Green with a view to renting it. In the evening he is entertained to dinner by Horace Plunkett with R. A. Anderson, James MacNeill, LR, and G. K. Chesterton.

27   GY returns to Galway. WBY speaks at a dinner at the Arts Club at which his and GY's healths are drunk. Writes a draft of 'Lines Written in Dejection'.

October

1   (Tue) In Dublin seeing various people and putting materials for *A Vision* into order. Writes to ask G. K. Chesterton to lecture at the Abbey. Takes MG's house in Stephen's Green for four months at a rent of £2.10s per week.

2   Cannot go over 73 Stephen's Green with SMY as he intends because Miss Delaney, who is acting as MG's agent, is not there, but they buy furniture for the house nevertheless.

4   Taken by Stephen Gwynn to see Samuels and Edward Shortt, the Chief Secretary for Ireland, as part of a campaign to get MG released from prison. WBY also asks that MG should be examined by an independent doctor. Discusses the revival of Synge's *Deirdre of the Sorrows* at the Abbey.

5   Publishes seven poems in the *Little Review*. The Yeatses move into 73 Stephen's Green.

7   Writes to Lord Haldane urging him to prevent the extension of conscription to Ireland.

8   GY leaves Ballylee to join WBY in Dublin. They resume regular sessions of automatic writing.

10   Attends the first meeting of the Dublin Drama League.

11   Writes a Preface to *Two Plays for Dancers*. Attends a dinner in honour of Chesterton and makes a speech.

13   Attends Chesterton's lecture at the Abbey; Shaw also speaks.

14   Persuades Gwynn to apply to the Chief Secretary for MG's release.

16   Sees LR's *The Whiteheaded Boy* at the Abbey.

18   Attends a meeting of the Lane Pictures Committee.

20   Attends a lecture on 'Equality' by Shaw at the Abbey Theatre.

24   Meets AG at the Abbey Theatre.

25   Attends a meeting of the Lane Picture Committee, with AG, Shaw, Sir Robert Woods, Ellen Duncan, Cruise O'Brien, Atkinson and Bodkin.

29   MG released from Holloway prison and sent to a sanatorium.

November

1	(Fri) Attends a meeting of the Lane Picture Committee at the Arts Club, with AG, Ruth Shine and others, which rescinds the decision to seek arbitration.
10	Session of automatic writing.
11	The First World War ends. WBY speaks to AE's Hermetic Society on his lunar symbolism.
17	Asks Sturge Moore to design the cover of *The Wild Swans at Coole*. Quinn cables that JBY has been knocked down in New York. GY, seven months pregnant, is taken seriously ill with pneumonia.
23	Writes 'Demon and Beast'.
24	Although banned from travelling to Ireland, MG arrives at 73 Stephen's Green, having escaped detection. WBY, worried by GY's perilous medical condition, refuses her admission and a bitter quarrel breaks out between them.
26	Moves into the Stephen's Green Club to make room for nurses for GY, who is still dangerously ill.
29	WBY sees Mrs Campbell in Dublin.

December

8	(Sun) GY gets up for the first time since being taken ill with pneumonia. WBY working on material for *A Vision*.
c.10	The Yeatses leave 73 Stephen's Green for 96 Stephen's Green.
11	Automatic scripts begin again after GY's illness.
14	General Election, in which Sinn Fein scores a resounding success.
16	The Yeatses go to Wicklow for some days so that GY can recuperate. WBY begins writing 'Towards Break of Day'. They return to Dublin for Christmas.

1919

January

4	(Sat) *The Dreaming of the Bones* (play; *VPl*, 762–79) published in the *Little Review* and *The Only Jealous of Emer* (play; *VPl*, 528–75) in *Poetry* (Chicago). Early this month GY's illness, the news of JBY's accident in New York, and his quarrel with MG causes WBY severe nervous exhaustion and eye trouble. Writes 'The Second Coming'.
5	Sends Quinn £35 for JBY's nurse.
9	The Yeatses go to the Spa Hotel in Lucan for rest and recuperation.
10	WBY receives £15 from Pound for his contributions to the *Little Review*. Begins to write 'On a Political Prisoner'.

c. 13	Returns to Dublin from Lucan.
16	Busy writing lyrics for the *Little Review*.
20	Begins rehearsals of *On Baile's Strand* and later lectures on *A Vision* material to a mystical group. SMY calls, alarmed at the prospect of JBY crossing the Atlantic while it is still heavily mined.
21	Sends Quinn £40 towards JBY's repatriation to Ireland.
26	Lectures at the Abbey on psychic research with Dr William Crawford of Belfast.
29	Friends again with MG. *Two Plays for Dancers* published. Speaks after T. C. Kingsmill Moore's inaugural address 'Socialism and War' at the Historical Society, Trinity College Dublin, and dines there afterwards.
30	Lectures at TCD. Finishes 'On a Political Prisoner'.
31	Speaks at the Arts Club on *A Vision* material.

February

2	(Sun) Rehearses *On Baile's Strand* at the Abbey, where he meets AG who reads him her new play *The Jester*. In the evening he debates at the Abbey with Professor John Howley on the Catholic attitudes to psychical research.
3	Attends the dress rehearsal of *On Baile's Strand* and is present at most performances over the coming days.
10	GY goes to stay with SMY in Dundrum. WBY develops a violent cold, which keeps him confined to the house, so he does not see AG off to London.
19	Fred O'Donovan leaves the Abbey to set up his own touring company.
22	WBY and GY leave 96 Stephen's Green; he stays at the Stephen's Green Club, while she moves into the Hibernian Hotel for a few days. They have let 18 Woburn Buildings to Douglas Goldring and his wife.
23	Chairs another debate on Spiritualism at the Abbey.
25	GY enters Smyth's private nursing home in Upper Fitzwilliam Street.
26	Anne Yeats born at 10 am. WBY visits the nursing home every evening until GY and Anne leave on 19 March.
28	Offers LR the managership of the Abbey after a misunderstanding with AG.

March

5	(Wed) Takes charge at the Abbey and directs rehearsals of MacNamara's *The Rebellion in Ballycullen*.
10	AG returns to Dublin and WBY consults her about the latest events at the Abbey.
11	The Macmillan edition of *The Wild Swans at Coole* published.

12	Dines with AG and Cruise O'Brien at the Arts Club. AG and WBY go on to hear James Stephens read his stories from the *Tain*, and WBY recites 'On a Political Prisoner' and 'The Rose Tree'.
13	Drops in to see AG on his way to a meeting of the Drama League.
16	Entertains ladies from Sligo to tea and consults the astrologer Cyril Fagan at the Arts Club. At about this time begins writing 'A Prayer for my Daughter'.
19	Takes AG to lunch, and in the evening sees her act the title role in *Cathleen ni Houlihan* at the Abbey. He, GY and Anne Yeats move to a furnished house, Dundrum Lodge, Dundrum, until late April.
20	Calls in at the Abbey where AG reads him *The Seagull*, a new play by F. H. O'Donnell.
21	Lunches with AG.
25	Gives Unwin permission to raise the price of *Poems* from 7*s*. 6*d*. to 10*s*. 6*d*.
29	Sees the last 3 Acts of *John Bull's Other Island* at the Abbey.
30	In Dublin for a debate with LR at the Abbey on 'The Abbey Theatre, Past and Future' and stays in the city for the night.
31	Consults LR about the legal consequences of Abbey plays being performed by new touring companies of former members, and attends an Abbey rehearsal. He and GY have a session of automatic writing.

April

1	(Tue) Begins writing 'A Prayer for my Daughter'.
8	The English edition of *The Cutting of an Agate* published. SMY and ECY throw a party for WBY and GY, attended by 50 people.
13	LR calls to collaborate on a press release about the Abbey.
20	Boyd interviews WBY about the Abbey for the *Irish Commonwealth*.
21	Has tea with AG and confesses that he is disappointed with the reception of *The Wild Swans at Coole*.
25	Attends a business meeting at the Abbey, after which he dines with AG at the Arts Club and they go on to see her *The Dragon* at the Abbey.
27	Anne Yeats christened at St. Mary's Church, Donnybrook.
30	WBY and GY unable to go to Ballylee as planned, so GY goes to stay with her sisters-in-law at Gurteen Dhas, while WBY moves into the Stephen's Green Club.

May

6	(Tue) Dines with Gogarty.
9	Crosses from Dublin to London, were he stays until 27 May. Calls to see Ricketts.
12	Sees a performance of Edmond Rostand's *Cyrano de Bergerac*.

13	WBY and his mother-in-law inspect 18 Woburn Buildings and find a good deal of damage and dirt. In the evening he dines with Dulac. GY arrives in Ballylee for some days.
15	Iseult Gonne joins GY at Ballylee
c.17	Sees a rehearsal of *The Player Queen*.
19	GY joins WBY in London.
25	Attends a performance of *The Player Queen* given by the Stage Society.
26	GY goes to Oxford. WBY attends the second performance of *The Player Queen* in London.
27	Joins GY at the Boar's Hill Hotel, near Oxford. They lease 4 Broad Street for the coming winter.
28	Sessions of automatic writing.
29	Session of automatic writing.

June

10	(Tue) WBY and GY stay with the Dulacs.
13	Sends Quinn £234 to pay JBY's debts.
14	The Yeatses travel to Ireland from London.
15–17	The Yeatses stay with the Gogartys in Dublin and see the architect Scott about work on Ballylee.
18	The Yeatses arrive in Ballylee for the summer, where they continue with the automatic writing.
25	WBY gives up the lease for 18 Woburn Buildings.
Late June	The Yeatses return briefly to Dublin to see Anne Yeats.

July

2	(Wed) Spends two days in Kilkenny researching Anne Hyde's burial place.
4	The Yeatses return to Dublin.
7	GY, Anne Yeats and her nurse return to Ballylee. WBY, still in Dublin, tries to get into TCD Library, which is closed for two weeks.
8	WBY spends the day wandering around Chapelizod.
9	Horace Plunkett calls to see WBY. Later WBY meets AE for a friendly chat, and tells him about GY's automatic writing. Is invited to lecture at a Japanese university for two years.
10	Reads in TCD Library, having obtained special permission.
11	Dictates an article. WBY and AE dine with Horace Plunkett at the O'Neills.
14	Returns to Ballylee.
23	Goes to Coole and reads AG a draft of 'If I were Four and Twenty'.
26	WBY and GY stay in Galway, on their way to a fishing holiday at Oughterard on Lough Corib, where they stay until 2 August and where WBY questions GY's spirit communicators on the nature of victimage and the ideal frequency of sexual intercourse.

August

2	(Sat) The Yeatses move back to Ballylee.
9	Visits Coole
17	The Yeatses stay with Gogarty at Renvyle, where GY sees the ghost of a young boy.
22	They return to Ballylee.
23	First part of 'If I were Four-and-Twenty' (essay; *Expl*, 263–80) published in the *Irish Statesman*.
29	WBY briefly visits Dublin from Ballylee.
30	In Dublin, sees LR and Harris about the future of the Sunday lectures at the Abbey. Second part of 'If I were Four-and-Twenty' published in the *Irish Statesman*.

September

2	(Tue) The Yeatses dine at Coole with Martyn and Professor Vendryès, the editor of the *Revue Celtique*. WBY stays the night and helps AG with her biography of Lane. During this month he writes 'An Image from a Past Life'.
13	At Coole with Vere O'Brien and Captain and Miss Ward. Later he argues with AG over Abbey finances.
22	The Yeatses stay in Dublin on their way back to Oxford.
23	GY and WBY dine with SM and ECY in Dublin.
24	GY, Anne Yeats and her nurse return to England, but WBY remains in Dublin, delayed by tonsillitis and a railway strike.

October

1	(Wed) Still ill in Dublin early this month with a bad attack of tonsillitis.
6	Gogarty takes him for a drive in the Wicklow mountains.
12	WBY manages to travel to Oxford and join his family and two Irish servants at 4 Broad Street.
27	L. A. G. Strong attends WBY's 'Monday Evening'.
28	The Yeatses go to London for his lecture and to arrange passports for their coming trip to USA. WBY calls on AG and reads her 'A People's Theatre', a letter-article addressed to her.
29	The Yeatses dine with Dulac at the Mont Blanc Restaurant in Gerrard Street and afterwards go to George's Club, probably the Lyceum.
30	WBY lectures in London. He also calls on Watt to discuss publication arrangements for *Four Plays for Dancers*, *The Player Queen*, and a book of essays.
31	Sees Ricketts.

November

2	(Sun) WBY calls on AG in London and she reads him extracts from the draft of her biography of Lane.

3	Returns to Oxford from London.
7	WBY's mother-in-law visits them in Oxford to see Anne.
8	'A Prayer for my Daughter' (poem; *VP*, 403–6) published in the *Irish Statesman*. Writing 'Under Saturn'.
19	Lectures to the Oxford University Dramatic Society on 'The People's Theatre'. Meets Richard Hughes.
22	Edward Shanks and Siegfried Sassoon call on WBY.
29	The first part of 'A People's Theatre' (letter; *Expl*, 244–53) published in the *Irish Statesman*.
30	Lectures on 'Recent Poetry' to a student society.

December

6	(Sat) The second part of 'A People's Theatre' (*Expl*, 253–9) published in the *Irish Statesman*.
14	The Yeatses stay with Ottoline Morrell at Garsington.
30	Anne Yeats and the servants return to Ireland; GY and WBY remain in Oxford, staying at the Cranston Hotel but using 4 Broad Street during the day.

1920

January

7	(Wed) The Yeatses move to London and stay at the Gwalia Hotel as their sailing has been delayed by an American dock strike. WBY spends time in the British Museum, reading recent writers on Blake.
13	With GY, sails for the USA on the *Carmania*; lectures in America until 29 May. During this tour WBY reads all Jane Austen's novels with great satisfaction.
24	They arrive in New York and stay at the Algonquin Hotel, where Quinn collects them to dine with JBY.
25	They go with JBY to Quinn's for lunch.
27	After an unsuccessful attempt at automatic writing at 5.25 pm, they spend the evening with Quinn.
29	They attend the Annual Dinner of the Poetry Society of America at the Hotel Astor. JBY, Jeanne Foster, Witter Bynner, Padraic Colum, Noguchi and Siegfried Sassoon are among those present.

February

1	(Sun) A session of automatic writing.
2	WBY lectures at the University of Toronto at 8.30 pm on 'The Theatre of the People'.
3	Gives a Poetry Reading at 8.30 pm to the Women's Directory, Montreal.

13	Lectures on 'The Theatre' at the Hampton Bookshop, Northampton, Massachusetts.
17	Lectures at 11 am on 'The Theatre' to the League for Political Education at the Carnegie Hall, New York.
18	Lectures on 'The Younger Generation of Poets' at 5.00 pm to Yale University, after which he dines with William Lyon Phelps.
19	Lectures on 'The Younger Generation of Poets' to the Fine Arts Society, Washington DC.
20	Lectures at the Brooklyn Institute on 'The Theatre', but is taken to the wrong venue and arrives half an hour late.
21	Attends a tiring luncheon at the League for Political Education.
22	Examines the architecture in 5th Avenue. Quinn arranges for him to dine at the St Regis with him and the editors of the *Dial*, Thayer and Seldes, but WBY is unable to attend because of illness. Quinn visits him at the Algonquin after the dinner.
23	WBY's lecture in Pittsburgh is cancelled. He stays in bed at the Algonquin until the evening. JBY visits in the afternoon and after he has left Quinn, who has cashed a cheque for the Yeatses, calls and learns that WBY has given an interview on Ulster. Marsh of the Macmillan Company calls and Quinn leaves at 5.00 pm, but returns at 7.15 pm to see the Yeatses to the train.
24	Lectures at 7.30 pm on 'The Theatre' at Oberline College and afterwards goes to Pittsburg.
29	The Yeatses arrive in Chicago.

March

1	(Mon) A session of automatic writing.
2	WBY lectures to the Friday Club in the afternoon and on 'Friends of my Youth' at 8.15 pm at the University of Chicago.
3	Harriet Monroe, the editor of *Poetry*, gives a dinner in Chicago in honour of the Yeatses.
9	WBY lectures to the Drama League, Oak Park, Illinois.
10	The Yeatses leave Chicago for the South West.
13	Lectures on the Theatre at Brigham Young University in Salt Lake City.
15	The Yeatses meet the elders of the Mormon Church, and WBY lectures on 'The Theatre' at the University of Utah.
19	Lectures on 'The Theatre of the People' to the Drama League at the Masonic Temple in Portland.
20	Junto Sato gives WBY his ancestral Japanese sword in Portland.
21	At a session of automatic writing in Portland, the 'communicators' discuss the ideal time for the conception of a new avatar.
22	The Yeatses leave Portland for San Francisco by an evening train.
23	Travelling by train to California.
24	Automatic writing on train. Lectures at Berkeley.

25	Lectures on the Theatre in San Francisco in the evening.
26	The Yeatses given a Reception by Mary Phelan in San Francisco.
28	Automatic writing in Pasadena.
29	8.20 pm automatic writing in Pasadena, but George's spirit communicator, Dionertes, informs them that in future such communication is to come through GY speaking in sleep, her words to be recorded by WBY.
30	Yeatses in Pasadena.
31	Lectures to the Hollywood Women's Club on Younger Poets in the afternoon.

April

2	(Fri) Gives a Poetry Reading to the Friday Morning Club, Los Angeles.
3	Lectures in the afternoon to the Los Angeles Center Drama League.
5	Lectures in the afternoon on 'Friends of my Youth' to the Ebell Club, Los Angeles.
6	Lectures to the Shakespeare Club, Pasadena. Iseult Gonne marries Francis Stuart in Ireland.
7	Lectures in Santa Barbara.
12	Lectures on 'Friends of My Youth' to the Lyceum Association, New Orleans.
13	The Yeatses leave New Orleans by train for San Antonio and automatic writing corrects some previous errors.
14	WBY lectures on 'The Theatre' to the Southern Association of College Women, San Antonio, Texas.
15	Lectures at Georgetown, Texas, and at the University of Texas at Austin.
16	Lectures in Waco, Texas.
17	Lectures at 2 pm to the Matheson Club in Dallas, where the Yeatses remain until 21 April.
18	Lectures in Sherman Texas.
21	The Yeatses leave Dallas for Missouri.
23	Lectures on 'The Theatre' to the Teachers College, Kirksville, Missouri.
26	Lectures in Nashville, Tennessee.
28	The Yeatses in Cleveland.
29	They hold a session of automatic writing on the train from Cleveland to New York.
30	The Yeatses return to the Algonquin Hotel, New York.

May

6	(Thu) WBY lectures in Jordan Hall, Boston, at 4.00 pm, and addresses the School of Expression alumni dinner in the evening.
7	Poetry Reading at Wellesley College, where he remains until 9 May.

10	Returns to New York, staying with Quinn for rest of the month.
11	The Yeatses dine with the lecture agent, Pond.
16	A session of automatic writing.
17	A session of automatic writing. Yeats and Quinn go to see de Valera.
18	WBY is recorded on a moving film in New York.
22	WBY and GY dine with JBY.
23	A session of automatic writing corrects earlier errors.
26	Quinn gives a dinner in his apartment for WBY, GY and JBY.
27	Dinner with Quinn.
28	The Yeatses arrive in Montreal.
29	They leave Montreal for England on the *Megantic*.

June

c.6	(Sun) The Yeatses arrive back in England and stay at 27 Royal Crescent, Holland Park, London, as their Oxford house has been let. GY goes to Dublin to see Anne. WBY buys a green parrot.
14	GY returns from Dublin with Anne Yeats and the family moves into Pound's flat in Church Street, Kensington, where WBY prepares *Four Plays for Dancers* for publication.
18	They go to see Mrs Pat Campbell in Philip Moeller's 3-Act comedy *Madam Sand* at the Duke of York's Theatre.
19	WBY calls on Sir Ian and Lady Hamilton at 1 Hyde Park Gardens, to introduce GY to them.
22	Sends material for *Michael Robartes and the Dancer* to the Cuala Press.
26	Hears that work has not yet begun on restoring Thoor Ballylee.
28	Sends copy for *Four Plays for Dancers* to Macmillan via Watt.
Late June	The Yeatses spend an evening with Tagore at Rothenstein's studio, where Tagore sings some of the songs from *Gitanjali* and Jelly d'Aranyi plays the violin.

July

1	(Thu) Calls on Ricketts.
3	Eric Morgan visits the Yeatses.
12	The Yeatses return to 4 Broad Street, Oxford.
23	WBY tries to enlist the help of the Sinn Fein member for South Galway in preventing the intimidation of their neighbours and to investigate a possible threatening letter to GY.
24	SMY comes to Oxford for an extended visit.
28	MG wires him to come and help sort out the marital problems that have arisen between Iseult and Francis Stuart.
29	WBY bumps into Lord Dunsany and his wife at the Euston Hotel; they catch the 8.40 pm boat train and WBY's luggage is searched at Holyhead for concealed firearms. The ferry is so crowded that WBY sleeps on the floor.

30	LR calls on him at the St Stephen's Green Club in Dublin in the morning and WBY catches the 3.30 pm train to Glenmalure, Wicklow.
31	At Glenmalure, both MG and Iseult give him an account of the quarrel with Francis Stuart. WBY persuades Iseult Gonne to enter a nursing home and collects depositions from neighbours and friends as evidence of Stuart's cruelty towards her. Finishes 'On a Picture of a Black Centaur by Edmund Dulac' (*VP*, 442), partly inspired by a picture by Cecil Salkeld, who is also at Glenmalure.

August

1	(Sun) Moves back to Dublin and stays at St Stephen's Green Club. Greatly upsets LR with his account of Iseult's marital problems.
2	Consults Dr Bethel Solomons about getting Iseult into a nursing home and sees LR at 4.30 pm.
4	MG and Iseult Gonne arrive in Dublin from Glenmalure; WBY meets them at the station and arranges for Iseult to go straight to the nursing home. He later calls at the office of the architect Scott to arrange an interview about the refurbishment of Ballylee.
5	Consults Desmond Fitzgerald about the letter threatening AG. Sees Kerrigan and Sara Allgood in Ervine's *Mixed Marriage* and his own *Cathleen ni Houlihan* at the Abbey.
6	George writes to tell him that she has had a miscarriage.
7	With MG, sees Iseult Gonne at the nursing home and dictates two letters for her to copy: one to Francis Stuart, the other to a solicitor. In the evening he consults MG about Iseult's affairs.
9	Sees MG in the morning about Iseult Gonne's affairs. In the afternoon discusses the refurbishment of Ballylee with the architect Scott. AG arrives in Dublin.
10	Sees MG and relays AG's advice that she should consult a doctor about Stuart's mental health.
12	Returns to England and meets GY in London, where they consult the spirit communicator Dionertes about recent events; he advises the conception of another child.
13	WBY and GY return to Oxford where he works hard at *A Vision*. Making Oxford friends, particularly Ottoline Morrell, and seeing a number of people who are passing through. Buys two canaries.
21	SMY returns to Dublin from Oxford.
22	Writes to Pound that 'Hugh Selwyn Mauberley' has moved him 'deeply' and to Watt to accept Macmillan's terms for *Four Plays for Dancers*.

September

4   (Sat) The Yeatses spend the weekend as guests at Ottoline
            Morrell's house, Garsington Manor. During the rest of the
            month WBY works at poems (including 'All Souls' Night'),
            prose, and Abbey affairs.
9   Suggests to Quinn that he should rent Garsington Manor.
28   Begins an unsuccessful campaign to persuade his father to
            return to Ireland from New York.
29   Writes to *The Times* to complain of British atrocities in Ireland,
            but his letter is not published. Late this month Asquith calls on
            him in Oxford and they discuss the Irish situation.

October

1   (Fri) Invites William Force Stead to dinner.
7   Finishes a version of his poem 'All Souls' Night'.
8   Arrives in Dublin with GY to have his tonsils removed by Gogarty.
            They dine with LR that evening at the Hibernian Hotel.
10   Dines with Plunkett and urges him and AE to get Asquith
            to mount a campaign against Black and Tan atrocities in
            Ireland.
13   Haemorrhages badly after his tonsillitis operation at the
            Elphis Nursing Home and becomes very ill.
17   Although still ill, returns to England to avoid a rail strike, and
            boards the ferry for the following morning's sailing.
18   MG visits him on the ferry before it sails. He takes three days
            on the journey home, sleeping at Holyhead and at Chester
            and going direct from Chester to Oxford. For the rest of the
            month he convalesces in Oxford, corrects proofs, and
            arranges the pictures in his study.
23   'Easter 1916' (poem; *VP*, 391–4) published in the *New
            Statesman*.

November

1   (Mon) Early this month he revises *The King's Threshold* and con-
            tinues writing 'All Souls' Night'.
6   'The Second Coming' and 'An Image from a Past Life' (poems,
            VP, 401–2, 389–90) published in the *Nation* and five poems
            appear in the *Dial*.
13   'A Meditation in Time of War', 'Towards Break of Day', and
            'On a Political Prisoner' (*VP*, 417–27, 398–9, 397) published
            in the *Nation*.
14   Finishes his revision of *The King's Threshold*, but abandons the
            idea of rewriting it in prose. Working on his Memoirs.
19   Ezra and Dorothy Pound begin a week's visit to the Yeatses and
            Dorothy stays on.

26	Sends AG 'Reprisals', a new poem about Robert Gregory, but she asks him not to publish it. Has corrected the first proofs of *Four Plays for Dancers*.
c.27	Sturge Moore visits the Yeatses.
c.29	Robert Bridges dines with the Yeatses.

December

1	(Wed) Takes the Chair at a dinner for Horace Plunkett given by the Oxford Irish Club and Plunkett goes back to the house with him afterwards.
9	A member of the Fabian Society tells him at lunch that Lloyd George will stay in power for 20 years.
11	WBY's mother-in-law, Nelly Tucker, comes to stay.
12	Hears from AG that the Abbey Theatre may have to close.
18	Has written 18,000 words of his memoirs in the last month, and is reading economics for a lecture to the Oxford University Irish Club.
20	Resumes contact with Frank Pearce Sturm.
23	Discusses his long-term publishing plans with Macmillan.
25	Ill with some kind of poisoning, possibly from a leaking gas-pipe.
27	Hears that Thoor Ballylee has been used by the Black and Tans and much damage done there. Begins to think of going for an extended period to Italy with GY, who is again pregnant.
30	GY goes to London to consult her solicitor about compensation for the damage at Ballylee and calls on the Pounds while she is there.

1921

January

6	(Thu) The Dulacs stay with the Yeatses in Oxford for a few days.
11	The Australian theatre director, Louis Esson, visits WBY.
15	Refuses to attend 'Warriors' Day' celebrations in London because of the behaviour of the Black and Tans in Ireland.
17	The Yeatses abandon their Italian plans because GY's mother is seriously ill. Reads AG's play *Aristotle's Bellows* but does not like it.
c.20–3	The Yeatses visit Wells and then go on to Glastonbury.
24	Moves with GY to stay at Stone Cottage.
25	Restates his artistic terms for acting as literary editor of the Cuala Press.
31	Stops over in London on his way back to Oxford from Sussex.

February

1	(Tue) Attends a performance of Ben Jonson's *Volpone* at the Phoenix Theatre, London. Huxley, Sassoon, Swinnerton, Ervine

and Shanks also in the audience. *Michael Robartes and the Dancer* published.

2   Returns to Oxford from London on the 1.35 pm train with LR.

8   Learns that accounts of the damage at Thoor Ballylee have been greatly exaggerated. GY is having a difficult pregnancy.

12   Sturm comes to stay. The Indian poetess Sarojini Naidu comes to tea.

17   WBY denounces British policy in Ireland in a speech at the Oxford Union.

22   Dines with Richard Hughes and the Brome Society in Balliol College at 8.30 pm.

28   Lunches with A. E. Coppard at the Brome Society.

29   The Yeatses in London for a few days.

Late Feb   The Yeatses let 4 Broad Street for four months from April to save money.

March

5   (Sat) 'All Souls' Night' (poem, *VP*, 470–4) published in the *London Mercury*.

6   WBY and GY stay the night with Ottoline Morrell at Garsington. Siegfried Sassoon is a fellow-guest.

7   WBY lunches with the Masefields at the Brome Society.

21   William Force Stead attends WBY's 'Monday Evening'. The Abbey, like other Dublin theatres, is forced to close for a week by the imposition of an 8 pm curfew.

31   Publishes a letter in the *TLS* about the Lane Pictures.

April

1   (Fri) Lets his house in Oxford and stays the night at the New Inn.

2   Moves into Minchin's Cottage, Shillingford, Berkshire. Anne Yeats ill with whooping cough.

9   Reading Eugénie Strong's *Apotheosis and After Life*, essays on art and religion in the Roman Empire.

May

3   (Tue) In London to deliver a series of lectures for the Abbey Fund. Sees Eva Fowler, and spends a dull evening at Ricketts' who renews a promise to design the cover for a volume of WBY's poems. WBY is rewriting a number of poems.

4   Sees AG and Mrs Huth Jackson in the afternoon; dines with Dulac in the evening, and later sees Christina Stoddart.

5   Lunch at the Queen's Restaurant with the Fagans, AE and Plunkett, and afterwards lectures at the Fagans' on behalf of the Abbey Theatre fund to which Plunkett subscribes £100. He sees Dr. W. Hammond about GD matters. Later WBY reads AG a version of 'Nineteen Hundred and Nineteen'.

8	In the morning goes to see the incumbent of St Paul's Church, Knightsbridge, with Mrs Huth Jackson. In the afternoon sees Eva Fowler.
10	Lunches with AG at Una Pope-Hennessy's and afterwards gives a lecture and a reading on behalf of the Abbey at Mrs Herbert Johnson's which raises £39.
12	Attends AG's lecture at the Fagans' on behalf of the Abbey, followed by a performance of *The Gaol Gate*.
24	Passes through London on his way to lecture in Lincoln. In London sees AG, his tailor, and a dancer at the New Oxford Music Hall.
25	Leaves London for Lincoln, where he gives two lectures.
26	Returns to Shillingford, where he is ill.

June

4	(Sat) The first part of 'Four Years' (autobiography; *Aut*, 113–39) published in the *London Mercury* and the *Dial*. Early this month WBY rereads Trollope's *The Warden* and *Barchester Towers* and continues his attempt to persuade JBY to return to Ireland.
10	Sees GY's doctor in Oxford, who tells him that not all children are so well behaved as Anne Yeats. Werner Laurie offers him £500 for the rights to a limited, signed edition of *Reveries over Childhood and Youth*.
28	*Selected Poems* published in New York.
29	The Yeatses move to Cuttlebrook House, Thame.

July

1	(Fri) Begins the enlargement of his memoirs for the Werner Laurie edition, while correcting the proofs for the Cuala edition.
2	The second part of 'Four Years' (autobiography; *Aut*, 139–63) published in the *London Mercury* and the *Dial*.
6	Force Stead visits the Yeatses.
11	A truce declared in the Anglo-Irish War.

August

6	(Sat) Final part of 'Four Years' (autobiography; *Aut*, 164–200) published in the *London Mercury* and the *Dial*.
22	Michael Yeats born in Thame, but becomes ill and is seen by a specialist later in the month. At about this time WBY writes 'A Prayer for my Son' (*VP*, 435–6).

September

3	(Sat) 'Thoughts upon the Present State of the World' (poem, later 'Nineteen Hundred and Nineteen'; *VP*, 428–33) published in the *Dail*.
9	Ottoline Morrell calls.

13	The Yeatses leave Thame for Dublin, where Michael is to have an operation. WBY writes 'The Wheel' (*VP*, 343).
14	In Dublin, staying at the Hibernian Hotel.
15	At Abbey rehearsals followed by tea with AG at the Hibernian Hotel.
16	Lunches with AG, sees AE, and has dinner with AG at the Gresham, where he speaks of moving to Italy.
18	WBY and GY lunch with SMY, ECY and Susan Mitchell at Gurteen Dhas.
19	Sees Horace Plunkett and prophesies 30 years of revolutionary politics.
21	Crosses to London.
23	Goes to Norwich from London to open Monck's Maddermarket Theatre and attends a production of *As You Like It* there.
29	WBY in London.
30	Returns to Oxford.

October

8	(Sat) Enlarging his memoirs and rereading Shelley.
25	The Yeatses take Michael Yeats to London for treatment for a triple hernia.
26	WBY sees a rehearsal of *The Land of Heart's Desire*, being produced by Allan Wade at the Kingsway Theatre.
27	WBY returns to Oxford, but GY remains in London to be near Michael Yeats.
28	*Four Plays for Dancers* published. WBY attends a lecture by Richard Ashe King in Oxford and sees him to the train.
29	GY telegraphs that Michael Yeats needs an operation. WBY sends AG and LR a revised version of *The King's Threshold* for a new production at the Abbey.
30	Michael Yeats undergoes an operation in London.
31	GY telegraphs that the operation is a success. WBY writes a new passage for *The King's Theshold*.

November

2	(Wed) Goes to London on way to Scotland and sees GY.
c.3	Attends a performance of *The Sleeping Beauty*.
5	WBY travels to Glasgow to begin a Scottish lecture tour.
6	Reading Hall Caine's biography of Rossetti and a book on Mormon history.
7	Lectures in a Glasgow church and afterwards a lost Middleton relative, a portrait painter, introduces himself, and they stay up talking and drinking whisky.
8	Dines with his newly-found Middleton relative.
10	Learns that his lecture at Aberdeen has been cancelled because of possible political hostility. Lunches with students at Glasgow

University and lectures to them on 'The Theatre'. Dines with Agnes Raeburn, a distant relative, in Glasgow and lectures afterwards.

14 Returns to Oxford on conclusion of his Scottish tour.

16 Michael Yeats leaves the London nursing home and returns to Oxford after his operation.

18 WBY meets Richard Ashe King at Oxford station and attends his lecture; King dines and stays the night with the Yeatses.

23 Attends Ashe King's third lecture in Oxford.

December

1 (Thu) WBY ill, confined to the house and unable to do much work for several days.

7 Sends LR a new ending to the prose *Hour-Glass*.

16 LR comes to stay until 20 December.

17 The Yeatses, Ottoline Morrell and LR lunch with the Duke and Duchess of Marlborough at Blenheim Palace.

18 Horace Plunkett calls in.

19 Suggests to AG that the Abbey should ask the new Irish Government to take them over as an Irish National Theatre.

20 Michael Yeats christened, with LR as godfather and Ottoline Morrell also present. Afterwards lunch, presents and champagne at the Yeatses.

*c.*21 *Four Years* published by the Cuala Press. The Anglo-Irish Treaty is debated by the Dail; WBY is in deep gloom about Ireland and suffering from a heavy cold.

26 Takes to his bed with severe influenza

1922

January

7 (Sat) The Dail ratifies the Treaty, leading to civil war in Ireland.

9 WBY proposes a new 6-volume collected edition of his work.

12 Revising his memoir for publication.

18 WBY and GY go to Paris to attend an Irish Race Conference, where he speaks on 'The Plays and Lyrics of Modern Ireland' on 23 January.

26 Leaves Paris for England where he lectures in Brighton.

27 Returns to Oxford. Hears a rumour that he might be appointed Minister for Arts in the new Irish Government.

February

1 (Wed) Receives a wire from Michael Rafferty, the Gort builder, saying that he is beginning work on Thoor Ballylee.

3 JBY dies in New York.

12	GY goes to Dublin to look for a house and also visits Ballylee to check on the progress of the building there. WBY stays in Oxford dictating new sections for his memoir to a typist.
14	GY takes out a lease on 82 Merrion Square. In Oxford, WBY goes to a performance of Ibsen's *The Pretenders*.
19	Sends ECY the final copy for *Seven Poems and a Fragment*.
20	GY returns to Oxford. WBY spends the rest of this month revising copy for *Later Poems* and *Plays in Prose and Verse* and getting new material typed.

March

8	(Wed) Speaks at the dinner of the Oxford University India Society. Is reading Joyce's *Ulysses*.
14	Sends Macmillan copy for *Later Poems* via Watt.
16	The Yeatses stay with Ottoline Morrell at Garsington, as the first stage in their move from Oxford.
17	WBY goes to London for the weekend prior to moving to Ireland and sees Dulac, Ricketts and other friends. He and GY attend a séance where a voice purporting to be JBY speaks of being happy.
20	WBY goes to Dublin while GY returns to Oxford to fetch the children and luggage. Sees LR and Gogarty.
21	Moves to the Stephen's Green Club from the Hibernian Hotel. Tries to persuade Hyde to write his memoirs for the Cuala Press.
23	Attends a performance of *The Hour-Glass* at the Abbey.
25	GY arrives in Dublin.
27	WBY goes to Coole, where he rewrites the song in *A Pot of Broth*, and AG reads George Sand's *Consuelo* to him.
28	Visits Ballylee to see how work is progressing.

April

*c.*7	(Fri) Moves to Ballylee from Coole. Civil War raging in Ireland. Abandons his reading of *Ulysses* for Trollope.
8	Sends corrected proofs of *The Wind Among the Reeds* to Macmillan via Watt.
9	Walks over to see AG in Coole.
13	Goes to Dublin with AG and calls on MG. Attends a board meeting at the Abbey, and later discusses the Irish political situation with AE.
14	Visits an exhibition at the Royal Irish Academy.
17	Returns to Ballylee.
30	Visits Coole; despondent at the state of Ireland.

May

1	(Mon) Writes a Preface for *Plays in Prose and Verse*.
2	A session of 'philosophic sleep', by which the 'communicators' now transmit their information through GY. These 'sleeps',

mostly concerned at this time with the progress of the soul after death, continue throughout the coming months.

6   The first part of 'More Memories' (autobiography; *Aut*, 199–219) published in the *London Mercury* and the *Dial*.

8   Goes to Coole to see AG, who reads him more of *Consuelo*.

13   Intruders try to force their way into Coole at 11 pm.

14   Goes to Coole to sit for a medallion by Spicer Simson.

15   Spicer Simson visits Ballylee and in the evening WBY walks back with him to Coole.

16   Lunches at Coole, where Simson finishes the medallion during the afternoon and does one of AG.

17   WBY sees the Commanding Officer of the Free State forces in Gort about the raid on Coole. Stays at Coole to protect AG.

18   Works in the morning; has a meeting with Free State officers and AG at Coole in the afternoon. Remains at Coole, where AG reads the beginning of her memoirs to him, and he stays up until midnight in case the raiders return.

20   Discusses books for the Gort Library with the local schoolmaster, Brady, who is visiting Coole.

21   Brady and his wife come to dinner at Coole.

22   Reads his memoirs to AG and discusses the American Civil War, which he regrets as having destroyed the fine civilization of the South.

26   Suggests AG should bring his anthology *A Book of Irish Verse* up to date, and she reads him more of her memoirs.

*c.*27   Finishes his memoirs, *The Trembling of the Veil*, and dispatches the MS to Werner Laurie. ECY sends him proofs of JBY's *Early Memories*.

28   Sends most of the final proofs of *Later Poems* to Macmillan via Watt. AG reads more of her memoirs to him, but he disparages the poetry of her friend Sir Alfred Lyall.

June

3   (Sat) *Seven Poems and a Fragment* published. The second part of 'More Memories' (autobiography; *Aut*, 219–35) appears in the *London Mercury* and the *Dial*.

4   Calls at Coole, where AG reads him more of her memoirs.

5   WBY and GY go to Coole to discuss his proposed Honorary Degree at Queen's University, Belfast.

7   AG calls in at Ballylee for tea.

8   WBY goes to stay at Coole, where he enjoys a peaceful time, and AG reads him more of her memoirs. He begins 'Meditations in Time of Civil War'.

16   WBY returns to Ballylee. The Irish general election results in victory for the pro-Treaty parties.

19	Writes a hostile report on *The Crimson in the Tri-Colour*, Sean O'Casey's first play.
21	AG calls at Ballylee with political news and finds WBY at work on 'Meditations in Time of Civil War'.
25	Calls at Coole and AG reads him her 'Folklore of the War and the Rising'.
28	AG's neighbours, the Scovells, are ordered out of the country by the Republicans and WBY delivers her letter on their behalf to the Commanding Officer of the Free State forces in Gort. AG reads him more of her memoirs.
29	Because of the disturbed state of the country, the Yeatses postpone a proposed trip to Dublin.
30	The Yeatses call on AG at Coole in the afternoon, bringing news of the fighting at the Four Courts in Dublin.

July

1	(Sat) The third part of 'More Memories' (autobiography; *Aut*, 236–55, 279–86) published in the *London Mercury* and the *Dial*. WBY stays the night at Coole and tells AG that he has always tried to satisfy the ear in his poetry. She reads *Consuelo* to him.
4	Hears wild rumours about the Civil War. Visits Coole where AG reads him extracts from his letters that she has been typing and reaches the end of *Consuelo*.
6	The Yeatses go to Coole with rumours of the fighting in Dublin; they stay to tea with the nine O'Malleys who have also called.
9	Visits AG at Coole; she reads him more of his letters and from George Sand's *The Countess of Rudolstadt*.
10	Takes another letter from AG to the Free State forces at Gort, telling them of threats to the Scovells. They send him to the Republican officer. He and GY go to tea with AG.
12	WBY calls at Coole with the rumour that there has been a settlement in the Civil War.
14	Anne Yeats ill. WBY calls at Coole. Writes and corrects a draft of Part VI of 'Meditations in Time of Civil War'.
15	WBY and GY lunch at Coole, where the first letters and newspapers for a fortnight have arrived. AG reads a good deal of *The Countess of Rudolstadt* to WBY.
16	WBY visits Coole and discusses the previous evening's ambush in Gort.
19	Calls at Coole with Part III of 'Meditations in Time of Civil War'.
20	Anne Yeats taken ill and needs treatment in Dublin.
21	GY manages to get a lift to Dublin and, after securing medical attention for Anne, goes on to Oxford to sort out problems about their former house there. WBY calls at Coole, where AG

reads more of *The Countess of Rudolstadt*, and at dinner they discuss Turgenev, whose books WBY detests for their insincerity.

22   Visits Coole with Michael Yeats and expresses confidence that the Free State government is working to a definite military plan.

23   Calls at Coole.

24   Staying at Coole, he and AG hear a bomb exploding. Back in Ballylee he hears gunfire for an hour. He returns to Coole at 7.00 pm and, since his eyes are bad, AG reads him a good deal of *The Countess of Rudolstadt* in the evening.

27   Staying at Coole, hears news of the assassination of Leslie Edmunds, of the Congested Districts Board, in an ambush.

29   On a drive to Ballylee from Coole, WBY sees a dead man in a car. AG reads more of *The Countess of Rudolstadt* to him.

30   Returns to Ballylee after his stay at Coole.

31   WBY and GY, back from her trip to Oxford, go to Coole for lunch and for the afternoon. WBY is pleased by the political and war news that GY has brought back from Dublin.

August

5   (Sat) The final part of 'More Memories' (autobiography; *Aut*, 291–318) published in the *London Mercury* and the *Dial*.

6   Calls at Coole where AG tells him of the rumour that the Ballylee bridge is to be blown up; goes to see the Commanding Officer in Gort about this and is told there is no danger.

12   Arthur Griffith dies unexpectedly of a cerebral haemorrhage.

15   At Coole, discusses death of Arthur Griffith.

16   Calls at Coole. Still writing 'Meditations in Time of Civil War' and tells AG that lyric poetry should be rooted in history or personal biography.

17   The Yeatses take Anne Yeats to Coole.

19   Ballylee bridge blown up by Republicans at midnight.

20   Goes to Coole and gives AG an account of the blowing up of the bridge.

25   Calls at Coole and discusses the assassination of Michael Collins on 22 August.

26   Visits Martyn, now an invalid at Tillyra.

September

1   (Fri) Calls at Coole and admires AG's translation of Pearse's poem 'Mise Eire'.

5   Calls at Coole, anxious that the Dail may lack resolve.

7   AG visits Ballylee.

8   WBY stays the night at Coole.

9   At Coole, reading Morley's *Life of Rousseau* with admiration but finding that Rousseau was all image.

11	At Coole, dispirited by the lack of peace in Ireland.
17	Goes to Dublin.
18	Returns to Ballylee.
19	Owing to the blowing up of the bridge, the river floods the ground floor of Thoor Ballylee for several hours. Takes the children to stay at Coole while he and GY are in Dublin, and stays the night there.
20	Goes to Dublin with GY to put 82 Merrion Square into order, and where he works on the text of *A Vision*.
26	The Yeats children leave Coole for Dublin.

October

6	(Fri) Sees William Cosgrave, President of the Irish Executive Council, and suggests that the Municipal Gallery should be housed in the state apartments of Dublin Castle.
18	At a reception at Gogarty's.
19	Horace Plunkett consults WBY about the future of the *Irish Homestead*.
20	*The Trembling of the Veil* published. Late this month WBY negotiates with the Irish Government for an Abbey subsidy.
30	A powerful bomb explodes in Merrion Square during WBY's 'Monday Evening', cracking a window in his house.

November

3	(Fri) *Later Poems* and *Plays in Prose and Verse* published.
4	*The Player Queen* (play; *VPl*, 715–61) published in the *Dial*. WBY makes a speech at the Arts Club about the state of Ireland.
5	Receives copies of *Later Poems* and *Plays in Prose and Verse* and is delighted with their design and by Ricketts' covers for them.
8	Meets AG at an Abbey rehearsal and takes her to the train for Foxrock, where she is staying with Horace Plunkett.
10	Sees AG in Dublin and tells her of the lack of discipline in the Free State Army. She lunches and dines with the Yeatses at 82 Merrion Square.
11	Reads AG his letter on the Abbey Theatre for *The Voice of Ireland*, and then the just-finished 7th part of 'Meditations in Time of Civil War'.
16	Leaves Dublin for a lecture tour in England.
17	Arrives in London and goes to see Ricketts in the evening.
18	Is snubbed by Gosse at the Savile Club. Sees Christina Stoddart in the evening and they discuss the GD and occult matters.
19	Dines with Dulac and Helen Beauclerk, Dulac's new mistress.
20	Lectures in Cardiff.
21	*The Player Queen* published.
22	Lectures in Sheffield.

23	Lectures in Leeds. Telegraphs Ernest Blythe asking unsuccessfully for clemency for Republican prisoners sentenced to death.
24	Spends a long weekend with the Morrells at Garsington, where he meets Bertrand Russell, David Cecil and L. A. G. Strong among others.
26	Has a tête-à-tête with Ottoline Morrell.
28	Returns to London, where he sees a production of Shelley's *The Cenci*.
29	Sees a matinée production of the *Medea*. Phones Dulac about masks for his plays, and goes to the Freemasons' Library about GD properties. Dines with Dulac and Helen Beauclerk in the evening.
30	Lunches with OS, who helps him choose a pair of evening shoes as a present for GY.

December

1	(Fri) Reading Eliot's *The Sacred Wood* and, more fitfully, Gogol. Dines with Ricketts and Shannon.
2	Has a hostile exchange with Gosse over James Joyce at the Savile Club. Buys reproductions of Blake's 105 designs for Dante for £10. Dines with Dulac and Helen Beauclerk. GY writes to tell him that the Irish Government wants permission to nominate him to the Senate.
3	Lunches with T. S. Eliot, with whom he is charmed, and they discuss Joyce, poetry and the parallel dream for three hours; WBY agrees to write an essay on Blake's Dante designs for the *Criterion*.
4	Lectures in Leicester, where he stays with Dr Robert Rattray and meets Professor Vachel Burch.
5	Goes to Birmingham and stays with the Cadburys.
6	Goes to Liverpool for a lecture. Lunches with an old friend J. G. Legge, with whom he is staying, and has tea with the Landon Studio Society.
7	Appointed to the Irish Senate by the Free State government.
c.8	Returns to Dublin and works every morning on the text of *A Vision*, which Werner Laurie is eager to publish.
11	Attends the opening ceremony at the Senate, taking the oath at 12.20 pm.
12	Speaks at the first meeting of the Senate in support of Lord Glenavy's nomination as Chairman. Desmond Fitzgerald comes to dinner.
13	Sees Cosgrave and advocates a committee to investigate the conditions in which Republican prisoners are being held.
20	Conferred with an Honorary DLitt from Trinity College, Dublin.
24	Bullets fired into the Yeatses' house, and a fragment from one hits GY.

31   Writes to Ernest Blythe asking him to reconsider a decision not to compensate the Gonnes for the seizure of their car by the Black and Tans.

1923

January

5   (Fri) Anne Yeats severely ill with scarlet fever. WBY hears that MG has been arrested by the Free State Government, and writes to Iseult offering help.

6   'Meditations in Time of Civil War' (poem, *VP*, 417–27) published in the *London Mercury* and the *Dial*.

9   Sees Tim Healy, the Governor General, about the Lane Pictures, and Healy dictates a letter on the subject to Lord Beaverbrook.

10   Speaks in the Senate on the formation of Standing Committees and is appointed to the Standing Committee on Standing Committees. Attends the wedding of his cousin, Hilda Pollexfen.

11   Lunches with Lord Glenavy, the chairman of the Senate.

14   Firing in the street near 82 Merrion Square.

16   Crosses to London to take up the question of the Lane Pictures with British politicians.

17   Arranges a number of interviews and lunches with Dulac.

19   Sees Henry Massingham about the Lane Pictures and arranges meetings with Lord Plymouth, Lord Peel, Lady Cunard and the Irish journalist Robert Lynd.

20   Sees Lionel Curtis, and later Lord and Lady Cunard, and Lord Buckmaster about the Lane Pictures. In the evening dines with Dulac and Helen Beauclerk.

21   Refuses an invitation to dine with Lady Cunard for fear of quarrelling with fellow-guest Filson Young; dines instead with Robert Lynd to seek journalistic support for the return of the Lane Pictures.

22   Lunches at Lady Cunard's with a large party.

23   Arranges with Eliot to substitute a chapter from 'The Trembling of the Veil' in the *Criterion*, for the article on Blake's Dante designs which he has not had time to begin. Hears from Eddie Marsh that the British Cabinet has asked Curtis to draw up a Report on the Lane Pictures. In the evening he returns briefly to Dublin to attend Senate meetings.

24   Speaks in the Senate in favour of an Anglo-Irish amnesty for military prisoners.

25   Tries at AG's request, but unsuccessfully, to have the flogging of Republican prisoners stopped. Votes in the Senate in favour of the Housing Scheme Grant.

26	Attends a meeting of the Senate Committee on Standing Committees. Returns to London by evening boat.
27	Works on the text of *A Vision*, and lunches at Ottoline Morrell's London house, although she is ill with a cold. Sees Gogarty who is thinking of leaving Ireland, and they go to tea with Lady Leslie.
28	Gogarty calls. WBY works on *A Vision*, has tea with the Morrells and goes to the theatre with Lady Cunard.
29	Takes Gogarty to dine with Dulac.
30	Sees Lord Peel at the India Office at 12 noon. Eddie Marsh tells him that the Cabinet will discuss the Lane Pictures in about 3 weeks. Lunches with Lady Cunard and dines with Gogarty.
31	Lunches with Lady Londonderry.

February

1	(Thu) Lunches with Lord Granard and dines at Lady Cunard's, where he discusses the Irish situation with Winston Churchill.
2	Begins regular sessions of dictating *A Vision* to his London typist. Dines with GY's grandmother, Edith Woodmass, who urges him to move the family to Chester.
3	Dictates more of *A Vision*.
5	Lunches with Lord Granard and Lord Southborough, and suggests a modification of the Anglo-Irish Treaty to end the Irish Civil War.
7	Returns to Dublin.
8	Speaks in the Senate against the sweeping powers of entry proposed by a new Enforcement of Law Bill.
9	Returns to London and talks to P. J. Hogan on the journey; in the evening goes to arrange séances at the College of Psychic Science.
10	Lunches with Lord Granard and hears that negotiations over his suggested modifications to the Treaty are going well.
11	Learns that negotiations are not going as well as Granard thought.
14	GY in London; they dine at the Mont Blanc in Gerrard Street and go to a séance with Mrs Cooper at 3 pm.
*c.*15	The Yeatses and Gogarty attend a party at the Lavery's.
18	GY returns to Dublin.
19	WBY meets Plunkett in London.
20	Returns to Dublin and has long discussion with AG about the Lane Pictures. They go together to a production of *Othello*.
21	Sees Langton Douglas. Votes in the Senate for an amendment to the Enforcement of Law Bill, making under-sheriffs accountable to judges. Later AG calls in on her way back to Coole, and they discuss the rumoured execution of Republican prisoners.

March

3	(Sat) GY ill with scarlet fever and WBY moves into the Stephen's Green Club for a few days.

*c.*9	Sees *The Land of Heart's Desire* at the Abbey.
14	Attends a meeting of the Senate Committee on Standing Committees. Speaks in the Senate in favour of a Bill to provide for Arthur Griffith's family.
15	Speaks in the Senate on the permanent location of the Irish parliament. Decides with AG that the Abbey should defy a Republican order that all Dublin theatres must close.
21	Votes in the Senate against an amendment to the Local Government Bill, giving County Councils the right to increase rates.
22	Speaks in the Senate on the proposal that Irish polling cards should include a photograph. GY convalescing after scarlet fever.
27	Sees James MacNeill about an Irish Parliamentary resolution on the Lane Pictures. Impressed with the Abbey's production of *A Doll's House*.
28	Speaks in the Senate on the Damage to Property Bill.

April

2	(Mon) Attends and admires a production of Goldsmith's *She Stoops to Conquer* at the Abbey.
3	Sees P. S. O'Hegarty about Post Office appointments.
8	Suffers from indigestion and headaches for several days.
11	Meets AG who is in Dublin.
12	AG dines with the Yeatses, who now have an armed guard, and they go on to the first production of O'Casey's *The Shadow of a Gunman* at the Abbey.
13	Intervenes in the Senate in a debate on the Damage to Property Bill and votes on an amendment.
14	Goes with AG to see MacNeill about the Government taking over the Abbey Theatre. AG lunches with the Yeatses.
16	WBY introduces the American poet Jackson to AG and she takes them both to tea with James Stephens. Receives an alarming report of current losses at a meeting of the Abbey Directors.
17	AG returns to Galway.
18	Speaks in the Senate on proposed compensation for personal injuries and damages sustained during the Anglo-Irish and Civil Wars.
19	Speaks in the Senate, advocating the appointment of a committee to consider whether Ireland should join the League of Nations. Later his proposal for a committee to edit and publish Irish manuscript material is accepted and he is appointed its Chairman.
26	Presides at the first meeting of the Committee on Irish Manuscripts. Late this month he writes 'The Crazed Moon' (*VP*, 487–8), begins *The Cat and the Moon*, a new Noh play, and continues working on *A Vision*.

May

1	(Tue) Chairs the second meeting of the Committee on Irish Manuscripts.
2	Meets AG on her way through Dublin to London and sees her off at the boat.
3	Consults government officials about the treatment of Iseult Gonne, now a Republican prisoner, and passes their assurances on to MG. Chairs the third meeting of the Committee on Irish Manuscripts.
4	Chairs a meeting of the Lyster Memorial Commitee.
9	Proposes a motion in the Senate that the Irish Government should press the British Government to return the Lane Pictures to Dublin.
12	Leaves Dublin for a lecture tour in Scotland.
21	Arrives in London from Scotland. Has a séance with a medium from Crewe in the morning, and in the evening with Powell, a Welsh medium, during which there are violent physical manifestations.
22	Hears that the Cuala Press has been raided and his sisters and two printers arrested.
24	In the morning visits AG who is in London and discusses the progress of the Lane Pictures campaign. In the afternoon calls to see OS who is nursing her sick husband.
26	Goes to Oxford to stay with Ottoline Morrell at Garsington.
28	Inscribes verses in Hazel Lavery's scrapbook at Garsington; she promises to introduce him to the Duke of Devonshire, who might help the Lane Pictures campaign. Returns to London in the evening.
29	Leaves London for Dublin.
30	Attends the Senate for a debate on the Unemployed Insurance Bill and speaks briefly in an Adjournment Debate.
31	Chairs the fourth meeting of the Committee on Irish Manuscripts.

June

1	(Fri) AG, in Dublin to consult her doctor about a lump in her breast, calls on the Yeatses, and later enters a nursing home.
2	AG undergoes an operation to remove her left breast.
3	WBY visits AG in hospital and discusses psychic research.
4	Visits AG in hospital and discusses the parlous state of Abbey finances and Sarah Harrison's allegations about the forging of Lane's will.
5	Attends the Senate and in the evening visits AG.
6	Opposes a proposal in the Senate that Senators' monthly allowances should depend on their attending at least half the meetings. Votes against an amendment to the Unemployed

Insurance Bill which would decrease the benefits to the unemployed.

7   Lunches with Gogarty, where he sees Cosgrave, O'Malley and Lady Fingall. In the afternoon speaks in the Senate against the censorship of films. Sees AG who sends him to consult James Stephens about housing the Lane Pictures at the National Galley. Gives £2. 2s. to the Lyster Memorial Fund.

8   Sees Cosgrave about uniting all Irish libraries and art collections under one head. AG moves from her nursing home to 82 Merrion Square.

9   In the afternoon Gogarty takes WBY to call on the Governor General, Tim Healy, to discuss the Lane Pictures.

11   Takes the recuperating AG for a walk; they meet James Stephens who shows them the pictures Martyn has presented to the National Gallery. In the evening Coffey and Tom Esmond call on WBY and discuss politics.

13   Joseph O'Neill calls on WBY.

14   WBY excited to find similarities between *A Vision* and Einstein's theories. Alice Stopford Green calls.

15   LR calls about the Abbey and Patrick Hogan, Minister for Agriculture, comes to lunch and discusses the state of the Civil War.

16   WBY accompanies AG back to Coole.

19   Leaves Coole, having talked much about his ideas in *A Vision*. Reading Ferdinand Ossendowski's *Beasts, Men and Gods*.

20   Votes in the Senate against an amendment to a National Insurance Bill.

*c.*24   Attends a lunch for Hilaire Belloc.

25   Speaks in the Senate on the National Insurance Bill.

26   At GY's 'incitement' invites Joyce to stay with him in Dublin.

27   Chairs the fifth meeting of the Committee on Irish Manuscripts. Over the coming weeks he works daily on *The Cat and the Moon*.

July

4   (Wed) Attends a stormy meeting of the National Gallery Board. In the afternoon he seconds a motion in the Senate calling for the release of an Irish political prisoner in Britain.

5   With LR sees Ernest Blythe about a state subsidy for the Abbey.

7   'A Biographical Fragment' (autobiography; *Aut*, 371–6; 576–9) published in the *Criterion*.

8   Dines with GY at the Jamesons' at Howth. His eyesight bad for several days.

11   Speaks in the Senate on the permanent location of the Irish Parliament.

17   Hears that SMY is in bad health. Attends a Senate Committee Meeting.

19	Goes to London to arrange a nursing home for SMY. While there he sees her doctors, as well as the artists Orpen and Shannon, Alec Martin and Lion of the St James' Theatre, who offers the Abbey an engagement.
23	Dines with Brendan Bracken and meets Lutyens and Godfrey Locker Lampson of the Home Office.
24	Returns to Dublin for a Senate committee.
25	GY and the children go to Coole while Ballylee is made ready, but WBY stays in Dublin.
26	Speaks in the Senate, urging the inspection of prisons.
30	Speaks in the Senate during the Committee Stage of the Public Safety Bill.
31	Votes in the Senate against an amendment to the Public Safety Bill.

August

1	(Wed) Votes in the Senate against amendments to the Public Safety Bill and to a Land Bill.
2	Attends an afternoon session of the Senate and urges a longer period of consideration for the Defence Forces Bill.
3	Attends morning and afternoon sessions of the Senate; votes for the second reading of the Public Safety Bill, speaks on the Indemnity Bill and on the definition of ancient monuments in the Land Bill.
c.12	The Yeatses go to stay at Coole.
16	The Yeatses leave Coole to return to Ballylee.
19	WBY calls at Coole in the afternoon and stays to dinner, discussing the political situation and Abbey affairs.
22	Calls at Coole and discusses the use of corporal punishment in Irish prisons.
23	Cuala Industries move into 82 Merrion Square.
24	Goes to Dublin with GY (who returns to Ballylee on the 25th).
27	Votes in the General Election.
30	Writes a Preface for Gogarty's *An Offering of Swans*.
31	Sends a first batch of corrected proofs of *Plays and Controversies* to Macmillan via Watt.

September

7	(Fri) Sends Werner Laurie the first instalment of *A Vision*.
c.10	Publication of JBY's *Early Memories*, with Preface by WBY. Moves into his new study at 82 Merrion Square and sends more proofs of *Plays and Controversies* to Macmillan.
12	AG comes to stay at 82 Merrion Square.
13	WBY and AG dine at Gogarty's.

16   Sees Cruise O'Brien who tells him that many of the Republicans want to take the Oath. Stays up until 3.00 am finishing a version of 'Leda and the Swan'.

17   Expounds his belief that the epoch of democracy is at an end to AG and an Anglican monk. Reads 'Leda and the Swan' to AG and later accompanies her to *The Dragon* at the Abbey.

18   AG reads WBY and LR her *The Story Brought by Brigit*. WBY drafts more versions of 'Leda and the Swan'.

19   AG leaves Merrion Square for Coole.

October

4   (Thu) Sends remaining proofs of *Plays and Controversies* to Macmillan.

11   Watt sends Laurie the agreement for *A Vision*.

12   Laurie asks Watt to coax WBY into writing a description of *A Vision* as no-one has the faintest idea what it is about.

15   Attends a meeting of the Drama League. Suffering from a violent cold, complicated by a minor operation on his nose which causes bleeding.

16   LR calls to help draft statements to the Government about the Abbey Theatre and the Lane Pictures. Horace Plunkett also calls.

22   Sends the final proofs of *Plays and Controversies* to Macmillan via Watt.

23   Toiling at the last chapter of *A Vision*. Late this month he sees Brendan Bracken in Dublin.

November

8   (Thu) AG comes to stay at 82 Merrion Square. WBY proposes the vote of thanks for W. Beare's Presidential Address on 'The Modern Novel' at the TCD Philosophical Society.

10   Dines with AG, LR, Alice Green and Tom Esmond at the Metropole. They go on the Abbey to see *John Bull's Other Island*.

11   AG tells WBY that she and others have written a letter to the press complaining of the treatment of the Republican hunger strikers and offers to leave 82 Merrion Square if this compromises him.

12   AE and Dermot MacManus call on WBY to discuss the hunger strike.

13   Sees Hugh Kennedy, the Irish Attorney General, about setting up an Artistic Committee to advise the new Government on official designs. Opposes AG's suggestion of a petition on behalf of the hunger strikers and they go on to the first performance of Gaelic plays at the Abbey.

14   Speaks in the Senate in praise of Plunkett's work for Irish agriculture. Later denounces the 'histrionics' of the Gaelic movement, although he wishes to see the country Irish-speaking.

15	Awarded the Nobel Prize for Literature and receives a telegram telling him this.
16	Discusses business arrangements at the Abbey with AG and LR.
26	Writes 'To Lennox Robinson' as a dedication to *Essays*.
27	*Plays and Controversies* published. Visits Lady Londonderry.
30	Goes to London on his way to Stockholm for the Nobel Prize ceremony. GY joins him a few days later.

December

6	(Thu) Sails from Harwich for Esberg on his way to Stockholm.
7	Arrives in Copenhagen, where he is interviewed by Danish journalists.
8	Arrives in Stockholm.
10	Presented with his Nobel diploma and medal by King Gustav and speaks at the Nobel Banquet.
11	Watches the celebrations for Crown Prince Adolf and his new wife Louise on their entry into Stockholm.
12	Attends a reception for Nobel prize-winners at the Royal Palace.
13	Delivers his Nobel lecture to the Swedish Royal Academy, followed by days of sightseeing in Stockholm, including a visit to the picture gallery of the National Museum.
14	Visits Stockholm Town Hall.
15	The American poet Robert Almon calls on WBY. Later the Yeatses see a performance of *Cathleen ni Houlihan* put on at the Royal Theatre, Stockholm, followed by *She Stoops to Conquer*.
16	Leaves Stockholm for London by way of Copenhagen, Amsterdam and Antwerp.
24	GY returns to Dublin, but WBY stays on in London and visits OS and SMY.
28	Dines with Dulac at the Ivy Restaurant.

1924

January

1	(Tue) Early this month WBY returns to Dublin and begins work on 'The Bounty of Sweden'. He uses the Nobel Prize money to pay off his and his sisters' debts, to finish furnishing 82 Merrion Square, and to improve his Library; the remaining £6000 he invests. Later this month Gogarty's *An Offering of Swans* is published with a Preface by WBY. Publishes 'The Gift of Harun Al-Rashid' in *English Life*.
15	Speaks in the Senate on Civil Service regulations, on the Irish language, and on the participation of Irish artists at the forthcoming British Empire Exhibition.
16	Returns corrected copy of *Later Poems* to Macmillan via Watt.
21	Dines out with GY.

23	Speaks in the Senate in favour of the inspection of prisons. Finishes 'The Bounty of Sweden'.
23	Speaks in the Senate in favour of pensions for judges obliged to retire early.
23	Attends the Senate for a debate on a Public Safety Bill.
25	Speaks to a large audience at the Royal Dublin Society.
28	Returns to writing *A Vision*, but is delayed by a great deal of proof-reading throughout February. Spends a dull evening at a new social club.
29	Invites Desmond Fitzgerald to dinner.
30	Attends the Senate for the committee stage of The Courts of Justice Bill.

February

6	(Wed) Attends a Board Meeting of the Irish National Gallery; later speaks in the Senate on the necessity for an independent judiciary and votes in favour of an amendment increasing the number of Circuit Judges from 8 to 10.
7	Speaks in the Senate during a debate on The Courts of Justice Bill.
8	Speaks in the Senate during the committee stage of The Courts of Justice Bill.
10	Returns a large part of the proofs of *Essays* to Macmillan via Watt.
11	Consults Jack Yeats over the advisability of ECY visiting SMY in her nursing home in England.
13	Returns a further tranche of proofs of *Essays* to Macmillan via Watt.
16	Advocates authoritarian views in an interview with the *Irish Times* (*UP* II. 433–6).
22	Returns a further tranche of proofs of *Essays* to Macmillan via Watt.

March

5	(Wed) Sends the corrected proofs of *Essays* to Macmillan via Watt. Speaks in the Senate at the report stage of The Courts of Justice Bill.
7	WBY accompanies AG to the Abbey to see O'Casey's *Juno and the Paycock*, which he has not seen before.
8	Attends AG's tea party for the players at the Abbey.
10	In the evening O'Casey, AG, Gogarty, AE, Alan Duncan and the American journalist Jewell attend WBY's 'Monday Evening'.
11	Dines at the Glenavys with GY and various government ministers.
12	Sends a further substantial tranche of the corrected proofs of *Essays* to Macmillan via Watt. Attends debates in the Senate in the afternoon. Sees off AG, who has been called back to Galway by the illness of her sister, from the Broadstone Station.
13	Votes on an amendment to a Fisheries Bill in the Senate.
15	Elected a Member of the Royal Irish Academy.

17	Sends a further tranche of the corrected proofs of *Essays* to Macmillan via Watt.
19	Speaks in the Senate on ministerial responsibility for the National Gallery and Museum.
30–1	Attends private Drama League performances of *At the Hawk's Well* at 82 Merrion Square.

April

2	(Wed) Attends a Board Meeting of the Irish National Gallery.
6	Goes to Coole where he writes more of 'The Bounty of Sweden'. AG reads Wilde's *The Picture of Dorian Gray* to him.
7	Hears that GY in Dublin is ill. Finishes a poem, possibly 'Wisdom' (*VP*, 440).
8	Visits Ballylee and finds it almost completely restored.
9	Dines at Coole with Bagot, a neighbouring landlord.
12	Return to Dublin from Coole delayed by missing the connection at Athenry and he goes on with AG to Galway where she is overseeing the selling-up of her late sister's house. Back in Dublin, dines at the United Arts Club with James Stephens, AG and Thomas MacGreevy.
14	Attends an Abbey Directors' Meeting which discusses mortgaging the Theatre.
15	Accompanies AG to the first performance of her *The Story Brought by Brigit* at the Abbey.
17	Lunches with AG during which they discuss the latest developments in the Lane Pictures campaign, and, later, evil and the nature of the soul.
18	Dines with AG at the United Arts Club, where she tries to persuade him to get Hyde appointed to the Senate.
19	Attends another performance of *The Story Brought by Brigit*, which he pronounces good but badly produced.
20	At afternoon party of the Douglases to meet the Australian Prime Minister and where he discusses the Lane Pictures with Cosgrave. In the evening he goes with GY and AG to Gogarty's.
22	Dines with AG at Clery's restaurant. Thinks he has finished *A Vision*, although he continues partial rewritings for several weeks. Begins organizing the Tailteann Games.
26	Attends Gogarty's dedication of two swans to the Liffey from TCD boathouse.

May

1	(Thu) Votes in a debate on Old Age Pensions in the Senate, and speaks on proposed sites for the Irish parliament (Oireachtas).
c.3	(Sat) Entertains Kevin O'Higgins at 32 Merrion Square.

5	GY goes to London. WBY begins writing *Calvary*.
6	*Essays* published. WBY goes to Coole, where he discusses the Boundary Question with AG and works on *A Vision*. In the evenings AG reads Disraeli's *Vivian Grey* to him.
9	Discusses the Irish Boundary question with AG and gives her an account of Pound's *Cantos*.
10	Visits Ballylee with AG, but cannot get in owing to a broken door.
11	Returns to Ballylee with the builder Rafferty and finds that it has been broken into but nothing stolen. AG urges him to press the government to release de Valera from prison.
12	Working hard at *A Vision*, and makes progress in bringing it together.
13	Rita Daly dines at Coole.
15	Returns to Dublin for an Arts Federation meeting.
19	Sees Cosgrave's Secretary about the Lane Pictures dispute.
21	Chairs the sixth meeting of the Committee on Irish Manuscripts. Speaks later in the Senate in favour of extending the session until all the bills, particularly one ensuring Irish copyrights in the USA, have been passed.
23	A reporter from the *Freeman's Journal* interviews WBY about the Lane Pictures.
24	The neurotic Sarah Harrison calls to see him about the Lane Pictures but he pretends to be out.
26	Pronounces *A Vision* far from finished.
31	Meets AG at the station on her arrival from Coole and they spend the evening discussing the campaign on behalf of the Lane Pictures.

June

3	(Tue) Attends the Annual General Meeting of the Abbey Directors. Meets Alice Stopford Green later, and spends the rest of the evening talking gossip and politics with AG.
4	Attends a Board Meeting of the Irish National Gallery. In the afternoon attends the Senate, where he urges adequate fire protection for the National Museum and presents the Final Report of the Committee on Irish Manuscripts.
5	Speaks in the Senate on Irish manuscripts.
7	'Leda and the Swan', 'The Lover Speaks' (later 'Owen Aherne and his Dancers'), and 'The Gift of Harun Al-Rashid' (poems; *VP*, 441, 449–50, 460–70) published in the *Dial*.
14	Attends a dinner given in honour of W. F. Barrett.
15	Puts 'The Bounty of Sweden' into order, writing a Preface and a new footnote.

16	Delivers 'The Bounty of Sweden' to the Cuala Press. Adds introductory sentences to Cherry Haughton's memoir of Synge for publication in the *Irish Statesman*. Plays golf with Healy, the editor of the *Irish Times*, and meets AG at the station on her way through Dublin to England.
17	Invites Pound to the Tailteann Games.
19	Speaks in the Senate on the need for adequate fire precautions in the building. Later this month he helps drum up subscribers and contributions for the short-lived publication *Tomorrow*.
25	Sees Desmond Fitzgerald about assisting Pound to visit Ireland, and, unsuccessfully, about importing Joyce's *Ulysses* (banned in Britain) into Ireland.
27	WBY and AG offer the Abbey Theatre to the Irish nation.

July

1	(Tue) Invites Joyce to the Tailteann Games.
2	Attends a Board Meeting of the Irish National Gallery. Opposes a proposal in the Senate that railway tickets, signs and notices should be printed in Irish as well as English.
3	Advocates in the Senate a tariff on German stained-glass until the exchange-rates are back in balance.
5	*The Cat and the Moon* (play, *VPl*, 378–9) published in the *Criterion* and the *Dial* and 'A Memory of Synge' (article; *UP* II. 436–7) in the *Irish Statesman*. Leaves a statement by Sarah Harrison on the Lane Pictures with Cosgrave's secretary.
9	Travels to Aberdeen to receive an Honorary Degree.
10	Honorary degree conferred by Aberdeen University.
11	Travels to London. Sees a Gauguin exhibition at the Leicester Gallery and later dines with Dulac.
12	Visits museums and galleries in London. In the evening goes to see Shaw's *St Joan*.
13	Lunches with OS and Dorothy Pound. Entertains Dulac and Helen Beauclerk to dinner at the Ivy.
14	In the morning consults Lutyens about fire protection in public buildings as part of his Senate work. Goes on to Garsington to stay with Ottoline Morrell.
15	Returns to London and sees Lionel Curtis at the Colonial Office about the Lane Pictures. Returns to Dublin by the night boat.
16	Speaks in the Senate on the urgent necessity of making the National Museum fire-proof.
17	AG arrives in Dublin and stays with the Yeatses. In the afternoon AG and WBY go to see Tim Healy at the Vice-Regal Lodge to discuss the Lane Pictures. They go on to the Government Offices in Merrion Street to see Desmond Fitzgerald and Eamon Duggan.
c.18	*The Cat and the Moon and Certain Poems* published.

19	AG and WBY interview witnesses about the Lane Pictures.
20	AG and WBY await word from the government about the Lane Pictures, but none comes. Gogarty calls in at dinner and they ask him to raise the matter with Cosgrave.
21	At AG's behest, WBY phones Duggan to enquire about developments in the Lane Pictures campaign and later delivers a letter from her to the Government Offices.
24	Sits on the Irish Film Appeal Board and is enraged by its predilection for censorship.
25	Distributes circulars among his friends, calling for subscriptions for the magazine *Tomorrow*.
27	Writes verse from 10 to 11.30, from 11.30 to 1.30 sits on a committee to set up a new Irish political party, and from 3.00 pm attends Senate debate on the Land Bill.
29	John Quinn dies in New York.
31	Dermot MacManus, Andrew Jameson and General O'Connell call at 82 Merrion Square to confer about the Defence Bill then going though the Dáil.

August

2	(Sat) 'To All Artists and Writers' (article; *UP* II. 438–9) published in *Tomorrow*. 'Compulsory Gaelic' (article; *UP* II. 439–49) published in the *Irish Statesman*.
2–10	WBY attends the celebrations connected with the Tailteann Games.
9	Presentation of gold medals for literary prizes at the Royal Irish Academy.
11	AE and L. A. G. Strong at WBY's 'Monday Evening'.
13	WBY and GY fail to get seats at the Abbey because of the success there of O'Casey's *The Shadow of a Gunman*.
*c.*14	Goes to London to make use of museums and libraries for information needed in *A Vision*, on which he works every day.
15	Dines with Dulac and Helen Beauclerk.
17	Visits Ricketts and Shannon at Chilham in Kent to consult Shannon about designing robes for Irish judges.
18	Delivers the contents of the new volume of the *Collected Edition* to Macmillan via Watt.
21	Back in London he meets Arthur Waley, Mrs Mathers and Compton Mackenzie, with whom he talks through the evening. Buys furniture for Merrion Square at Heals.
23	Dines with Dulac.
25	Buys more furniture at Heals. Dines with Dulac, Helen Beauclerk and an American journalist at the Ivy.
26	Dines with Shannon and discusses his proposed design for Irish judges' robes.

27   Buys toys for his children at Harrods. Has a séance with
        Mrs Cowper. In the evening dines with Dulac and Helen
        Beauclerk.
28   Dines with Ricketts and Shannon and has further discussions
        on Shannon's proposed design for Irish judges' robes.
29   Dines with OS.

September
1   (Mon) Moves from the Savile to the Arts Club, Dover Street.
        Working on *A Vision* in the London Library. Dines with Dulac
        and a Dr Crimp.
2   Sees Archer's *The Green Goddess.*
4   Meets AG, in London for hearings about the Lane Pictures, and
        discusses their evidence with her and Ruth Shine. Later takes
        AG to see *The Great Adventure.*
5   WBY and AG present evidence to the Committee on the Lane
        Pictures at the Foreign Office. Afterwards WBY takes AG to
        lunch at Gatti's, and in the evening dines with Shannon.
6   'The Bounty of Sweden' (autobiography; *Aut*, 531–72) published
        in the *London Mercury* and the *Dial*. In the afternoon meets Mrs
        John Penlington, who has written on Japanese drama.
8   Crosses to Dublin by a late boat.
20   Writes a Preface for H. P. R. Finberg's translation of Villiers de
        l'Isle-Adam's *Axël.*
22   AG comes to stay at 82 Merrion Square and WBY entertains her,
        AE, Gogarty, Stephens and Geoffrey Phibbs at his 'Monday
        Evening', where they discuss poetry.
23   Meets Eoin O'Duffy, the Chief of Police, at Gogarty's and proposes
        that an official History of the Anglo-Irish War should be written.
24   Accompanies AG to a performance of George Shiels' *Paul
        Twyning* at the Abbey.
25   Discusses the forthcoming Abbey programme and vetoes AG's
        suggestion that her *The Image* should be produced. In the
        evening AG takes him to see *The Merchant of Venice* produced at
        the Father Matthew Hall by Frank Fay.
26   Attends a meeting of the Drama League at 82 Merrion Square
        with LR.
30   Sends H. P. R. Finberg the introduction to Villiers de l'Isle-
        Adam's *Axël.*

October
1   (Wed) Attends a Board Meeting of the Irish National Gallery.
7   Subscribes to a clavichord for Robert Bridges. Sends a first
        tranche of corrected proofs of *Early Poems and Stories* to
        Macmillan via Watt.

10	Goes to stay at Coole with GY and tells AG that he has been rereading 'The Wanderings of Oisin'. While at Coole he works on *A Vision* and rewrites old poems, including 'A Cradle Song' and 'The Dedication to a Book of Stories', and in evening AG reads Conrad's *The Arrow of Gold* to him.
12	Sends a further tranche of corrected proofs for *Early Poems and Stories* to Macmillan via Watt.
13	Visits Ballylee with GY.
15	Sends more corrected proofs for *Early Poems and Stories* to Macmillan via Watt.
16	GY and WBY leave Coole for Dublin.
17	Speaks in the Senate on the Boundary Question and reconciliation with Northern Ireland. After the speech he suffers acute pain and his doctor tells him he has high blood pressure and instructs him to give up lecturing, writing, and public speaking for a while, and take exercise.
21	AG comes to stay at 82 Merrion Square for an emergency committee meeting of the Carnegie Trust, and WBY, furious at her account of LR being forced to resign from the Trust because of his supposedly obscene story in *Tomorrow*, goes to see AE and has a row.
22	AG gives him an account of a second meeting of the Carnegie Committee, and discusses his health.
23	In the evening AG reads him a letter and poems by Lyle Donaghy. Later she leaves for Coole.
27	WBY sends a further tranche of corrected proofs for *Early Poems and Stories* to Macmillan via Watt.
29	Goes to stay at Coole, where he works on *A Vision*, and revises old poems. In the evenings AG reads Trollope's *Phineas Finn* to him.
30	Sends a further tranche of corrected proofs for *Early Poems and Stories* to Macmillan via Watt. AG types his revised version of 'The Dedication to a Book of Stories' and later reads him plays sent in to the Abbey.
31	AG reads him more plays submitted to the Abbey, and they disagree over the revival of her *The Image*.

November

3	(Mon) Discusses *A Vision*, the antithesis between Christ and Buddha, and occult matters with AG. Rewriting 'The Lamentation of the Old Pensioner' (*VP*, 131–2).
8	'An Old Poem Re-Written' (poem, later 'The Dedication to a Book of Stories selected from the Irish Novelists'; *VP*, 129–30) published in the *Irish Statesman*.
9	Develops a bad cold, but has rewritten some of his stories and poems over the last weeks, including 'The Crucifixion of the Outcast', as well as working on *A Vision*. Sends a further tranche

of corrected proofs and revises for *Early Poems and Stories* to Macmillan via Watt.

10	The Dalys of Castle Daly pay a visit to Coole.
12	Rewrites 'The Sorrow of Love'.
14	AG makes fair copies of WBY's much corrected 'Cuchulain's Fight with the Sea' for the printers.
15	Leaves Coole for Dublin.
16	Sends a further tranche of corrected proofs and revises for *Early Poems and Stories* to Macmillan via Watt.
17	AG is in Dublin about Abbey finances and stays at 82 Merrion Square.
18	WBY has a heated discussion with Bryan Cooper, arguing that Irish Protestants have been too accommodating to Catholics in the new state.
19	His doctor tells him that his blood pressure is still too high.
21	Sends more revises for *Early Poems and Stories* to Macmillan via Watt. Leaves Dublin for London.
22	Spends the day reading Maupassant's *Bel-Ami* by the Savile Club fire.
25	Consults Watt about his publishing affairs.
26	Goes to stay in Sidmouth, Devon, with GY's mother and step-father. Plays golf and continues work on *A Vision*.
28	Sees Ibsen's *A Doll's House* in Sidmouth, performed by a band of itinerant actors.

December

6	(Sat) Returns to London from Sidmouth and meets GY at Garlands Hotel. While in London he sees his oculist.
*c.*8	Leaves London for Dublin.
16	Sends the Dedication and further corrected proofs for *Early Poems and Stories* to Macmillan via Watt.
19	Appeals to the Senate to ensure that the fine ceilings are not harmed during renovations to the chamber.
21	Sends further corrected proofs for *Early Poems and Stories* to Macmillan via Watt.
22	Attends a Board Meeting of the Irish National Gallery.
31	Sends further corrected proofs for *Early Poems and Stories* to Macmillan via Watt.

1925

January

4	(Sun) Leaves Dublin for Sicily with GY.
5	While passing through London he delivers further corrected proofs for *Early Poems and Stories* to Macmillan via Watt. For rest

of the month he travels in Sicily and southern Italy with GY and Pound.

23	The Yeatses in Naples, where they remain for two weeks.

February

1	(Sun) Sends further corrected proofs for *Early Poems and Stories* to Macmillan via Watt.
13	In Capri and enjoying 'perfect weather'.
16	Goes to Rome for a week.
c.22	Leaves Rome for London, where he sees the publisher Werner Laurie about the MS of *A Vision*.
c.24	Crosses to Dublin and is feeling much better.
25	Official opening of the Cuala Industries' showroom at 133 Lower Baggot Street; they subsequently move out of 32 Merrion Square.
c.27	Sees Senator S. L. Brown about the Lane Picture dispute.

March

12	(Thu) Sends further corrected proofs for *Early Poems and Stories* to Macmillan via Watt.
14	'An Undelivered Speech' (speech; *UP* II, 449–52) published in the *Irish Statesman*.
25	Sees a rehearsal of LR's new play *Portrait* and spends the evening with LR and MacGreevy. GY is in London seeing her mother.
26	Sees another rehearsal of LR's *Portrait* in the afternoon.
28	In the evening consults Desmond Fitzgerald about a Government subsidy for the Abbey, and they discuss LR's position in the Theatre.
30	Visits SMY in Dundrum at 3 pm to discuss Cuala debts.
31	Attends the Senate and intervenes briefly in a discussion on procedure.

April

1	(Wed) Attends a Board Meeting of the Irish National Gallery.
c.9–13	Sybil, sister of Erskine Childers, stays with the Yeatses.
17	Suggests that Macmillan should republish Le Fanu's *Through a Glass Darkly*, illustrated by Norah McGuinness.
19	Attends the Dublin Drama League's production of Strindberg's *The Spook Sonata* and Schnitzler's *The Wedding Morning* at the Abbey.
c.21	Offers to pay off the Cuala Press's £1,500 overdraft.
22	Finishes *A Vision*, hands it to GY to draw the diagrams and forward to the publisher, Laurie, clears his desk, and begins to write letters again. Starts to plan out his play *The Resurrection*. In the evening sees Shaw's *Fanny's First Play* at the Abbey.
30	Complains of the acoustics at the Senate and votes on the Dundalk Harbour and Port Bill.

May

6   (Wed) Votes in the Senate on the Treasonable Offences Bill.

7   Goes to see Iseult Gonne who is in hospital after a serious operation and continues to see her daily until she is discharged on 12 May. Later in the day, Gogarty calls. WBY has begun writing *The Resurrection*.

13   Spends the day going through his papers, and in the evening he and GY are guests at dinner party given by Lady Desart. Excited by an article on Oswald Spengler in the *Dial*.

14   Goes to Coole, where he works on *The Resurrection* and reads Plato's *Timaeus*.

15   Reads AG his article 'The Need for Audacity of Thought'.

22   Has finished *The Resurrection*, apart from the lyrics, and reads it to AG.

23   Begins writing a lyrical introduction to *The Resurrection*. Is reading Pater's *Plato and Platonism*.

24   Begins writing the first of 'Two Songs from a Play'.

25   Finishes a version of 'Two Songs from a Play'.

26   Returns to Dublin from Coole.

June

3   (Wed) Attends a Board Meeting of the Irish National Gallery.

5   AG comes to stay and they attend two meetings at the Abbey, the second to raise the salaries of the actors and staff.

6   Consults AG as to whether LR should be made Managing Director of the Abbey, and the appointment by the government of George O'Brien as a Director.

8   Ernest Blythe dines with the Yeatses and AG and discusses the return of the Lane Pictures.

9   Dr Cassidy calls to discuss a scheme for an Abbey tour to Vienna.

10   WBY speaks in the Senate on the need to protect historic monuments as cultural and economic assets. Phones Senator Brown to come round to discuss the Lane Pictures with him and AG. Reads AG his speech on divorce.

11   Causes controversy in the Senate and the country with a speech against the prohibition of divorce in Ireland. Writes 'The Three Monuments' (*VP*, 460) at this time.

19   AG, disturbed by the Report of the British Commission on the Lane Pictures, comes up to Dublin unexpectedly and stays with the Yeatses. They phone Lord Glenavy to enlist his help in the matter.

20   AG and WBY work on papers relating to the Lane Pictures.

21   Helps AG with her campaign over the Lane Pictures. In the evening Gogarty calls and reads his new play to them.

22	WBY urges the Irish Government to appoint a Swedish expert as director of all art and technical education in Ireland.
23	AG reads a version of her play *Dave* to WBY and GY.
25	Proofs of *A Vision* arrive. WBY is appointed to the Joint Committee of the Senate and Dáil to consider the terms of the Commercial and Industrial Property (Protection) Bill. AG leaves for London.

July

1	(Wed) Proposes AG for the Senate, but she is defeated.
c.2	*The Bounty of Sweden* published.
6	An urgent summons to the Senate prevents him seeing Ernest Rhys, who is in Dublin.
9	AG returns from London and gives WBY an account of the latest round in her campaign over the Lane Pictures. WBY tells her that he is trying to form a new Unionist party in the Senate.
10	Attends a meeting of the literary advisers to the *Irish Statesman* with Plunkett, AE, Edmund Curtis and two Fellows of TCD. AG returns to Coole.
14	The Yeatses go to Thoor Ballylee; WBY has a cold but is correcting proofs of *A Vision* and writing 'The Tower'.
16	His cold better, he visits Coole and tells AG that he is still planning his new political party.
25	Calls on AG and stays the night at Coole. She reads him several chapters of Trollope's *Phineas Finn*, and he looks through the works of the historian Lecky to get ideas for his new party.
28	Calls at Coole to help AG with her commentary on the Irish Government's reply to the Report of the Lane Commission. He stays the night, and they continue work the following day.
29	Is writing the second part of 'The Tower'.

August

4	(Tue) Goes to Coole to consult AG about his forthcoming Address at the Abbey.
6	Goes to Dublin.
8	Gives an Address on the history and achievements of the Abbey Theatre during a supper at the Theatre to thank Ernest Blythe and the Irish Government for their subsidy.
9	Defends himself in the *Sunday Times* against Gosse's charge that his Nobel Prize speech was inaccurate and in bad taste. Late this month he goes to Switzerland with GY and LR to lecture for the travel agent Henry Lunn in Mürren.
28	The Yeatses and LR meet up with Thomas MacGreevy in Milan.

September

| c.9 | (Wed) Returns to Dublin from Switzerland. Works on remaining proofs of *A Vision*. |

18	Goes to Coole to discuss George O'Brien's objection to the Abbey's production of O'Casey's *The Plough and the Stars*.
21	Returns to Dublin with AG.
22	Attends a long Emergency Meeting of the Abbey Directors which discusses the dispute over *The Plough and the Stars* and decides to introduce majority voting at further meetings. Afterwards he reads parts of *A Vision* to AG. Publication of *Early Poems and Stories*.
23	Accompanies GY and AG to an early colour film, *The Wanderer of the Waste Land*, based on a novel by Zane Grey.
24	Attends a further Directors' Meeting at the Abbey. After discussion, they decide that LR should be asked to take over from Michael J. Dolan as the main producer of plays at the Theatre.
*c.*25	Returns to Ballylee, where he remains for three weeks, finishing 'The Tower' and reading Murasaki Shikibu's *The Tale of Genji*.
30	Visits Coole.

October

4	(Sun) Calls at Coole and tells AG that he has finished the third part of 'The Tower'.
7	Finishes 'The Tower'.
12	The Yeatses leave Ballylee for Dublin.
13	WBY's Canadian cousin, Grace Yeats, calls to see him. He spends the middle of the month finishing page-proofs of *A Vision* and revising *Reveries over Childhood and Youth* and *The Trembling of the Veil* for a new combined edition.
29	Pays off the Cuala Industries' debts of £2,010. 11*s*. 1*d*.
31	Attends a children's party for Anne Yeats. GY goes to London to supervise a sale of Cuala goods.

November

2	(Mon) Gogarty calls in at WBY's 'Monday Evening'; Ryan, the philanthropist, is also there.
3	Sees his accountant to finalize details for clearing the Cuala debts.
4	Iseult Gonne and her husband Francis Stuart call in the evening and they discuss Stuart's next book.
5	Dines with the O'Neills. Has finished revising *Autobiographies*.
8	Lunches with Andrew Jameson.
*c.*10	Speaks at a meeting of the TCD Historical Society.
11	GY returns from London.
12	Inspects schools in the morning and sits in the Senate in the afternoon.
25	Works on drafts of his forthcoming after-dinner speech to the ILS.
26	Arrives in London from Dublin after 'a cold & windy passage'.
27	Thomas MacGreevy calls to see him.

28   Meets OS and his mother-in-law in the afternoon and dines at
             the Ivy with Dulac and Arthur Waley in the evening.
29   Leaves the Savile Club because of the cold and moves into the
             Knightsbridge Hotel. Sees GY's grandmother, Edith Woodmass.
30   Guest of honour at a dinner given by the ILS at the Florence
             Restaurant and makes a speech on Irish Education.

December
1   (Tue) Dines at the PEN Club in London.
2   Lectures for Sturge Moore at Bedales School in Hampshire.
5   First part of 'The Child and the State' (article; *UP* II. 454–8) pub-
             lished in the *Irish Statesman*.
5–7   Goes to Oxford, and thence to stay with Ottoline Morrell at
             Garsington. Ethel Sands, Edward Sackville-West, Sassoon and
             Gilbert Spencer there, and David Cecil comes for lunch on
             7 December.
7   Leaves Garsington and returns to Dublin.
8   Deep in Bertrand Russell's *The ABC of Relativity*.
9   Present at the opening of the Second Triennial Period of the
             Senate. Votes for the successful re-election of Lord Glenavy as
             Chairman but fails by one vote to have James Douglas elected
             Vice-Chairman.
12   Second part of 'The Child and the State' published in the *Irish
             Statesman* (article; UP II, 458–61).
14   Votes in the Senate against an amendment to the Shannon
             Electrification Scheme.
16   Votes in the Senate for the second and third readings of a Bill to
             confirm the amended Treaty between Ireland and Britain.
17   In the Senate speaks against sex-discrimination in civil service
             appointments and votes against the second readings of the Civil
             Service Regulation (Amendment) Bill and the Local Elections
             Postponement Bill.
22   Anne Yeats ill with pneumonia.
26   AG comes up to Dublin for the Abbey's 21st birthday celebrations.
27   Collects AG in a taxi to celebrate the Abbey Theatre's 21st birth-
             day, with performances of *The Hour-Glass*, *Hyacinth Halvey* and
             The Shadow of the Glen and many speeches.
28   Attends an entertainment given by the Dublin 'Round Table'
             for the directors, actors and staff of the Abbey Theatre.

1926

January
2   (Sat) Reading Walter McDonald's *Reminiscences of a Maynooth
             Professor*.

5	Reading Bertrand Russell's *The Problems of Philosophy*.
7	Meets AG on her arrival in Dublin and takes her to the Abbey while he dines out.
11	O'Casey withdraws *The Plough and the Stars* from the Abbey because the actress Eileen Crowe refuses to say some of his lines; WBY insists that Crowe give up the part and rehearsals resume. Reads AG some of his latest poems from the sequence 'A Man Young and Old'. Consults a General about the design of banners for Irish regiments.
15	*A Vision* published. WBY advises the publisher Laurie not to send review copies to any Irish papers apart from the *Irish Statesman*.
22	LR takes WBY and GY to the cinema to see *The Gold Rush*.
31	Writes 'The Death of the Hare', Part IV of 'A Man Young and Old' (*VP*, 453).

February

3	(Wed) Attends a Board Meeting of the Irish National Gallery. That evening the Yeatses dine at the Vice-Regal Lodge, where Tim Healy advises him how best to approach the British Government over the return of the Lane Pictures.
6	'The Need for Audacity of Thought' (article; *UP* II. 461–5) published in the *Dial*. Writes 'Chosen'.
7	Pays a tailor's bill of £45. 18s.
8	The Yeatses hold a large dinner at Jammets Restaurant and WBY goes to the Abbey for the first production of *The Plough and the Stars*, which causes great controversy.
11	Nominated to the Joint Library Committee of the Irish Parliament. Republican sympathizers rush the Abbey stage in protest against *The Plough and the Stars*; the actors fight them off, the police are called, and someone throws a shoe at WBY, who addresses the rioters from the stage. The musician Walter Rummell arrives to stay with the Yeatses.
12	WBY meets AG on her arrival in Dublin and gives her an account of the demonstrations at the Abbey. They go on to a performance of *The Plough and the Stars*, which has police protection.
13	The IRA try to kidnap the Abbey actor Barry Fitzgerald in protest at *The Plough and the Stars*, and the company is put under police guard. They remain in theatre between the afternoon and evening performances and WBY falls asleep while Rummel entertains them on the piano.
14	Attends a Drama League production of Eugene O'Neill's *In the Zone* and G. K. Chesterton's *Magic* at the Abbey.
18	Writing a version of Sophocles' *Oedipus Rex*.
21	Thanks Grierson for his *The Background of English Literature*, which he has been reading constantly for weeks, especially the

essay on Byron. Has also been rereading Grierson's edition of Donne.

23   Defends the Abbey Theatre against charges of political and religious bias in a speech to the Dublin Literary Society.

March

3   (Wed) Congratulates the Government in the Senate on its intention to appoint only experts to the committee charged with designing the new Irish coinage.

7   In the morning attends Susan Mitchell's funeral. Corresponds with Kennedy, the Lord Chief Justice, about the design of robes for Irish judges.

14   Attends a Drama League production of Shaw's *Heartbreak House* at the Abbey with GY and annoys her by disparaging it.

21   WBY and GY lunch with the Sisters of Mercy at St Otteran's School, Waterford.

22   Inspects St Otteran's School, the inspiration for 'Among School Children'. About this time writes 'Father and Child' (*VP*, 531).

24   Speaks at length in the Senate on the School Attendance Bill, urging the provision of adequate school buildings and meals for pupils, advocating the Montessori method of education, and insisting that the interests of the child must not be subordinated to nationalist or religious ideologies.

27   Speaks at the unveiling of a memorial plaque to T. W. Lyster at the National Library of Ireland (*UP* II. 470–2).

30   Speaks in the Senate in favour of increased spending on education.

April

2   (Fri) AG and her granddaughters arrive at 82 Merrion Square and she and WBY discuss the Lane Pictures, the political situation, and Irish judges' robes.

3   'More Songs from an Old Countryman' (poems; later 'A Man Young and Old'; *VP*, 454–7, 458–9) published in the *London Mercury* and the first part of 'A Defence of the Abbey Theatre' (speech; *UP* II. 465–70) in the *Irish Statesman*. Early this month WBY suffers a slight rupture and catches measles. He reads A. N. Whitehead's *Science and the Modern World* and corrects the first two books of his autobiographies for publication in one volume.

12   Disgusted by MacNamara's comedy *Look at the Heffernans!* at the Abbey and phones MacNamara to denounce it.

22   Hears that Republicans are planning to blow up the Abbey Theatre as a reprisal for the production of *The Plough and the Stars*.

28   Speaks in the Senate against an amendment to the Schools Attendance Bill and denounces the deficiencies in Irish education.

May

1   (Sat) The second part of 'A Defence of the Abbey Theatre' published in the *Irish Statesman*. WBY is reading Benedetto Croce's philosophy.

2   Speaks before the Dublin Drama League's performances of his Noh plays *The Only Jealousy of Emer* and *The Cat and the Moon*.

3   Attends a Board Meeting of the Irish National Gallery.

6   AG comes to stay.

8   Discusses the nature of Comedy with AG.

10   Accompanies AG to a meeting of the Abbey Directors, which radically rearranges the Company's salary and promotion structures.

12   Consults AG about the financial arrangements under which Sara Allgood is to be re-engaged at the Abbey. Votes in the Senate against an amendment to the Enforcement of Court Orders Bill.

17   Attends the Senate and later leaves Dublin for Ballylee, where he begins writing 'A Woman Young and Old'. He is reading Baudelaire and Stephen MacKenna's translation of Plotinus' *The Enneads*.

18   Visits Coole and reads his *Oedipus the King* to AG.

19   Helps entertain the Vere O'Brien party who call for tea at Coole. Appointed chairman of the committee on coinage design. He is full of enthusiasm for the Protestant Anglo-Irish eighteenth century and looking up his Cromwellian ancestors.

20   Leaves Coole for Ballylee.

25   Writes 'First Love', Part I of 'A Man Young and Old' (*VP*, 451) and is reading Shaw's *Back to Methuselah*.

26   Visits Coole for lunch and tells AG that he has begun 'Among School Children' and is thinking out 'The Seven Sages'.

31   Goes to Dublin from Ballylee for a meeting of the Senate.

June

2   (Wed) Attends a Board Meeting of the Irish National Gallery.

3   Votes in the Senate for the second reading of the Railways Bill.

4   Returns to Ballylee with LR. Over the coming weeks the Gogarty family, WBY's uncle Isaac and his cousins, Hilda and Guy, visit Ballylee. Writing 'A Last Confession.'

5   The final part of 'A Defence of the Abbey Theatre' published in the *Irish Statesman*.

6   The Yeatses and LR go to Coole for tea and stay on to dinner, at which they discuss the plays to be produced during the Autumn Abbey season.

14   Writing 'Among School Children'.

15   Goes to Dublin and speaks in the Senate against President Cosgrave's resolution to debar certain State employees from election to either House of the Irish Parliament.

16	Buys Oswald Spengler's *The Decline of the West* and discovers remarkable similarities to *A Vision*. Votes in the Senate against an amendment to increase the hours of shop-opening.
17	Chairs the first meeting of the Committee on Irish Coinage.
*c.*18	Returns to Ballylee.
21	Calls at Coole and discusses the Lane Pictures, the Abbey Company's salaries and Oswald Spengler.
24	Goes to Dublin with AG to mount a press attack on King George V for opening the Tate Gallery while the Lane Picture question is still *sub judice*. They see Ernest Blythe.
25	Discusses the protest over the King's conduct with AG and Professor William Thrift and at 3.00 pm goes with AG to the Dáil, where the matter is raised. In the evening he dictates interviews for the Dublin press and at 11.00 pm takes one version to the *Irish Times*.
26	Returns to Ballylee.
28	Calls at Coole to discuss his forthcoming speech in the Senate on the Lane Pictures and reads AG a poem, probably the revised version of 'Chosen' (*VP*, 534–5).
30	Chairs the second meeting of the Committee on Coinage. The Report of the Joint Committee on the Commercial and Industrial Property (Protection) Bill is laid before the Senate and Dáil.

July

1	(Thu) Iseult Gonne calls and tells the Yeatses that she is expecting a baby. WBY is reading Spengler's *Decline of the West* with great excitement.
2	Votes in the Senate against an amendment to the Local Authorities Bill. Returns to Ballylee from Dublin and continues writing 'The Friends of his Youth', Part VII of 'A Man Young and Old' (*VP*, 455–6).
4	Calls at Coole and stays to dinner, discussing the Lane Pictures with AG.
7	Goes to Dublin to attend a Board Meeting of the Irish National Gallery.
8	Chairs the third meeting of the Committee on Coinage.
12	Calls to Coole; tells AG that Cosgrave has proposed the building of a new Municipal Gallery and reads her a version of his forthcoming Senate speech about the Lane Pictures. They agree to raise LR's salary to £400 p.a.
14	Delivers a long speech in the Senate on the Lane Pictures, which criticizes George V for opening a new wing of the Tate Gallery before the status of the pictures has been resolved.
15	Attends an extraordinary meeting of the Board of the Irish National Gallery to consider what action should be taken over

the refusal of the British Parliament to return the Lane Pictures to Dublin.

16	Returns to Ballylee.
17	Calls at Coole and stays to dinner. Pronounces himself pleased with his Senate speech, and he and AG write letters appointing LR manager of the Abbey and Michael Dolan teacher in the School of Acting.
22	Speaks in the Senate in favour of a new design for Irish judges' robes, but his proposal is defeated. Chairs the fourth meeting of the Committee on Coinage.
23	Begins to compose the poem 'Meeting'.
26	Calls at Coole and co-signs AG's letter to *The Times* refuting MacColl's assertions that at the time of his death Lane was undecided as to the final destination of his Pictures. The letter is published on 29 July.
31	Yeats visits Coole for lunch, eager to write another letter to *The Times* refuting MacColl. AG reads him two acts of her rewritten *Sancho's Master*.

August

2	(Mon) The Yeats family return to Dublin for the Dublin Horse Show.
c.4	*Estrangement* published.
5	Chairs the fifth meeting of the Committee on Coinage.
7	At LR's where he meets Josephine MacNeill, wife of the Irish High Commissioner in London, who tells him her husband wants to bring out a pamphlet on the Lane Pictures.
8	Asks Andrew Jameson to join the Lane Pictures Committee and AG to write a new pamphlet on the dispute.
17	Chairs the sixth meeting of the Committee on Coinage. The Yeatses spend the middle of the month at Howth.
21	Stays at Muckross House, Co. Kerry, to write verse away from Dublin distractions. Shane Leslie is a fellow guest. WBY writes 'Parting' and 'Her Vision in the Wood' and finishes 'A Last Confession' and 'Meeting' (*VP*, 535–6, 536–7, 538, 539).
30	Returns to Dublin where Shane Leslie and his wife, LR, and AE attend his 'Monday Evening'.
31	Sits with AG before another operation for breast cancer. Later chairs a meeting of the Coinage Committee.

September

2	(Thu) Chairs another meeting of the Committee on Coinage. Visits AG in hospital. *The Land of Heart's Desire* broadcast by BBC Belfast. Is busy early this month revising his recent poems

and seeing AG's pamphlet, *Case for the Return of Sir Hugh Lane's Pictures to Dublin*, through the press.

4   Visits AG in hospital and they discuss her pamphlet on the Lane Pictures.

6   Visits AG in hospital.

20   Back in Ballylee, he visits AG, recovering from her operation at Coole, and they go through the proofs of her pamphlet on the Lane Pictures.

22–3   Reading George Shiels' new play, *Cartney and Kevney*, and reviewing his development as a dramatist.

23   At Coole, where AG reads him the third act of her new play, *Sancho's Master*.

26   Writing 'Sailing to Byzantium'. Late this month he is reading Croce, writing 'Among School Children' and correcting proofs of *Autobiographies*.

c.29   Returns to Dublin from Ballyllee.

October

2   (Sat) The first part of 'Estrangement' (autobiography; *Aut*, 461–78) published in the *London Mercury*.

3   Lectures in Liverpool.

4   In London, staying at the Orchard Hotel. Spends most of this visit on the campaign for the Lane Pictures. He introduces Lady Londonderry to James MacNeill, the Irish High Commissioner, persuades her to form an Organizing Committee, and arranges for sympathetic journalists to review AG's recent pamphlet.

8   Sees Shotaro Oshima, his Japanese translator. Has tea with Thomas MacGreevy.

11   Dines with Cecil Harmsworth.

12   Consults Tom MacGreevy about his application for the Directorship of the Irish National Gallery.

17   Has dinner and spends the night at Lord Beaverbrook's country house at Leatherhead, where he discusses the Lane Pictures with several journalists.

18   Sees Manning Robertson in London and meets members of the British Labour Party at the Irish High Commission. Meets Birrell and Kevin O'Higgins at the Lavery's in the evening and also Lord D'Abernon, a governor of the Tate Gallery.

19   Returns to Dublin and takes to his bed with a bad cold.

c.23   Michael Yeats enters a nursing home for an operation on an ear duct.

November

2   (Tue) Meets Jameson and Brown to organize a Dublin Lane Pictures Committee.

5	*Autobiographies* published.
6	The second part of 'Estrangement' (*Aut*, 478–95) published in the *London Mercury*.
7	Goes to London.
15	Spends the morning reading the works of the German psychologist Wilhelm Wundt at the London Library; lunches at the Irish High Commission, where he meets Kevin O'Higgins and Bracken. Sees Manning Robertson to arrange a public dinner. *The Shadowy Waters* broadcast by BBC Belfast.
16	Lunches with Bracken to meet Lutyens, who offers to design a Gallery in Dublin for the Lane Pictures if the bridge site is adopted.
17	Consults Winston Churchill, who promises his support in the Lane Pictures campaign and advises him on who else to approach.
18	Returns to Dublin, travelling by day. Sees Gogarty in the evening, who warns him of the dangers to Senators of travelling in Irish country districts.
19	Begins to bring his memoirs up to date.
21	Reading Lady Londonderry's memoir of her father, Henry Chaplin.
24	Attends the first meeting of the Dublin Lane Pictures Committee.
25	Chairs a meeting of the Committee on Coinage.
29	Writes 'Her Triumph' (*VP*, 533–4).
30	Gives an 'At Home' for the Swedish architect, Ragnar Ostberg.

December

1	(Wed) Busy early this month with the production of *Oedipus the King* at the Abbey and composing new poems for the sequence 'A Woman Young and Old'.
7	Finishes 'The Empty Cup', Part V of 'A Man Young and Old' (*VP*, 454). Attends the first production of *Oedipus the King*.
8	Phones the Talbot Press about the wrong attribution of AG's portrait in their *Irish Life and Landscapes*. At 3 pm McCormick and LR call to help him make cuts to *Oedipus*; at 4 pm he has a consultation about the new Irish Copyright Bill.
c.12	Suggests to Norah McGuinness that she should illustrate some of his poems in the style of Byzantine wall-pictures and spends the evening looking through photographs of Sicilian mosaics with her.
14	Recommends Norah McGuinness to Macmillan as illustrator of his poems.
15	Votes in the Senate for the Ultimate Financial Settlement between Ireland and Britain. Begins writing *Oedipus at Colonus*.
17	Sees Sam Brown about the Lane Pictures campaign.

19   Consults the Society of Authors about the new Irish Copyright Bill.

29   Half way through *Oedipus at Colonus*.

1927

January

4   (Tue) LR calls in the evening to show WBY a successful rewriting of his play *The Round Table*, and with a plot for a new play.

6   WBY finishes the dialogue for *Oedipus at Colonus*. In the middle of this month he is prostrate with arthritis in his right leg, for which he gets a daily massage.

22   Catches influenza from LR.

25   Finds that the influenza has relieved his arthritis.

27   AG comes up to Dublin.

29   AG moves from her Dublin hotel to stay with the Yeatses in Merrion Square. Informs him that she and Margaret Gregory are selling Coole Park.

31   WBY a little better and comes downstairs for a while. AG reads him Trollope's *The Claverings* and helps with his revision of *Oedipus at Colonus*.

February

1   (Tue) AG again helps WBY revise *Oedipus at Colonus*.

2   Signs a public protest against the piracy of Joyce's *Ulysses*.

7   The representative of an American printer calls with samples of banknotes, in the hope of persuading WBY to adopt them for the new Irish currency. AE, AG and S. L. Brown attend his 'Monday Evening'.

8   LR comes to dinner and Frank O'Connor calls in later.

9   Takes AG to see *Beau Geste* at the cinema.

10   LR again at dinner with the dramatist and new Abbey actor Rutherford Mayne.

11   AG goes down with influenza at the Yeatses' house.

13   AG better; she continues reading *The Claverings* to WBY and attends his 'Monday Evening' with AE and General O'Connell, who airs his proposal to proclaim George V the King of Ireland.

14   WBY and the Coinage Committee judge the designs submitted for the new Irish coinage and choose those by the English artist Percy Metcalfe. S. L. Brown calls to discuss the Lane Pictures campaign with WBY and AG. WBY resigns from the Dublin Arts Club.

16   AG reads her play *Dave* to WBY and afterwards continues with her reading of *The Claverings*.

19   Writes a chorus for *Oedipus at Colonus*.

21	AG and WBY finish work on *Oedipus* and he thanks her for helping him put it into natural speech.
23	Votes in the Senate against an amendment to the Local Government Bill.
24	Speaks in the Senate on the need to protect Irish writers' copyright in the USA.
26	AG leaves Merrion Square for Coole. A revised edition of *Poems* published late this month.

March

7	(Mon) Consults an Irish scholar about the proposed changes to Irish copyright provisions.
9	Speaks in the Senate in favour of turning Merrion Square into a public park.
11	A long and impassioned speech by WBY in the Senate defeats a proposed amendment to the Industrial and Commercial Property (Protection) Bill, which would have denied Irish authors copyright in Ireland if they did not print their works there.
12	Recommences writing *Oedipus at Colonus*. Is reading Angelo Crespi's *Contemporary Thought of Italy*.
13	Writes 'From "Oedipus at Colonus"', Part XI of 'A Man Young and Old' (*VP*, 459).
14	AG comes to stay at Merrion Square on her way to Liverpool and accompanies WBY to the Abbey to see her *Sancho's Master*.
18	AG returns to Merrion Square from Liverpool.
20	The Abbey Company returns from America. AG reads WBY Trollope's *An Autobiography*.
21	AG returns to Coole.
24	Writes 'Colonus' Praise' (*VP*, 446–7). Late this month WBY is slowly revising *Oedipus at Colonus* and reading Plato.

April

4	(Mon) Addresses the Dublin Rotary Club on the Lane Pictures.
6	Attends a Board Meeting of the Irish National Gallery.
7	Speaks again in the Senate in favour of turning Merrion Square into a public park.
8	Votes in the Senate in favour of an amendment to the Juries Bill allowing women to serve on juries.
12	'The Lake Isle of Innisfree' broadcast by BBC London.
25	Goes to London on Lane Pictures business. Sees the MP Charles Howard Bury, Harmsworth and others.
30	Consults Lord Haldane, who recommends a high-level deputation to Baldwin. Cecil Harmsworth and his wife dine with WBY at the Ivy Restaurant to meet Dulac and Helen Beauclerk.

May

2	(Mon) Sees Lord Birkenhead about the Lane Pictures.
3	Returns to Dublin.
4	Speaks in the Senate on the protection of Irish copyrights in both America and Ireland, and votes for an amendment to the Barrow Drainage Bill.
7	'Four Songs from the Young Countryman' and 'Two Songs from the Old Countryman' (poems, *VP*, 451–3, 454–5) published in the *London Mercury*.
10	Meets AG on her arrival in Dublin and takes her straight to the Abbey by taxi to see her play *Dave*. She stays at Merrion Square.
11	Again accompanies AG to the Abbey to see *Dave* and Shaw's *Fanny's First Play*.
12	AG returns to Coole. WBY votes in the Senate for an amendment to the Barrow Drainage Bill.
13	Poems by Yeats broadcast by BBC London.
14	Chairs a meeting of the Provisional Committee to advise British Authors Productions Ltd on Irish films.
16	Goes to London overnight by way of Holyhead.
17	LR calls on him in London to discuss the Irish Film Committee. WBY meets Cecil Harmsworth that afternoon and later sees OS and Dorothy Shakespear.
20	Consults Harold Macmillan about future publishing plans and dines with Dulac.
21	Goes to Cambridge to see a matinée production of *The Player Queen* at the Festival Theatre and likes it so much that he stays on for the evening performance. Sees Ninette de Valois dance for the first time.
22	Returns to London, where over the next few days he dines with Cecil Harmsworth and Dulac and attends two lunch parties.
26	Dines at the annual TCD London dinner as a guest of Cecil Harmsworth and is asked to make a speech. Sounds out Harmsworth on the possibility of English journalistic support for the Irish Government.
30	In the afternoon sees Cecil Harmsworth to continue discussions about English journalistic support for the Free State Government.
31	Returns to Dublin.

June

1	(Wed) Writes a Preface for *Sophocles' King Oedipus*. Attends a Board Meeting of the Irish National Gallery.
4	*The Resurrection* (play, *VPl*, 900–36) published in the *Adelphi*, and 'The Tower' (poem, *VP*, 409–16) in the *Criterion*.

9	Chairs a meeting of the Provisional Committee to advise British Authors Productions Ltd on Irish films.
15	Goes to Coole.
17	Reads part of 'A Woman Young and Old' to AG. Later this month moves to Ballylee, where, with the children away, he reads Hegel and writes verse, including the poems 'A First Confession' (*VP*, 532–3) and 'Consolation' (*VP*, 534). Part of the wood panelling in the Tower catches fire and burns the ceiling in WBY's study.
25	Visits Coole and tells AG that he is writing poems for 'A Woman Young and Old' and thinking of a play in which Christ meets Judas.
27	Returns to Dublin to visit the dentist. Continued bleeding forces him to abandon his 'Monday Evening' guests, LR, Cruise O'Brien, Seamus O'Sullivan and an American visitor, and return to the dentist.
28	At the dentist again. LR calls later in the afternoon. WBY returns to Galway at the end of the month.

July

1	(Fri) Visits Coole in the evening, where he dines with the Warrens and AG's great-nephew Desmond Shawe-Taylor.
2	WBY and GY dine at Coole with Desmond Shawe-Taylor and they discuss Theocritus.
5	WBY stays at Coole.
7	Goes up to Dublin for a meeting of the Film Committee. AG accompanies him to visit her doctor and stays at Merrion Square.
10	News of the assassination of Kevin O'Higgins reaches the Yeatses just as they are about to dine at the Gresham Hotel and they walk about the streets of Dublin in deep shock until bedtime.
12	The Senate assembles to pay respects to Kevin O'Higgins.
13	WBY processes with the rest of the Senate to O'Higgins' funeral at St Andrews Church and from there to Glasnevin Cemetery.
14	Returns to Ballylee, where he finishes the series of poems 'A Woman Young and Old' and begins 'A Dialogue of Self and Soul'.
15	Visits Coole. Spends the rest of this month and most of August mainly in Ballyllee, but goes up to Dublin for meetings of the Senate. He reads Toyohiko Kagawa's novel *Before the Dawn* and D. T. Suzuki's *Essays in Zen Buddhism*. Entertains Kazumi Yano, who is translating *The Wanderings of Oisin* into Japanese.

August

4	(Thu) Visits Coole.
6	'Among School Children' (poem, *VP*, 443–6) published in the *London Mercury* and the *Dial*. Writing 'Blood and the Moon' (*VP*, 480–2).

9	In Dublin for a meeting of the Senate, where he votes in favour of the draconian emergency Public Safety Bill.
10	Intervenes briefly in the Senate during the debate over the Public Safety Bill and votes against 5 amendments that would moderate its provisions.
c.11	Returns to Ballylee.
13	De Valera takes the Oath and enters the Dáil. WBY visits Coole and discusses Tolstoy and the political situation. He begins to revise *A Vision* in the middle of the month. *October Blast* is published.
24	Gets soaked walking from Ballylee to Coole but reads from *October Blast* to AG's visitors and discusses the need for an intellectual belief. Stays to dinner.
26	Goes from Ballylee to Dublin for the production of his two Oedipus plays.

September

3	(Sat) The Yeatses go to Wicklow for the weekend.
5	Invites the Dutch poet Pieter Nicolaas van Eyck to lunch.
c.6	WBY suddenly wakens out of despondency.
12	Attends the first production of *Oedipus at Colonus* at the Abbey. In the middle of the month he reads Benedetto Croce's *Philosophy of the Practical, Aesthetic as Science of Expression and General Linguistic* and *Logic as the Science of the Pure Concept*.
c.13	James R. Wells, President of the publishers Crosby Gaige, calls to suggest a limited edition of new poems by WBY. Begins writing 'Death' (*VP*, 476).
15	Begins writing 'From the "Antigone"'.
16	Sends Macmillan the copy text for *The Tower*.
c.20	Excited by pictures of Hildo Krop's theatrical masks.
22	'Aedh wishes for the Cloths of Heaven' broadcast by BBC Bournemouth. WBY is busy later this month working on poems, including 'A Dialogue of Self and Soul' (*VP*, 477–9) and 'In Memory of Eva Gore-Booth and Con Markiewicz' (*VP*, 475–6), for the special edition by James Wells. Sees Cosgrave in an unsuccessful attempt to get Sean MacBride out of gaol on parole.

October

1	(Sat) Attends a noisy and cantankerous dinner at a restaurant with Tom MacGreevy, LR and Dolly Travers-Smith.
3	Finishes 'In Memory of Eva Gore-Booth and Con Markiewicz' and is writing 'Symbols' (*VP*, 484) .
5	Attends a Board Meeting of the Irish National Gallery.
c.10	Taken ill with a severe and exhausting cold which turns to pneumonia and lasts until 25 October.

26	Rewrites 'A Dream of a Blessed Spirit' while correcting a new edition of *Poems* and retitles it 'The Countess Cathleen in Paradise'.
27	AG comes to Dublin to see WBY before he goes south for the Winter.
29	AG helps WBY with the proofs of *Oedipus the King*.
31	AG visits for the evening and reads him some of her essays about Coole, 'Figures in Clay'.

November

1	(Tue) AG returns to Coole.
3	WBY and GY cross to London.
4	They sail for Gibraltar on the SS *Morea*.
9	The Yeatses reach Gibraltar and go to the Hotel Reina Christina in Algeciras.
11	Publication of *Stories of Red Hanrahan and the Secret Rose*, illustrated by Norah McGuinness.
13	First opening of the Peacock Theatre in Dublin.
14	The Yeatses travel by car from Algeciras to Seville, where his lung begins to bleed and he fears that he is dying.
15	WBY finishes correcting the proofs of *The Tower*. He is reading Bertrand Russell daily and walking in the Alcazar.
18	Is reading Wyndham Lewis's *Time and Western Man* with growing admiration.
23	The Yeatses leave Seville for Cannes, stopping over in Madrid and Barcelona. Begins light work again, writing a little verse every morning.
25	The Yeatses book into the Hotel Château St Georges in Cannes.

December

1	(Thu) Seriously ill in Cannes with congestion of the lungs. Allowed to do no work and only light reading.
14	GY returns to London to fetch the children, while WBY remains in Cannes. Writing first drafts of 'Oil and Blood'.
15	In London GY discovers that Michael Yeats is seriously ill and consults a specialist who immediately transfers him to a hospital.
22	GY returns to Cannes with Anne Yeats.
23	Michael Yeats arrives in Cannes. Late this month WBY continues with his reading of *Time and Western Man* and also reads Lewis's *The Art of Being Ruled*. Finishing 'A Dialogue of Self and Soul'.

1928

January

| 1 | (Sun) LR remains in Cannes until around the 12 January discussing possible productions of Shakespeare and of AG's *Grania* |

at the Abbey. Fellow guests from the Russian Embassy in Paris try unsuccessfully to have the Yeatses thrown out of the Hotel Château St Georges on the grounds that WBY has infectious consumption. He is reading the last chapters of *Time and Western Man* over and over again, and spending most of the day in bed.

11   Sits out all morning in the hotel garden. The doctor in Cannes tells him his bad health is due to years of overwork and that his recovery will be slow. In the evening GY reads him extracts from André Maurois's biography of Disraeli.

12   Urges Macmillan to publish a volume of plays by LR.

13   A bout of influenza causes a recurrence of inflammation of the lungs. In the middle of the month WBY puts 82 Merrion Square in the hands of a Dublin estate agent since his chronic ill-health will make winters abroad desirable. Michael Yeats is sent to a school in Switzerland having been diagnosed as suffering from a tubercular gland.

17   GY makes WBY dictate a prose version of *The Only Jealousy of Emer* as the scenario for a ballet (later *Fighting the Waves*) for the use of Ninette de Valois, and afterwards takes him to lunch in Cannes.

February

1   (Wed) Spends the early part of the month recovering from another attack of influenza and reading Robert Browning's *Paracelsus* and the *Autobiography* of St Theresa. Finishes 'From the "Antigone"' (*VP*, 540) and writes 'Before the World was Made'.

8   Watches the Battle of the Flowers in Cannes.

*c.*9   The Yeatses motor along the coast to have lunch and tea with Mrs Lucy Phillimore.

13   Anne and her nurse leave Cannes for Dublin.

14   *The Tower* is published and WBY is astonished by its bitterness. WBY, GY, and Michael Yeats move from Cannes to Rapallo to look for an apartment; they stop in Mentone on the way to get a second opinion on his health, which confirms the diagnosis of the Cannes doctor.

17   The Yeatses arrive in Rapallo and take rooms at the Albergo Rapallo. Later this month WBY finds that his exhaustion is gone; he walks by the sea in the mornings, returns to bed in the afternoons, spends the evenings with the Pounds or alone with GY, and then reads detective or western stories in bed from 10 to *c.*11.30 pm. Pound helps him to punctuate his new poems.

23   GY leaves WBY in Rapallo while she takes Michael Yeats to school in Switzerland.

24   Pound spends several hours explaining the structure of the *Cantos* to him.

25	In the morning Dorothy Pound takes WBY to the Library in quest of more detective stories; in the evening the Pounds take him to dine with Gertrude Stein.
26	Pound continues to explain his *Cantos* to WBY and reads him Cavalcanti; they dine together most nights.
28	Walks for almost an hour without fatigue. Reads Pound's translations of Cavalcanti, prior to dining with him.

March

1	(Thu) Early this month the Yeatses take a flat in Rapallo. WBY works on alternate days, revising *A Vision* and writing *A Packet for Ezra Pound*.
2	GY returns to Rapallo from Switzerland.
12	Sends AG a copy of 'Before the World was Made' (*VP*, 531–2).
13	*The Land of Heart's Desire* broadcast by BBC London.
17	GY signs a five-year lease on a newly-built fourth-floor apartment at 12 via Americhe, Rapallo. 'The Ballad of Father Gilligan' broadcast by BBC London.
20	'The Ballad of Moll Magee' broadcast by BBC London.
27	WBY's version of *Sophocles' King Oedipus* is published.
30	The Yeatses travel from Rapallo to Villars-sur-Bey in Switzerland to see Michael Yeats.

April

7	(Sat) 'The Death of Synge' in the *London Mercury* (autobiography; *Aut*, 499–527). Early this month WBY continues to revise *A Vision* and write *A Packet for Ezra Pound* under the inspiration of Cavalcanti.
*c.*9	The Yeatses return to Dublin from Switzerland by way of Paris (where they lunch with MacGreevy), Cherbourg and Cobh.
16	Consults two Dublin doctors about his health; they prescribe pills and start him on a course of three injections monthly. His general routine is to write all morning in bed and get up for lunch.
17	Reads and dislikes O'Casey's *The Silver Tassie*.
20	Writes to tell O'Casey that he dislikes *The Silver Tassie*.
23	Percy Metcalfe stays with him in Dublin.
28	Has tea with Katharine Tynan in Dalkey.

May

3	(Thu) AG comes to stay at Merrion Square and goes with WBY to see T. C. Murray's *The Blind Wolf* at the Abbey.
4	His doctor tells him his blood pressure is at its lowest for years.
6	He and LR oppose AG's suggestion that Sara Allgood should be re-engaged at the Abbey.
7	AG reads him one of her essays on Coole for possible publication by Cuala.

9	Accompanies GY, AG and LR to the Abbey to see *The Plough and the Stars*.
12	Invites the Hones to dinner.
13	The Yeatses and AG go to a party at LR's house. In the evening AG begins to read Trollope's *Dr. Wortle's School* to him.
14	Attends a Directors' Meeting at the Abbey which agrees to Sara Allgood's re-engagement, but at half the salary she has asked for.
17	AG continues reading *Dr. Wortle's School* to WBY until LR calls at 10 pm.
18	LR and AG to dinner with Miss Cunningham who translates *verbatim* a German play on Robert Emmet for them.
19	Dines with Gogarty to meet the editor of an American magazine.
20	The Yeatses hold an 'At Home' from 4 to 7 pm.
21	Holds a dinner party prior to his 'Monday Evening', which is attended by AG, Gogarty, the Blythes, Philip Hanson and Arland Ussher.
22	AG finishes reading *Dr. Wortle's School*.
23	Dines at the Shelbourne with AG, AE and Lucy Phillimore. Attends Shelah Richards' production of Margaret Kennedy's *The Constant Nymph* at the Abbey, but dislikes the play.
24	AG returns to Coole. At the end of this month the sale of 82 Merrion Square to the architect R. M. Butler for £1,500 is finalised.

June

1	(Fri) Engages in a public controversy over the Abbey's rejection of O'Casey's *The Silver Tassie*.
4	Walter Starkie consults WBY about the dispute with O'Casey and they decided to publish the whole correspondence relating to it. WBY signs a contract with Crosby Gaige for the American publication of *Oedipus at Colonus* for £150.
c.5	*The Death of Synge* published.
6	Attends a Board Meeting of the Irish National Gallery.
15	Meets AG, up from Coole, at the station and takes her to Merrion Square.
16	AG reads him a letter from de Valera in support of the return of the Lane Pictures.
17	WBY visits London for a few days while GY goes to Switzerland to collect Michael Yeats from School.
23	In London, meets the Sitwells.

July

1	(Sun) Very tired after the journey back from London and spends a couple of days in bed. A psychic message tells him he has time to finish his work. Trying desperately to finish the revised *A Vision*.

4	Votes in the Senate for the Constitution Amendment Bill.
6	*The Shadowy Waters* broadcast by BBC Belfast.
10	Votes in the Senate for the second reading of the Constitution Amendment Bill.
11	Votes in the Senate at the committee stage of the Constitution Amendment Bill.
12	Votes again in the Senate for the Constitution Amendment Bill.
18	Taken ill while speaking in the Senate on the Constitution Amendment Bill.
c.23	Vacates 82 Merrion Square and moves temporarily to Howth while GY arranges their new apartment at 42 Fitzwilliam Square.
24	Protests on hearing that the Municipal Gallery is thinking of acquiring a painting by Frank Dicksee.
25	Makes his last Senate appearance but does not speak.
26	WBY, AE and Starkie call as a deputation on the Minister for Finance, Ernest Blythe, to urge the setting up of an Irish Academy.

August

1	(Wed) Early this month he moves into 42 Fitzwilliam Square. Wyndham Lewis sends him a copy of *Childermass*, of which he admires the first 100 pages. Sees Shaw in Dublin and they discusses Expressionism.
12	Writes to Wyndham Lewis for the first time. Finishes his course of 12 injections.
14	Goes to Coole in search of tranquillity in which to write up his report on the new Irish coinage. Also finishes *A Packet for Ezra Pound* and revises *The Player Queen*.
15	Emil Gottgetreu, a young German, turns up at Coole and infuriates WBY at lunch with his praise of Charlie Chaplin, Ernst Toller and Upton Sinclair. In the evening AG reads WBY Denis Johnston's play *The Old Lady Says 'No!'*.
16	Discusses Buddhism with Poppy Guthrie and the Warrens who are visiting Coole for tea. AG is reading Trollope's *Orley Farm* to him.
19	AG gives up reading *Orley Farm* because the print is too small and replaces it with Trollope's *Rachel Ray*. She also reads him her essay on 'The Garden' which he wants to publish with others as *Coole*.
20	Reading Emil Ludwig's *Bismarck*.
22	Publishes a letter in the *Irish Independent* denouncing the proposed Irish Censorship Bill.
23	Francis Macnamara calls at Coole with his daughter and gossips with WBY, mainly about Augustus John.
24	WBY reads 'Sailing to Byzantium', 'Among School Children' and the third part of 'The Tower' to a large party at Coole, including the Clancys and the Revd Madden, Protestant Chaplain at the Curragh.

25	Photographs of the new Irish coinage reach Coole, and WBY dictates an essay on them to AG.
26	Reads Shane Leslie's *The Skull of Swift*. Denounces Irish education to AG for having produced an island of moral cowards. Writes to tell Pound that he cannot use his translation of Cavalcanti in *A Packet for Ezra Pound*. In the afternoon helps act as host to large party from St Clerans who come to Coole for tea. AG reads him *Rachel Ray* in evening. WBY is also reading Radclyffe Hall's *The Well of Loneliness*.
27	Visits Guy Gough at Lough Cultra with AG and is delighted by all that he sees there. 'The Ballad of Father Gilligan' broadcast by BBC London.
28	Hears that Anne Yeats is ill in Dublin. Finishes his essay on the Coinage. Thomas Kiernan and his wife visit Coole.
29	Sends Thomas Bodkin a copy of his Coinage essay. After dinner AG reads him George Shiels' play *Mountain Dew* and they discuss ways of improving it. Has decided not to allow his name to go forward for election to the Senate. 'The Ballad of Moll Magee' broadcast by BBC London.
30	AG reads him more of her essays for *Coole*.
31	Leaves Coole for Dublin.

September

1	(Sat) Stays for the weekend with Lucy Phillimore in Wicklow but has a furious argument with her over literature and politics. Anne Yeats is much better.
10	AG calls on the Yeatses in Fitzwilliam Square and finds WBY angry because Walter Starkie has poached all his 'Monday Evening' guests. In the middle of this month WBY engages in a controversy over the proposed Irish censorship laws.
15	GY leaves to take Anne back to school in Switzerland, returning to Dublin on 19 September.
22	'The Censorship and St. Thomas Aquinas' (article; *UP* II. 477–80) published in the *Irish Statesman*.
29	'Irish Censorship' (article; *UP* II. 480–5) published in the *Spectator*.

October

3	(Wed) Consults Senator Brown about the establishment of an Irish Academy of Literature to which appeals against censorship could be made.
14	WBY and GY at Coole; WBY combative over the Censorship Bill and reading Swift.
15	The Yeatses leave Coole for Dublin.
17	WBY leaves Dublin for London by the morning boat.

23	Meets GY in Stafford for two days to visit Jean and John Hall, friends they made in Algeciras.
30	Lunches with Denis Gwynn to discuss his biography of Edward Martyn.
31	Leaves London for Rapallo.

November

3	(Sat) WBY and GY arrive in Rapallo and stay at the Hotel Mignon until their apartment is ready. WBY becomes over-excited through reading nothing but Swift. Later he begins to write 'At Algeciras'.
23	The Yeatses' furniture arrives from Dublin. WBY is finishing off *A Packet for Ezra Pound*.
27	GY moves into their apartment, Via Americhe 12–8, Rapallo.
28	WBY moves into the new apartment.

December

c.19	(Wed) James MacNeill, the new Irish Governor General, and his wife visit WBY in Rapallo and show him a set of the new coinage. WBY donates £50 to try to keep the *Irish Statesman* afloat.
25	Tom MacGreevy spends Christmas with the Yeatses in Rapallo.
28	MacGreevy leaves Rapallo having made great friends with Pound.

1929

January

3	(Thu) The Yeats family visit Rome for a week; WBY laid up for a few days with fatigue.
12	WBY and GY back in Rapallo, where he sees Pound daily, 'disagree-ing about everything'. In the middle of the month he writes a number of prose drafts for poems as well as a version of *Resurrection*.
22	Drafts an essay on 'The Artist as Victim'.
23	Writing 'Mohini Chatterjee' (*VP*, 495–6) and early versions of 'At Algeciras' (*VP*, 493–4) and 'The Nineteenth Century and After' as part of a lyric sequence, 'Meditations Upon Death'.
28	GY ill with influenza.
29	WBY invites Richard Aldington and Brigit Patmore to call after dinner.

February

4	(Mon) Finishes 'At Algeciras'.
6	Begins writing 'Words for Music, Perhaps'.
9	Revising 'Mohini Chatterjee'.
12	Writes 'Mad as the Mist and Snow'. An attack of rheumatism in the middle of the month confines him to bed. He purchases vol. II of Spengler's *The Decline of the West* and reads it with admiration.

14–24   Writes 'Three Things'.
24   Writes 'Crazy Jane on the King'. Later this month he gives up
             reading Robert Browning and turns to William Morris. LR visits
             for a week on his way back from the USA.

March

1   (Fri) Has a dream which provides the theme for 'Crazy Jane
             Grown Old looks at the Dancers'.
2   Dines with Pound to meet Gerhart Hauptmann, George Antheil and
             Basil Bunting and they discuss Antheil's music for *Fighting the
             Waves*, *At the Hawk's Well* and *The Only Jealousy of Emer*. WBY sees
             Sam Brown, who is in Rapallo. Has finished 'The Nineteenth
             Century and After' (*VP*, 485) and writes 'Crazy Jane and the Bishop'.
6   Finishes 'Crazy Jane Grown Old looks at the Dancers'.
8   Writes 'Those Dancing Days are Gone' (*VP*, 524–5).
9   Has completed five poems for 'Words for Music Perhaps',
             including 'Three Things'.
*c.*14   Brief visit to Lucy Phillimore in Monte Carlo. In the middle of
             this month he tires himself reading the proofs of *A Packet for
             Ezra Pound*. He reads Sturge Moore's *Armour for Aphrodite* and
             vol. II of *The Decline of the West* in bed every morning and
             writes poetry in the afternoon. Also begins reading Wyndham
             Lewis's *Tarr*.
18   Extracts from WBY and AG broadcast in 'The Irish Programme'
             by the BBC National service.
20   Writes 'Lullaby'.
27   Writes 'I care not what the sailors say', later retitled 'Crazy Jane
             Reproved'. Antheil plays WBY his music for *Fighting the Waves*.
28   GY goes to Switzerland to see the children. WBY writing
             'Cracked Mary and the Bishop', later 'Crazy Jane and the Bishop'.
29   Finishes 'Lullaby' and begins 'Girl's Song' ('I went out alone').
             Has written 11 lyrics in the last two months, 9 of them for
             'Words for Music Perhaps'.

April

1   (Mon) Begins to write 'A Young Men's Song'; still reading
             Spengler, Morris and Sturge Moore.
10   Writes a satirical squib on Mrs Phillimore. Sees a good deal of
             Antheil and Basil Bunting.
17   Pound, back from Venice, calls on WBY and they discuss
             Spengler and Frobenius. Writes 'Love's Loneliness'.
*c.*20   The Yeatses dine with Hauptmann at his villa.
27   The Yeatses leave Rapallo for London, via Cherbourg, staying
             overnight in Paris where they have tea with Betty Duncan and
             where WBY apparently calls on Joyce.

29	They arrive in London; GY returns immediately to Dublin, but WBY stays on at the Savile Club. In the course of the next 17 days he sees OS, Dulac (twice), Sturge Moore (twice), Ottoline Morrell (twice) and visits two mediums.
30	Calls on OS.

May

1	(Wed) Attends the 'Ghost Club' with Everard Feilding and reveals the truth about the origins of *A Vision*.
3	Calls on Ricketts.
4	Meets Wyndham Lewis for the first time, for tea.
6	Entertains Dulac, Helen Beauclerk, and Ninette de Valois to dinner at the Ivy restaurant.
7	Dines with OS at 7.30 pm.
*c.*8	Sees Ottoline Morrell.
10	A new edition of *Poems* published by Ernest Benn Ltd., who have taken over the rights from Unwin.
16	Returns to Dublin from London.
19	Goes to see Jack Yeats and admires his new pictures. Later this month the proof-correction for his *Selected Poems* sets him rewriting old poems.
*c.*26	The Yeatses dine at the Vice-Regal Lodge.
28	A dozen short poems broadcast by the BBC National service.
*c.*29	Accompanies AG to the Peacock Theatre to see Micheál MacLiammóir in *An Unknown Soldier* and AG invites MacLiammóir to lunch to meet WBY.

June

1	(Sat) The German writer George Sylvester Viereck and AG visit the Yeatses.
2	WBY gives a luncheon party for Viereck.
13	LR drives the Yeatses to stay at the Royal Hotel, Glendalough, because WBY is not sleeping well, and they all celebrate WBY's 64th birthday there. While in Glendalough the Yeatses go to see Iseult Gonne and Francis Stuart. WBY revises *A Vision* and corrects 'Crazy Jane and King George'.
21	The Yeatses return to Fitzwilliam Square.
29	Begins writing 'Tom the Lunatic'.

July

1	(Mon) Spends early July helping to prepare Gogarty's *Wild Apples* for the Cuala Press. Attends the conferring of an honorary degree on John Galsworthy at TCD and discusses Joyce with him afterwards.
9	Sees Denis Johnston's play *The Old Lady Says 'No!'* at the Gate Theatre.

13	Goes to stay with AG at Coole, where he works on *A Vision*; in the evening AG reads him Trollope's *The American Senator*.
16	WBY and AG drive to Castle Taylor to visit her kinsman Michael Shawe-Taylor; they also call in to Tillyra but find the Hemphills away.
17	Visitors from Lough Cultra call.
21	LR and Rutherford Mayne come to tea and dinner at Coole.
23	Shots fired into Castle Taylor. Later this month a Dutchwoman, probably Rebecca Brugsma, who is writing on WBY, comes to Coole for two days and plies him with questions.
30	Yano offers WBY a chair in Formosa (Taiwan) at £1,000 a year plus accommodation and travelling expenses.

August

4	(Sun) Visits Tillyra with AG.
6	Leaves Coole for Dublin.
7	Attends a rehearsal of *Fighting the Waves*.
8	GY vetoes idea of the Professorship in Formosa. In the middle of the month WBY entertains Hildo Krop and shows him round Dublin. He is writing 'I am of Ireland'.
13	Attends the first performance of *Fighting the Waves* at the Abbey.
17	AG comes to Dublin to see *Fighting the Waves*.
18	At the Abbey with AG.
20	A number of American visitors come to tea.
c.24	*A Packet for Ezra Pound* published.
27	WBY goes to stay at Markree Castle, near Collooney, Sligo, while GY takes the children to stay in Coole. WBY is writing 'Coole Park'.

September

5	(Thu) The Yeatses meet up at Ewing's Golf Links Hotel at Rosses Point for a short family holiday.
7	Working on 'Coole Park, 1929'.
c.10	The Yeatses return to Dublin.
c.18	Goes to stay at Coole for a week, where he writes 'Swift's Epitaph' and 'Coole Park, 1929'.
20	*The Pot of Broth* broadcast by the BBC National service.
25	Returns to Dublin from Coole.
30	Trying to finish 'Coole Park, 1929'.

October

1	(Tue) *The Winding Stair* published by the Fountain Press, New York.
2	'Three Things' (poem; *VP*, 521) published in the *New Republic*.
7	Attends the first night of LR's play, *Ever the Twain*, before which GY throws a dinner party at Jammet's Restaurant, attended by WBY, AG, Andrew Jameson and Bryan Cooper.

8	*Selected Poems: Lyrical and Narrative* published by Macmillan.
9	*Three Things* published in Faber's 'Ariel Poems' series.
10	Attends a revival of *King Oedipus* at the Abbey.
11	Expounds his political and philosophical ideas at a meeting of the Dublin Hermetic Society.
23	Leaves Dublin for London.
24	Spends the afternoon with the MacKenzies and discusses GD affairs.
25	Goes to Bristol to consult the Hermes Temple of the GD there.
27	Returns to London.
28	Sees Dickson to discuss GD matters.
29	Dines with Dulac. Writing 'Crazy Jane on the Day of Judgement'.
30	Dines with Lord Beaverbrook.

November

*c.*1	(Fri) Sees Shaw's *The Apple Cart* at the Queen's Theatre.
3	Has tea with Ottoline Morrell, where he meets Sara Allgood. Suffers a haemorrhage of the lungs in the evening just before dining with Carnegie Dickson, who examines him; they again discuss GD matters.
4	His doctor refers him to R. A. Young, a specialist, about his lungs; Young forbids him to attend O'Casey's *The Silver Tassie* and tells him to postpone his departure for Rapallo by a fortnight.
5	Dines with Dulac. Revises his Preface to Gogarty's *Wild Apples*.
7	Has his lungs X-rayed. He is embarking on a study of Coleridge's prose and verse.
11	Hears that the X-rays show nothing alarming.
14	Lunches with Mrs Hall and enlists her help in the agitation over the Lane Pictures. Has tea with Gerald Heard.
16	Coughs blood again and stays in bed.
19	The Yeatses move from the Knightsbridge Hotel to the Grosvenor and hold a dinner party for the Dulacs, Gerald Heard, Dolly Travers-Smith and other friends.
21	WBY and GY leave London for Rapallo.
*c.*23	Writes 'After Long Silence'. Late this month he suffers a nervous collapse in Rapallo and remains in bed in the mornings, only managing an hour's work a day.
29	The Yeatses meet Siegfried Sassoon and Stephen Tennant.

December

6	(Fri) Pound calls.
8	Begins gradually to get his strength back. Sees Hauptmann again.
16	His energy returns temporarily and he manages to write letters with his own hand.

24   Suffers a serious relapse, with a high temperature and delirium. Basil Bunting calls daily but Pound stays away, fearing infection.
26   Writes a feverish letter to LR, resigning from the Abbey, but GY burns it.
29   His illness (Malta Fever which is not finally diagnosed until late January), becomes dangerous and he makes an emergency will, witnessed by Pound and Bunting.

1930

January
1   (Wed) Critically ill in Rapallo throughout this month and into February.
5   Temperature drops slightly.
22   Dr Niccola Pende, a specialist from Genoa, diagnoses Malta Fever and prescribes injections, arsenic and a special diet.

February
14   (Fri) Out of bed for the first time since his illness, he sits in a wheelchair for half an hour, but is unable to walk or stand alone.
20   Writes his first letter since falling ill. His blood pressure is down and he has grown a beard. Hauptmann is sending him champagne, his appetite is returning, and he now gets up every afternoon for an hour.
28   Has begun to go down to the town and visit the Café Arum for a cocktail with either Pound, Hauptmann, or S. L. Brown, and then back to bed.

March
4   (Tue) Turns to cowboy stories, having exhausted his supply of detective novels. Pound calls for the first time since he fell ill.
10   Is well enough to dispense with the services of a nurse.
16   The Abbey's Belfast production of *Cathleen ni Houilihan* broadcast by the BBC National service.
17   Has Sam Brown to tea. GY is reading Morris to him.
20   Feels really convalescent and beginning to read serious literature again: Edith Sitwell's *Alexander Pope* and Alice Drayton Greenwood's *Horace Walpole's World*.

April
2   (Wed) The Yeatses move to a hotel in Portofina Vetta in the mountains five miles from Rapallo, where he reads Swift's *Letters* and the *Journal to Stella*, and becomes obsessed by Swift, Bolingbroke and Pope. Publication of Gogarty's *Wild Apples* with WBY's Preface.

*c.*4	Pound visits the hotel and they argue about Confucius.
7	In Portofino where he begins a journal which he continues until November and which is later published as 'Pages from a Diary in 1930' (*Expl*, 289–340).
*c.*12	Back in Rapallo he falls into a routine of working for an hour in bed after breakfast for two or three days, and then stopping work altogether for two or three days. He reads Swift until 12 noon most mornings, after which he gets up. In the afternoon he goes out for an hour and then lies down for an hour, reading nothing heavier than a detective story; at night GY reads him one of Morris's prose stories.
*c.*18–24	The Masefields visit the Yeatses in Rapallo.
30	Writes first prose draft of his poem 'Byzantium'.

May

8	(Thu) GY goes to Genoa to meet the children returning from school in Switzerland.
22	WBY has his beard shaved off.
23	Begins writing verse for the first time since the onset of Malta Fever.
24	Takes an hour's walk and spends most of the following day in bed.
25	Writes to congratulate Masefield on his appointment as Poet Laureate.

June

4	(Wed) Jack Yeats sends him an inscribed copy of his *Sligo*. Rereading Coleridge.
7	Goes swimming for the first time since his illness.
13	The Yeatses go to Portofino Vetta.
15	WBY stays on in Portofino while GY takes the children back to school in Switzerland.
*c.*17	WBY and GY return to Rapallo.
28	Wyndham Lewis has sent WBY *The Apes of God* and he and GY argue about it until 11.30 pm.

July

3	(Thu) Leaves Genoa by sea to arrive in Dublin, via London, on 17 July.
5	Boat calls in to Algiers.
9	The Yeatses dock in Southampton and go to London, where WBY remains while GY returns to Dublin.
10	Dines with Elsa Ducat. While in London he sees Ottoline Morrell, James Joyce and Emilie Grigsby, among others.
17	Leaves London for Dublin.
22	Lord and Lady Longford drive WBY to Renvyle from Dublin and they stay overnight at Packenham Hall.

23	Arrives at Renvyle House Hotel, Co. Galway to have his portrait painted by Augustus John. Lord and Lady Longford are also guests at the hotel.
27	John lays aside his first portrait of WBY and begins a second, larger, picture.
30–1	John takes two days off painting to go to Galway races, and WBY tries to finish *A Vision*. Lucy Phillimore arrives to stay in Renvyle.

August

1	(Fri) John remains a third day at Galway races.
6	John finishes his portraits and WBY leaves Renvyle for Coole, where he finds that AG has discovered a cancerous growth.
10	Accompanies AG to Dublin where they hold an Abbey meeting with LR, after which she is admitted to a Dublin nursing home for an operation; WBY visits her daily. Revises 'The Crazed Moon'.
22	AG returns to Coole from Dublin.
23	WBY attends a dress rehearsal of *The Hour-Glass* at the Abbey. Begins to plan *The Words upon the Window Pane*.
25	Attends a revival of *The Hour-Glass*, which is a huge success.

September

4	(Thu) Has drafted a very full scenario for *The Words upon the Window Pane*. Early this month WBY attends his uncle Isaac's funeral.
10	WBY arrives at Coole, where he writes 'For Anne Gregory'.
13	Correcting *Stories of Michael Robartes* and writing notes in his diary, including a 'Letter to Michael's Schoolmaster'. Begins *The Words upon the Window Pane*. Gives Anne Gregory 'For Anne Gregory', which AG makes him recite numerous times.
15	Reading Hone's as yet unpublished *Bishop Berkeley* and rejects the notion of Berkeley as a saint and sage.
17	AG finishes reading Trollope's *Cousin Henry* and then moves onto his *Mr. Scarborough's Family*, followed by *Ayala's Angel*. WBY writing 'Byzantium'.
18	Reads a version of *The Words upon the Window Pane* to AG.
20	Reading the Japanese social reformer Toyohiko Kagawa.
23	GY pays a flying visit to Coole, bringing Swift's poems for WBY and a fair copy of *Stories of Michael Robartes*; she returns to Dublin *c.*25 September.
28	Reads AG another version of *The Words upon the Window Pane*. 'The Lake Isle of Innisfree' broadcast by BBC National Service.
30	Discusses Irish politics with Michael Shawe-Taylor, who has called at Coole.

October

| 4 | (Sat) Finishes *Words upon the Window Pane*. Seven of his poems published in the *New Republic*. |

*c.*7	GY comes to Coole and tidies up the Ballylee garden while there.
17	WBY leaves Coole for Dublin. Dictates *A Vision* and other works every morning and is finishing 'Crazy Jane on the Day of Judgement' and 'Veronica's Napkin'.
27	Sees the first half of a disappointing production of *King Lear* at the Abbey.
29	Sees the second half of *King Lear*. Puts *The Words upon the Window Pane* into rehearsal.

November

1	(Sat) Arrives in London from Dublin. Sees Ottoline Morrell and Dulac. Eight of his poems published in the *London Mercury*.
3	Visits Oxford to stay with Masefield, who on 5 November organizes a recitation of his poems. Sees the poet John Cournos in Oxford.
5	Visits May Morris at Kelmscott.
7	Returns to London, where he meets Virginia Woolf and Walter de la Mare at Ottoline Morrell's house in Gower Street.
8	Writes 'Spilt Milk' and over the coming days sees Sturge Moore, Dulac and James Stephens.
12	Leaves London for Dublin. 'A Song for Music' (later, 'Those Dancing Days are Gone'), 'Cracked Mary and the Bishop', 'Cracked Mary and the Dancers', 'Cracked Mary Reproved' (poems, *VP*, 524–5, 513, 514, 509) published in the *New Republic*.
17	The first production of *The Words upon the Window Pane* at the Abbey proves a success and WBY takes a curtain-call. Begins to write an introduction to the play, and thinks of a book of four introductions to be called *Wheels and Butterflies*.
20	Tells Joseph Hone that he wants Protestant Ireland to base its culture on Burke, Swift and Berkeley.
21	Meets AG at Broadstone Station and takes her to the Abbey to see *The Words upon the Window Pane*.
27	A selection of WBY's poems, read by Sara Allgood with a commentary by Desmond MacCarthy, broadcast by the BBC National Service.
29	The Yeats children return from school in Switzerland.
30	AG visits WBY, who reads her his detailed and damning criticism of Denis Johnston's Abbey production of *King Lear*.

December

1	(Mon) Early this month he sees a production of *The Merchant of Venice* at the Gate and congratulates Hilton Edwards on his performance as Shylock. Later in the month he consults Macmillan about an edition de luxe of his works.

1931

January
2	(Fri) Death of Frank Fay. WBY spends early January revising his work for the edition de luxe.
5	Adds a final stanza to 'Two Songs from a Play'.
6	Returns to work on *A Vision*.
14	'Meditations upon Death' (poem; *VP*, 493–4) published in the *New Republic*. In the middle of the month the Yeatses lease Joseph Hone's house at Killiney.
19	Attends a performance of *Fighting the Waves* at the Vice Regal Lodge, with the Governor General, the American ambassador, AG, government ministers and most of fashionable Dublin.
20	Dines with AG at the Kildare Street Club.
22	Goes to Coole, where he stays until 9 February; Margaret and Anne Gregory come to dinner.
24	Writing a preface for Hone's *Bishop Berkeley*. AG reads him Trollope's *Cousin Henry*, and lends him Macaulay's essay 'Memoir of Goldsmith', and other books by and about Oliver Goldsmith, whom he continues to read for the rest of the visit.

February
5	(Thu) Lord Monteagle stays at Coole until 7 February. WBY is making further revisions to *A Vision*, writing 'Coole Park and Ballylee, 1931', and reading Trevelyan's *Blenheim*.
9	Returns to Dublin and stays at the Standard Hotel because his children have measles.
10	WBY and LR hunt for the MS of a mislaid play by Sean O'Neill. In the evening he sees Gogarty and is writing 'The Choice'.
11	Sees John Guinan's new play, *The Rune of Healing*, at the Abbey.
13	Moves into the Hone's house at South Hill, Killiney, where the Yeatses remain until May; GY is delayed in Dublin since Anne Yeats is too ill to be moved. WBY begins dictating material for the edition de luxe to Alan Duncan, who has come from Paris to act as his secretary for a month.
18	LR calls in the evening to discuss O'Neill's lost play and a possible Abbey subscription for Frank Fay's widow and family.
19	GY and Anne Yeats join WBY and Michael Yeats at South Hill, Killiney. WBY is not sleeping well later this month and his doctor orders him to stop working.

March
2	(Mon) Finishes his revisions to the typed copy of *A Vision*, which Alan Duncan makes legible over the next two days.
4	Begins dictating a new version of *The Resurrection* to Alan Duncan.

| 10 | Starts to dictate his Introduction to *The Words upon the Window Pane* to Alan Duncan and continues for several weeks. |

April

3	(Fri) Death in London of Katharine Tynan Hinkson.
c.7	WBY suffers from a sore throat for several days.
11	Dines with LR and Blythe to discuss an Academy of Letters.
24	Writes a squib 'Upon a Recent Incident'. Still working at his essays for the edition de luxe.
c.26	LR reads Jack Yeats's play *The Old Sea Road* to WBY but they agree that it is not suitable for the Abbey.
27	Attends the first night of Denis Johnston's *The Moon in the Yellow River* at the Abbey.

May

3	(Sun) Signs a contract with Macmillan for the edition de luxe.
9	AG arrives in Dublin to see *Oedipus* at the Abbey.
10	The Yeatses have guests in the afternoon; in the evening WBY dines with AG at the Standard Hotel.
11	Lunches at Fitzwilliam Square with AG, LR and the new Abbey director, Walter Starkie, to discuss tactics at the afternoon meeting. In the middle of the month WBY sells stock to pay off the Cuala overdraft, which the bank is threatening to foreclose; he undertakes to pay SMY half her annual salary, and these arrangements greatly reduce his disposable income.
22	Leaves Dublin for London taking six of the seven volumes of the edition de luxe for Macmillan.
23	Dines with OS at Hatchett's Restaurant, Piccadilly, after which they go to the Royal Academy. In the evening he dines with the Dulacs.
24	Goes to Oxford.
26	Conferred with an Honorary D.Litt at Oxford University, followed by dinner at Wadham College during which he reads from *The Tower* and *The Winding Stair*. Meets Walter Starkie's sister, Enid.
27	Lunches in Oxford with William Force Stead, after which he returns to London. Hears that his flat in Rapallo has been burgled.
28	Sees Watt about his publishing affairs.

June

1	(Mon) Delivers the bulk of the MS for the proposed edition de luxe to Macmillan at 11 am and offers him three further books. Learns that Macmillan will not publish the edition de luxe until the Autumn of 1932 but will pay advances on each volume.
3	Calls on Mrs Travers-Smith.
c.6	Meets Shree Purohit Swami at the Sturge Moores'.
7	Dines with Ottoline Morrell.
8	Writes a version of 'Crazy Jane on God'.

| 9 | Returns to Dublin, where he continues writing his Introduction for Hone's *Bishop Berkeley*. |
| 17 | Sees AG, who has been in Dublin to consult her doctor, to the train. Later in the month the Yeatses entertain actors from the Swedish State Company, who are in Dublin to see an Abbey performance. |

July

1	(Wed) Early this month he helps AG to sort out inefficiencies at the Abbey, as a result of which Ervine has received no royalties for his plays.
8	Writes 'Crazy Jane on God'.
12	Has finished the Introduction for Hone and is writing lyrics again.
13	(also 14) Meets Hone and Rossi.
23	Writes to congratulate LR on his engagement to Dorothy (Dolly) Travers-Smith.
27	Finishes 'Tom the Lunatic.'
28	At Coole with Jack and Cottie Yeats; AG in bad health and WBY stays until 7 August.
29	Writes 'Tom at Cruachan'.

August

2	(Sun) Reading H. S. Ede's *The Savage Messiah*, an account of Henri Gaudier-Brzeska's relationship with Sophie Brzeska.
9	AG's daughter-in-law suggests to WBY that the ailing AG needs a constant companion.
13	In Dublin for dinner with the MacNeills at Vice-Regal Lodge.
c.14	Returns to Coole, bringing Rossi with him.
16	The insensitive McLaughlin at Coole irritates WBY. WBY is writing 'The Dancer at Cruachan and Cro-Patrick'.
17	WBY looks after Americans who are at Coole.
18	Rossi leaves Coole and the journalist Mrs Brandenburg arrives. WBY writes a late version of 'The Results of Thought'.
19	Writes 'The Delphic Oracle upon Plotinus'.
24	GY and the Yeats children arrive in Coole.
28	GY and the children leave Coole; WBY remains and Mrs Leach (Rita Daly) calls. Finishes 'The Results of Thought' and writes 'Remorse for Intemperate Speech'.

September

3	(Thu) Writing 'The Mother of God'.
4	Leaves Coole for Dublin.
8	Talks about his version of *Oedipus the King* for the BBC in Belfast and later the same evening broadcasts a short selection of his poems.
10	Returns to Coole.

12	Rewriting 'The Mother of God'. Robin Flower, Gaelic scholar and translator, at Coole.
17	WBY returns to Dublin for the Abbey Ball and AG accompanies him to see her doctor. WBY remains in Dublin dealing with business arising out of the Abbey's financial situation and its forthcoming American tour.
21	At the Abbey with GY for first night of *The Cat and the Moon*.
22	Has LR and Walter Starkie to dinner.
23	Addresses the Abbey Company about the financial position and the future. Meets Peadar O'Donnell at the Abbey.
24	Goes to Renvyle, Galway, where he sees two of his plays.
25	Leaves Renvyle for Coole.
26	Dines at Lough Cultra with AG, Margaret and the young Gregorys.
28	Advises AG to put her papers into order.

October

1	(Thu) Accompanies AG to Dublin where she consults her doctor about a lump in her breast.
2	At Gogarty's in the evening with AE and deplores the contemporary lack of appreciation of oratory.
3	The first part of 'The Words upon the Window Pane: A Commentary' (essay; *Expl*, 343–63) published in the *Dublin Magazine*. WBY attends a packed last performance by the Abbey Company before they leave for an American tour.
5	Escorts AG back to Coole. Working well, writing 'The Great Year' for *A Vision*, and reading Ludwig Fischer's *The Structure of Thought*.
7	The Abbey Company leave for their tour of the USA.
9	Hears his first radio broadcast, Gerald Heard speaking on 'This Surprising World'.
c.11	Writes 'Old Tom Again'.
15	Publication of Hone and Rossi's *Bishop Berkeley* with WBY's Introduction.
16	AE arrives in Coole but is called back prematurely to Dublin on 19 October because his son is going to England. Late this month WBY continues work on *A Vision*, writes an Introduction to *The Words upon the Window Pane*, and tries to persuade AE to rewrite Shree Purohit's *An Indian Monk*. AG reads Trollope to him every evening.

November

7	(Sat) A further instalment of 'The Words upon the Window Pane: A Commentary' published in the *Dublin Magazine*.
9	Goes to Dublin, where he starts rehearsing the Abbey's Second Company in *The Dreaming of the Bones*.

10	Meets Ninette de Valois.
13	Colum and the Starkies dine with the Yeatses.
14	Returns to Coole; AG suffers a nose-bleed which lasts two hours.
15	AG better and reads WBY Trollope's *Can You Forgive Her* in the evening. He is writing 'Quarrel in Old Age'.
c.20	Experiences a profound mystical experience after dark in the woods of Coole, which inspires 'Crazy Jane talks with the Bishop' and 'Crazy Jane and Jack the Journeyman'. He is writing commentaries on his plays to be published in *Wheels and Butterflies*.
27	Mistakenly goes to Dublin for production of *The Dreaming of the Bones* but discovers he is a week too early and returns to Coole.

December

4	(Fri) Goes to Dublin for a dress rehearsal of *The Dreaming of the Bones*.
5	A further instalment of 'The Words upon the Window Pane: A Commentary' published in the *Dublin Magazine*.
6	Attends the first production of *The Dreaming of the Bones* and takes a curtain call.
c.8	Returns to Coole with GY to whom he dictates the MS of the revised *A Vision*.
14	GY returns to Dublin, taking the MS of *A Vision* with her. WBY begins to write 'Vacillation.'
22	Has written the first 3 stanzas of 'Vacillation' and is reading Balzac and Shelley's *Prometheus Unbound*.
25	Spends Christmas with AG at Coole. In late December he is afflicted with a bad cold which persists into January.

1932

January

1	(Fri) Recovering from his cold and thinks he has found a new lyrical theme.
2	A further instalment of 'The Words upon the Window Pane: A Commentary' published in the *Dublin Magazine*. Writes Part VII of 'Vacillation' (still entitled 'Wisdom').
5	Has written three sections of 'Vacillation'.
6	The Abbey Patent renewed by the Governor General of the Irish Free State in the name of WBY and AG.
7	Begins an article on contemporary Ireland for the *Spectator*.
10	Tells GY that he has completed four parts of 'Vacillation'.
c.16	Returns briefly to Dublin.
17	Finishes his *Spectator* article.

19	Goes back to Coole.
24	Has finished 'Vacillation', which now has seven parts.
26	Finishes 'The Three Movements' (*VP*, 485).
29	Writes a blurb for Francis Stuart's *Pigeon Irish*.
30	'Ireland, 1921–1931' (article; *UP* II. 486–90) published in the *Spectator*. Finishes 'The Seven Sages'.

February

1	(Mon) Turning his introductory verses to *Coole* into a longer poem, 'Coole Park and Ballylee, 1931'.
3	Aodh de Blácam attacks WBY and other Anglo-Irish writers in the Irish Press for attempting to restore the eighteenth century and create division in Ireland.
6	A further instalment of 'The Words upon the Window Pane: A Commentary' is published in the *Dublin Magazine*.
8	Receives the first part of *An Indian Monk* in MS and thinks it a masterpiece. He is writing an article on AE.
9	Reads the MS of Rossi's introduction to *Swift* with admiration.
13	Finishes 'Coole Park and Ballylee, 1931'.
15	Leaves Coole for Dublin.
16	Votes Fine Gael in the general election, but de Valera and Fianna Fáil win a majority for the first time.
22	Interviewed by a correspondent from the *Manchester Guardian* about his opposition to the banning of Liam O'Flaherty's *The Puritan*. Dines at the American Embassy.
24	Returns to Coole.

March

5	(Sat) *Stories of Michael Robartes and His Friends* published. The final instalment of 'The Words upon the Window Pane: A Commentary' (*Expl*, 363–9) published in the *Dublin Magazine*. WBY goes up to Dublin on Abbey business and in the evening Peadar O'Donnell calls to read him a play.
*c.*6	Lunches with the actress Ruth Draper and Walter Starkie and his wife at Fitzwilliam Square.
*c.*8	Returns to Coole with pain-killing drugs for AG.
10	Second part of the MS of *An Indian Monk* arrives and overwhelms WBY.
16	Sends Cuala the copy text for *New Poems* via GY. AG is reading Charlotte Brontë's *Shirley* to him.
26	Goes to Dublin, where he sees Francis Stuart.
30	Crosses to London, where he stays at the Savile Club.
31	Visits the Irish High Commission. Later, sees Sturge Moore, the Swami and Gwyneth Foden and tries to patch up a quarrel between Moore and the Swami.

April

1   (Fri) Lunches with George Tulloch, and in the afternoon sees
            the publisher Hutchinson on behalf of AG. While in London he
            acts as an unofficial go-between in the Anglo-Irish controversy
            over the Oath of Allegiance.

2   The first part of 'Introduction to *Fighting the Waves* ' (essay,
            Expl, 370–91) published in the *Dublin Magazine*. Goes through
            the final section of the MS of *An Indian Monk* with Sturge
            Moore.

3   Attends a Complimentary Dinner in his honour, given by the
            ILS at Romano's.

5   Sees Lavery for lunch, has tea with OS and dines with Dulac.

6   Interviewed by a *Daily Express* journalist from 11 am to
            12 noon; from 12 noon to 1.40 pm the Irish High
            Commissioner calls to instruct him on what to say on the Oath
            question. From 1.40 to 4.30 pm he lunches with Shaw to
            discuss setting up an Irish Academy of Letters. In the late after-
            noon Lady Lavery sees him about the Oath and in the evening
            he goes to a meeting of the Ghost Club.

7   Lunches with the Swami and Gwyneth Foden at 1.00 pm and
            goes to Lady Ottoline Morrell's in the late afternoon.

8   At 3.00 pm meets Malcolm MacDonald and Sir Richard Harding
            at a house in Queen's Gate to put the Irish case against the
            Oath. He dines later with Sturge Moore.

9   The Irish High Commissioner calls to question WBY about his
            meeting with MacDonald and Harding. Has tea with Edith
            Sitwell and dines with OS. 'My Friend's Book' (review; *E & I*,
            412–18) published in the *Spectator*.

10   Dines at the Athenaeum and goes on to broadcast a selection of
            his poems about women for the BBC.

12   Works with Sturge Moore on *An Indian Monk* and dines with
            him. Goes on to Ottoline Morrell's and later sees the Swami.

13   Visits Macmillan & Co., where he learns that they have begun
            to print the edition de luxe.

14   Leaves the MS of *An Indian Monk* with Macmillan. Dines with OS.

15   Lunches with Shaw and discusses arrangements for the Irish
            Academy of Letters, for which Shaw gives him £50.

17   Tea with Gwyneth Foden.

18   Lunches with Sturge Moore. At 4.00 pm introduces the Swami
            to Dulac.

19   Sees Sturge Moore and scolds him about his quarrel with the
            Swami.

20   Returns to Dublin, where he is busy organizing the Irish
            Academy of Letters.

22	Spends the morning hunting for an old detached house. GY types the Shaw–Yeats letter of invitation to potential members of the Irish Academy of Letters.
26	Sees Keller, the Abbey lawyer, who advises him to register the Academy of Letters under the Friendly Societies Act.
27	Goes to Coole.

May

7	(Sat) The second part of 'Introduction to *Fighting the Waves*' published in the *Dublin Magazine*.
8	For the first time in months AG manages to sit outside for a while with WBY.
9	AG tells him that a lump in her breast has grown larger and WBY writes to Slattery, her Dublin doctor.
10	Slattery wires that he will be out of Dublin for a week.
12	WBY goes to Dublin to meet the Abbey Company on its return from America.
*c.*13	Signs an agreement to publish AG's diaries and letters.
16	Meets Starkie and LR to discuss a proposed Abbey tour in 1932.
15	Makes an offer for Riversdale, a detached house in the Dublin suburb of Rathfarnham.
22	Sees Slattery, who tells him that an operation is not necessary for AG; that afternoon he visits Michael Yeats's school and takes him for a drive. Dines that evening in Delgany, and AG's solicitor phones at 11.15 pm to tell him that AG is sinking fast.
23	Travels to Coole by 7.30 am train, but is informed at Gort station that AG has died in the night. He takes a room at Glynn's Hotel and goes to pay his respects at Coole. At Margaret Gregory's request he moves into Coole.
25	Attends AG's funeral at the New Cemetery in Galway.

June

2	(Thu) Writes a draft of 'Stream and Sun at Glendalough'.
4	The final part of 'Introduction to *Fighting the Waves*' is published in the *Dublin Magazine*. He asks Sturge Moore if he will edit AG's autobiography. Spends much of this month correcting proofs of the new Macmillan edition de luxe.
19	Writes a memorial essay, 'The Death of Lady Gregory', at the Royal Hotel, Glendalough.
23	Finishes 'Stream and Sun at Glendalough'.
27	GY takes possession of the new house, Riversdale.
30	Attends a long Directors' meeting at the Abbey, and then has his sisters to lunch to discuss designs for Cuala. GY is preparing Riversdale for their move there.

July

7	(Thu) GY sends him to the Royal Hotel, Glendalough, to be out of the way while she arranges the move to Riversdale. He is reading Virginia Woolf's *Orlando* and Frank O'Connor's *The Saint and Mary Kate*.
12	Dines with Iseult and Francis Stuart. He is working on the lectures for his coming American tour.
13	Entertains Iseult and Francis Stuart to dinner.
14	Dines again with Iseult and Francis Stuart.
15	The Royal Hotel is so noisy that he goes to stay with the Stuarts at Larragh.
18	Returns to Dublin, where he stays at the Kildare Street Club.
19	Sees LR.
*c.*21	Moves to his last Irish home, Riversdale, Willbrook, Rathfarnham, Dublin.
25	Attends the first night of LR's *All's Over Then?* at the Abbey.
30	Finishes an essay on Shelley's *Prometheus Unbound*.

August

1	(Mon) Spends much of this month working on the rules and constitution of the Irish Academy of Letters with AE and Frank O'Connor.
8–9	Most of the contents of Coole are auctioned.
12	Begins to correct the proofs of *An Indian Monk*.

September

1	(Thu) Sends out the letter of invitation, co-signed with Shaw, to the founding members of the Irish Academy of Letters.
2	Writes to Joyce, urging him to accept nomination to the Academy of Letters.
5	Sends the Swami his Introduction to *An Indian Monk*.
14	First meeting of the Irish Academy of Letters elects officers; WBY is empowered to use his own judgement in raising money in America and elsewhere for the Academy.
18	Announces the founding of the Irish Academy of Letters at a public meeting at the Peacock Theatre.
*c.*25	At a séance given by Mrs Duncan.
27	Attends a meeting at AE's house to discuss arrangements for the Academy of Letters.
28	Attends a another séance.
30	Sees Keller, AG's Dublin lawyer, about the publication of her Autobiography, Diaries, and Correspondence.

October

4	(Tue) Attends a Board Meeting of the Abbey Theatre.
6	Goes to Manchester.

7	Lectures in Manchester.
8	Travels to London and consults Kiernan at the Savile Club about the publication of AG's biographical writings.
10	Sees Lavery at 4.30 pm.
11	Catches a cold which confines him to bed for a day and a half, and persists throughout his stay in London.
13	Lunches with Sturge Moore.
14	GY arrives in London.
18	To tea with Emilie Grigsby and dines with Ellis Roberts.
19	Sees Huntington at 11 am about the publication of AG's memoirs and Macmillan at 4 pm about his own publishing plans.
20	Sees Alan Duncan in the morning, then Shaw on Academy business, and later visits Ottoline Morrell.
21	Sails on the *Europa* from Southampton for his last tour of the USA, with Alan Duncan as his secretary.
26	Arrives in New York in dense fog and only reaches his hotel at midnight.
27	Several interviews followed by dinner at the Authors' Club, of which he is made an honorary member.
28	More interviews and has his portrait drawn; sees a representative of the Macmillan Company about his books, and in the evening makes a brief speech after the Abbey's performance of *The Words upon the Window Pane*.
29	Sees Judge Campbell at 10.30 am and goes to stay with Mrs Harrison Williams for the weekend.
30	Returns to New York late at night.
31	Sets out on his lecturing tour.

November

1	(Tue) Lectures in Bangor, Maine. He is reading D. H. Lawrence's novels with great excitement.
4	Lectures on 'New Ireland' at Colby College.
5	Returns to New York.
7	Leaves New York for the mid-west.
10	Lectures at 8 pm on 'New Ireland' to the Oratorical Association, Ann Arbor.
11	Makes arrangements in Detroit for the forthcoming Abbey visit there, and later tours the Ford factory and museum.
14	*Words for Music Perhaps* published. WBY arrives in Cleveland.
15	Lectures on 'My Own Poetry' at Kent State University.
16	Leaves Cleveland for Cincinnati, arriving in the evening.
18	'Remorse for Intemperate Speech' (poem; *VP*, 506) published in the *Spectator*. Spends the weekend at the home of W. T. H. Howe in Cincinnati, where James Stephens is also staying.
20	Speaks to a gathering of Howe's friends in Cincinnati.

23   Lectures at 8.30 pm on 'The Irish National Theatre' to the Canadian Authors' Foundation in Toronto.
24   Visits his Toronto relatives.
25   Sees a performance of O'Neill's *Mourning Becomes Electra*.
26   Leaves Toronto for Montreal.
27   Lunches with the Montreal PEN Club and later lectures on 'New Ireland' to the People's Forum, Montreal.
28   Lectures at 4.15 pm on 'New Ireland' to the Women's Canadian Club, Montreal.
29   Alan Duncan begins driving him from Montreal to Boston. WBY stops off to lecture at 8.30 pm on 'New Ireland' at Dartmouth College.

December
1   (Thu) Lectures at Colgate University, Hamilton, New York.
2   Lectures in Groton, Connecticut. 'For Anne Gregory', 'Symbols', 'Swift's Epitaph' (poems; *VP*, 492, 484, 493) published in the *Spectator*.
3   Arrives in Boston.
4   Arrives in New York at 3.20 pm.
6   Lectures on 'New Ireland' at 11.00 am to the League for Political Education, and on the same subject at 8.15 pm to Columbia University.
7   Lectures on 'New Ireland' at Bryn Mawr College.
8   Lectures on 'The Irish National Theatre' to Wellesley College.
9   Returns to Boston.
11   Attends a séance with Margery Crandon in Boston.
12   Delivers an evening lecture in Boston.
14   Arrives in New York, where he keeps fit by swimming most days.
15   Lectures to the Brooklyn Institute to raise funds for the Irish Academy.
16   Dines with the Thomas J. O'Neill in New York, and gives a poetry reading.
17   Lectures in a private house in New York on behalf of the Irish Academy.
18   Lectures in New York on behalf of the Irish Academy.
19   Lunches with Mrs Robinson, who makes a donation to the Irish Academy.
22   Sees representative of the Macmillan Company to discuss his American copyrights and to try to persuade them to improve the covers and design of his American editions.
23   Delighted when Horace Reynolds sends him photographic copies of his early articles in American newspapers and gives him permission to republish them as *Letters to the New Island*.
25   Christmas Dinner with Irving Bush, New York.

| 27 | Visits the Metropolitan Museum, New York. |
| 29 | Attends the opening of Jack Yeats's exhibition of paintings at the Museum of Irish Art, and attends a reception at the Brabizon. |

1933

January

3	(Tue) Speaks at a Dutch Treat Luncheon in New York.
4	Stays with the Crandons for four days in Boston, sitting to séances with Margery Crandon every day.
9	Lectures at Notre Dame, Indiana.
*c.*11	Back in New York, lunches with the theatre agent French, and then sees a wealthy woman about endowing the Irish Academy.
12	Lunches with William Button, President of the American Society for Psychical Research, in New York.
15	Attends a benefit performance of his *King Oedipus*.
16	Attends a dinner to raise funds for the Irish Academy. While in New York he discusses his publishing affairs with George Brett of Macmillan, and consults lecture agencies on behalf of the Swami.
22	Sails from New York on the *Bremen*.
27	Arrives in Southampton and travels to London, staying at the Euston Hotel. Sees the Swami with Alan Duncan to persuade him not to undertake an American lecturing tour.
28	Returns to Dublin.
29	Sees AE about plans for the Irish Academy.

February

1	(Wed) Sees a copy of *Words for Music Perhaps* for the first time.
*c.*3	Confined to bed by influenza.
19	Lectures on behalf of the Irish Academy. Is rereading Balzac's *Louis Lambert* and begins a commentary on it.
22	AE calls to see him about Irish Academy.
26	Instructs Watt not to renew his agreement with Benn for *Poems*.

March

1	(Wed) Defies the Fianna Fáil government's attempt to impose its candidate on the Abbey Board and to censor the plays taken on overseas tours.
8	Has an hour's satisfactory interview with de Valera about his government's attitude to the Abbey.
9	Has finished his essay on *Louis Lambert* and is much occupied with Abbey business and organizing the Irish Academy.
15	Starts 'Parnell's Funeral'.
17	'Prometheus Unbound' (article; *E & I*, 419–25) published in the *Spectator*.

29   Signs an agreement with Macmillan for *Collected Poems*. Trying to work out a social philosophy for Ireland based on his 'Four Philosophic Positions'.

April

2   (Sun) Delighted to accept Macmillan's suggestion that his long poems should be placed at the end of the *Collected Poems*. Finishing 'Parnell's Funeral'.

19   Travels to London, where he stays at the Savile Club.

20   Sees OS. While in London he discusses a proposed biography of AG and spends most mornings reading her diaries; he also sees Dulac several times, as well as Shaw.

28   Lunches with Lady Lavery.

May

2   (Tue) Sees Watt and asks him to arrange terms for WBY to write AG's biography.

3   Sees Macmillan.

7   Returns to Dublin.

9   Walks out of the first production of Denis Johnston's *A Bride for the Unicorn* at the Gate Theatre.

12   Reading the *Aphorisms of Yoga* translated by the Swami and goes on to read T. E. Hulme's *Speculations* and D. H. Lawrence's *Lady Chatterley's Lover* later this month.

27   The Yeatses hold an 'At Home' from 4.00 pm.

29   Sees AE at 4 pm about arranging an Academy deputation to protest against the banning of Shaw's *The Adventure of the Black Girl in Her Search for God*. The deputation, under his leadership, calls on the Minister of Justice the following day.

31   Contributes £3 to the 'Army Comrades'.

June

1   (Thu) Goes to London, where he reads AG's MSS extensively and sees Watt, Dulac and OS.

2   'The Great Blasket' (review; *UP* II. 492–4) published in the *Spectator*.

5   Goes to Oxford, where he reads his poems at the English Club.

6   Dines at Christ Church College as the guest of George Cooke, the Professor of Hebrew.

7   Leaves Oxford for Cambridge.

8   Presented with an Honorary Degree by Cambridge University.

9   Arrives in London.

13   Has a long, pleasant lunch at Emilie Grigsby's. In the evening gives a dinner party at the Savile to celebrate his 68th birthday with the Swedish Ambassador, Dulac, Squire, James Stephens, Kiernan and the music critic W. J. Turner among the guests.

14   Attends an 'At Home' at the Swami's house.

15   Sees Huntington of the publishers Putnams about the publication of AG's biographical works and dictates a letter to Margaret Gregory, who is causing difficulties about this.

18   Visits the British Museum to see the Oriental Collections.

24   Returns to Dublin.

July

7   (Fri) Signe Toksvig (Mrs Hackett) visits the Yeatses and meets Dolly Robinson there. WBY also sees Joseph Hone and discusses Swift with him.

17   Dermot MacManus brings Eoin O'Duffy to see WBY about possible Blue shirt resistance to de Valera. WBY advises action only if a constitutional crisis arises, after which the government should be put into the hands of the ablest men.

29   Sees P. J. Ruttledge, the Minister of Justice, at the Abbey and again raises the banning of Shaw's story with him.

August

1   (Tue) Writes the Preface for *Letters to the New Island*.

9   Speaks at the first Annual General Meeting of the Irish Academy of Letters at the Peacock Theatre.

12   A mass parade in Dublin by O'Duffy's supporters is banned by the government and the Blueshirt Movement goes into decline.

September

9   (Sat) Goes with his family to stay with Dermot MacManus in Granard, Longford, where they remain until 14 September.

19   *The Winding Stair and Other Poems* published.

27   Finishes Hamsa's MS of *The Holy Mountain*, which has taken him seven weeks to read.

October

14   (Sat) GY goes into a trance in which the sprit Dionertes instructs WBY to hate God.

November

1   (Wed) Spends the early part of the month writing *The King of the Great Clock Tower*. In the middle of the month he discusses Austin Clarke's proposed biography with him.

14   *Collected Poems* published in New York.

28   The English edition of *Collected Poems* published. Late this month WBY writes 'Three Songs to the Same Tune'.

30   Begins writing 'Three Marching Songs'.

December

4   (Mon) Goes to London.

5   Lunches with OS and later attends a PEN Club dinner.

c.8	Catches a bad cold and remains in bed for some days. While in London he sees the Dulacs, the medallist Maurice Lambert and John Squire.
21	Returns to Dublin, where he slowly recovers from his cold and works on *The King of the Great Clock Tower*. Margaret Gregory returns his letters to AG.

1934

January

1	(Mon) Gives a dinner party for F. R. Higgins and his wife, ECY and SMY, with fireworks for his children. Early this month he puts the last touches to *The King of the Great Clock Tower* and then turns to *A Vision*.
4	R. Nesbitt Keller phones at 5.00 pm to reveal that AG's *Autobiography* is to be published immediately.
9	WBY sees Molly Childers at 7.30 pm.
10	Attends a séance.
11	Dictates to Pet Wilson, his typist, from 3.00 pm.
13	Dictates to his typist in the afternoon and later attends a séance given by Newell.
15	Spends the afternoon dictating to his typist.
17	Shaw declines to act as judge for the Harmsworth prize.
20	Faber accept Shree Hamsa's book, later entitled *The Holy Mountain*.
24	*Letters to the New Island* published.
26	Sees Flecker's *Don Juan* at the Gate Theatre.
27	Writes to ask Masefield to act as judge of the Harmsworth Prize. Over-excitement caused by writing *The King of the Great Clock Tower* and revising *A Vision* obliges him to give up reading for two days.
30	Sees Starkie at 2 pm about Abbey affairs.
31	Meets the musician Arthur Duff for tea at the Kildare Street Club to discuss music for *The King of the Great Clock Tower*. He is still writing 'Three Songs to the Same Tune' (*VP*, 543–9).

February

1	(Thu) Sees Starkie at 2 pm and attends a Directors' Meeting at the Abbey at 5.00 pm. Absorbed in Abbey administration and work on AG's papers.
2	Attends a council meeting of the Academy of Letters and announces that Masefield will act as judge for Harmsworth Prize; dines at the Standard Hotel at 7.30 pm.
5	Sees Bodkin and they agree to commission Maurice Lambert's design, 'Aengus & the Birds', for the Irish Academy's most prestigious medal.

6	Sees Keller about AG's diaries and letters at 3.30 pm and goes on to a Council Meeting of the Academy at 5.00 pm.
14	Awarded the Goethe–Plakette (Goethe Medal) by the Frankfurt Council.
15	Lunches with the MacNeills at 1 pm and dines with Iseult Gonne at the Kildare Street Club at 8 pm.
16	Sees Starkie and afterwards dictates to his typist. Attends a council meeting of the Academy at 5.30 pm and then goes to the Abbey.
20	Sees Starkie at the Dublin Art School.
23	Writes to Macmillan about the edition de luxe and sends them copy text for *Wheels and Butterflies*. 'Three Songs to the Same Tune' (poem; *VP*, 543–9) published in the *Spectator*.
27	Finishes 'Three Marching Songs' and becomes absorbed in writing *Dramatis Personae*.

March

2	(Fri) Attends a meeting of the Academy at 8.30 pm.
6	Delighted with Macmillan's proposal to publish a *Collected Plays* in uniform with *Collected Poems*. Goes to Cuala at 4.15 pm.
7	Tells Sturm he has finished *A Vision*; he has also completed the George Moore section of *Dramatis Personae*.
14	Attends a council meeting of the Academy at Higgins' house.
15	Sees Gogarty for lunch at 1.30 pm.
16	Leaves Dublin for Belfast for a BBC broadcast.
17	Broadcasts 'A Programme of Irish Music and Humour and Poetry by W. B. Yeats Spoken by himself' for the BBC in Belfast.
18	Lunches with Wilson in Belfast.
20	Back in Dublin, he sees Starkie about Abbey and Academy affairs.
21	Sees Starkie.
22	Attends a general meeting of the Academy at 3.30 pm.
23	Sees Eamon de Valera.
28	Sees Starkie.
30	Sees LR, Starkie and Padraic Colum.

April

4	(Wed) Leaves Dublin for London for a Steinach operation, a procedure that was thought to increase sexual potency. 'The Growth of a Poet' (article; *UP* II. 495–9) published in the *Listener*.
5	Has a consultation with Norman Haire at 12 noon after which he undergoes Steinach operation at the Beaumont House Hospital.
c.8	*The Words upon the Window Pane* published.
10	GY visits WBY in London after his operation.
19	Travels back to Dublin, staying at Chester overnight.
20	Arrives back in Dublin. Works in bed during the following mornings.

27	Returns the proofs of *The Holy Mountain* to the Swami.

May

1	(Tue) Engaged early this month in a controversy over the choice of the Englishman Lambert as the designer of the Irish Academy medal.
10	Feeling better after his operation; blood pressure down and less irritable. He is rereading George Moore and finding him amusing and tragic.

June

1	(Fri) Receives the final proofs of *The Holy Mountain*. Later he dictates to his typist.
*c.*2	Meets McGillycuddy at Gogarty's and they discuss Eugene O'Neill's forthcoming visit to Ireland.
4	Sees J. H. Pollock about the use of quotations in his book on WBY. Writes to thank the Ober–Burgermeister of Frankfurt for the award of the Goethe–Plakette.
6	WBY and GY depart from Cork for Cherbourg on their way to Rapallo to clear their apartment and bring back some of their furniture to Dublin. They remain in Italy until 25 June.
25	WBY travels to London from Italy; GY goes to see her mother in Sidmouth, Devon.
29	Sees Gwyneth Foden and the Swami in the afternoon and dines with OS and Dorothy Pound at 7.30 pm.
30	Consults Dr Smith about his blood pressure and goes on to sees Turner. Later he meets Ottoline Morrell and Dulac and then has tea with OS at 4.30 pm. James Stephens dines with him at 7.30 pm.

July

1	(Sun) Has tea with Ottoline Morrell.
2	Has tea with Emilie Grigsby.
3	Lunches with Ottoline Morrell at 1.30 pm and dines with Dulac at 7.30 pm.
*c.*5	Leaves London for Dublin.
7	'Louis Lambert' (essay; *E & I*, 438–7) published in the *London Mercury*.
9	Dines at the Kildare Street Club and then attends the first Abbey performance of Shaw's *On the Rocks*, which does not end until after 11 pm.
10	Attends a Directors' Meeting at the Abbey. At about this time the Yeatses' furniture from Rapallo arrives in Dublin.
11	Attends the council of the Academy at 8.00 pm.
24	Sends OS a copy of the recently written 'Ribh denounces Patrick' (*VP*, 556). Has also just written 'Ribh at the Tomb of

Baile and Aillinn' (*VP*, 554–5). Attends a rehearsal of his new dance play, *The King of the Great Clock Tower*.

25   Attends a rehearsal at the Abbey at 5.30 pm.

29   Attends a rehearsal at the Abbey.

30   At the Abbey for the first night of *The King of the Great Clock Tower* and a revival of *The Resurrection*.

August

4   (Sat) Writes a preface to *Wheels and Butterflies*. Early this month he also writes a number of 'Supernatural Songs', partly to make up sufficient copy for his Cuala book. He also reads Baron Corvo's *Hadrian VII* with admiration.

6   Finishes 'The Four Ages of Man' (*VP*, 561). In the middle of the month he writes 'Church and State'.

*c.*22   Writing 'Conjunctions' (*VP*, 562).

*c.*23   Writing 'He and She' (*VP*, 559), which he finishes on 25 August.

31   Sends Macmillan the final version of his Introduction to *Wheels and Butterflies*.

September

10   (Mon) Returns proofs of *Collected Plays* to Macmillan and composes a squib on Norah McGuinness.

23   Attends a rehearsal of W. R. Fearon's *Parnell of Avondale* at 1.00 pm.

25   The classicist E. R. Dodds comes to tea.

26   WBY explains that in his symbolism the 'hawk is the straight road of logic, the butterfly the crooked road of intuition' (to Force Stead).

27   Lunches at the Gresham Hotel. Academy dinner in the evening.

29   The Abbey Company leave for an American tour.

October

1   (Mon) WBY attends the first night of *Parnell of Avondale* performed by the Second Abbey Company.

3   The Yeatses cross to London.

4   WBY phones Margot Collis, who has written to him in Dublin about founding a poet's theatre, to arrange a meeting.

6   *The King of the Great Clock Tower* (play; *VPl*, 990–1011) published in *Life and Letters*. The Yeatses leave London for Rome to attend the 4th Congress of the Alessandro Volta Foundation, staying at the Albergo Palazzo and Ambasciatore.

7   WBY attends the welcoming reception hosted by Francesco Orestano of the Royal Academy of Italy at 5.30 pm in the Hotel des Ambassadeurs.

10   Lunches with Gordon Craig; in the afternoon attends a stormy meeting of the Volta Congress during which Craig intervenes

	and Marinetti orates. At 9.00 pm he attends a performance of D'Annunzio's *Figlia di Jorio* at the Teatro Argentina.
16	Leaves Rome; GY stays on and returns direct to Ireland on 20 October. WBY sea-sick crossing the Channel.
17	Arrives in London, taking a self-contained flat in Seymour Street for a week. Rewriting *The King of the Great Clock Tower* to give Margot Collis a speaking part.
18	WBY phones Margot Collis before 11.00 am and asks her to keep the day for him.
19	'A Parnellite at Parnell's Funeral' (poem; *VP*, 541–3) published in the *Spectator*.
19–23	Busy seeing dancers, musicians and actors for a new theatrical project (later the Group Theatre). Asked to edit *The Oxford Book of Modern Verse* (*OBMV*).
22	Begins writing *A Full Moon in March*.
23	Has tea with OS.
25	At Ottoline Morrell's where he meets Virginia Woolf and speaks of the occult, Balzac, Stendhal, Tolstoy and Proust, and of getting the Irish back to the eighteenth-century writers; he advises Woolf to read Swift's *Drapier's Letters*.
26	Discusses the Group Theatre project with a gathering of friends at the Dulacs in the evening.
29	Sees Eliot and agrees to write a Preface for Purohit Swami's translations from the Mandookya Upanishad for the *Criterion*.
30	Agrees to join the Group Theatre. Sees Margot Collis at 3.00 pm.
31	Leaves London for Dublin.

November

2	(Fri) 'Old Age' (poem, later 'A Payer for Old Age'; *VP*, 553) published in the *Spectator*. Continues work on *A Full Moon in March*.
12	Impressed by a production of Molière's *School for Wives* at the Abbey.
13	Publication of *Wheels and Butterflies*. Meets LR, Bladon Peak and James Bould to discuss the next Abbey production.
c.14	The musician Harry Partch calls about setting WBY's *Oedipus* to music and they discuss the relationship between words and music.
17	Spends the morning correcting Margot Collis's poems and later goes for a walk with F. R. Higgins.
18	Partch calls on WBY again.
21	Writes to Dulac and Dolmetsch to introduce and recommend Partch.
23	Attends an Academy meeting. 'Vain Hope' (poem, later 'Church and State'; *VP*, 553–4) published in the *Spectator*.
24	Writes the 1st stanza of his poem 'Margot'.

25	In a gloom because he cannot finish 'Margot' and so GY arranges with him to see Gogarty; he dines at the Kildare Street Club and goes on to see Gogarty at 9.00 pm, where he hears Rabelaisian stories of the Dublin slums.
26	Works on 'Margot' then dines with Dermot MacManus and goes on with the poem in bed, finishing it just before dawn. Writes to John Hayward to thank him for an edition of Swift and describes his increasing interest in Swift.
27	Attends a council of the Academy at the Abbey at 4.00 pm.
29	Dictates to his typist at 3.00 pm.
30	*Collected Plays* published. Goes to the Abbey at 12.30 pm.

December

1	(Sat) 'Ribh at the Tomb of Baile and Aillinn', 'Ribh prefers an Older Theology', 'Ribh considers Christian Love insufficient', 'He and She', 'The Four Ages of Man', 'Conjunctions', 'A Needle's Eye' and 'Meru' published in the *London Mercury* and *Poetry* (Chicago). WBY sees Higgins at 4 pm.
3	Has tea with Pollock at 4.30 pm and attends the first night of the Abbey production of Pirandello's *Six Characters in search of an Author.*
4	Attends a Directors' Meeting at the Abbey at 4 pm.
5	Attends an Academy of Letters Dinner.
7	Crosses to London, where he takes a room in Seymour Street but goes to the Savile Club for lunch and his letters. 'The Singing Head and the Lady' (poem; *VP*, 789–90) published in the *Spectator.*
11	Dines at the Dulacs' with Margot Collis.
12	Sees Sir John Squire.
13	Dines with Ashley Dukes to discuss the Group Theatre.
14	Lunches with T. S. Eliot at 71 Pall Mall. *The King of the Great Clock Tower* published by Cuala.
*c.*15	Re-meets his former mistress Alick Schepeler in a London Street but cannot remember her name.
19	Sees Watt to discuss terms for the publication of *The King of the Great Clock Tower* in England. Later arranges a tentative timetable for Group Theatre productions in April. Going daily to Norman Haire for injections.
20	Gets Margot Collis to recite to Ottoline Morrell and friends.
23	Reads *A Full Moon in March* to Rupert Doone.
*c.*26	Meets Ethel Mannin and begins an affair with her.
27	Attends the first meeting of the Group Theatre Committee with Dulac, Rupert Doone, T. S. Eliot and Margot Collis, who acts as secretary.
28	Sees Watt about his publishing plans.

30   Writes to Mannin that the knowledge he is still sexually active has brought him sanity and peace.
31   Given an injection by Norman Haire at 12.45 pm. Lunches with Ethel Mannin at the Ivy Restaurant at 1.30 pm and goes on to a meeting of the Group Theatre Committee at Dulac's studio.

1935

January
2   (Wed) Meets Ethel Mannin at his Seymour Street lodgings and at 6.00 pm takes her to meet the Swami before dining with her, Dulac and Haire at the Ivy. WBY dictates *Dramatis Personae* for an hour a day while in London.
3   Dines with Ethel Mannin at the Ivy.
5   Sees Ethel Mannin in the evening.
8   Attends an evening meeting of the Group Theatre Committee at Dulac's to complete the preliminary arrangements for the plays.
9   Gives a dinner party at the Ivy.
11   Meets his proposed biographer, Oliver Edwards, at 1.30 pm in the Savile and returns to Dublin in the evening.
c.12   Collapses with renewed congestion of lungs and is confined to bed; his illness persists until early March.
27   Suffers a relapse while arguing with Margaret Gough's solicitor over AG's papers and starts spitting blood, panting and shivering.
28   X-rayed by Dr Shaw and Dr Stewart.
29   GY is told that the X-rays show an enlargement of the heart.

February
1   (Fri) 'The Wicked Hawthorn Tree' (poem; *VP*, 788) published as *A Broadside*.
13   WBY is improving daily and can now sit up in a chair once or twice a day for half an hour, although he still has fluid on the lung and a slightly strained heart. In the middle of the month he becomes absorbed in the theme of self-sacrifice and its destructive nature. Later in February he begins another rereading of Balzac and also starts to read *The Arabian Nights*. His doctor allows him to correct proof-sheets of *Dramatis Personae,* and he is trying to understand the Eliot and Auden schools of poetry for *OBMV*.
25   A letter from O'Casey, commiserating about his illness, ends the long breach between them.

March
2   (Sat) *A Full Moon in March* (play; *VPl*, 978–89) published in *Poetry* (Chicago).

4	WBY feels much better and is able to play croquet with Anne Yeats.
13	Trouble between Doone and Ashley Dukes over the production of Group Theatre plays.
23	Sends Macmillan the diagrams for *A Vision*.
25	Crosses to London.
26	Moves back into his Seymour Street flat where there is no gas fire and he catches cold.
27	Wakes up with a sore throat and exhaustion; nevertheless he sees Dulac and Ashley Dukes and completes much essential business.
28	Is prostrate with illness but the doctor assures him he will recover in a few days.
29	A violent cold keeps him in bed and his doctor, who comes daily to give him injections, diagnoses nervous exhaustion following a bronchial infection.
30	Remains in bed.

April

2	(Tue) Writes to Ethel Mannin in praise of Ernst Toller's plays.
3–4	Two busy days seeing the Swami and people about the theatre project.
4	Sees Bladon Peake, potential director in the Group Theatre. In the evening dines with Dulac.
8	Wires Auden to come up from Birmingham to settle a point about his play and they have a long lunch at the Ivy. Afterwards Olivia Onions calls. WBY is working at his *Criterion* essay and reading steadily for the *OBMV*.
*c.*9	The Group Theatre project is apparently dead because Eliot's *Murder in the Cathedral* cannot be performed before its production in Canterbury.
11	WBY invites Dukes to dine at the Savile and they restart the Group Theatre.
12	Slowly casting off his cold and trying to get Higgins's *Arable Holdings* reviewed in London.
15	Dictates his essay for the *Criterion* to his London typist, Louise Jacobs.
19	Moves into Gwyneth Foden's flat at 19 Lancaster Gate Terrace. Dines with Dulac, who realizes how ill he is and wires to GY to come over. From 20 April to 13 May he is seriously ill in London with a second attack of congestion of the lungs; he moves back to 17 Lancaster Gate where he is confined to his room and forbidden all work.

May

1	(Wed) 'The Rose Tree' (poem; *VP*, 396) published as *A Broadside*.
*c.*17	Dines with O'Casey in London.

29	Sees O'Casey, Margot Collis and Eliot and reads them poems by Dorothy Wellesley (DW).
31	Writes to Maurice Bowra about Symbolism and the 1890s.

June

1	(Sat) Orders DW's *Poems of Ten Years* and is much impressed by a production of *Job* at Sadler's Wells.
3	Ottoline Morrell drives WBY to stay for the first time with DW at Penns in the Rocks; he stays overnight and returns to London on 4 June.
7	WBY has Ethel Mannin to dine at Lancaster Gate; Edmund Dulac and Helen Beauclerk come in later.
8	Sets off for Dublin; delayed a day because there was no berth on the steamer.
9	Arrives back in Dublin.
10–14	Working on proofs, revising DW's poetry and reading Sackville-West for inclusion in *OBMV*. Writes to ask DW's advice on *OBMV*.
13	To mark WBY's 70th birthday the family, including SMY, ECY, Jack and Cottie Yeats hold a celebratory dinner at Riversdale. Among the presents is a vellum book of congratulation containing the names of 129 writers and artists, accompanied by a Rossetti drawing. The BBC in London celebrates his birthday by broadcasting a selection of his favourite lyric poems, read by Audrey Moran.
16	The Abbey company returns to Dublin from the USA.
17	WBY is reading the poems of Sackville-West, DW and Edith and Sacheverell Sitwell for *OBMV*. Finds that the second puberty produced by the Steinach operation has put his imagination into ferment.
24	His doctor orders complete celibacy for the moment and administers a bromide. He refuses an invitation to lecture at Harvard and wants to cut himself off from public life, to plunge into impersonal poetry and to rid his soul of the bitterness caused by the frustration of his work in Ireland.
26	Orders a large number of books from Bumpas for his work on *OBMV*.
27	Guest of honour at a PEN banquet to mark his 70th birthday at the Hibernian Hotel. His extended family, including his aunt are among the 250 guests. WBY, Masefield, Hackett, O'Faoláin and Desmond MacCarthy gives speeches and Julian Bell, Constance Masefield and Moya Llewellyn Davies are also present.

July

5	(Fri) Harry Clifton gives him a piece of lapis lazuli, later the inspiration for his poem 'Lapis Lazuli'.

6	'Mandookya Upanishad with an Introduction by William Butler Yeats' (essay; *E & I*, 474–85) published in the *Criterion*. WBY reading Elinor Wylie for *OBMV*.
12–13	Writes numerous letters, thanking friends for their birthday greetings and gifts.
17	AE (George Russell) dies in Bournemouth.
18	Appoints Hugh Hunt producer at the Abbey on Masefield's recommendation.
20	Attends AE's funeral in Dublin, meeting the coffin from the Mail Boat at 6.30 am.
24	Returns galley proofs of *A Vision*.
29	Writes to Holloway about the composition of *The Player Queen*. Feels really well for the first time since leaving London.

August

7	(Wed) Holloway sees WBY at the Abbey with GY and they discuss alterations to the vestibule.
10	In the evening sees Higgins and reads him DW's poems.
12	Attends the first Abbey production of *The Silver Tassie*. Over the next few days writes to AG's executors and publisher about her literary remains.
13	Crosses to England with Anne Yeats.
14	He and Anne Yeats arrive at Penns in the Rocks.
18	Plays croquet with Anne Yeats, DW and her guests. Discusses his selection of DW's poetry for Faber and she advises him on his selection of Kipling for *OBMV*.
23	Returns to London with Anne Yeats; he stays on at the Savile, while she goes to Stratford; over the coming days he reads 45 books in the British Museum and consults Norman Haire about his heart.
24	Lunches with Eliot and gives him the selection from DW's poetry. In the evening he dines at the Dulacs, where he reads DW's poem 'Fire' to them and their guests.
28	Dines with Eliot and DW at the Ivy Restaurant at 7.00 pm.
30	Returns overnight to Dublin by way of Liverpool.

September

1	(Sun) Attends Martin Browne's lecture at the Abbey on Eliot's *Murder in the Cathedral* with verse spoken by Robert Speaight. Early this month the Abbey comes under clerical attack over its production of *The Silver Tassie*.
8	Spends the day reading Pound for *OBVM*, finding him 'the sexless American professor for all his violence' (to DW).
9	Works all morning at *A Full Moon in March* and sends it to Margot Collis. Sees people on Abbey business.
14–15	Reading W. J. Turner's poetry for *OBMV*.
15	Sends Macmillan the proofs of *A Full Moon in March*.

16	At the Abbey with GY for the first night of Higgins's *A Deuce o'Jacks* and a revival of *Maurice Harte*; O'Casey and the Longfords also present.
19	Absorbed in *OBMV*, which is almost finished.
20	Has a business lunch and attends four committee meetings in the afternoon.

October

12	(Sat) Discovers a small lump on his tongue.
15	Consults a surgeon who advises an operation.
16	Undergoes an operation to remove the lump on his tongue.
18	Learns that the lump is benign.
23	Begins a course of injections.
24	Leaves Dublin for London by night boat via Liverpool.
25	Sees Turner.
27	In London for a special 'birthday' production of *The Player Queen* at the Little Theatre. Afterwards he motors to Penns in the Rocks with DW and Hilda Matheson.
29	Returns to London and dines with Dulac.
30	Given the second in his course of injections by Carnegie Dickson, after which he returns to Penns in the Rocks.

November

2	(Sat) The first part of 'Dramatis Personae' (autobiography, *Aut*, 383–407) serialized in the *London Mercury*.
3	Returns to London from Penns in the Rocks. Sees the Swami and Mrs Foden to discuss where to go for their collaboration on the *Upanishads*.
4	Discusses the financial terms for *OBMV* with Watt. Sees Turner's play, *The Man Who Ate the Popomack*.
5	Has tea with Ottoline Morrell. Sees Eliot's *Murder in the Cathedral* at the Mercury Theatre.
6	Has the third in his series of injections.
8	Returns to Dublin from London. Deep in his work and writing in bed every morning from 9.30 am until noon.
22	*A Full Moon in March* published.
28	Travels to Liverpool *en route* for Majorca, where he and Shree Purohit Swami are to collaborate on translations from the *Upanishads*.
30	Sails from Liverpool for Majorca at 11 am with the Swami and Gwyneth Foden.

December

| 1 | (Sun) Rough seas keep WBY in bed for three days. |
| 7 | The second part of 'Dramatis Personae' (autobiography, *Aut*, |

407–34) serialized in the *London Mercury*. 'The Soldier Takes Pride' (poem; *VP*, 547–9) published as *A Broadside*.

9 *Dramatis Personae* published. WBY arrives in Gibraltar.

11 Recites his poems at a ship's concert.

12 His boat arrives two days late in Majorca and WBY, the Swami and Gwyneth Foden stay in a Parma hotel. Has tea with the British Consul, Alan Hillgarth, and sends the Introduction for *OBMV* to GY.

13 WBY and his party move to the Hotel Terramar, where he begins writing *The Herne's Egg* in the mornings and going through the Swami's translations from the *Upanishads* in the afternoons.

16 Finishes a first prose scenario of *The Herne's Egg*.

20 Finishes a more elaborate scenario of *The Herne's Egg*.

21 Begins writing *The Herne's Egg* in verse.

30 Has finished and is copying out the first act of *The Herne's Egg*. The Hillgarths lunch with WBY and the Swami at the Hotel Terramar.

1936

January

4 (Sat) Third part of 'Dramatis Personae' (autobiography, *Aut*, 434–58) serialized in the *London Mercury*. Early this month WBY is writing verse, including 'Why should not Old Men be Mad?' (*VP*, 625–6), and helping the Swami translate the *Upanishads*. Finishes Act I and a scene of Act 2 of *The Herne's Egg*.

c.11 Taken ill with breathing difficulties and sees a doctor, who forbids creative work but permits him to continue with the *Upanishads*.

16 Feels better and gets up; he is reading T. E. Lawrence's *The Odyssey of Homer* continually.

23 Sits in the sunshine for 3 hours and revises DW's poems.

27 Suffers a severe collapse with nephritis and a heart problem which causes difficulty in breathing.

29 Consults a doctor who orders complete rest and confines him to bed. Dictates a letter asking GY to come to Majorca to nurse him but, on the doctor's instructions, the Swami telegraphs her to come out at once.

29–31 WBY critically ill and London papers report his imminent death.

February

2 (Sun) GY arrives in Majorca at 8 in the morning, having flown to Barcelona, and consults WBY's doctor. The Hillgarths bring

him pillows, a padded bed-rest, a bed table, 15 detective and cowboy stories and a bed-pan. WBY's slow recovery from illness is not complete until mid-April.

March

10   (Tue) WBY's doctors recommend a change in diet and a slight change of drugs. Dulac sends him out a wheelchair.

19   Anne Yeats sails for Majorca from Liverpool.

21   Michael Yeats is confirmed in the Church of Ireland at St Columba's College, with ECY representing the family.

23   GY and WBY move from the Hotel Terramar to a near-by villa, Casa Pastor. He is reading Huxley's *Those Barren Leaves* and Victoria Sackville-West's *The Edwardians*. Works a little every morning on the *Upanishads*.

April

1   (Wed) Early this month Michael Yeats joins his family in Majorca.

5   WBY puts on his ordinary clothes for the first time since late January.

18   His doctor informs him that his body is back to normal.

20   Begins his Introduction to *The Ten Principal Upanishads*. Later this month, having finished *The Upanishads*, WBY and the Swami begin a translation of the *Aphorisms of Yoga*. WBY also returns to work on *The Herne's Egg*. His bust is being sculpted by Mary Klauder.

May

1   (Fri) Early this month he continues revising DW's poems and reading Turner's autobiographical *Blow for Balloons*.

12   *Dramatis Personae, Estrangement, The Death of Synge, The Bounty of Sweden* published in one volume by the Macmillan Company (NY). The English edition appears on 15 May.

15   Margot Collis arrives unexpectedly at 6.30 am suffering a fit of insanity and bringing her poems for WBY's opinion. She subsequently sails to Barcelona, where she falls through a roof and breaks her knee-cap, and whence the Yeatses are summoned by the British Consul to help her. WBY sends her home in charge of a nurse, partly at his own expense.

16   Back in Majorca, WBY sees Shree Purohit Swami off for India. Writing 'A Crazed Girl' (*VP*, 578).

26   WBY, GY and Anne Yeats leave Majorca by steamer for London.

June

2   (Tue) The Yeatses arrive in London.

6   Publication of *Selections from the Poems of Dorothy Wellesley* with WBY's Introduction. WBY goes to stay with DW in Sussex where

he finishes a version of *The Herne's Egg*. Turner comes down for a night and they plan a new series of *Broadsides* with DW.

10	Revising Margot Collis's poems for publication in the *London Mercury*.
13	Margot Collis visits him in Sussex.
19	Proofs of *OBMV* reach WBY.
21	Travels to London from Sussex with Rothenstein, who has also been staying with DW. Sees Turner.
22	Sees Sturge Moore and Dulac, who tells him that, contrary to Gwyneth Foden's allegations, the police are not investigating the Swami.
24	Goes through Turner's poems with him for *Broadsides*, getting rid of vague rhetoric.
25	Reads *The Herne's Egg* to Dulac, Turner and Margot Collis.
27	Sees Elizabeth Pelham and Alan Hillgarth about Gwyneth Foden's libelling of the Swami.
28	Meets Clifford Bax by chance.
29	GY meets him at Holyhead and accompanies him back to Dublin, where he is greeted by a welcoming committee on the pier which includes Gogarty, Higgins, Hayes, Walter Starkie and Frank O'Connor.

July

4	(Sat) 'Prefatory Notes on the Author', later the first section of the Introduction to Margot Ruddock (Collis's) *The Lemon Tree*, published in the *London Mercury*.
5	Finishes a revised version of *The Herne's Egg*.
6	Begins 'The Three Bushes'.
7	Finishes the first draft of 'The Three Bushes'. In the afternoon he asks GY to take over management of the Cuala Press but she refuses.
8	Finishes the final version of 'The Three Bushes'.
c.12	Ottoline and Philip Morrell come to tea at Riversdale. Later this month he advises DW on the rewriting of her version of 'The Three Bushes' and falls into a daily routine in which he gets up at 4.00 am to correct proofs until 5.30 am, returns to bed, breakfasts at 7.30 am and then writes poetry until 12 noon. In the afternoon he is taken for a spin in his wheelchair.
20	Starts poem, 'Lapis Lazuli'.
25	Finishes 'Lapis Lazuli'. Higgins calls in the evening.
27	Writes the poem 'Huddon, Duddon and Daniel O'Leary' for the beginning of *A Vision*.
30	Begins 'To Dorothy Wellesley'.

August

2   (Sun) Reads out the MS of *The Herne's Egg* to GY who types it.

3   Continues dictating *The Herne's Egg* to GY. Gogarty calls to see him.

5   Sends a corrected version of 'To Dorothy Wellesley' to DW.

10   Greeted with applause at a packed Abbey Theatre, where his *Deirdre* is being revived with Jean Forbes-Robertson in the title-role.

11   Orders *Deirdre* to be withdrawn in disgust at Jean Forbes-Robertson's performance. In the middle of the month he suffers a relapse in health; his doctor prescribes digitalis, but WBY ascribes his recovery to the adoption of a milk and fruit diet. Probably writes 'A Nativity' (*VP*, 625) at this time.

23   Writing his talk for the BBC. Sees Frank O'Connor in the evening.

September

4   (Fri) Returns the proofs of *OBMV* to the Clarendon Press.

8   Sends 'Come Gather round me, Parnellites' to DW. Spends the middle of the month correcting proofs of *A Vision*, and dealing with final queries about the text of *OBMV*.

28   Travels to London and strikes up an acquaintance with 'Gypsy Nina' in the train. Stays at the Savile Club.

October

1   (Thu) Reads *The Herne's Egg* to Robert Speaight, Martin Browne, Turner and Margot Collis in Dulac's studio. Afterwards takes Margot Collis out to dinner and tires himself talking until 10.30 pm.

2   Gives a dinner party at the Ivy to introduce Ethel Mannin to the Dulacs.

4   Reading Huxley's *Eyeless in Gaza*.

5   Goes to stay with DW at Penns in the Rocks.

7   Writes extra pages for his talk at the BBC's request.

8   Rehearses his BBC talk at Penns in the Rocks. In the evening Rothenstein's son and daughter-in-law come to stay, and DW persuades WBY to read poetry to them.

11   Driven up to London for his BBC broadcast 'Modern Poetry'.

12   Is driven back to Penns in the Rocks with Turner.

14   'Modern Poetry' (broadcast; *E & I*, 491–508) published in the *Listener*.

17   Is driven up from Sussex to London.

18   Has Margot Collis to tea.

19   A violent cold keeps him in bed at the Savile Club.

21   Recovered from this, he has a long lunch with Elizabeth Pelham and later dines with Dulac.

22	Gives lunch to Hilda Matheson of the BBC to discuss further broadcasts; later sees Turner and they rehearse a programme of verse with Margot Collis and Watkins. Hears that the Mercury Theatre wants to produce his play.
23	Calls on Watt and discusses the contents of Macmillan's proposed edition de luxe of his works. Sees Dulac.
24	Returns to Penns in the Rocks.
26	Returns to London and sees OS.
*c.*28	Returns to London from Penns in the Rocks.
29	Sees Faber and Faber about the publication date of *The Ten Principal Upanishads*, and calls on Dent to arrange the publication of Margot Collis's poems.

November

1	(Sun) Sees OS. In evening goes with the Dulacs to see the Group Theatre's production of Louis MacNeice's *Agamemnon* at the Westminster Theatre. At about this time he applies for membership of the Eugenics Society.
3	Returns to Dublin, GY meeting him at Holyhead. Begins to correct the proofs of *The Ten Principal Upanishads* and sort out the various copyright fees for poems published in *OBMV*.
9	Writes 'The Lover's Song' (*VP*, 574).
10	Sends Macmillan a list of contents for the edition de luxe via Watt.
14	Maloney's *The Forged Casement Diaries* puts him into a rage and he begins 'Roger Casement' (*VP*, 581–2).
16	Goes to the dentist.
19	*The Oxford Book of Modern Verse* published and causes controversy.
20	Finishes 'The Lady's First Song' (*VP*, 572). Goes on to write 'The Chambermaid's First Song' (*VP*, 574), 'The Chambermaid's Second Song' (*VP*, 575), and 'An Acre of Grass' (*VP*, 575–6).
27	Finishes correcting the last galley proofs of *A Vision* and *The Ten Principal Upanishads*. Sends a version of 'Roger Casement' (*VP*, 581–2) to the *Irish Times* but it is not published.

December

1	(Fri) Attends a dinner given by Patrick McCartan, who is organizing an American Committee to raise money for WBY.
5	Reading Turner's *Henry Airbubble in Search of a Circumference*.
7	Revises 'Roger Casement' to omit Gilbert Murray's name.
8	GY sends the corrected and enlarged version of 'The Three Bushes' to Watt.
9	Finishes 'The Spur' (*VP*, 591). In the middle of the month writes 'The Ghost of Roger Casement' and descends into a black mood

over the Casement diaries, the reception of *OBMV*, and the declining state of Europe.

25   The Abbey stage designer Tanya Moiseiwitsch spends Christmas with the Yeatses.

26   Goes into a mental darkness, a feeling of utter solitude, which keeps him in bed for three days.

29   Recovers from his depression and writes 'Imitated from the Japanese' (*VP*, 567) while dressing. In the evening Higgins calls and they discuss the critical attacks on *OBMV*.

1937

January

2   (Sat) 'The Three Bushes' (poem; *VP*, 569–75) published in the *London Mercury*. Early this month WBY returns the proofs of *The Ten Principal Upanishads* to Faber and writes 'The Curse of Cromwell' (*VP*, 580–1), 'Sweet Dancer' (*VP*, 568) and probably 'What Then?' (*VP*, 576–7). 'Come Gather round me, Parnellites' (poem; *VP*, 586–7) published as *A Broadside*.

7   A radio set, purchased by WBY through the BBC, arrives at Riversdale.

12   Lunches with Kiernan to discuss broadcasting on Irish Radio.

21   Finishes 'The Great Day', 'Parnell', and 'What Was Lost'.

22   Writing 'The O'Rahilly' (*VP*, 584–5). Sees Higgins and Moya Llewellyn Davies for lunch and attends a meeting of the Abbey Directors in the afternoon.

23   Dines at Gogarty's to meet Col. Theodore Roosevelt.

27   Sends Scribner's Sons, via Watt, the list of contents for the collected 'Dublin Edition' of his works.

28   Confined to bed by an attack of influenza.

February

1   (Mon) Listens to a broadcast of his poems from the Abbey stage by Radio Eireann which is a technical disappointment.

2   Publishes 'Roger Casement' (*VP*, 581–2) in the *Irish Press*.

3   Publicly thanked by representatives of the Irish government for his poem on Roger Casement.

7   No longer infectious from influenza; Dermot MacManus comes to discuss politics and the Spanish Civil War. Over the coming days he does no creative work but revises proofs of *The Ten Principal Upanishads* and suffers a digestive attack.

13   Publishes another version of 'Roger Casement' in the *Irish Press*, revised in the light of a letter from Alfred Noyes.

16	Elected a member of the Athenaeum.
21	Consults Higgins about an improved broadcast from the Abbey stage.

March

4	(Thu) Goes to London, staying for the first time in the Athenaeum and remaining until 24 April, seeing as many people as he can. 'The Three Bushes' published as *A Broadside*. Ottoline Morrell quarrels with him for mentioning Turner's attack on her in *OBMV*. WBY in a strange excitable state in London.
25	Holds a rehearsal for his broadcast 'In the Poet's Pub' with Turner and George Barnes.
26	Writing 'The Wild Old Wicked Man' (*VP*, 587–90).
30	Robert Nichols brings Aldous Huxley to see him. At 2.30 pm he rehearses his BBC broadcast, 'In the Poet's Garden'.
31	Measured for a suit at Jaeger's. Has tea with AEFH, to whom he is reconciled after 27 years.

April

2	(Fri) At 2.30 pm attends the final rehearsal for his BBC programme, 'In the Poet's Pub', which is broadcast at 9.20 pm that evening. 'What Then?' published in the *Erasmian* during this month.
3	Goes to Penns in the Rocks. Turner also stays there during the week.
9	Lady Sibyl Colefax visits Penns in the Rocks, also Frederick Ashton and H. A. L. Fisher. Writes a version of 'The Gyres'.
10	Goes to London.
11	Begins a 'General Introduction' for the Scribner Collected Edition of his works. Correcting page-proofs of *A Vision*.
13	Attends a BBC rehearsal.
16	Has tea with John Berryman. At this time he begins a friendship with Edith Shackleton Heald (ESH).
18	Publication of *The Ten Principal Upanishads* translated by Shree Purohit Swami and WBY, and with a Preface by WBY.
21	Dines with Richard Church and Margot Collis.
22	Attends the final rehearsal of his BBC programme, 'In the Poet's Parlour', which is broadcast at 10.20 pm.
24	Returns to Dublin, where he dedicates himself to revising the proofs of *A Vision*. Begins 'The Old Stone Cross' (*VP*, 598–9).

May

3	(Mon) Finishes correcting the proof sheets of *A Vision*.
4	Higgins comes in to discuss future numbers of *Broadsides*.
11	Higgins calls to continue his discussion about the *Broadsides* and to sing his latest ballads.

| 26 | WBY announces his retirement from public life at an open meeting of the Irish Academy and afterwards attends the Academy Dinner from 7.30 to 11.30 pm, where he hears 'The Three Bushes' and other of his poems sung. |

June

1	(Tue) Sees Higgins.
6	Gives a garden party for Anne Yeats.
8	Goes to London, where he remains until 21 July. *Nine One-Act Plays* published.
9	Revises 'The O'Rahilly' and a preface for Scribner's Collected Edition. Sees Dulac and lunches with ESH at the Athenaeum.
10	Sees Elizabeth Pelham.
12	Dines with Dulac and George Barnes to discuss his next broadcast.
13	Drives with the Dulacs to visit ESH in Steyning, Sussex.
14	ESH motors WBY to Penns in the Rocks.
16	Return to London and moves from the Athenaeum to a service flat at 52 Holland Park.
17	Dines with ESH at the Coronet Restaurant, Notting Hill Gate.
18	Lunches with ESH, Hilda Matheson and Turner at the L'Escargot Restaurant.
19	Receives £600 from his American Committee through Patrick McCartan.
21	Delivers the copy for Vol. IV of the Scribner Collected Edition to Watt. Has tea with Anne Yeats who is in London.
22	Calls on Macmillan and arranges details of his forthcoming publications. Attends the first rehearsal of his BBC programme, 'My Own Poetry'.
23	Introduces the designer Diana Murphy to ESH and Nora Shackleton Heald over tea at the Athenaeum.
24	Attends a rehearsal of his BBC programme from 5.30 to 6.30 pm and has a violent row with Dulac; he is then motored to Steyning to stay with ESH.
28	Returns to London from Steyning.
29	Has Richard Church to dine at the Athenaeum with Margot Collis.

July

| 1 | (Thu) A stormy BBC rehearsal leads to a quarrel with Dulac that lasts for a fortnight. The BBC take publicity photographs. Having finished three prefaces for the Scribner edition, his head is full of subjects for poetry. |
| 3 | Has a meeting with ESH which is a great joy. Gives an interview to the *News Chronicle* and later broadcasts a programme 'My Own Poetry' for the BBC at 10 pm. |

6	ESH motors him from London to stay with DW at Penns in the Rocks. During the visit DW has a severe nervous collapse and becomes *distrait*.
7	Elizabeth Pelham visits Penns in the Rocks and tells him that the Swami's 'Master', Shree Hamsa, has died.
8–10	Writes a manifesto against the modern musician's treatment of words, which becomes the Introduction to the bound volume of *Broadsides*.
12	ESH motors him from Penns in the Rocks to her house in Steyning.
*c.*13	Meets the poet and artist David Jones at tea at Lady Chichester's house and praises his *In Parenthesis* in fulsome terms.
15	A friendly letter from Dulac ends their quarrel.
18	Leaves Steyning for London, staying at the Athenaeum.
19	Harry Clifton introduces him to an American medium whom he is paying for psychic help in a romantic intrigue.
20	Crosses by night boat to Dublin.
22	Writes every morning and in the next fortnight finishes six poems and writes a new one, finishes an essay, and corrects the proofs of *The Herne's Egg*.
23	Higgins calls, indignant about the singer used in WBY's BBC broadcast.
24	Writes drafts of 'A Model for the Laureate'.
26	Rewrites 'A Model for the Laureate' and sends copies to ESH and DW. Begins 'Colonel Martin' and finds he is writing more poetry than he has ever written in the same space of time.

August

1	(Sun) 'The Curse of Cromwell' (poem; *VP*, 580–1) published as *A Broadside*. ECY calls to show him embroidery designs by Diana Murphy.
2	He is in good health again and all his work is finished.
8	Sees Frank O'Connor.
9	AEFH dies.
10	Finishes 'Colonel Martin' (*VP*, 594–7) and begins writing 'Those Images' (*VP*, 600–1). A visit to the Municipal Gallery inspires his poem 'The Municipal Gallery Revisited'.
16	Attends the Abbey to see *The Playboy of the Western World* and receives an enthusiastic reception.
17	Speaks after an Academy banquet at the Dolphin Hotel of his gratitude to McCartan and his American benefactors.
18	His American benefactors offer to rebuild the Abbey Theatre. WBY rewrites those songs of his sung at the Academy banquet.

| 25 | Begins writing 'The Municipal Gallery Revisited' (*VP*, 601–4). |

September

4	(Sat) Finishes 'The Municipal Gallery Revisited'.
6	Negotiates a new financial arrangement for Cuala with the Bank.
9	Sails to Holyhead, where he spends the night.
11	Travels from Holyhead to London, staying at the Athenaeum.
15	Goes to stay with ESH in Steyning.
17	*The Words upon the Window Pane* shown on BBC television.
c.20	Driven to Oxford to replace a false tooth.
21	Goes into Brighton for work on his dental plate.
22	Is motored from Steyning to stay with DW at Penns in the Rocks.
25	Turner and Hilda Matheson come to Penns in the Rocks.
26	Returns to London.
28	Attends a performance of Shakespeare's *Richard II*.
30	Invites Diana Murphy to tea to discuss embroidery designs for Cuala. Has dinner with Dulac.

October

1	(Fri) 'A Pilgrim' (poem; *VP*, 592–3) published as *A Broadside*. WBY's London doctor reports that his health is much better.
4	Lunches with George Barnes of the BBC to discuss more broadcasts. Calls to see Watt to discuss the *Aphorisms of Yoga*, Scribner's Collected Edition of his works, and the American rights of *A Vision*.
5	Rothenstein lunches and afterwards sketches him at his new studio. Dines with Dulac.
6	Does a broadcasting test at the BBC.
7	The revised edition of *A Vision* is published. WBY returns to stay with ESH at Steyning.
12	Begins 'The Circus Animals' Desertion' (*VP*, 629–30) after seeking a theme for nearly five weeks and goes on to find other themes, probably including that for 'Long-legged Fly' (*VP*, 617–18).
20	Returns to London.
22	Goes back to Steyning.
27	Returns to London, where he dines with Dulac and Helen Beauclerk.
28	Rehearses his BBC programme.
29	Assisted by Margot Collis, he broadcasts the programme 'My Own Poetry Again' for the BBC at 10.45 pm.

November

| 1 | (Mon) Returns to Dublin and begins to put Cuala Industries on a sounder financial footing. Early this month he also rewrites his Introduction to the Swami's *Aphorisms of Yoga*, |

tries to defuse a dispute in the Abbey between Frank O'Connor and LR, and arranges for the publication of *On the Boiler*.

16	Presents a statement on the future of the Cuala Press.
c.18	Sees a revival of George Shiel's *Cartney and Kevney* at the Abbey.
22	*The Words upon the Window Pane* broadcast by BBC radio.
28	Sees ECY about the reform of Cuala Industries. He is suffering from a chill and his doctor sees him regularly on Thursdays.

December

4	(Sat) 'Colonel Martin' (poem; *VP*, 594–7) published as *A Broadside*.
14	*Essays 1931 to 1936* published.
15	Frank O'Connor calls.
25	Renews his subscription to the Eugenics Society and asks its advice on essays he is writing for *On the Boiler*.

1938

January

5	(Wed) Leaves Dublin for London, accompanied by GY and Michael Yeats.
7	Leaves London for Monte Carlo with ESH.
8	Passes through Paris with ESH on his way to Monte Carlo.
9	Arrives in Monte Carlo.
11	A violent attack of indigestion prostrates him for a week.
21	*The Herne's Egg* published.
22	Moves to Menton where he corrects proofs of *New Poems*, writes *On the Boiler*, and reads Jack Yeats's *A Charmed Life*.

February

4	(Fri) GY arrives in Menton and ESH leaves for Paris. WBY establishes a routine in which he writes poetry in the mornings and GY pushes him in a wheelchair by the sea in the afternoons.
5	Writing 'The Apparitions' (*VP*, 624) and afterwards 'The Statesman's Holiday' (*VP*, 626–7) and 'A Bronze Head' (*VP*, 618–19).
8	GY types part of the MS of *On the Boiler*.
c.16	Sees an exhibition of Gwen Le Gallienne's paintings.
23	Visits the dentist.
24	In bed with a slight cold.
25	Calls on Richard Le Gallienne.
27	Sends a privately-printed pamphlet to his American benefactors as a token of gratitude.

March

1	(Tue) Moves to the Hotel Idéal-Séjour, Cap-Martin.
4	Revises 'The Apparitions' and begins two other poems.

5	'To a Friend' (later 'To Dorothy Wellesley'), 'The Great Day', 'Parnell', 'What Was Lost', The Spur', 'Sweet Dancer', 'The Old Stone Cross', 'Those Images', 'Lapis Lazuli', 'The Wild Old Wicked Man', 'An Acre of Grass', 'Are You Content' (poems; *VP*, 579, 590–1, 568, 598–9, 600–1, 565–7, 587–90, 575–6, 604–5) published in the *London Mercury*.
23	Returns to London from France and dines at the Grosvenor Hotel with ESH.
24	Goes to Penns in the Rocks and reads DW his new poems and *On the Boiler*.
25	Turner and Hilda Matheson at Penns in the Rocks. Revises 'Long-legged Fly'.
29	ESH motors him to Steyning where he begins his play *The Death of Cuchulain*.
30	Corrects proofs of the *Aphorisms of Yoga*.

April

2	(Sat) The medium Harry Price comes to tea at Steyning.
9	Writes a version of 'The Statues'.
12	Goes to London, staying at the Athenaeum, to discuss broadcasts with George Barnes of the BBC, and hears a recording of 'In the The Poet's Pub'. Dines with Dulac.
13	Lunches with Elizabeth Pelham and her sister, after which he reads them *On the Boiler* and remains talking for five-and-a-half hours.
14	Returns to Steyning where he revises *On the Boiler* and his recent poems.
18	Elizabeth Pelham comes to visit him in Steyning.
20	Visits Rothenstein.
21	Goes to London in afternoon, staying at the Athenaeum.
23	Turner motors him to Penns in the Rocks where he writes a poetic version of *The Death of Cuchulain*.
24	Meets the astronomer Sir James Jeans at Penns in the Rocks.
25	*The Shadowy Waters* shown on BBC television.
27	Turner and the BBC producer Spackman visit WBY at Penns in the Rocks.

May

1	(Sun) ESH calls over to see him.
3	Goes to London for two days, staying at the Athenaeum; sees Cecil Harmsworth about Cuala in afternoon and dines with Dulac in the evening.
4	*The Shadowy Waters*, with a different cast, repeated on BBC television.
5	Finishes a version of *The Death of Cuchulain*.

6	Is motored to Oxford by ESH, staying at the Mitre.
7	Gives a luncheon party at Wadham College for Maurice Bowra and later dines with John Sparrow in All Souls.
8	Writes the poem 'What is the explanation of it all?' (*YA* 5, 212–13), and returns from Oxford to Steyning.
11	Goes to London to see Arnold Toynbee.
13	Returns to Dublin and works every morning on *The Death of Cuchulain*.
18	*New Poems* published.
24	Writes 'Politics' (*VP*, 631).

June

2	(Thu) Summons a special meeting of the Abbey Board to dismiss Hugh Hunt as manager. Revising 'The Statues' (*VP*, 610–11) and writing 'In Tara's Halls' (*VP*, 609). *Aphorisms of Yoga* with WBY's Introduction is published later this month.
10	Attends a special meeting of the Abbey Board, which asks Frank O'Connor to withdraw his resignation.
13	Attends a meeting of Abbey Board to discuss a replacement for Hugh Hunt. This crisis undermines his already indifferent health over the coming weeks, although later this month he entertains Gogarty, Montgomery Hyde and the Austrian diplomat Baron Franckenstein.
23	The Welsh poet Vernon Watkins calls to see him.
24	Attends a meeting of the Abbey Board. Later this month Padraic and Mary Colum, home briefly from America, come to tea.

July

1	(Fri) Chairs a meeting of the Abbey Board.
4	Receives the second instalment of the money collected for him by his American benefactors.
5	Has tea with Shotaro Oshima.
8	Goes to London, where he stays at the Athenaeum and sees Turner.
12	ESH motors him down to Steyning; he begins to write 'Crazy Jane on the Mountain' (*VP*, 628).
16	The Shackletons invite the Dulacs to Steyning for the weekend.
19	Leaves Steyning for Penns in the Rocks. Hilda Matheson is also there.
21	Begins writing 'John Kinsella's Lament for Mrs. Mary Moore' (*VP*, 620–1).
22	Turner comes to stay at Penns in the Rocks.
25	Moves from Penns in the Rocks to Steyning.
28	Visits Shelley's old house, Field Place, and the church where the Shelleys are buried.

| 29 | Finishes 'John Kinsella's Lament for Mrs. Mary Moore' and begins 'High Talk' (*VP*, 622–3) and probably 'The Man and the Echo' (*VP*, 632–3). |

August

2	(Tue) He is motored to Elizabeth Pelham's for tea.
4	'"I Became an Author"' (article; *UP* II. 506–9) published in the *Listener*. Writing News for the Delphic Oracle'.
8	Motors to London from Steyning and catches the train to Chester, where GY meets him and accompanies him to Dublin.
9	Writing 'Under Ben Bulben' (*VP*, 636–40), inspired by William Rose's *Rainer Maria Rilke: Aspects of his Mind and Poetry*. Suffering from swollen ankles.
10	Attends the first night of *Purgatory*, designed by Anne Yeats, at the Abbey Theatre and takes a curtain call.
11	Goes to see *On Baile's Strand* at the Abbey.
26	Entertains MG and Ethel Mannin to tea.
28	Dines at the Shelbourne Hotel with Ethel Mannin and her new lover Reginald Reynolds.

September

| 4 | (Sun) Finishes 'Under Ben Bulben' (*VP*, 636–40). In the later part of this month WBY tries to reorganize Cuala Industries into a limited liability company, but is frustrated by the procrastination of the accountant and the illness of ECY. |
| 30 | Shares the general relief at the Munich agreement. |

October

1	(Sat) Working on the papers necessary to convert Cuala into a limited liability company, which have at last arrived. Writing *The Death of Cuchulain*.
3	OS dies.
6	Cuala Industries becomes a limited company with WBY, ECY, GY and F. R. Higgins as directors.
8	Confined to his room with lumbago. Reading Ethel Mannin's novel *Darkness my Bride*.
11	Gogarty calls to see him.
12	Chairs first meeting of the reconstituted Cuala Board, which appoints Frank O'Connor auditor and makes a preliminary distribution of shares in the company.
18	His visit to England delayed by a visit to the dentist. Makes late corrections to 'Three Songs to the One Burden'.
c.24	Decides to bring out another series of *Broadsides*.
25	Crosses to England.
26	Upset by reading MG's autobiography, *A Servant of the Queen*.
27	Arrives in Steyning by an evening train.

November

11   (Fri) Moves from Steyning to Penns in the Rocks.

14   Goes to London, staying at the Savile Club.

15   Has dinner in London with Pound, Turner, ESH and her sister Nora.

16   Returns to Steyning in the evening.

24   Goes back to London, staying at the Athenaeum.

25   GY arrives in London and they have lunch with DW at Carlton Gardens and go afterwards to see Shaw's *Geneva*.

26   WBY and GY leave for the South of France on the evening ferry train.

28   The Yeatses book into a hotel in Beaulieu-sur-Mer but, driven from it after an hour by the noise of children and trains, they book into the Hotel Idéal-Séjour at Cap-Martin.

December

3   (Sat) 'Hound Voice', 'High Talk', 'John Kinsella's Lament for Mrs. Mary Moore', 'Apparitions', 'A Nativity' (poems; *VP*, 621–2, 622–3, 620–1, 624, 625) published in the *London Mercury*. WBY is correcting proofs of *On the Boiler* and dining with DW every second or third day at her villa above Beaulieu, where he meets the pianist Schnabel and discusses Stefan George and Rilke.

21   DW and Hilda Matheson call upon the Yeatses.

22   Michael Yeats arrives in Cap-Martin to join his parents.

25   The Yeatses spend Christmas Day with DW and Hilda Matheson.

1939

January

7   (Sat) 'The Man and the Echo', 'The Circus Animals' Desertion', and 'Politics' (poems, *VP*, 632–3, 629–30, 631) published in the *London Mercury*. WBY finishing *The Death of Cuchulain* and begins writing 'Cuchulain Comforted' (*VP*, 634–5) at 3 am, inspired by a dream.

8   Dismisses Higgins as editor of *Broadsides*.

11   Hilda Matheson and Turner and his wife call on the Yeatses.

13   Finishes 'Cuchulain Comforted'. Dines with DW, Hilda Matheson and the Turners at DW's villa at Beaulieu-sur-Mer.

15   Michael Yeats returns to Ireland.

21   Finishes 'The Black Tower' (*VP*, 635–6).

22   Dictates corrections to *The Death of Cuchulain* and writes to AG's executor about the publication of her diaries. Dermod and Mabel O'Brien call on WBY and find him in an expansive mood.

24   Too tired to join the Turners for dinner prior to their departure for London.

26	DW calls and realizes that WBY is dying; she returns in the afternoon and evening. He manages to dictate corrections for *The Death of Cuchulain* and 'Under Ben Bulben' to GY.
27	In much pain from his heart; given morphine and sinks into a coma. ESH arrives from Paris in the evening.
28	Dies at 2.30 pm in the Hotel Idéal-Séjour, Cap-Martin.
29	WBY's body taken to the cemetery chapel at Roquebrune.
30	Buried at Roquebrune at 3 pm according to the Anglican rite with GY, DW, ESH, Hilda Matheson and Mabel and Dermod O'Brien as mourners.

Index

Abbey School of Acting (later the Second Abbey Company), 149, 151, 152, 153, 154, 155, 159, 161, 163, 173, 249, 275, 289

Abbey Theatre, 92, 94, 96, 97, 104, 106, 107, 108, 109, 110, 111, 112, 113, 114, 115, 116, 117, 118, 119, 120, 121, 122, 123, 125, 126, 127, 128, 129, 131, 132, 133, 134, 135, 136, 137, 138, 139, 140, 141, 142, 143, 144, 145, 146, 147, 148, 149, 150, 151, 152, 153, 154, 155, 158, 159, 160, 162, 163, 164, 167, 168, 169, 170, 173, 174, 175, 177, 178, 179, 180, 181, 183, 184, 185, 192, 195, 198, 199, 200, 201, 203, 204, 206, 212, 213, 214, 215, 216, 217, 218, 222, 226, 227, 228, 229, 230, 231, 232, 233, 234, 235, 236, 237, 238, 239, 240, 241, 242, 243, 244, 245, 246, 247, 248, 249, 251, 253, 258, 259, 260, 267, 268, 270, 271, 272, 273, 274, 275, 277, 279, 280, 281, 283, 285, 286, 287, 288, 289, 290, 291, 295, 296, 300, 302, 303, 305, 307, 309, 310; American Tours, 110, 148, 149, 150, 151, 152, 153, 157, 158, 160, 161, 162, 163, 164, 165, 166, 170, 171, 173, 174, 180, 182, 186, 187, 188, 189, 191, 194, 253, 275, 279, 281, 289, 294; British Tours, 102, 105–6, 110, 111, 112, 115, 120, 121, 130, 131, 134, 139, 140, 146, 147, 148, 149, 154, 155, 157, 164, 165, 168, 174, 177, 178, 179; Irish Tours, 106, 121, 122, 127, 129, 145; Consultations Committee, 118, 120, 123, 125, 142, 144, 148

Aberdeen, Lady, Ishbel Maria Marjoribanks (1857–1939), Liberal, humanitarian, wife of Lord Aberdeen, 114

Aberdeen, Sir John Campbell Hamilton-Gordon, Earl, later 1st Marquis of (1847–1934), Lord-Lieutenant of Ireland 1886 and 1905–15, 132

Academic Committee of the Royal Society of Literature, 139, 140, 141, 147, 148, 149, 153, 154, 156, 159, 161, 162

Academy, The, 62, 77, 84

Adolf Bernadotte, Crown Prince, from 1950 King, of Sweden (1882–1973), 231

AE, *see* Russell, George William.

Aeschylus, (c. 525–c. 456 BC), Greek dramatist, 94, 111; Oresteian Trilogy, 94; *The Persians*, 111

Aesop, 6th-century BC Greek fabulist, 13

Ainley, Henry Hinchliffe (1879–1945), actor-manager, 184

Alcock, Miss, theatre producer, 176

Aldington, Richard (1892–1962), poet and novelist, 263

Alessandro Volta Foundation, 289

Alexander, George (1858–1918), actor manager, 72

Alexandra, Queen Consort of King Edward VII (1844–1925), 95, 184

Allgood, Molly, *see* O'Neill, Maire

Allgood, Sara (1883–1950), actress, 107, 119, 122, 123, 125, 127, 131, 137, 138, 141, 142, 145, 147, 177, 180, 211, 247, 259, 260, 267, 271

Alma-Tadema, Laurence (1864–1940), writer and translator, 47

Almon, Robert, American poet, 231

Alviella, Comte Goblet d', French anthropologist, 49; *The Migration of Symbols*, 49

America, 151

Amhurst, Miss, London social hostess, 156

Anderson, Robert Andrew (1891–1942), agriculturist, 201

Anglo-Saxon, The, 68

Anstey, F., pseud. of Thomas Anstey Guthrie (1856–1934), British

Wilde, Oscar (1854–1900), Irish
playwright, author, critic and wit, 6,
15, 19, 21, 35, 101, 110; *A Florentine
Tragedy*, 106; *The Picture of Dorian
Gray*, 233; *Salomé*, 100, 106
Wilde, Sir William Robert Wills
(1815–76); oculist, folklorist and
father Oscar, 13; *Irish Popular
Superstitions*, 13
Williams, Mrs Harrison, American
hostess, 281
Williams, Herbert, American publisher, 93
Williams, William Carlos (1883–1963),
American poet and novelist, 138
Wilson, A. P., Abbey manager, 173, 178,
179, 180
Wilson, Christopher ('Chris')
(1874–1919), British composer and
conductor, 75
Wilson, David, novelist and occultist,
190, 191, 192
Wilson, Pet, WBY's Dublin typist, 286
Wimborne, Alice Katherine Sibell, née
Grosvenor, 182
Wimborne, Ivor Churchill-Guest, 1st
Viscount (1873–1939), British
politician and Lord Lieutenant of
Ireland, 181
Winter, John Strange, pseud. of Mrs
Arthur Stannard, née Henrietta
Palmer (1856–1911), 16
Wise, Edith Mary (1863–1938), WBY's
cousin, 19
Withers, Percy (1867–1945), medical
practitioner and teacher of English,
156
Witt, Sir Robert Clermont (d. 1952), art
administrator and art critic, 179, 180,
181
Woodmass, Edith Alice (1848–1927),
GY's grandmother, 225, 244
Woods, Sir Robert (1865–1938), surgeon
and MP, 201
Woolf, Virginia (1882–1941), British
novelist, 271, 290; *Orlando*, 280
Wordsworth, William (1770–1850),
Romantic poet, 159, 176; *The
Excursion*, 177; *The Prelude*, 177
Worlde and the Childe, The, 154
Wreidt, Etta, American medium, 164,
165, 174, 180

Wright, Udolphus ('Dossy') (1887–1952),
electrician, stage manager, and
bit-part actor at the Abbey, 180
Wundt, Wilhelm, German scholar, 251
Wycherly, Margaret (1884–1956),
London-born actress, 94, 97
Wylie, Elinor, née Hoyt (1885–1928),
American poet, 295
Wynne, Frances Alice (1863–93), Irish
poet, 22

Yano, Kazumi, Hojin Yano (b. 1893),
Japanese poet, critic and translator,
255, 266
Yeats, Anne (1919–2001), painter and
WBY's daughter, 203, 204, 205, 206,
207, 210, 214, 215, 218, 220, 221,
222, 224, 229, 243, 244, 257, 258,
262, 263, 264, 266, 269, 271, 272,
274, 286, 295, 298, 304, 310
Yeats, Bertha George, née Hyde-Lees
(GY), xv; 164, 165, 167, 175, 176,
182, 191, 192, 194, 195, 196, 197,
198, 199, 200, 201, 202, 203, 204,
205, 206, 207, 208, 209, 210, 211,
212, 213, 214, 216, 218, 219, 220,
221, 222, 223, 225, 226, 228, 229,
231, 232, 233, 234, 236, 238, 239,
240, 241, 242, 243, 245, 246, 255,
257, 258, 259, 260, 261, 262, 263,
264, 265, 266, 267, 268, 269, 270,
271, 272, 274, 275, 276, 277, 279,
281, 285, 287, 288, 289, 290, 291,
292, 293, 295, 297, 298, 299, 300,
301, 304, 307, 310, 311, 312
Yeats, Elizabeth Corbet (ECY), xv; 3, 9,
14, 15, 40, 61, 80, 86, 97, 106, 107,
108, 122, 129, 137, 142, 163, 165,
166, 175, 182, 193, 198, 204, 206,
216, 218, 219, 227, 231, 232, 279,
286, 294, 298, 305, 307, 310
Yeats, Grace Butler (1898–1997),
Canadian cousin of WBY's, 243
Yeats, Isaac Butt (1848–1930), WBY's
paternal uncle, 247, 270
Yeats, Jane Grace, née Corbet (1811–76),
WBY's paternal grandmother, 4
Yeats, Jane Grace (1875–76), WBY's
sister, 4
Yeats, John Butler (JBY), xv; 3, 4, 5, 7, 9,
11, 13, 15, 16, 19, 36, 38, 39, 51, 56,